MW00635618

PRAISE FOR *THE CRASH OF FLIGHT 3804*

"The most extraordinary historical account of pipeline politics and the blood-drenched Great Game for Oil ever written. Investigative reporter Charlotte Dennett's tenacious, decades-long quest to uncover the truth about the death of her father — America's first master spy in the Middle East — has resulted in a riveting saga replete with previously hidden details about the powerful characters, countries, and corporations locked in vicious perpetual competition to control the world's oil. No book connects the dots like this one, and with such fascinating clarity. Urgent reading for anyone looking to understand who and what brought us into the War on Terror era and how the groundwork for future wars is being laid."

— KRISTINA BORJESSON, author of *Feet to the Fire*;
creator and cohost of The Whistleblower Newsroom

"Dennett has crafted a page turner that reads like a thriller. Ironically, her father's warning echoes throughout the book: 'God help us if we ever send troops to the Middle East.' Decades on, his daughter has picked up the torch to illuminate how America's addiction to endless wars is actually the ongoing covert battle for energy still being played out in Afghanistan, Georgia, Russia, Iran, Iraq, Syria, Gaza, Yemen, and other explosive regions of the world. And the tragedy continues. *Bravissima* for Dennett's courageous, compelling, and unnerving work!"

— TERENCE WARD, author of *The Wahhabi Code*

"As a retired US Army colonel and diplomat . . . I found this book to be fascinating — filled with a treasure trove of details about the beginning of the oil wars in the Middle East and continuing to today with the United States 'guarding' Syria's oil fields as it attempts to overthrow Syria's Assad government. The book . . . tracks the deals, missteps, and wars for oil. The detailed maps show pipeline routes over the decades and are themselves a remarkable way to track the political dynamics of the region!"

— ANN WRIGHT, retired colonel,
US Army/Army Reserves; former US diplomat

"Charlotte Dennett has a fascinating personal saga to share and a mystery to solve. This book offers the hidden backstory to the history of US involvement in the Middle East. It is the type of broad and deep historical dig that is so badly needed, and it helps us see the bigger picture behind policies and failures that affect us today. Suddenly, all these wars make sense."

— RUSS BAKER, author of *Family of Secrets*;
founder and editor-in-chief, *WhoWhatWhy*

"Investigative journalist Charlotte Dennett is onto something big. As an outsider researching her master spy father's 1947 death at the dawning of the Great Game for Oil, she takes on the CIA's notorious secrecy with fierce determination. That leads Dennett to the highest echelons of the agency while looking for answers and, intriguingly, the CIA makes it clear they want her on their side. Dennett's telling is a 'ghost story' beginning at the foundation of the CIA that still haunts us today as the world her father died for disintegrates into chaos. One cannot help but wonder that if her father had lived, could his nuanced vision for the Middle East have altered the disastrous course the United States is on now?"

— PAUL FITZGERALD AND ELIZABETH GOULD,
authors of *Invisible History*

"A mix of curiosity and loyalty — to family and country — drove Charlotte Dennett to find out if the 'humaneness' ascribed to her spymaster father by his Harvard professor could have persisted in the dog-eat-dog espionage surrounding post-WWII access to Middle East oil. She found abundant material to answer that question and many others about the early death of her father and about the origins of the endless wars that have come to characterize the region he loved. We are gifted with an intriguing, personal account of the Great Game for Oil and its countless and continuing casualties."

— RAY MCGOVERN, cofounder, Veteran Intelligence
Professionals for Sanity; former CIA analyst

"A father's death and perhaps murder by 'allies' while pursuing a vital mission for the United States. A daughter's lifelong search for truth and justice. Spies. Fortune-seekers. A cast of royals, brigands, bankers, patriots, and other history-makers struggling to control oil wealth from Central Asia to the Middle East to Northern Africa over the past century. Compelling country-by-country current analysis by an expert reporter and historian. Revelations about the 'pipeline politics' that constantly create headlines about endless war, war crimes, terrorism, and ethnic cleansing, but remain little understood by Westerners, including major media. All of that is combined in this page-turning memoir, culminating in a surprise ending. In brief, this is a masterpiece."

— ANDREW KREIG, editor, Justice Integrity Project;
author of *Presidential Puppetry*

THE CRASH OF
FLIGHT 3804

A LOST SPY, A DAUGHTER'S QUEST, AND THE DEADLY POLITICS OF THE GREAT GAME FOR OIL

CHARLOTTE DENNETT

FOREWORD BY DANIEL C. DENNETT, III

Chelsea Green Publishing
White River Junction, Vermont
London, UK

Maps by John Van Hoesen, copyright © 2020 by Chelsea Green Publishing.

Project Manager: Patricia Stone
Developmental Editor: Joni Praded
Copy Editor: Nancy Ringer
Proofreader: Eliani Torres
Indexer: Shana Milkie
Designer: Melissa Jacobson

Printed in the United States of America.
First printing March 2020.
10 9 8 7 6 5 4 3 2 1   20 21 22 23 24

Our Commitment to Green Publishing
Chelsea Green sees publishing as a tool for cultural change and ecological stewardship. We strive to align our book manufacturing practices with our editorial mission and to reduce the impact of our business enterprise in the environment. We print our books and catalogs on chlorine-free recycled paper, using vegetable-based inks whenever possible. This book may cost slightly more because it was printed on paper that contains recycled fiber, and we hope you'll agree that it's worth it. *The Crash of Flight 3804* was printed on paper supplied by Sheridan that is made of recycled materials and other controlled sources.

ISBN 978-1-60358-877-5 (hardcover) | ISBN 978-1-60358-878-2 (ebook) |
  ISBN 978-1-60358-879-9 (audio book)

Library of Congress Cataloging-in-Publication Data is available upon request.

Chelsea Green Publishing
85 North Main Street, Suite 120
White River Junction, VT 05001

Somerset House
London, UK

www.chelseagreen.com

To the memory of my father, Daniel C. Dennett,
and the women who sought to preserve his legacy:
my mother, Ruth Leck Dennett, and
my grandmother, Elisabeth Redfern Dennett.

To Jerry, my beloved husband, mentor, and friend.

And to all who fight to preserve this Earth
and to bring an end to its endless wars.

CONTENTS

LIST OF MAPS

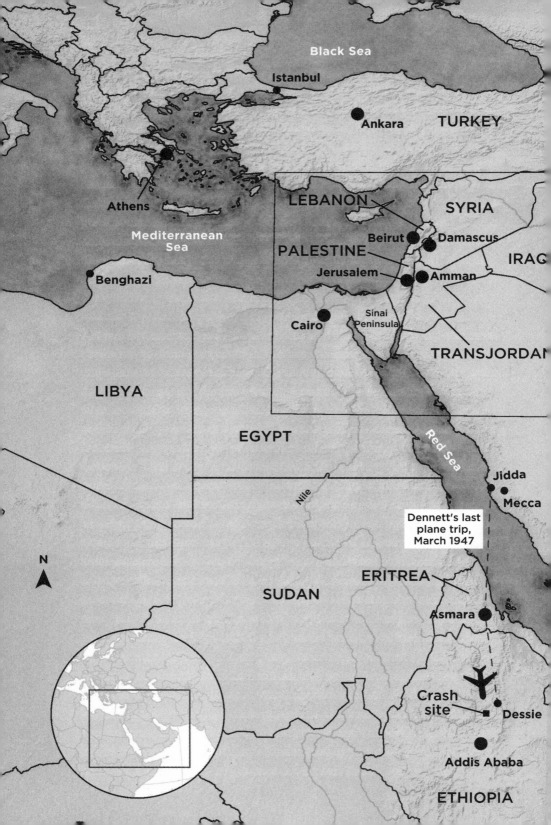

The Middle East and
the Great Game for Oil

This map introduces the reader to the most dangerous turf of the Great Game for Oil in the Middle East, from World War II to the present. When American master spy Daniel Dennett was sent to the region in 1944, Lebanon was advertised as the "Gateway to the Middle East." He learned to see the region otherwise — as oilmen saw it, with Lebanon, along with Syria and Palestine (soon to be Israel) as the "Gateway to Middle East Oil." The focus then, as now, was on an area known as "the Rectangle," shown here over the land bridge that connects these gateway countries on the Eastern Mediterranean with the major oil-exporting countries of Iraq, Iran, and Saudi Arabia. Palestine and Syria hosted, respectively, the terminal points of British- and French-controlled pipelines built in the early 1930s that connected to the oil of Iraq. Dennett's job was to negotiate the route of the newest pipeline, the American-controlled Trans-Arabian Pipeline, from Dhahran across Arabia to a terminal point in either Palestine or Lebanon — much to the alarm of the French, the British, and the Russians. After a top-secret mission to Saudi Arabia, he boarded a plane in Jidda destined for Ethiopia for more oil discussions, but the plane crashed near Dessie, Ethiopia. A seasoned player in pipeline politics, Dennett likely became one of America's first victims of the Great Game for Oil. Today, the game is more deadly than ever, with endless wars throughout the region. *Map source:* Robert Fisk, *The Great War for Civilization* (New York: Vintage Books, 2005), xiv–xv.

FOREWORD

There are the things the grown-ups know but never talk about, and then there are the children who discover these fascinating facts and blurt them out — usually to the dismay and embarrassment of their elders. A recent example was when the spoiled brat in the White House announced on October 6, 2019, that all American troops would be promptly withdrawn from Syria, abandoning our allies, the Kurds. Then, three weeks later, he abruptly changed course. With candor that betrayed his cluelessness, Donald Trump announced that American troops would be sent into Syria after all to "secure the oil"! Yes, it's all about the oil, and has been for decades, but hush! We aren't supposed to talk about that.

The Great Game for Oil is one of civilization's dirty secrets, except that it is well known by leaders, including elected presidents, dictators, foreign ministers, economic advisors, and oil company executives and their representatives. It's also known by intrepid spies and journalists. My father was one of those spies and my sister Charlotte is one of those journalists. She has spent decades sleuthing, sometimes at considerable personal risk, trying to get to the bottom of the intrigues that led to our father's death in a suspicious plane crash in Ethiopia in 1947, when she was just a baby in Beirut and our father was the United States' first master spy in the Middle East.

Along the way in her journey, Charlotte has fought for the release of CIA documents that uncovered early plays in that Great Game for Oil. Ultimately those documents showed how Big Oil, intelligence, and military powers began to write, in those post–World War II years, a new future for the Middle East, which our father had dedicated his career to understanding. The tale Charlotte tells in this book is full of surprises, some of them shocking. It spans decades and nations and explores links connecting figures like Winston Churchill, Dick Cheney, Recep Tayyip Erdoğan, Vladimir Putin, and Kim Philby, the famous British spy who was practicing his craft in Beirut and the Middle East at the same time as our father.

Kim Philby's story, in fact, is one that underscores the challenges of writing about covert operations. A few years after our father was killed, Philby, a senior officer in the British Secret Intelligence Service (SIS), fell under suspicion of being a double agent, a highly placed traitor working for the Soviet KGB. A secret tribunal was held by SIS, but in 1951, Philby was found not guilty on the evidence presented. Although SIS had been unable to convict him, they quite reasonably refused to reinstate him to his most sensitive position. He resigned and moved to Lebanon to work as a journalist. In 1963, a Soviet defector to London confirmed Philby's double-agent role, and when the SIS went to Beirut to confront him, he fled to Moscow, where he spent the remainder of his life working for the KGB.

Or did he? When Philby first showed up in Moscow, he was (apparently) suspected by the KGB of being a British plant — a *triple* agent, if you like. Was he? For years a story circulated in intelligence circles to this effect. The idea was that when SIS "exonerated" Philby in 1951, they found a brilliant way of dealing with their delicate problem of trust. Many have imagined a directive something like this:

> *Congratulations, Kim, old chap! We always thought you were loyal to our cause. And for your next assignment, we would like you to pretend to resign from SIS — bitter over our failure to reinstate you fully, don't you see — and move to Beirut and take up a position as a journalist in exile. In due course we intend to give you reason to "flee" to Moscow, where you will eventually be appreciated by your comrades because you can spill a lot of relatively innocuous insider information you already know, and we'll provide you with carefully controlled gifts of intelligence — and disinformation — that the Russians will be glad to accept, even when they have their doubts. Once you're in their good graces, we'd like you to start telling us everything you can about what they're up to, what questions they ask you, and so forth.*

Once SIS had given Philby this new assignment, the story goes, their worries were over. It just *didn't matter* whether he was truly a British patriot pretending to be a disgruntled agent, or truly a loyal Soviet agent pretending to be a loyal British agent (pretending to be a disgruntled agent). He would behave in exactly the same way in either case; his activities would be interpretable and predictable from either of two mirror-image, intentional-stance profiles. In one, he would deeply believe that the British cause was worth risking his life for and, in the other, he would deeply believe that he had a golden opportunity to be a hero of the Soviet Union by pretending that he deeply believed that the British cause is worth risking his life for, and so on. The Soviets, meanwhile, would no doubt draw the same inference and not bother trying to figure out if Philby was really a double agent or a triple agent or a quadruple agent. Philby, according to this story, had been deftly turned into a sort of human telephone. He was a mere conduit of information that both sides could exploit for whatever purposes they could dream up, relying on him to be a high-fidelity transmitter of whatever information they gave him, without worrying about where his ultimate loyalties lay.

In 1980, when Philby's standing with his overseers in Moscow was improving (apparently), I was a visiting fellow at All Souls College in Oxford. Another visiting fellow at the time happened to be Sir Maurice Oldfield, the retired head of MI6, the agency responsible for counterespionage outside Great Britain, and one of the spymasters responsible for Philby's trajectory. (Sir Maurice was the model for Ian Fleming's "M" in the James Bond novels.) One night after dinner, I asked him whether this story I had heard was true, and he replied quite testily that it was a lot of rubbish. He wished people would just let poor Philby live out his days in Moscow in peace and quiet. I replied that I was pleased to get his answer, but we both had to recognize that it was also what he would have told me had the story been true! Sir Maurice glowered and said nothing.

Sorting through subterfuge is a systemic problem that arises in spycraft. In May of 2019, when I joined my sister and other members of our family as guests at CIA headquarters in Langley, Virginia, to honor our father as the CIA's first fallen star, I was surprised to find that they had a gift shop where one may buy souvenirs. Side by side on the wall were two sweatshirts with CIA insignias and the mottos: YE SHALL KNOW THE TRUTH, AND THE TRUTH SHALL SET YOU FREE and ADMIT NOTHING. DENY EVERYTHING.

Every journalist who tries to ferret out the truth about spy activity recognizes that there will always be unverifiable loose ends and a real possibility that further layers lie beneath the layers you uncover. But still, getting as much of the truth as we can is definitely worth the effort.

Charlotte has been a patient investigator, exploring those loose ends with precision. She has also been been curious and unafraid — two traits that once caused a CIA psychologist to ask her why she didn't join the agency. But those traits also apply to journalism. She began her career in the Arab world. In 1975, she dodged bullets and reported on the beginning of the Lebanese civil war. She interviewed victims of the Shah of Iran's oppression and diplomat families who began to question the official story of the hostage takeover of the American embassy in 1979. She later risked her life with her husband in the Amazon in order to chronicle the destruction of the rainforest and its indigenous peoples during the darkest time of Latin American dictators. But the Middle East has always had a special hold on her, as did the need to know what exactly happened to her father.

In the process, she uncovered a larger story, too — about what happened to the peoples of the Middle East when the search for oil "at all costs" in the post-World War II period resulted in unimaginable human suffering through deadly wars that continue to this day. Sadly, our father was prescient when he warned, "God help us if we ever send troops to the Middle East."

This book uncovers real patterns in history, patterns that continue to shape major events that will affect us all, and we remain ignorant of them at our own peril.

Daniel C. Dennett, III
Cape Elizabeth, Maine
November 15, 2019

CHAPTER ONE

Tracking TAPLINE

On the afternoon of March 24, 1947, a team of American investigators combed through the wreckage of a C-47 military transport plane that had crashed into the side of a mountain near remote Dessie, Ethiopia, killing all six Americans aboard.[1] Four of the men on Flight 3804's manifest had been enlisted men. The other two were civilians: the Cairo-based US petroleum attaché and the Beirut-based US cultural attaché — my father, Daniel Dennett, who used his State Department position as a cover for his work for the Central Intelligence Group (CIG), predecessor to the Central Intelligence Agency (CIA). Dennett had just come from a mission to American oil installations in Saudi Arabia. There, he had been trying to determine the final route of the Trans-Arabian Pipeline, which would transport oil across the Arabian Peninsula to a terminal point on the shores of the Eastern Mediterranean, in either Palestine or Lebanon.

The plane was carrying heavy cargo — 2,000 pounds of top secret radio equipment as well as an aerial camera. The passengers were destined for Addis Ababa and meetings with officials of Sinclair Oil. This American oil company had recently won an exclusive concession from Emperor Haile Selassie to explore for oil throughout all of Ethiopia.

Investigators found the communications equipment smashed into many pieces, a cause for great concern back in Washington, DC. But lying in the rubble untouched by the impact of the crash was a book, titled simply *This Fascinating Oil Business*. The author, Max Ball, was an oilman who had written the book in 1939, when anticipation of America becoming a major oil power in the Middle East was heightened thanks to its 1933 exclusive oil concession in Saudi Arabia. His goal, Ball explained, was to "uproot some cherished notions" about the oil business, plainly stating, among other things, that "the oil industry is no monopoly but a dog-eat-dog competition, with too many dogs."[2]

It would take me many years to fully appreciate just how ugly — indeed, deadly — that dog-eat-dog competition could get, and how oil pipelines and espionage have played a major role in the many conflicts in the Middle East. Over the course of five decades I made annual trips to the US National Archives in College Park, Maryland, to pore over Daniel Dennett's declassified reports for the wartime Office of Strategic Services (OSS) and its immediate postwar successor, the CIG, trying to understand the events leading up to the plane crash and the nature of his work as American's top master spy in the Middle East. Perhaps because I never knew my father — I was six weeks old when he died — I felt compelled to "discover" him through his writings. But what propelled me more than anything was the growing suspicion that the plane crash had not been an accident caused by bad weather, as was tentatively reported in an accident report I found at the archives. "The plane crashed into the side of the mountain because clouds obscured the mountains," my mother would explain. I never questioned her further, not wanting to upset her. It was only after her death in 1972, when I was in my early twenties and working as a roving correspondent throughout the Middle East, that I realized that I needed to know more about my father and the circumstances leading up to the plane crash.

Decades later, in 1995, I tracked down a CIA officer at Fort Myer, just outside Washington, DC, who had served in the Middle East after the war and knew of my father. Dennett's death was "a great loss," he admitted. "He knew more about the Middle East than our man in Egypt," whose knowledge, he joked, "went back two thousand years." Then he turned serious. "We always thought it was sabotage, but we could never prove it."

A Life-Changing Discovery
My introduction to pipeline politics actually began in late 1975, after I left Lebanon, then ravaged by civil war, and my job as a reporter for the *Daily Star*, an English-language newspaper in Beirut, to return to the States. I had been shot at during the buildup to the civil war, and I decided that I was not keen on losing my life at a young age in a war that made no sense. I joined my brother, also named Daniel Dennett, and his family for Christmas dinner at their home in North Andover, Massachusetts. After regaling them with tales of my travels throughout the Middle East, I was suddenly struck by the realization that I had been retracing many of the steps of our late father when he was sleuthing in the Middle East in the mid-1940s under the code name "Carat."[3]

My Christmas-dinner epiphany prompted me to venture up into the attic to search for an old steamer trunk I had found in my mother's attic as a youngster. Back then, it had beckoned me to open it, but as I dimly recalled, I had been distracted by my grandmother's exotic costumes from her days as a biology teacher at a Christian college for girls in Constantinople (now Istanbul) in 1900. They had been draped over the trunk, and so I paid little attention to what lay inside.

After my mother's death, the steamer trunk was transferred to my brother's attic, where I happily found it under a sunlit eave. This time, with an anticipation I couldn't have begun to match in childhood, I opened it and found — to my astonishment — a blanket wrapped around a scrapbook crammed full of photographs of Turkey at the turn of the century. Beneath it lay three more scrapbooks. One traced my father's youth through public high school, then Harvard and, upon graduation, teaching assignments at the American University of Beirut in the early 1930s; the other two were full of photos and letters from my father and mother in Beirut to my grandparents in Winchester, Massachusetts, dating from 1944 to 1947.

I immediately pulled out the last scrapbook and carefully turned one brittle page after another, looking for letters and newspaper clippings that led up to the time of his death. Sure enough, there was the fateful telegram to my mother informing her of the plane crash in Ethiopia. After that came a frayed yellow obituary from the *Winchester Star*, which stated that my father had been on a "vacation junket" to Ethiopia. Better yet, inserted into the pages of the scrapbook were two folded documents, one identified in my mother's handwriting as "Dan's last report" and the other, "Dan's last letter home."

For a few minutes I sat very still, realizing that these were the final reports from my father about his last days on earth. I was too excited to contemplate the fact that my mother had never told me of their existence, or that she and her mother-in-law had prepared these scrapbooks for someone in the family to eventually discover as a treasure trove of my father's life and death — in short, his legacy.

Pasted into the scrapbook were letters of condolence from his professors and his peers. His German professor at Harvard, John Waltz, wrote, "In my nearly 50 years of experience with college students, few have made such a strong and lasting impression upon me as your son. . . . He seemed to me to represent the best New England traditions: open mindedness, fairness, tolerance, [and] humaneness and did not depart from them in the most trying times. He had wise intellectual and artistic interests. He was the type of man that is most needed in America at the present time and in the immediate future." It helped to read those words, to learn from someone other than family members that there had been good qualities to the man, at least when he was a student. But I couldn't help wondering: Had he been tolerant and humane as a spy? After all, my attic discovery occurred at a time when all sorts of sordid revelations were being reported about the CIA in the aftermath of the Vietnam War. Did they apply to the CIA's predecessor organizations as well? Did they apply to my father?

I found a telegram from the director of the Office of Near Eastern and African Affairs at the Department of State, Loy Henderson, stating that Dennett's "record of service was outstanding." That kind of tribute could perhaps be expected — although I later learned that Henderson was a very big fish in the State Department and, in a break with protocol, often received many of Dennett's secret reports directly, without review by intermediaries, a rare practice.

Perhaps most interesting was a letter from the American minister to Saudi Arabia, J. Rives Childs, reporting to the American minister* in Beirut, Lowell Pinkerton, that "Dennett arrived [in Riyadh] about March 14 from Dhahran and was of great help to us in the information he was able to give me *concerning the pipeline negotiations*. He had an exceptional mind and indicated by his eagerness to learn and willingness to impart his knowledge that he possessed exceptional qualifications as an Officer of Our Government."[4] (emphasis added)

Reading through my father's last letter and his last report, I concluded that his mission to Saudi Arabia was fraught with political intrigue. He was charged with inspecting American oil installations at the headquarters of the Arabian American Oil Company (Aramco) in Dhahran and determining where the Trans-Arabian Pipeline (also known as TAPLINE) should cross the Arabian Peninsula, what countries it would traverse, and where it should terminate on the Eastern Mediterranean coast.

His official report to Minister Childs described a top TAPLINE negotiator expressing deep frustration — not with the Saudis, but with the Syrians over their reluctance to grant pipeline transit rights over Syrian territory on the terms offered by the American oilmen. TAPLINE's William Lenahan

---

* During and immediately after World War II, ambassadors to the Middle East were referred to as "ministers" and the embassies were called "legations."

"was in a gloomy and angry mood," Dennett wrote. "He was finished with the Syrians. . . . Shortly after we reached Dhahran he told me that he had been criticized by Aramco and Standard officials for talking too freely about the pipeline project [to me]. He asked me under no circumstances to reveal while I was in Dhahran that I knew anything about or was interested in the pipeline negotiations. I agreed." (Being a loyal government employee, however, Dennett ignored Lenahan's warning and, as noted by Childs, gave a detailed report on his visit to Saudi Arabia.)[5]

My father's last letter to my mother was more intimate and colorful, expressing his awe and fascination with this new American enterprise and the walled-off, suburban-like community it had created in the middle of the desert, sitting on top of one of the richest oil finds in the world. He mused over the future of Arabia and noted, "The most interesting thing of all was seeing the plans now under foot for building new Arab towns, laying on electricity, drinking water, medical and hospital services, good sanitation. . . . No one knows just how large the biggest [oil] field is, but they have drilled 27 wells so far over an area 15 miles long and 8 wide and they haven't drilled a dry well yet."

His letter ended cryptically. He was not heading back to Beirut as originally planned. "For reasons I will tell you later," he reported to my mother, "I am going to Ethiopia. . . ."

From the contents of his last report and last letter home, I concluded that, in contradiction of his obituary, his subsequent flight to Ethiopia was no "vacation junket." Did government officials tell my grandparents what to leave in and what to leave out of the obituary? Or did they self-censor because they knew (or did they?) that he was on a top secret intelligence mission? Was this why there was no mention of his trip to Saudi Arabia? I couldn't ask my grandparents, who were long gone, or my mother. Where could I go for answers?

There was no World Wide Web at this time. But of course there were libraries. Thankfully, the Howe Memorial Library of the University of Vermont was located in nearby Burlington. I went straight to its reference department on the first floor, which housed thick multivolume indexes to the *New York Times*. I pulled out the 1947 volume and began to search for articles on the Middle East and Saudi Arabia. What turned up was truly eye opening.

An article in the Sunday *Times*, dated March 2, 1947, appeared three weeks before the airplane crash under this headline: "Pipeline for U.S.

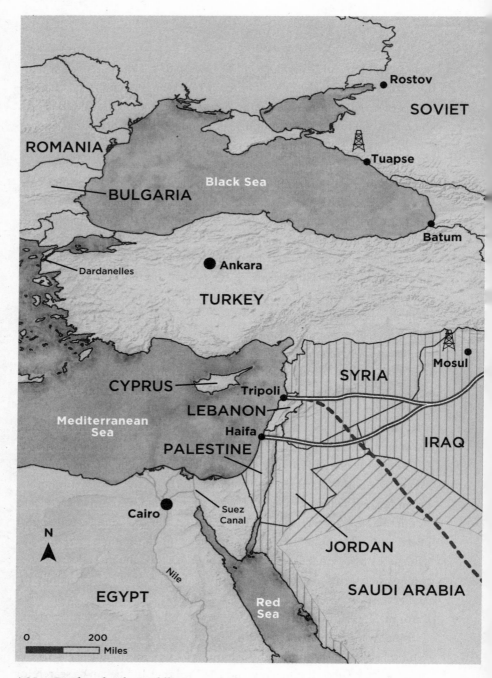

A New Pipeline for the Middle East

This map is adapted from an extraordinary map published in the *New York Times* just two weeks before the 1947 plane crash that killed Daniel Dennett. That original map provided my first introduction to pipeline politics. Like this one, it showed a projected route of the Trans-Arabian Pipeline, but its accompanying

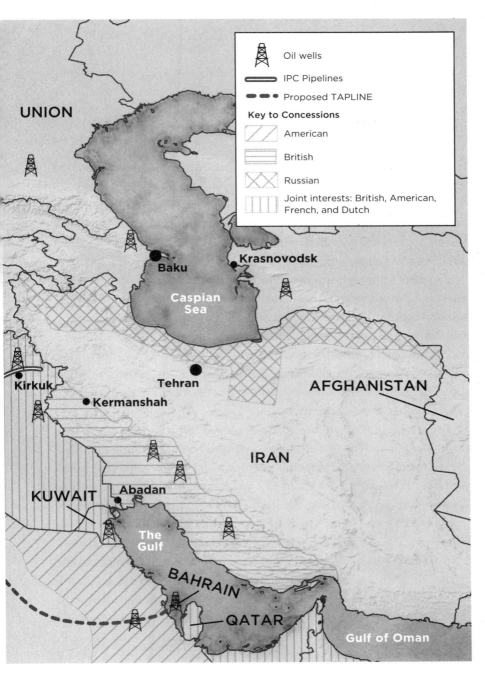

UNION

Baku

Krasnovodsk

Caspian
Sea

Kirkuk

Tehran

Kermanshah

AFGHANISTAN

IRAN

KUWAIT Abadan

The
Gulf

BAHRAIN

QATAR

Gulf of Oman

Oil wells

IPC Pipelines

Proposed TAPLINE

Key to Concessions

American

British

Russian

Joint interests: British, American,
French, and Dutch

article, "Pipeline for U.S. Adds to Middle East Issues," put the pipeline and Dennett's last mission to Saudi Arabia into a larger context: a big-power rivalry over
oil, especially with Russia, that has continued to this day. The map also showed the
two branches of the older Iraq Petroleum Company (IPC) pipelines, constructed
in the early 1930s, which had equally profound significance to Middle East issues.[6]

Adds to Middle East Issues: Oil Concessions Raise Questions Involving Position of Russia." It could not have been more to the point, and as I write now, over seven decades later, I can't help but marvel over its relevance to today's concerns with Russia.

Datelined Cairo, and written by Clifton Daniel (later to be President Harry Truman's son-in-law), it began: "By 1950 more than one hundred million American dollars will have been laid out across the Arabian *and Syrian deserts* and the territories of four Middle East countries in the form of a pipeline from Saudi Arabia to the Mediterranean coast [emphasis added; apparently, the developing problem of transit rights across Syria was not known to the reporter]."

The next paragraph was even more telling: "Protection of that investment and the military and economic security that it represents inevitably will become one of the prime objectives of American foreign policy in this area, which already has become a pivot of world politics and one of the main focal points of rivalry between East and West." The East, of course, was the Soviet Union, another rising superpower after World War II. Clearly, the Soviets' growing influence in the Middle East was being seen as a matter of national security.

Two paragraphs down, the article described this pipeline ("one of the world's largest and longest") as being a possible source of conflict between the United States and Great Britain. It meant "laying down another major American interest in the Middle East parallel to that of the British. The Anglo-American partnership, rattled this week by the renewal of faultfinding on the Palestine issue, will be further consolidated or — another possibility — new areas of contention between the two countries will be created."

If the mention of Palestine was not enough to heighten my interest, the article brought another major player, France, into the possible fray: "France has formally demanded to know why she, a partner with the British, Americans, and Dutch in the Iraq Petroleum Company, was left out of the recent deal by the partners to share in the extraction and sale of Arabian oil."

This was my first hint of rivalry among America's erstwhile allies over postwar oil in the Middle East.

But perhaps the best part of the article was the map that accompanied it. Titled "A New Pipeline for the Middle East," it showed the dotted line of the projected pipeline extending west across Saudi Arabia, Jordan, and Syria to a terminal point in Lebanon. The line ran across the British-controlled

Iraq Petroleum Company (IPC) pipeline that terminated in Haifa, Palestine, and into the French-controlled IPC pipeline that terminated in northern Lebanon near the Syrian border. Both pipelines were branches of the IPC pipeline originating in oil fields near Kirkuk, Iraq, and built in the early 1930s. Seen from the bird's-eye vantage point of a map reader, it looked as though the proposed Trans-Arabian Pipeline was butting a proverbial camel's nose under the tent of two colonial powers, which (as I soon learned) did not welcome the intrusion.

Pipeline Maps Are Worth a Thousand Words

Thus began my fascination with pipeline maps. You know the saying: A picture is worth a thousand words. Well, the same goes for maps.

If this March 2, 1947, article and map weren't enough to get me going, in that same Sunday edition the *New York Times* ran yet another article with another map that put big-power rivalry in the Middle East in a larger context. Appearing in the "News of the Week" section, this second map bore the title "Focal Points on the World Map — as Some Great Decisions Impend."

The focal points were actually worldwide spheres of influence, and what leapt out from this map was the prominent position of Great Britain controlling all the important coastlands of the Middle East, from the Eastern Mediterranean through the Suez Canal, down to the Red Sea, and rounding the Horn of Africa, covering the southern tip of the Arabian Peninsula (including what is now Yemen) and both sides of the Persian Gulf (now commonly referred to as "the Gulf" to satisfy Arab sensibilities, the Arabs having long protested the "one-sided" labeling of the waterway, which is bordered by Iran on the east and the Arabian Peninsula on the west).[7] I had never seen such a vivid illustration of British monopoly over the Middle East in order to protect its trade and tanker routes to India.* Yet there was one significant exception: There, smack in the middle of the Arabian Peninsula, like a dark inkblot plopped down in the midst of Great Britain's sphere of

---

* I would later learn that when Winston Churchill, as First Lord of the Admiralty on the eve of World War I, converted the Royal Navy's fuel from coal (of which Britain had ample supplies) to the more energy-efficient oil (of which it had none), he predicted that he would have to "take arms against a sea of troubles" to gain access to oil. This map showed the result of that prediction: Not only did Britain control the Middle Eastern waterways to guarantee its ships a safe passage to India, but it was also protecting the route of oil tankers delivering precious oil to its navy and for its industrial development.

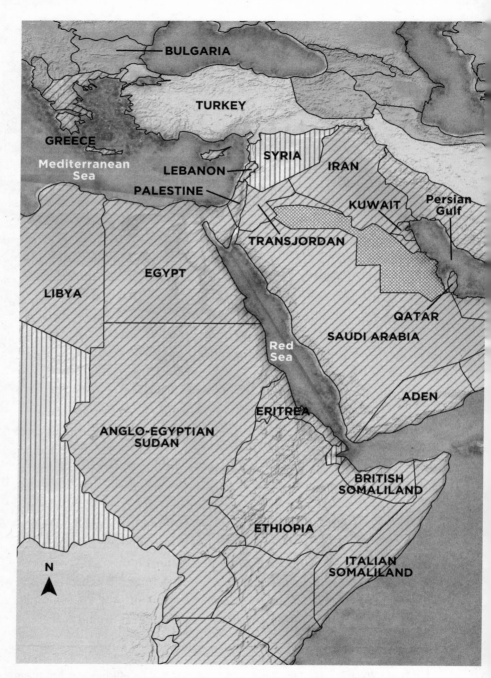

Focal Points on the World Map: The British Sphere of Influence in the Middle East
This map, too, is adapted from a *New York Times* map published on March 2, 1947.
Its most noticeable aspect is the British sphere of influence, revealing Britain's
exclusive colonial control over the countries bordering waterways of strategic
importance to the British Empire. That control was needed for the protection of

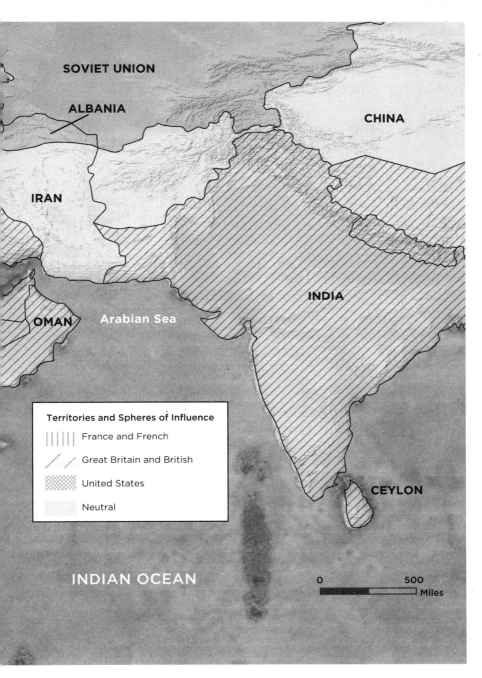

SOVIET UNION

ALBANIA

CHINA

IRAN

OMAN
Arabian Sea

INDIA

Territories and Spheres of Influence

| | | | | | France and French

/ / Great Britain and British

United States

Neutral

CEYLON

INDIAN OCEAN

0   500
                      Miles

its trade route to India as well as oil tanker routes from the Eastern Mediterranean through the Suez Canal, down the Red Sea, around the Bab el Mandeb Strait to the Gulf of Aden (bordering Yemen), and on to the Gulf and the Indian Ocean. Equally significant is the small (but soon to grow) sphere of US influence in the Middle East shown here as occupying a large section of Saudi Arabia.[8]

influence, was the American sphere of influence. And according to the *New York Times* article accompanying this map, the greatest impending decision in the postwar era was how that sphere of influence might change. The article's title read, "Our World Role: A Crucial Debate Opens."

World War II had changed the balance of power in the Middle East, with Great Britain's power significantly reduced and the United States' power greatly increased. A look at the two *New York Times* maps reveals the difference: Britain's direct colonial hold over the region's waterways, depicted in the "Focal Points on the World Map" map, had ceded to joint interests (British, American, French, Netherlands), as depicted in the "New Pipeline for the Middle East" map. Hovering to the north of the Middle East like a giant sleeping bear was the vast territory of the Soviet Union. Its geographic location — much closer to the Middle East than either Great Britain or the United States — was clearly a matter of intense concern. The Soviet Union was already occupying the northern part of oil-rich Iran. The article laid out the contours of the world's "debate," noting "rivalry of East versus West, or communism vs capitalism," along with the fact that Great Britain had been seriously weakened from the war and "could no longer keep up with all its commitments." This required "greater American economic participation in the Mediterranean and the Middle East, where Britain's influence is now pitted against Russia."

Here, in stark print, were the beginning signals of the Cold War. Ten days later, President Harry Truman announced the Truman Doctrine, designed to shield Greece and Turkey from Soviet penetration. The creation of the Central Intelligence Agency would soon follow with the passage of the National Security Act of 1947.

This was the historical context I had been looking for, and it shaped my inquiry into my father's death. My parents' letters home in 1946 and early 1947 clearly indicated that he saw Soviet Russia as the United States' biggest enemy in the postwar Middle East. But as declassified OSS documents at the National Archives would soon reveal, Great Britain and France (both resentful over America's displacement of their colonial influence in the Middle East) were not above suspicion. And lying at the heart of intensifying postwar rivalries among former allies was the Trans-Arabian Pipeline.

In fact, TAPLINE's ramifications would extend all the way to Europe. Its promise of delivering vast quantities of oil to an energy-starved postwar Europe would help secure the reindustrialization of western Europe through the Marshall Plan without using Western hemisphere oil resources that had already been diminished since the war.[9] It stood to reason that by replacing coal as a fuel source for many European industries, TAPLINE would also help break the hold of communist-controlled labor unions over the region's coal industry. Back then, a battle between superpowers over competing sources of energy was beginning to flare up. The very survival of Western capitalism seemed to depend on the success of TAPLINE, forcing Dennett, as the top diplomat-spy in the Middle East, to become expert in the intrigues of what I call the Great Game for Oil.

The Great Game Heats Up

When the OSS sent Daniel Dennett to Beirut, Lebanon, in the spring of 1944, his mission was to engage in counterintelligence work. That meant protecting American and Allied intelligence operations against infiltration by the Germans. But when he arrived, he discovered that all German agents had been "cleaned up." Instead, he soon found himself in the middle of a covert battle for cultural, political, and economic influence in the Middle East, pitting him against America's wartime allies — the British, the French, and the Russians. The State Department had warned him that he would find a veritable "free-for-all" among the allies as the war began to wind down, but he was still shocked (Anglophile that he was) to discover that the British were the biggest danger among the three allies when he first arrived. In his first report to his OSS superior, Turner McBaine, on May 12, 1944, Dennett described how, while "living his cover" as the cultural attaché, he learned that the British were fully engaged in cultural warfare against the Americans in their efforts to penetrate the American University of Beirut and the Aleppo College of Syria with British teachers and propaganda.[10] McBaine would have to wait for Carat's political and economic reporting to kick in, but when it did, the intelligence he gathered was bound to circulate beyond the US government. Whether Dennett knew it or not, McBaine also served as chief counsel to Standard Oil of California (Socal, later Chevron), one of the main partners in Aramco, which held the exclusive oil concession in Saudi Arabia.

From the time of its announcement to the press in February 1944, the Trans-Arabian Pipeline loomed large in the consciousness of every Arab leader and every foreign diplomat and spy stationed in Lebanon, Syria, and Saudi Arabia. Its construction, completed in 1950, would change the balance of power in the whole Middle East and, for that matter, the whole world. It would help firmly establish the United States as a global superpower.

During a brief visit to Washington, DC, following the death of Franklin D. Roosevelt in 1945, my father revealed to a family friend that his life was in danger. As he boarded a plane for Beirut, he turned to his friend and soberly commented, "I may not come home alive. Please look after my wife and children in case that happens."

When he returned to Beirut, he found that French authorities had used a disturbance in a Lebanese village as a pretext to send troop reinforcements into Syria and Lebanon and brutally bomb Damascus. Dennett, who now employed at least twenty subagents in the region, quickly learned the true motive behind the French invasion: to control air and naval bases in the region that protected French-owned oil interests.[11]

By October 1945, Dennett and his colleagues had to contend with yet another challenge: appeasing Saudi Arabia's King Abdulaziz Ibn Saud. Two months before Roosevelt died, he had met with the monarch at Great Bitter Lake in Egypt in February 1945 and repeated his promise that no action would be taken on the status of Palestine without "prior consultation" with the Arabs. Now, according to Colonel William Eddy, then American minister to Saudi Arabia and the translator during the Bitter Lake discussions, Ibn Saud "could not reconcile" Roosevelt's promise with a "reported proposal by the United States that 100,000 [surviving European] Jews should be admitted to Palestine now without prior consultation." Colonel Eddy passed on to the State Department's Loy Henderson his dire warning: "If the growing suspicion should be confirmed that the US Government is flirting with a Palestine policy friendly to political Zionism and therefore (in Arab opinion) hostile to the Arabs, United States enterprises in Saudi Arabia will be seriously handicapped." In addition, "the King would not agree to have the oil from his country carried in a pipeline which terminates in Jewish controlled area, thereby making his country contribute to the livelihood and prosperity of Zionists."[12]

This stark example of Saudi involvement in pipeline politics would torment Carat and other foreign service personnel throughout the next year. As Carat affirmed to his superiors after completing his training, his mission to the Middle East was to "protect the oil at all costs." Now that mission appeared to be endangered by political Zionists on the one hand and, on the other, by Arab nationalists who were angry with the United States for having broken FDR's promise of "prior consultation."[13] He seemed stuck in a no-win situation.

On August 3, 1946, threats to Dennett's life became tangible. Terrorists bombed the US Legation in Beirut, including his office, and to a much lesser extent the British Legation. This was the first bombing of a US legation in the Middle East. Dennett rushed to the scene, crawled over the ruins of his office, and was relieved to find his safe still intact with top secret documents inside. The British immediately told him that Zionists were responsible. After all, a Zionist group had taken responsibility for the recent bombing of the British administrative and military headquarters for Palestine in the King David Hotel in Jerusalem. But Dennett's sources reported that the bombing in Beirut was "very amateurish," showing "very little planning," and certainly nothing "like the skill apparent in the bombing of the King David Hotel." Washington responded favorably to his reports, thanking him for his "voluminous material" (sent in five separate consecutive reports) and expressing the hope that "you will be able to piece together the true picture of the 'behind-the-scenes intrigue.' Naturally, we are most interested in the possibility that an outside Power may be involved." [14]

Carat began to suspect the British, taking a cue from Washington's memo, which had noted, "We cannot help but wonder why the British are taking no action. . . . It would seem that if they are actually doing nothing, they must have had excellent reasons for reaching such a decision."[15] But he also had to admit that, in the current climate, the Russians could not be ruled out. Just a week before the bombing, Dennett had written Washington's OSS that "we now agree that Lebanon has become the center in the Arab World for communist propaganda and activity. . . . The present [Lebanese] government is weak, fearful and easily intimidated by foreign powers."[16] He had asked for increased security at the embassy, but it never arrived.

These events and the intrigue surrounding them did not bode well if Lebanon was to become the terminal point for the Trans-Arabian Pipeline. Dennett found an agent to infiltrate the Lebanese Communist Party but found only cold comfort there. He learned, through one of his agent's discussions with the Soviet chargé d'affaires in Damascus, Vladimir Kiriev, that both the Russians and the French had started a "whispering campaign" against American diplomats in Beirut. According to the agent's report to Dennett, Kiriev described the Franco-Russian whisper campaign as accusing the US Legation of being "a large espionage outfit" bent on "kicking

France out [of Lebanon] in order to take her place." Kiriev summed it up succinctly: "America wants oil and mandate." This agent's report prompted Carat to warn Washington that "we expect increased French-Soviet attempts to penetrate the Legation."[17]

The bombing — which came with the threat that American oil installations would be next — occurred just one week before the United States convinced the Lebanese government to sign an agreement granting transit rights for the Trans-Arabian Pipeline. With Lebanon on board as a terminal point, the United States was one step closer to realizing its plan of connecting Saudi Arabia to Lebanon via a pipeline to the Mediterranean Sea and further cementing American interests in the region. The only remaining hurdle was getting Syria to grant transit rights for the pipeline to pass through the Golan Heights before reaching Lebanon.

Dennett's last official report, written following his trip to Saudi Arabia in March 1947, described how American oilmen had been quarreling over whether the final Mediterranean terminal point of the Trans-Arabian Pipeline should be in Haifa, Palestine (a destination not only opposed by Ibn Saud but also wracked by violence as Great Britain desperately fought Zionist Irgun paramilitary fighters over who should control Palestine), or in the Lebanese port town of Sidon, south of Beirut. Either way, the pipeline would have to pass through Syria, and the Syrians were balking on granting transit rights. The reason: President Harry Truman's final endorsement of sending 100,000 Jewish European refugees — survivors of the Holocaust — to Palestine. The president of Syria objected, having been openly critical of America's pro-Zionist policy in Palestine.[18]

Dennett did not live to see how the Syrian problem was resolved. He warned of Lenahan's frustrations with Syria during his trip to Saudi Arabia and then shifted his focus to Ethiopia, another region of intense big-power rivalry. He told a close friend in the United States that he had always dreamed of going to Ethiopia, a comment that, in the aftermath of the crash, would leave his friend overwhelmed with feelings of guilt for not having urged caution.

The Great Game in Ethiopia

From the outset of my quest, I wondered why my father had been heading to Ethiopia following his trip to Saudi Arabia. And why was the US petroleum attaché for the Middle East also on board that flight?

Once again, visits to the National Archives and perusal of declassified OSS documents answered my questions.

At the end of World War II, Emperor Haile Selassie was anxious to rid Ethiopia of Britain's stranglehold over his country's commerce, foreign affairs, and communications — a stranglehold that had existed since the British liberated the country from the Italians. He turned to the United States and an American oil company for help. In August 1945, he signed an exclusive concession with the American Sinclair Oil Company to explore Ethiopia for oil. If this were not enough of an affront to British interests, the emperor also entertained US proposals to set up an Ethiopia-owned airline managed by the American company Transcontinental & Western Air (TWA) to operate throughout the country, despite a 1942 military convention that had allowed only British military aircraft and personnel to fly freely into, over, and out of Ethiopia. Under the 1942 convention, British civil aircraft were to have a monopoly over commercial traffic. This restriction, reported John Spencer, an American legal advisor to the emperor, was of "particular concern" to the US State Department, "which feared that this provision would effectively exclude US carriers." Later in August 1945, a representative of TWA, Jack Nichols, headed to Addis Ababa to finalize arrangements with the emperor for setting up what would be called Ethiopian Air Lines. But he never made it.

Reported Spencer, "[Nichols's] plane crashed against an uncharted mountain peak in northern Ethiopia. It was only on September 8 that the contract was concluded, following a tense negotiating session lasting well into the night."[19] Perhaps not coincidentally, the flight path taken by Nichols's plane was identical to the one followed in March 1947 by the C-47 flight that killed Dennett and five other Americans.

With Ethiopian Air Lines finally established, Spencer set about acquiring aerial photos of Ethiopia to assist Sinclair Oil in charting pipeline routes. "A base map has been printed and several areas of most interest have been printed on this map, together with possible pipeline routes, rail distances etc.," he wrote in December 1946. "Sinclair is continuing its efforts to obtain air photos and if they are not available from any source an investigation will be made to determine the feasibility of flying over the area and obtaining photos thru a private undertaking on the part of Sinclair."

At this time, the Soviets were also coming on strong in Ethiopia, planning to build a hospital and establish public health services. They had also been carefully monitoring American moves in nearby Saudi Arabia. According to the Soviet newspaper *Izvestia*, they viewed the pipeline project as a dangerous "auxiliary enterprise of the American system of worldwide military bases," a reference to ongoing American efforts to establish an air base in Saudi Arabia.[20]

This was no idle fear. Cairo-based US military attaché Colonel William McNown had been scheduled to accompany Dennett and the five other Americans on the final leg of their trip to Ethiopia, but at the last minute he chose to get off the plane in Jidda, Saudi Arabia, to meet with the Saudis over setting up a US military base in Taif, near Jidda. The American militarization of the Middle East, in this case to protect the Trans-Arabian Pipeline, had just begun.

Regime Change in Syria as the Covert Energy Battle Takes Off

I have often contemplated what my father would have thought about postwar developments in the Middle East. He had warned, before his posting to Lebanon in 1944, "God help us if we ever send troops to the Middle East." I am grateful that he did not live to see the day when the newly created CIA responded to TAPLINE officials' declarations that Syrian intransigence over transit rights for the pipeline could not be tolerated. In 1949, the CIA overthrew then Syrian president Shukri al-Quwatli in its first-ever coup d'etat and replaced him with an army officer who promptly approved the pipeline route across Syrian territory.[21] The stakes were huge: guaranteed American transportation of Saudi oil to markets in Europe — at the expense of the Soviets.

Construction of the pipeline began shortly after the coup and was completed in December 1950. Its terminal point was in Sidon, Lebanon. It was closed down briefly by the Saudis during the Arab-Israeli War of 1967, when Israelis took control of Syria's Golan Heights, including the 25-mile stretch of the pipeline that passed through the region. The Saudis soon reopened it, and it survived without further incidents until 1969, when the Popular Front for the Liberation of Palestine (PFLP) dynamited it, causing hundreds of tons of oil to flow into the Sea of Galilee. It was closed again during the 1973 Yom Kippur War until mid-1974, only to become the target of anti-American militants during the Lebanese civil war that began in 1975. The pipeline finally closed in 1983, at a time when modern supertankers sharply cut the cost of shipping oil from Saudi Arabia through the Gulf, greatly reducing the flow of oil to a still-embattled Lebanon.[22]

The evolving story of TAPLINE opened my eyes to the central but often hidden role of oil and pipeline geopolitics in international affairs, and how secret and dangerous this intersection can be. It also sparked a further journey, one to understand how the espionage that led to my father's death not only continued but ended up shaping the future of US foreign policy and the structure of world order in an ongoing Great Game for Oil.

As the remaining chapters will show, a covert battle for energy is still being played out in Afghanistan, Georgia, Ukraine, Russia, Iran, Iraq, Syria, Gaza, Yemen, and other explosive regions of the world. The tragedy continues. But first, I need to set the stage for what happened between 1975, when my quest began, and the mid-1990s, when pipeline politics exploded onto the world scene after the dissolution of the Soviet Union. By drawing on my own experiences as a journalist in the Middle East, I have gained new insights into how oil was shaping US foreign policy in the postwar era, and why powerful interests in the United States did not — and do not — want the American people to truly understand this reality. Millions of lives have been lost, both military and civilian. As the tragedies have continued, so has the ignorance. The correlation is clear. The protest slogan "No blood for oil!" — first voiced by European Jews who escaped to Palestine in 1945 — would have to be contained.

CHAPTER TWO

Seeking Truth, Finding Oil

Many people can recall a harrowing event in their lives, one that forever shaped their outlook on their surroundings, the people they associate with, their career path, and their very identity. For me, it was the day a sniper's bullet barely missed me on a street outside a school in a suburb of Beirut. Looking back, I realize that my near brush with death forced me to grapple with the need for truth-telling in the face of danger — both as a reporter and as an individual.

My harrowing event occurred in March 1975, when I was heading to a friend's house in a communal taxi along the well-traveled route to the Beirut International Airport. Suddenly a large armored tank appeared in the street, heading toward us, its turret swinging wildly, ready to shoot off rounds at any minute. Pandemonium broke out in the taxi. "Unduk hon! Unduk hon! Min fadluk!" I yelled out in my sparse Arabic. (Stop here! Stop here! Please!) Everyone spilled out of the cab, and I raced down a narrow street in search of shelter. I found it in what appeared to be an elementary school next to a church. For the next six hours I lay on my belly underneath a desk, scribbling in a reporter's notebook while watching parents dodge bullets as they pulled their screaming children to safety.

As dusk fell, a young man who had seen me cowering under the desk as he rescued his niece came back to warn me: "A curfew will soon be imposed. You have a choice: Stay here and risk the school being overtaken by armed men who only know you as an American. Or you can come with me. You will be the last to leave. My car is parked across the street. We can make a run for it now." He held out his hand. I hesitated for a second, then took it. As we raced out of the school I noticed bloodstains near the entrance. "Over there!" he urged, gesturing toward his car, and as we dashed across the street, I heard the loud crack of a gun. A bullet whizzed by. His grip tightened and we kept running. He pushed me into the backseat of his car. "Get down. Get down!" he ordered, and then he sped his car backward down the street and away from the fighting.

My escape didn't end there. My rescuer took me to his uncle's apartment and explained that I was a visitor to the school. "Ahlan wa sahlan," his uncle said. (You are welcome.) After a few minutes, I asked if I could use a phone. He nodded, showed me to the phone, and left the room as I frantically dialed in to my newspaper, the *Daily Star*. With notes in hand, I recited my observations from under the desk to the editor and then hung up. Turning around, I found my host approaching me, this time scowling. "My nephew said you were a visitor. Who were you talking to and what were you saying? How do I know you are not a spy?"

I explained that I was a reporter for the *Daily Star*. I had taken refuge at the school when the fighting broke out, I said. I felt that I had to tell my story.

He was unconvinced. "I am sorry, but you must explain to me which side you are on. Depending on what you say, you may stay here for dinner or I will have to ask you to leave."

Another choice! Again, I made a quick calculation. I knew I was in an area near the airport that was heavily populated with Palestinian refugees.

"I have no idea who is fighting out there," I said, which was true. "I suppose it is government forces, and that they are fighting Palestinians." (The previous week, from the rooftop of my Beirut apartment, I had seen the Lebanese air force fly overhead in French Mirage jets and fire down on Palestinian refugee camps.)* The long civil war that would pit Lebanese Christians against Lebanese Shiite Muslims as well as Muslim and Christian Palestinians had not yet started, but tensions were at the exploding point. I paused, then took the leap, my gut instinct telling me to speak

---

* Seven years later, as the civil war still raged, Lebanese Maronite Christians belonging to the right-wing Christian Phalangist party entered the Sabra and Shatila refugee camps and slaughtered hundreds of men, women, and children, most of them Palestinians and Lebanese Shiites. An Israeli journalist, Seth Anziska, has recently released declassified documents showing the extent of collaboration between the Phalangists and then Israeli defense minister Ariel Sharon to rid Lebanon of Palestinians. Concluded Anziska, "Far from cementing Israel's regional hegemony, the 1982 [stage of the Lebanese Civil] War ultimately undercut Israeli and American influence in the Middle East, while transforming perceptions of both Zionism and Palestinian nationalism around the globe." See "Sabra and Shatila: New Revelations," *New York Review of Books*, September 17, 2018.

honestly while knowing that the wrong answer would have me out on the streets and into danger again. "I am for the Palestinians."

He looked intently into my eyes, then nodded and smiled. "In that case, you may stay." My host and his family treated me to a wonderful dinner and gave me a spare room. The following day, the *Daily Star* sent a team to fetch me and drive me back home.

Now, over forty years later, I look back on that incident and try to distill its full meaning, especially in the context of the Age of Trump, when attacks on the media as "fake news" by a habitually lying president have become commonplace. Telling the truth had been drummed into me in childhood by my mother (despite the fact that my father was a spy who, by profession, was taught how to lie!), and her admonitions stayed with me for my entire adult life. I realize that there are times when telling the truth can be an invitation to certain death, as when a hate-filled right-wing assailant holds a knife to one's throat near a mosque and asks, "Are you a Muslim?" Or when a crazed anti-Semite wielding a gun might confront someone outside a synagogue and ask, "Are you a Jew?" But as a young white American journalist, such extreme circumstances did not present themselves to me. I strove to report the truth and document it carefully, not only because it was the right thing to do but because readers expected it of me — and also because it saved my publisher from a libel suit. I would come to learn, however, that truth-telling did not always go hand in hand with reportage on the Middle East. As you will come to read in this book, there have been notable exceptions — brave journalists who risked their lives and their careers to tell the real story of what is going on in the Middle East. To them I owe much of what is in this book.

The Incomplete Truth

When I met my future husband in New York City in 1976, I told him, "The Middle East is the most censored region in the world." I didn't fully understand then that oil had something to do with the poor coverage of the Middle East in the Western press. It would take me decades to understand how conflicts in Lebanon, Israel/Palestine, and Syria fit into the Great Game for Oil, a deadly game that employed colonial divide-and-rule tactics to gain control over a region, pitting Arabs against Jews, Shiites against Sunnis, and Christians against Muslims. Today, most of the people in the Middle East are fully aware of the oil connection. Even some seventy years ago, when European Jews who had managed to escape Hitler's genocide took to staging protests in Palestine on behalf of the millions left behind, they either suspected or knew that the West's failure to rescue millions from the Holocaust had something to do with Saudi Arabia and the West's dependence on its oil.* Hence, their slogan, "No blood for oil!"

In the early 1970s, during my reporting days for the *Daily Star* and, before that, the English-language magazine *Middle East Sketch*, oil was a regular factor in the news. How could it not be? Saudi oil money was visibly transforming Beirut from a scenic, orange-rooftopped "Paris of the Middle East" into a freewheeling mecca of land speculation, where monolithic high-rises competing for views of the magnificent Mediterranean Sea were crowding out and eventually replacing the gracious porticoed homes of Lebanon's Ottoman and French colonial past.

During the summer, anyone flying Middle East Airlines to Beirut would invariably see black-robed Saudi women disappear into the plane's bathrooms halfway through the flight. There they would shed their veils and abayas and return to their seats dressed like elegant Parisian models. Accompanied by their husbands or male relatives, they were happy to escape Saudi Arabia's searing summer heat and looked forward to cooling off in Lebanon's mountains. In the evening, the Saudis would descend into the city to party in Beirut's fabulous nightclubs or gamble in the nearby Casino du Liban, freed from the ultra-strict restraints of their native country and its Wahhabi sect's prohibition of alcohol and Western dress styles.

Talk of oil was all around me, though only in a superficial way. Then, in 1973, the Arab oil-producing countries made world news when they declared an oil embargo against the United States and other Western countries for supporting Israel in the so-called Yom Kippur or October War. That was one of the few times when Americans got a small splash of

---

* As indicated in the previous chapter, the Saudi king explicitly rejected Haifa, Palestine, as the terminal point for the Trans-Arabian Pipeline in 1946. Even earlier, in 1944, Ibn Saud's opposition to Jewish immigration to Palestine and to Zionism in general was "well known," according to US Secretary of State Edward Reilly Stettinius Jr., who reminded President Roosevelt on December 13, 1944, that "recent pro-Zionist statements in this country" could have "a very definite bearing upon the future of the immensely valuable American oil concession in Saudi Arabia . . . " See *Foreign Relations of the United States*, 1944, volume V, Palestine, ed. E. R. Perkins, et al. (Washington, DC: US Government Printing Office, 1965), document 705.

oil reality as they lined up at the pump waiting for rationed gasoline. I was in Abu Dhabi at the very time that the boycott was announced by Sheikh Zayed bin Sultan al-Nahyan, ruler of Abu Dhabi and president of the United Arab Emirates. The embargo ended in March 1974 after Secretary of State Henry Kissinger negotiated an Israeli withdrawal from Egypt's Sinai Peninsula and peace talks between Syria and Israel had commenced.

"What Charlotte Couldn't Write"

As fate would have it, my early career as a journalist had me traveling to all the burgeoning oil countries on either side of the Gulf, with the exception of Saudi Arabia, where foreign women were not allowed to enter. The publisher of the *Middle East Sketch*, an Armenian entrepreneur named Bedros Kazandjian, knew there was money to be made by putting out colorful special issues celebrating the remarkable transformation of nomadic Bedouin societies into modern city-states thanks to their newfound oil wealth. My job as a roving correspondent was to document the phenomenon in places where most Western journalists had never been nor heard of: Bahrain, Kuwait, Oman, Abu Dhabi, Dubai, and the United Arab Emirates.

Today, as I look back at the first words I wrote about Abu Dhabi in 1973, I see how the oil connection had already clearly captured my imagination. In a piece I titled "Five Years from Blastoff," I wrote, "Once again the world's most precious commodity — petroleum — has launched a small, poverty-stricken country into space age modernity and affluence. Less than a decade ago . . . the southern Gulf sheikhdom of Abu Dhabi offered little more than two oases lost in an otherwise forbidden desert wasteland. . . . Abu Dhabi town, once a dismal setting of make-shift fishermen's shacks, a ruler's palace and a couple of mosques, is quickly becoming a futuristic vision of ultra-modern buildings, well-planned, four-lane dual carriageways and immense roundabouts, and a constantly evolving skyline."

I soon learned, however, that my publisher was far more interested in the ad revenues that could be derived from his glossy "country promotionals" than he was in what I wrote. Sometimes he would visit me and my beautiful blond British colleague, Christine Wood (who sold the ads), during our travels. He invariably asked Christine how she was doing, but not me. It was clear that I could write anything I wanted as long as it was not critical of the host governments I was covering. He certainly was not interested in publishing the truth about the growing corruption among the ruling sheikhs in the Gulf states or their repression of dissidents. So I wrote about modern welfare states providing annual subsidies and free education and health care to their citizens, about clashing cultures as mothers faced young daughters seeking freedom from the veil, and about the challenges facing architects in creating modern apartments that could accommodate old customs (mimicking, for instance, the gender-separate living quarters found in Bedouin tents). All fascinating — but not the whole story, which ended up in a file I called "What Charlotte couldn't write."

Iran presented another challenge to truth-seeking in that era. The *Sketch* sent me there in 1973 to cover the 2,500-year anniversary of the Persian Empire. Shah Reza Pahlavi, whom the CIA placed on the Peacock Throne in 1953 following the overthrow of the democratically elected nationalist prime minister, Mohammad Mosaddegh, chose the occasion to herald his peaceful "White Revolution" in rapidly modernizing his country. His aim, with US encouragement, was to use Iran's growing oil wealth to Westernize, even secularize, the country and break it free from the conservative mullahs who ruled the rural interior of Iran and adhered to their old religious ways.

What the festivities did *not* show, however, was the way the shah forced change on his citizens — not peacefully but coercively. To counter anticipated resistance in both cities and towns, he relied on his dreaded secret police, known as SAVAK. While in Tehran, I was shocked to see men in dark suits and dark glasses surveying every street corner and crowd for signs of a disturbance. Young college students, upon learning that I was American, pleaded with me to "tell the truth about our country" and expose the tyrannical rule of the US-backed shah. They told me about an explosion in a university chemistry lab that had killed dissident students; about a movie theater fire that had killed all the young people inside because the exit doors were locked; about universities being plied with drugs to keep students pacified in "opium dens"; about how the shah's sister, Princess Ashraf, was rumored to be a trafficker in opium.[1]

I had to relegate these stories to my "What Charlotte couldn't write" file, having recently seen how BBC reporters were declared personae non gratae for writing critically about the shah. But my day would come. Those stories would finally come to light a few years later, in the aftermath of the 1979 Iran hostage crisis, when the shah, having been deposed, was allowed to enter the United States for medical treatment, and Iranians seized the American Embassy in Tehran and took fifty-two Americans hostage in protest. But that was still a way off, and in the meantime, the world — and my search for the truth behind my father's life and death — tumbled onward.

From the Middle East to Latin America and Back Again

On April 13, 1975, right-wing Christian militiamen in Lebanon ambushed a busload of Palestinians, killing all within. I was in England on vacation when I heard the news, and I knew instantly that this was the spark that would start a civil war. By this time I had quit the *Middle East Sketch* and become a reporter for the Beirut *Daily Star*. Unlike my experience at the *Sketch*, as a reporter for the *Daily Star* I was allowed to write freely about contentious politics in Lebanon, including the mounting tensions between different factions. Just before I had left Beirut, a man in British intelligence had passed information on to my colleague Christine that I was a marked woman and should not return to Beirut. Having already escaped a bullet, I decided to stay out of Lebanon for the time being and return to the United States until the fighting subsided — unable to fathom that the war would last fifteen years.

I found an apartment in New York and began nosing around the United Nations looking for stories. The Middle East was fresh in my mind and very much in the news, what with rising oil prices following the 1973 October "Yom Kippur" War and the Arab oil boycott that followed it, the highly controversial 1974 appearance and address to the UN General Assembly by Yasir Arafat of the Palestine Liberation Organization, and the start of the Lebanese civil war. My future husband, also a freelance journalist, was also looking for stories at the UN.

But it was not the Middle East that brought Gerard "Jerry" Colby and me together. Rather, it was a story he had picked up at the UN from an Argentine journalist who had recently returned from the Brazilian Amazon. The journalist described shocking incidents of murderous attacks on Amazonian Indians and said that American evangelical missionaries working among the tribes were looking the other way. The missionaries, known in the United States as the Wycliffe Bible Translators and abroad by the deceptively secular scientific name they used, the Summer Institute of Linguistics (SIL), were working among some of the very tribes that had been hit by unknown assailants. Some Latin Americans suspected the missionaries of being allied with the CIA. Every one of the SIL missionary bases (dubbed "Scarsdales in the Amazon") came equipped with suburban ranch-style homes, manicured lawns, and tall radio towers overlooking landing strips where short takeoff and landing (STOL) aircraft of the type that had been used in Vietnam could land on a dime in the middle of the jungle.

As Americans, Jerry and I had to ask ourselves whether our compatriots in the Amazon (whether evangelical missionaries or CIA operatives) were caught up in or even complicit in the genocide of over 100,000 Amazonian Indians that took place during the 1960s and 1970s. Thus began an investigation that would absorb the next eighteen years of our lives. When we embarked on our initial six-month investigation in Latin America in June 1976, oil in the Amazon was not centermost in our minds. Nevertheless, we knew that the American oil company Texaco provided airplanes to SIL missionaries in Ecuador, and once in Ecuador, we found ourselves following the route of an American oil pipeline snaking through the jungle on the way to Limoncocha, SIL's main missionary base in the Ecuadorian Amazon. But it would take at least five years of research in presidential libraries and the National Archives before we discovered the role of Nelson Rockefeller, heir to John D. Rockefeller's formidable oil empire, in developing the Amazon (and much of Latin America's interior), starting as FDR's coordinator of inter-American affairs during World War II.

Eventually, the pieces would fall into place — and they would have relevance well beyond the Amazon and the Western Hemisphere. Much as in the conquest of the American West, wealthy ranchers, miners, and oilmen found missionaries to be useful in pacifying indigenous tribes who occupied land that they coveted. The SIL missionaries used their secular name and their scientific linguistic techniques to convince rulers in Catholic South America that their ability to teach literacy to indigenous peoples was key to integrating them into "Western" society. It seemed not to matter that the Protestant evangelical missionaries first taught Amazonian tribes to read and write in their own tribal languages by translating the Bible into their native tongues. What mattered to the host governments was that the Indians would next learn Spanish (or Portuguese in Brazil), and this would help further tribal loyalty to the government or government forces that aided foreign penetration onto the Indians' oil- and mineral-rich lands. Christ's message to turn the other cheek aided in pacification schemes, as did offerings of modern medicine to cure new diseases brought in by outsiders.

By 1995, when our book was published by HarperCollins, we finally had arrived at a title that encapsulated our findings: *Thy Will Be Done: The Conquest of the Amazon: Nelson Rockefeller and Evangelism in the Age of Oil.* One reviewer would call it "a methodology of conquest." Indeed, the techniques used in and lessons gleaned from the conquest of the Amazon could be applied to many parts of the world, albeit with adaptations. We followed the trail of US evangelical missionaries and spies from Latin America to Southeast Asia and Africa and inevitably found oil and fundamentalism as common denominators of conquest. The Middle East, being primarily Muslim, proved to be a harder nut to crack. Islam forbade its followers from converting to Christianity. More sophisticated techniques would have to be used to pacify the thousands of warring tribes in the oil-rich Middle East.

Investigating the CIA and the OSS

During our eighteen-year investigation, as Jerry and I "followed the money" in our search for what and who was behind the conquest of the Amazon, we would from time to time come across information that prompted us to look at the Middle East, and specifically, my father.

In the summer of 1976, just months after I had discovered my father's last report and last letter home at my brother's house over Christmas, Jerry and I were getting ready to leave for the Amazon. Several books had recently been published about the CIA in the wake of revelations about its involvement in the Vietnam War. Americans were learning for the first time about some of the CIA's dark underside, including its clandestine support of missionaries in Southeast Asia. I had told Jerry that my father had worked with the OSS, the predecessor of the CIA, but that I knew little about these organizations. After reading Victor Marchetti and John Marks's groundbreaking book, *The CIA and the Cult of Intelligence* in preparation for our trip, I got to wondering what my father might have been up to, and whether his work in any way paralleled the patterns of CIA operations that we were seeing in both Latin America and Southeast Asia.

I sent a letter to one of my parents' best friends, asking her to tell me about my father, his character, his political views, and what she knew about his work for the OSS. Hendrika Rynbergen was a tall, ungainly, and much-beloved retired nurse at Massachusetts General Hospital who had visited my father in Lebanon in the early 1930s, when he taught English at the American University of Beirut. She sent back to me a three-page typed letter. She described him as being rather obnoxiously opinionated when she first knew him, "so brilliant but in many ways naïve, especially when he came to Beirut, right out of Harvard, that I could never make up my mind whether to believe him or laugh at him." He eventually matured, she admitted, but the two of them invariably got into heated political arguments. "I was always a bit of a firebrand," she wrote. "He dug so much I threw my drink at him!" She recalled my father visiting her at Mass General and noticing the swastika — up until Hitler's regime an ancient symbol of health — on the smokestack. "I never heard the last of it until it was removed by popular subscription." A decade later, when he was "getting instructions from the hush-hush OSS," she found him to be "utterly intrigued by the shenanigans and dying to tell me about them, but could only hint." She knew little about the circumstances of his death. "Whether any sabotage was involved, I do not know," she wrote. "Of course the CIA — or perhaps it was then the OSS — was on the trail. I was called out of class one day to be interrogated by a government agent and I know your mother was met [by agents] on the boat when she landed with you in the U.S." Her words supported my suspicion that there was more to the plane crash than had been explained in my father's obituary.

When Jerry and I returned from Latin America, we again briefly deviated from our Amazon project upon hearing that my father's best friend from childhood, Sherman Russell, was in failing health and was not expected to live beyond six months.

We traveled to his old Victorian home in Winchester, Massachusetts, the town where I was raised by my mother, an editor at Ginn and Company publishers, and a beloved caretaker, Edna Anderson (my "second mother"). It was a rather gloomy place inside, dark and heavily draped. Its creaky floors were lined by worn Oriental rugs, suggesting that Sherm may have spent some time in the Middle East, perhaps visiting my parents. They were very close friends; my parents had even named me after Sherm's mother, Charlotte, although the family joke was that I was named after Charlotte the Donkey, a favorite pet of the British naval officer — another close friend — who had been in charge in Beirut when my parents were there. After my father's death, Sherm was a regular visitor to our house in Winchester and at one point was looked upon as a possible suitor to my mother. That never happened, most likely because Sherm turned out to be gay.

I noticed that a portrait of Lady Astor (a personal gift to Sherm) stared out from a wall in Sherm's living room, a reminder that his family, the Russells, breathed the same rarefied air as the Boston Brahmins. Sherm lay on a bed in the living room. Now wizened, bald, and dying from lung cancer, he beamed and motioned us to sit next to his bed. "See the fireplace over there?" he asked after fond greetings. "Your father and I used to blow the smoke up the chimney so his father, always the good doctor, wouldn't detect it. I guess I signed my death warrant back then." I silently agreed, having noticed that the armchair in which I sat sported a big black hole in the upholstery on one arm, ostensibly serving as a makeshift ashtray.

"Sherm," I ventured, "we were hoping you could tell us about Father while he was working with the OSS."

His long, handsome face squinched up into a grin — or was it a grimace? (He always did this when he reminisced about my father. He had a flair for the dramatic.) "Your father never lied to me," he said, his face dropping into a serious frown. "I believed him when he told me he was the highest placed American intelligence officer in the Middle East. He held the rank equivalent to colonel."

"Do you know what caused the plane crash?"

Sherm was emphatic in his response. "Your father told me, before his death, that the Russians were after him, so I always assumed it was the Russians."

"You mean you think it was sabotage?" I asked.

"Damn right it was. The plane blew up."

"How do you know this?"

Tired, he couldn't remember. We left shortly afterward, and a month later he was dead.

Heading home that evening, I thought back to the 1947 *New York Times* article I had read about the Trans-Arabian Pipeline and its subtitle: "Oil Concessions Raise Questions Involving Position of Russia." I wondered — what exactly was the position of Russia back then? Clearly, Russia was a former wartime-ally-turned-foe with covetous eyes (like other allies) on the Middle East. Were the Russians so frightened about America's rising power in the Middle East that they would have killed my father, and the five other Americans on that plane?

I read through the *Times* article again. It showed the United States as a rising power in the Middle East as a result of its control over Saudi oil.

The article anticipated "East-West rivalry" over oil, but it was not until the very last paragraph that I got a clue to another part of the Middle East that had both the Soviets and Americans deeply concerned, and that was Iran. The United States was seeking an oil concession in southeastern Iran, the article stated, "far from the Soviet sphere of influence but adjoining the British concession." A look at the map accompanying the article (see page 6) showed the Soviet sphere of influence extending beneath the Azerbaijan Soviet Socialist Republic and its oil-rich capital of Baku into northern Iran, all along the southern border of the Caspian Sea. "Moscow," the article concluded, "would surely consider the adjoining British and American concession as another Anglo-American conspiracy."

So here, clearly, was another vital staging ground for the Great Game to play out in the postwar era. I knew what had happened in Iran in 1953: a CIA-sponsored coup overthrew Iran's democratically elected prime minister, Mohammad Mosaddegh, who had nationalized Iran's oil and refused to sour relations with the Russians. What I didn't consider was the possibility that the stage had conceivably been set for that regime change as far back as March 1947, when President Truman announced the Truman Doctrine. This anti-Soviet strategy's goal was to curtail the spread of communism in Greece and Turkey, but it had broader implications: the beginning of the Cold War and its extension into the Middle East.

I was too focused on understanding the years 1944 to the day of my father's death in 1947 to fully grasp the broader context of the Cold War. But this, too, would change, and in a most unexpected way.

Revolution in Iran

In January 1979, political turmoil brought on by nationwide strikes and demonstrations throughout Iran exploded into a full-fledged revolution to bring down the shah. By January 16, these uprisings forced his removal from office. I was among the many who rejoiced over this news, having personally witnessed the suffering of Iranians under his rule. The fact that an Islamist cleric by the name of Ayatollah Khomeini would emerge as Iran's new leader was of no immediate concern to me. All Iranians, from secular leftist nationalists to conservative Islamists, were united in their joy over the shah's overthrow, the subsequent abolition of SAVAK, and the release of political prisoners and in their determination to see the shah held accountable for his crimes.

The exiled shah sought refuge first in Egypt, then in Morocco, then in the Bahamas, and finally in Mexico, where an American doctor noted that he was suffering from advanced cancer. What happened next would change the trajectory of history. Despite his reluctance, US president Jimmy Carter yielded to pressure to admit the shah into the United States for medical treatment. ("Fuck the shah!" he was overhead muttering in frustration.)[2] That pressure was coming from former Secretary of State Henry Kissinger, a protégé of former Vice President Nelson Rockefeller, and Chase banker David Rockefeller, Nelson's brother. The State Department had warned President Carter that such an action would cause Iranians to storm the American Embassy in Iran, and sure enough, on November 4, 1979, Iranian students did just that, taking hostage fifty-two Americans, including marines, diplomats, CIA officers, and other US staff. Recalling the US-sponsored overthrow of Mosaddegh, the students loudly chanted, "Death to America!"

Over the next 444 days, the so-called Iran hostage crisis gripped the country in a frenzy of political finger-pointing, most of it directed at President Carter for his inability to negotiate the hostages' release — or to remove them by force. The State Department, meanwhile, worked over-time to keep a lid on dissenting voices from the hostages' families, some of whom were beginning to question the causes of the crisis and the admin-istration's frustrating delays in solving it. I began to take notice of the few families who spoke out. As the daughter of a diplomat, I couldn't help but feel sympathy for them, especially with my personal knowledge of what had transpired under the shah. Little had been reported in the American press — until, that is, *60 Minutes* produced a special on the shah ("The Iran File") on March 2, 1980, four months into the crisis.

The show's Mike Wallace blew open the sordid details of the shah's reign of terror — his use of torture, his secret police collaboration with the CIA, and the intrigue that led to his admission into the United States at the urging of David Rockefeller and Henry Kissinger. As I sat, transfixed, watching the revelations in my New York apartment, two hostage fam-ily members were jumping for joy in their Virginia home. Bonnie and Luzette Graves, wife and daughter of hostage and Public Affairs Officer John Graves, were galvanized into action after suffering from months of stonewalling by the State Department's Family Liaison Action Group (FLAG). On the Monday following the *60 Minutes* report, they held a press conference in their suburban living room. Before a group of stunned reporters, Bonnie Graves declared, "It takes a strong nation to be able to say I'm sorry. What we need is a total reexamination of our foreign policy." What she said next stunned me, too: "We must cease our neocolonialist activities that feed the fires that breed terrorism."

Those were pretty strong words coming from a diplomat's family. Where, I wondered, did she get her views? And what did she know that we may not have known? I called her, explained my background, and asked for an interview. She accepted.

Here was my chance to not only give an unusual twist to the Iran hostage crisis — discussing it from the vantage point of a dissenting diplomat's family — but also honor my pledge to the Iranian students who had begged me four years earlier to tell the truth about the shah's Iran. The result was my cover story in *The Nation*, "The Hostage Families: Suffering in Silence." Published on December 13, 1980, it chronicled the ordeal of several "silenced" families. It began with a call for truth: "Truth is the first casualty of war, and in the diplomatic war between the United States and Iran over the hostages, the Carter Administration quickly put that adage into practice. An official curtain of silence was lowered around the hostages and their families, which had the effect — if not the intent — of muffling all criticism of Administration policy."

What was the Carter administration afraid of? The official line from FLAG was that any criticism would endanger the lives of the hostages. But Bonnie Graves, I discovered, had a unique take on the silencing, one that originated not from her own ponderings, but from a rather cryptic letter sent to her from her hostage husband. The letter, in one succinct sentence, said: "Watch out for Rockefeller, Kissinger, and Helms." (All three were close to the shah. Richard Helms, who had directed the CIA from 1966 to 1973 and then served as the US ambassador to Iran, ran a consulting company that helped Iranians with American business deals.)

Bonnie Graves assured me that her husband's statement was not out of character. John Graves had been an opponent of the Vietnam War. He believed that the United States had no business interfering in a civil conflict, an opinion that caused his reassignment out of Vietnam as an officer with the United States Information Service (as the United States Information Agency was then known overseas). He accepted his assignment to Tehran, almost a decade later, as his last. He planned to retire soon.

It did not take long for Bonnie Graves to figure out the meaning of her husband's warning. Shortly after she and her daughter went public, they were contacted by congressman George Hansen of Idaho, a Reagan Republican. Hansen was the chair of the House Banking Committee and had made two self-appointed diplomatic missions to Tehran. He said that he had collected "massive information" during these trips about "illegal banking activities" conducted by the shah with David Rockefeller's Chase Manhattan Bank. He subsequently informed Congress about his view as to why the Carter administration had immediately frozen Iran's assets following the shah's ousting and the hostage takeover, seizing $8 billion worth of Iranian assets deposited in American banks, chief among them Chase. As I later wrote in the *Nation* piece, "Chase had handled up to $20 billion a year of Iranian oil revenues during the reign of the Shah, but by the summer of 1979 the Khomeini Government had begun to withdraw large blocks of Iranian funds from Chase's branches in Europe."

If that weren't concerning enough to Chase executives, most notably CEO David Rockefeller, Chase had led an international consortium of banks in arranging up to $1.3 billion in loans to the shah's government, in violation of the shah's own constitution and against the advice of Chase's own lawyers in Tehran. "Once the new revolutionary government came into power," I wrote, "it was within its legal right to challenge at any time the validity of those loans." What if angry Chase shareholders felt obliged to file lawsuits against Chase for ignoring the advice of its lawyers? I could envision the lawyers sweating over this very realistic hypothetical. As David Rockefeller himself was fond of saying when confronted with a major crisis, something had to be done.

Some people — including the Graveses — wondered whether the seizure of hostages had been a setup from the beginning. The Khomeini government — which had overthrown the American-supported shah — had begun to draw down the massive Iranian accounts held by Chase's European banks. Did someone want those withdrawals to stop? The State Department had warned Washington that there would be trouble at the embassy if the shah was admitted into the United States for medical treatment. Rockefeller and Kissinger ignored the warning and pressured the reluctant Carter to take in the ailing monarch. Hostage takers stormed the embassy in protest, and almost on cue, the Carter administration immediately froze all Iranian funds in Chase's European banks. The hostages were released on day 444 under murky circumstances, but the assets would remain frozen for years.*

So here was another crucial element for understanding the Great Game: the connection between Big Banks and Big Oil and the behind-the-scenes maneuverings of very powerful people. The name Rockefeller had popped up in connection to Iran. It would soon consume our research for *Thy Will Be Done* once we discovered, some four years into our investigation, the role of Nelson Rockefeller in charting postwar foreign policy in Latin America.

We had the National Archives and Records Administration (NARA) to thank for exploring that connection: Rockefeller's papers from his days as FDR's coordinator of inter-American affairs had been recently declassified and were available at NARA's main facility in College Park, Maryland. What we had not anticipated was the role the National Archives would play in unlocking many of the secrets of my father's life.

Finding Carat at the National Archives

Quite by chance, while Jerry and I were sitting in the reading room of the National Archives in 1993, waiting for materials on Latin America, Jerry noticed a book on the shelf about the OSS written by former OSS operative and CIA agent Kermit Roosevelt. Jerry checked the index, found the section for the Middle East, and began reading. The OSS officer assigned to Beirut, Roosevelt wrote, was highly prized. His field reports often went straight to Washington, which was rare. His code name was Carat. We put more of the biographical pieces together and realized that Roosevelt was talking about my father. This was our first clue that maybe Sherm was right. Maybe Daniel Dennett had indeed been a high-level spy.[†]

---

* Release of $4.2 billion in previously frozen assets was contingent on Iran's agreement in 2013 to limit uranium enrichment and allow international inspectors to gain access to sensitive sites. See the Council on Foreign Relations background paper on international sanctions against Iran, "International Sanctions on Iran," by Z. Laub, July 15, 2015, https://www.cfr.org/backgrounder/international-sanctions-iran. Once again we find Big Banks having a hand in foreign policy: It was David Rockefeller who helped facilitate the controversial Iran nuclear deal. See the update to the new ebook edition of *Thy Will Be Done: The Conquest of the Amazon: Nelson Rockefeller and Evangelism in the Age of Oil*, by Gerard Colby with the author (New York: Open Road Media, 2017).

† Only very recently did we learn that the man who replaced my father was Kermit's cousin, Archie Roosevelt.

That same year, quite out of the blue, we received a call from a fellow researcher at the National Archives named Timothy Naftali. (Naftali would go on to become the archivist of the Nixon Presidential Library and, more recently, a CNN analytical contributor.) His news was breathtaking. While researching his book on the OSS and its highest-level counterintelligence branch (named X-2, after the British designation for double cross), he had stumbled onto my father's official OSS reports.

"They are quite detailed," he explained. "Your father was quite the writer and his reports are fascinating." The reports had been declassified and were in four boxes at the National Archives. He gave us the finding aids and the box numbers, and we made a beeline for Washington. (We always moved fast on a breakthrough, knowing that our subjects might die or the information might dry up or get reclassified or disappear altogether.)

Dennett's reports were out of order, in some disarray, and interspersed between CIA "withdrawal slips" that indicated that many of his reports were still classified. The thrill of finding anything at all — especially reports designating him as "Carat" — was enough to keep us there for an entire week. After the first go-through, the following picture emerged about his counterintelligence work, which must have been as much a surprise to him as it was to us: His rivals were not the Germans but the British, the French, and the Russians. "There will be a real free-for-all here," he wrote, using the same term his Washington handlers had used to describe the situation shortly before his arrival in 1944, and "we must figure out who is working for whom." Over the next year, that free-for-all became increasingly dangerous; his reports recorded assassination attempts on Lebanese leaders, riots, attempts to overthrow the (pro-US) Lebanese government, the bomb attack on the American Legation, and the bomber's message that American oil installations in Lebanon would be next.

It was only then, during my father's subsequent investigation of the bombing in August 1946, that we found any mention of oil in any of his reports. Had it slipped through the censor's pen? His final report — the one I found in my brother's attic about his trip to Saudi Arabia in March 1947 to determine the best route for TAPLINE — was not in any of the National Archives' file folders, of course. It was our precious secret — something we knew that the government didn't know we knew — and it kept us asking for more.

We had to wonder: What were all those withdrawal slips in the four Dennett boxes about? And why would documents that were over sixty years old have to remain classified? In 1993 I filed my first request for declassification of my father's reports at the National Archives.

By then, Operation Desert Storm, the first American war in Iraq (also called the Gulf War, 1990–91), had come to its inglorious end. As information dribbled in from various sources telling us that President George H. W. Bush's administration had created a false scare story to convince Congress to support Desert Storm, I began to realize that my own concerns about the war — that the US invasion of Iraq was terribly wrong and would lead to disaster — were being validated. Saddam Hussein, president of Iraq, had sent Iraqi forces to occupy Kuwait in response, he said, to Kuwait stealing oil from a shared oil field along the Iraq-Kuwait border. He claimed that Kuwait was "slant-drilling" for oil into Iraqi territory.[3] We soon learned that the US ambassador to Iraq, April Glaspie, had reportedly led Hussein to believe that the United States would not object if his troops went into Kuwait.[4] Furthermore, the Bush administration had highlighted Hussein's record of atrocities against his own citizens and claimed that Kuwaitis were suffering similar treatment. We heard, for example, riveting testimony about Iraqi forces removing Kuwaiti babies from incubators and leaving them to die; later, we learned that the testimony had been delivered by the daughter of the Kuwaiti ambassador to the United States, who had been coached in the lie by a prominent Washington, DC, PR firm.[5]

With my ongoing education in pipeline politics, it was easy to see how oil, and the United States' need to ensure and secure a steady supply of it, was the primary motivation behind the Gulf War. Most of the rest of the world agreed with me, though the Bush administration tried to downplay the influence of oil and highlight the humanitarian aspect of America's intervention, painting the United States as the hero fighting against the bully. I vowed that I would try to reveal the truth behind this war, beginning with talks to community groups. But little did I realize then how powerfully my father's warning against sending troops to the Middle East would resonate for decades to come. Like others, I was witnessing the onset of a new era: the era of endless wars.

CHAPTER THREE

Afghanistan
The "Graveyard of Empires"

The publication of *Thy Will Be Done* in 1995 required me to shift my focus back to Latin America, but I began to look more closely at the manner in which very powerful forces worked in this country and abroad, and more specifically, how they often manipulated God-fearing fundamentalists to pacify potential opponents in territories ripe for conquest. This global insight would eventually lead me back to the Muslim world and the role that Islamic fundamentalism played in fracturing the Middle East. What I found should not have surprised me. The same dynamics were at play, only deadlier: big powers used different jihadist groups to inflict horrific damage on resource-rich yet highly vulnerable peoples.

This understanding came gradually, of course. It was clear, from our book tours in the United States, that most Americans had no idea of the power dynamics behind evangelical movements and organizations, precisely because religion does not get the same scrutiny as other social phenomena in universities and the media.[1]

Jerry and I found ourselves repeatedly warning our audiences about the growing power and influence of politicized ultraconservative evangelicals in South America as well as in rural areas of the United States. One particularly riveting moment occurred when we were doing a radio interview in conservative Orange County, California, where the Wycliffe Bible Translators had its first headquarters. While we were explaining how fundamentalist missionaries were being used by corporate powers and US government agencies to pacify indigenous peoples resisting incursions onto their lands, a woman sitting opposite us in a glassed-in control room began to weep. We learned later that she was an evangelical, and she was heartbroken to hear that her evangelical peers had been duped by their leaders (who knew better) into thinking they were simply doing God's work, when in fact they were benefiting some powerful forces bent on exploiting the resources beneath indigenous lands.

As a feminist, I myself had personally encountered the power of corporate-funded, evangelically allied leaders such as Phyllis Schlafly of Stop ERA and Beverly LaHaye of Concerned Women for America, who were fighting the Equal Rights Amendment both nationally and in Vermont, where Jerry and I had taken up residence in 1984. During this time of increasing assaults on the women's movement, it occurred to me that evangelicals played the same role in this country as they did in Latin America, only in the United States their role was to pacify women who were increasingly standing up to corporate power. This notion was reinforced when anti-ERA forces, including Schlafly, swarmed into Vermont in 1986 and launched a brutal propaganda campaign to convince rural voters that, among other purported evils, "ERA equals AIDS." Eleanor Smeal, the fiery president of the National Organization for Women who had come to Vermont to assist in the Vermont ERA campaign, described how she encountered primly dressed "church ladies" handing out antifeminist literature at ERA rallies across the country. "Who are these women?" she asked a local politician at one point, only to learn that they were secretly financed by insurance companies who benefited from discriminatory practices in women's health care, especially by charging women more than men for medical insurance covering (i.e., prenatal and maternity care in hospitals). Insurance companies had been instrumental in defeating a national ERA, and, Smeal warned, they could do the same in Vermont.

Years after the Vermont ERA campaign was narrowly defeated, it was Smeal who provided me with yet another new insight into fundamentalism. She was then the head of the Feminist Majority Foundation and the organizer of the giant three-day Feminist Expo 2000 in Baltimore, Maryland, and she had invited me to speak about evangelism at the Expo after reading *Thy Will Be Done*. But when Smeal caught up with me inside the enormous Expo auditorium in Baltimore, she wanted to talk about something altogether different, something that would eventually carry me back to my search for answers to the Daniel Dennett mystery. "Charlotte, are you following what's going on with the Taliban in Afghanistan?" she asked.

Before I could say, "Well, no . . . ," she followed up with a one-liner that would resonate for years: "It's all about oil and fundamentalism!" Then she hurried off to a panel presentation, leaving me standing in suspended animation, oblivious to the swirl of women around me as they headed off to their next round of workshops.

Afghanistan was not then on my radar screen, or at least not fully. I certainly had heard of the Taliban and knew that they practiced an extreme medieval form of Islam in Afghanistan based on sharia law, which was much like the ultraconservative Islam followed by Saudi Arabia's Wahhabi sect.[2] I also knew that the Taliban had managed to conquer much of Afghanistan in the late 1990s and impose their extreme laws on the population, banning music, TV, sports, and other forms of entertainment. They were best known for mistreating women and expelling Afghan girls from their schools. But the oil connection? What was that about?

The answers flowed in shortly afterward thanks to the publication in 2000 of a book titled *Taliban: Militant Islam, Oil and Fundamentalism in Central Asia*. Its author was a Pakistani journalist named Ahmed Rashid who had covered Afghanistan for the past twenty years. He had become fascinated by Afghanistan's people and history, not least because they had managed to ward off two powerful empires — British and Soviet — in the twentieth century.

Afghanistan in fact was the birthplace of the original Great Game of the nineteenth century, when the British and Russians used their respective diplomats and spies to protect their territories from rival imperial intrusions — the British at all times safeguarding their trade routes to India from the Russians while pushing toward Afghanistan, and the Russians determined to prevent British claims on Russia's neighboring territories in Central Asia. Afghanistan stood as a buffer between the two competing empires. Yet as Rashid noted, the real Great Game played out as both empires raced to build and control the railways: "The Russians built railway lines across Central Asia to their borders with Afghanistan, Persia and China while the British built railway lines across India to their border with Afghanistan."[3] In the modern age, though, the Great Game began to play out differently. The turmoil that would engulf Afghanistan between 1992 and 1997 was borne out of "intense competition between the regional states [of Central Asia] and Western oil companies as to who would build the lucrative pipelines which are needed to transport the energy to markets in Europe and Asia." This rivalry, said Rashid, had in effect become "a New Great Game."[4]

To me, this concept was pivotal. During my years of research into my father's death, I had become intimately familiar with the term Great Game, having concluded that my father was likely one of its first American victims in the twentieth-century Middle East as the Great Game pivoted from rail lines, so prominent during the nineteenth century, to pipelines. The term can be traced back to the sixteenth century, when it applied to card games involving risk and, more generally, to associations with risk, chance, and deception. It was later popularized by famed British author Rudyard Kipling in his 1901 novel about a British colonial officer in India, titled simply *Kim*. Kipling's character would inspire a real British colonial officer named Harry St. John Philby to name his son Kim. And Kim Philby would go on to become the most famous spy and double agent of the twentieth century. Fittingly enough, St. John Philby and Kim Philby (both in Saudi Arabia in early 1947) would have an impact on my father's life . . . and possibly his death.

Rashid's work helped me see the connections between the railways of the nineteenth and early twentieth centuries and the pipelines of the twentieth and twenty-first centuries. Both were vital commercial arteries for distributing the fossil fuels that powered industrialization and military might. And in both cases, controlling their routes became the subject of intense secrecy, espionage, and conflicts that often led to war.

Afghanistan held a special position in the Great Games — old and new — because it did not easily yield to foreign invaders. For this reason, it had come to be known as the Graveyard of Empires. Three intersecting factors made the country hard to conquer, according to international relations analyst Akhilesh Pillalamarri. First, there is the simple matter of geography. Situated on the main land route between Iran, Central Asia, and India, Pillalamarri explains, the country "has been invaded many times and settled by a plethora of tribes, many mutually hostile to each other and outsiders." Second, those frequent invasions coupled with tribalism in the region contributed to pervasive lawlessness. Third, its rugged physical terrain, marked by extremely high and jagged mountains, made Afghanistan as a whole difficult to conquer and rule.[5]

In the 1990s, the modern-day Great Game involved a dance between dictators and oil barons. The dictators were the rulers of Afghanistan and the leaders of the former Soviet republics of Turkmenistan, Uzbekistan, and Kazakhstan, all of which formed a semicircle around Afghanistan to its north and lay in close proximity to the oil and gas riches of the Caspian Sea. They had accumulated wealth and power with heavy US assistance after the dismemberment of the Soviet Union in 1991. (The map on page 72 shows this area.)

The oil barons were two competing oil companies, the Argentine-owned Bridas and the American-owned Unocal (Union Oil Company of California). Both were vying for concessions and pipelines in and around the Caspian Sea. The race was on for what was considered to be, at the time, the last untapped reserves of energy in the world. Since this region of Central Asia is landlocked, the challenge would be transporting the oil and gas overland by pipelines.

Rashid's Quest

Ahmed Rashid discovered the oil connection as he was trying to learn more about Afghanistan's mysterious Taliban warriors. He was well aware that mujahideen warriors backed by the CIA had helped rout the Soviets from Afghanistan during the 1980s, but he was less familiar with the Taliban, who emerged suddenly as a fighting force in 1994, their warriors taking control of Afghanistan's second largest city, Kandahar, in November. At the time, Afghanistan was "in a state of virtual disintegration," Rashid observed, with warlords fighting "in a bewildering array of alliances, betrayals and bloodshed" and the country divided into fiefdoms. Disillusioned by the factionalism and growing corruption of the mujahideen who had fought the Soviets, the Taliban sought to "purify" the Islamic way of life and enforce a strict interpretation of Islamic law. They drew their recruits largely from refugee camps in Pakistan located along the border with Afghanistan. There, young Afghan refugees were educated in Saudi- and Pakistani-funded schools, or *madrassas*, that indoctrinated them about the ideal Islamic society created by the Prophet Mohammad 1400 years ago.[6] In Afghanistan, their ranks were drawn from the Pashtun, Afghanistan's majority ethnic group, which had once ruled Afghanistan for three hundred years. The Pashtun had recently lost influence to other tribes, but in a bid for what today looks like a "Make Afghanistan Great Again" campaign, they galvanized Pashtun nationalism and in 1995 gained control of Kandahar Province, strategically located in the southern part of the country next to Pakistan. The following year they laid siege to and captured Afghanistan's largest city and capital, Kabul.

This impressive and unexpected feat shocked the world and piqued the interest of Rashid, who began to make repeated forays from his base in Pakistan into Afghanistan to report on the Taliban phenomenon. During this period they had gained a reputation for being able to pacify warring tribes in Kandahar and neighboring provinces, bringing relative peace and security to the region.

When Rashid arrived in the city of Kandahar (capital of Kandahar Province) in March 1997, he was more determined than ever to find out "who they were, what motivated them, who supported them and how they had arrived at this violent, extreme interpretation of Islam."[7] He had expected to cover a rather salutary event — the Taliban's removal of their ban on soccer, symbolized by the rebuilding of the city's large soccer stadium. What he learned, to his horror, was that the newly inaugurated stadium was to play host to a public execution. Along with 10,000 men and boys (no females allowed), he saw Taliban guards march a shackled prisoner to the center of the stadium. The prisoner, Rashid learned, was accused of murdering his neighbor. Befitting the Taliban tradition of allowing relatives of the victim to exact vengeance, the guards placed a Kalashnikov into the hands of a relative, who promptly fired three rounds into the prisoner's back. This was clearly a public display of Taliban power, complete with a pre-execution speech to the crowd by a Taliban judge describing the history of the case and extolling the importance of Islamic punishment.

The following day, Rashid sought out the governor of Kandahar for an interview. As he approached the governor's mansion, he witnessed a silver-haired man impeccably dressed in Western attire emerge from the governor's office. Accompanying him were two other businessmen with bulging briefcases. As Rashid describes it, "They looked as though they had just concluded a deal on Wall Street, rather than holding negotiations with a band of Islamic guerrillas. . . . The last thing [they] wanted was to be seen by a journalist coming out of a Taliban leader's office."

They brushed off Rashid's effort to talk with them, claiming they had to catch a plane.

The silver-haired man, Rashid learned, was Carlos Bulgheroni, an Argentine of Italian descent who was chairman of Bridas. During the past year, Rashid had begun to seek information on this little-known oil company, wondering what it was doing in a country that had no oil. Three months after his strange encounter with Bulgheroni at the governor's mansion, he caught up with the executive and persuaded him to sit down for an interview.

Bulgheroni decided to open up. After the collapse of the Soviet Union, he explained, he sought out oil and gas ventures in western Siberia. He concluded that there were too many logistical problems and so turned to Turkmenistan, one of the former Soviet republics that was now open for business with the West. Bridas became the first Western company to invest in Turkmenistan, obtaining several oil and gas leases in 1992 and 1993. After discovering a large gas field in that country in 1995, Bridas concluded that the best way to get the gas to market was by running a pipeline from Turkmenistan through Afghanistan and on to Pakistan and India.

Between 1995 and 1996, Bulgheroni took constant flights to Afghanistan, visiting warlords who, he hoped, would not only approve of his idea but also help safeguard the route of the pipeline.[8] He also persuaded the war-weary government in Kabul that the pipeline would help bring peace, stability, and revenues to the country. In 1996, the government signed a thirty-year agreement with Bridas, which promised to build the pipeline with assistance from an international consortium. One of the international companies that Bulgheroni drew in was Unocal, a US oil company that had proven experience in Asia and boasted a very big name as one of its consultants: former Secretary of State Henry Kissinger.

Bulgheroni thought Unocal would be a good match for the project, not realizing that its bid to snare the pipeline contract would be Bridas's undoing.

The Fall of the Soviet Union and the Rise of Pipeline Politics

Bridas was at a significant disadvantage in the unfolding Great Game. Although it was the third-largest independent oil and gas company in Latin America, it had no experience in Asia and was no match for a large US oil company, one that was advised by the world-famous Kissinger. I wondered who among the players knew that Kissinger had long acted as a consigliere to very powerful Standard Oil heirs, Nelson Rockefeller and his brother, Chase banker David Rockefeller. The warning from hostage John Graves — "Watch out for Rockefeller, Kissinger, and Helms" — rang in my ears as I recalled the 1979 Iran hostage crisis.

By 2000, when Rashid's book was published, Nelson Rockefeller was long dead, but the family's investments in Big Oil around the world continued to be prodigious. ExxonMobil and Chevron, both offspring of the original Standard Oil Trust, had learned the lessons advanced by John D. Rockefeller Sr. as he built up his formidable oil empire: "Let the wildcatters go at it" first when developing a new oil prospect. After the little guys had done all the hard work of exploring and drilling, one of Rockefeller's Standard Oil companies would swoop down and buy out the wildcatters. This still holds true today. As the director of the Ghana National Petroleum Corporation once commented right before ExxonMobil took over a big block of oil in Ghana, "They are the big boys. They wait for you to develop the fields, and then they come in when they believe the prospectivity is within their range."[9]

Knowing this pattern, I was not surprised to learn that in 2005 Unocal would be bought out by Chevron, one of the most powerful oil companies in the world, which had built its fortune in Saudi Arabia. The scale, expertise, advanced machinery, and formidable foreign policy experience of Big Oil almost inevitably triumphed over smaller bidders when countries sized up whom they wanted to exploit their resources.*

Perhaps Chevron's interest in Unocal was piqued when Turkmenistan's president, Saparmurat Niyazov, decided to side with Unocal over Bridas to build the oil pipeline from Turkmenistan through Afghanistan. Unocal engaged in a full-court press with Niyazov, convincing him that vast riches would accrue to Turkmenistan and turn it into "the new Kuwait."[10] A deal with Unocal would have the backing of the United States and help him stand up against intimidation from his former masters, the Russians. Though Turkmenistan had been independent from Russia for four years, Russia still owned the pipelines that transported the country's enormous gas and oil wealth (159 trillion cubic feet of gas, 32 billion barrels of oil) to foreign markets. Niyazov's battle with the Russians over pipelines finally ended with a shutdown of the fields. His landlocked country was sitting atop stranded riches that had nowhere to go.

---

* In 1911, President Theodore Roosevelt responded to outraged cries against Rockefeller's monopolistic Standard Oil Trust (deriding it as "the Octopus") by breaking it up. The original Standard Oil of New Jersey, Standard Oil of New York, and Standard Oil of California would become Exxon, Mobil, and Chevron (the latter having pulled off the oil coup of the twentieth century by obtaining the exclusive concession in Saudi Arabia). After the fall of the Soviet Union in December 1991, all three were actively seeking to invest in Russia and in the former Soviet republics bordering the Caspian Sea. So, too, was Unocal, then the twentieth-largest American oil company (which in 2005 was bought out by Chevron).

In the United States, the Clinton administration was solidly behind Unocal's vision: two pipelines, one for oil and the other for gas, that would wind through western and southern Afghanistan and end up in Pakistan. Unocal's proposed project, according to its chief negotiator, was a "no brainer, if only you set politics aside." As Pulitzer Prize–winning journalist Steve Coll pointed out in another groundbreaking book on Afghanistan, *Ghost Wars*, "As the weeks passed, however, the politics only thickened."[11]

On October 25, 1995, President Niyazov invited both Bridas and Unocal representatives to New York to meet with him while he was attending sessions at the United Nations. In a public signing ceremony that included Kissinger, but no Afghans, Niyazov brazenly signed the pipeline agreement with Unocal and its partner, Saudi Arabia's Delta Oil Company, while shocked Bridas executives looked on in dismay. But Bridas was not about to give up. It had succeeded in winning over Pakistan's leader, Benazir Bhutto, into supporting the Bridas pipeline project. The New Great Game was now off and running.

Finding the Taliban-CIA-Unocal Link

It was not until a year later, after the Taliban's dramatic capture of Kabul in the summer of 1996, that Rashid began to investigate whether the Americans, and by extension Unocal, were backing the Taliban either financially or militarily. Rashid also searched for the reasons behind a developing rift in the region that pitted major powers against one another. On one side, backing the Taliban, were the United States, Saudi Arabia, and Pakistan, along with their allies Uzbekistan, Turkmenistan, and Azerbaijan. On the other side were Iran, Russia, and the former Soviet republics of Kazakhstan, Krgystan, and Tajikistan.

Rashid's findings, which he published in his book *Taliban*, became for me not just a startling revelation about modern-day pipeline politics but also my first signal that there were other pipeline trackers out there trying to cut through obfuscation after obfuscation to get at the truth. In his own investigation, Rashid discovered that "the strategy over pipelines had become the driving force behind Washington's interest in the Taliban." Washington's pipeline strategy, in turn, had triggered a "counter-reaction from Russia and Iran."

Getting to this understanding, he wrote, had been extremely difficult, akin to "entering a labyrinth, where nobody spoke the truth or divulged their real motives or interests." Rashid found himself having to act like a detective rather than a journalist because there were very few clues, and gaining access to "the real players in the game" had been difficult. The reason, he ultimately concluded, was that "policy was not being driven by politicians and diplomats, but by the secretive oil companies and intelligence services of the regional states."[12]

No wonder our elected leaders and our diplomats — traditional sources for journalists — were not always reliable for getting at the truth about what was really going on. They often didn't know. And this put journalists at a disadvantage. No wonder, too, that Americans are so woefully misinformed about the Middle East.

Oil companies, Rashid continued, "were the most secretive of all — a legacy of the fierce competition they indulged in around the world." That competition was fierce because of the prize at stake: billions in oil revenues and profits. "To spell out where they would drill next or which pipeline route they favoured, or even whom they had lunch with an hour earlier, was giving the game away to the enemy — rival oil companies."[13]

Rashid's blinding revelations got me thinking about the pressures that Carat had endured as he played the Great Game for Oil to keep foreign spies and foreign oil companies at bay. Whose interests did he ultimately serve? He was instructed to "protect the oil at all costs," which meant shielding American oil interests from foreign competitors and spies. That was where espionage and oil intersected. But what if the oil companies went too far in their ruthless quest to secure the oil? What if they tried to twist intelligence to get the United States embroiled in foreign wars to advance the companies' commercial interests, as clearly happened in Afghanistan and Iraq?

How Great Game Scheming
Can Produce Unintended Consequences

History is replete with examples of big powers implementing grand schemes that end up producing unintended consequences. One such scheme was to bring together thousands of Islamic fundamentalists from around the world and indoctrinate them in camps and schools (madrassas) in Pakistan and Afghanistan about the culture and valor of Islamic jihadism. The end game, which brought the CIA together with Pakistani and Saudi intelligence services, was to spread Islamism in Central Asia along the southern tier of the Soviet Union and bring down the Soviet Union.[14] The person who most openly took credit for this scheme was Zbigniew Brzezinski, a Polish émigré and die-hard anticommunist who had been integrated into David Rockefeller's tight circle of advisors and confidants in the early 1970s.

In 1972, Rockefeller had been conferring with executives of Chase Bank in several world capitals about international investments, having realized (as he writes in his *Memoirs*) that "the United States, although still dominant, had declined relatively in terms of its economic power; Western Europe and Japan, on the other hand, had recovered remarkably well since the devastation of World War II and had achieved dramatic economic growth." David was not one to sit idly by and watch any further erosion of American power and prestige, and he concluded, in typical Rockefellerian fashion, that "something had to be done." While omitting from his analysis the explosion of anti-American sentiment and actions in Latin America and America's losing the war in Vietnam, in which he had staked a great deal by backing President Lyndon Johnson, he concluded that he needed to forge a group of like-minded leaders representing the "three centers of democratic capitalism — North America, Europe, and Japan." He recruited Brzezinski, then a professor of Russian studies at Columbia University, to join him in setting up a meeting of five Europeans and four Japanese at Rockefeller's family estate in New York's Pocantico Hills. Out of this came the Trilateral Commission, with Brzezinski agreeing to be its executive director.

Rockefeller went about assembling "the best minds in America," as did the Europeans and the Japanese for their respective delegations, and the Trilateral Commission grew to include "union leaders, corporate CEOs, prominent Democrats and Republicans, distinguished academics, university presidents and the not-for-profits overseas."[15] And presidents.

In 1972, Jimmy Carter, then the Democratic governor of Georgia, attended the first meeting of the Trilateral Commission and apparently was so inspired that when he was elected president in 1977, he decided to fill his cabinet with Trilateralists, including Brzezinski as his national security advisor. Brzezinski would later describe how Carter, as early as 1978, "approved proposals by my staff to undertake, for example, a comprehensive, covert action program designed to help the non-Russian nations in the Soviet Union to pursue more actively their desire for independence — a program in effect to destabilize the Soviet Union."[16]

A related program conceived by Brzezinski and aimed at further destabilizing the Soviet Union was the CIA's covert funding of Islamist fundamentalists (the mujahideen) against the Marxist regime of Hafizullah Amin in Afghanistan. In 1979, in an effort to stem the resulting Islamist insurgency against Amin's secular reforms, the Soviet Union invaded Afghanistan. By doing so, the Soviets walked into Brzezinski's trap to create a "Soviet Vietnam." Pummeled by repeated guerrilla attacks by the US-supported mujahideen, the Soviets finally withdrew in 1989. Within two years, the greatly weakened Soviet Union dissolved.

The unintended consequence for the West — that the mujahideen would end up turning against the United States, as the Taliban did in Afghanistan — apparently caused Brzezinski no regrets. When interviewed by the French weekly *Nouvel Observateur* in 1998 about his role in arming Islamic fundamentalists, he famously stated:

> *Regret what? The secret operation was an excellent idea. It drew the Russians into the Afghan trap and you want me to regret it? On the day that the Soviets officially crossed the borders, I wrote to President Carter, saying in essence, "We now have the opportunity of giving to the USSR its Vietnam War." ... What is more important in world history: the Taliban or the collapse of the Soviet empire? Some agitated Muslims, or the liberation of Central Europe and the end of the Cold War?*[17]

Author Peter Dale Scott wryly observes the timing of the Brzezinski-Carter plan to draw the Soviets into Afghanistan in 1979: "In the history of oil exploration, this occurred at a time when U.S. oil companies, shaken up by the power of OPEC in the 1973 oil crisis, were casting eyes on the potential for oil and gas exploration in the Caspian Basin."[18] The region's massive oil and gas deposits in 1973 belonged to the Soviet Union. With the USSR's dissolution in 1991, the countries surrounding the Caspian were liberated from Soviet control, opening them up to all sorts of Western entreaties to develop them and their resources, and even to help them establish formal independence and declare themselves Central Asian "democratic republics."

Between 1991 and 1995, Washington had focused on working to develop better relations with the Russians. This was a delicate period of mutual adjustment, one that might require bringing Russia into NATO, while being careful not to antagonize Russia's long-term interests in Central Asia. At the same time, the American oil companies, along with some members of the foreign policy establishment, were keen on developing the oil fields in western Siberia and in the former Soviet republics around the Caspian Sea. In 1995, following the signing ceremony with Turkmenistan's President Niyazov, Unocal began planning the Central Asia Oil Pipeline Project (CAOPP) to build a 1,500-mile oil pipeline from Turkmenistan to Pakistan's coast, using existing (Soviet-era) pipelines to collect oil from Russia, Kazakhstan, Uzbekistan, and Turkmenistan to feed the oil into the CAOPP pipeline.[19] In short, this meant creating an energy corridor.

Unocal also proposed a *gas* pipeline from the Daulatabad gas fields in southern Turkmenistan (on the border with Afghanistan) to central Pakistan, giving Russia's state-owned gas company, Gazprom, a 10 percent share. Unocal executives proclaimed the deal a "win-win" for Russia: Not only would Gazprom get a share, but the pipeline would give Russia new outlets for its Siberian oil.[20]

But Unocal's rosy assessment, based on friendly relations with Russia, turned out to be premature.

The Clinton administration, which took over in 1993, began to chart a different course with Russia as early as 1995, when Russia's mounting economic and social problems began to take a toll on the country's stability. The administration began to snub the greatly weakened giant and its ally Iran. It had once considered softening the sanctions against Iran that dated back to the 1979 hostage crisis in order to run pipelines from Central Asia to Iran.[21] But now it began to isolate Iran and Russia and instead help the Caspian states of Turkmenistan, Uzbekistan, and Azerbaijan develop their own oil and mineral wealth in order to free them from dependence on Russia.[22] Needless to say, the Russians took notice.

Bridas also suffered at this time. In March 1996, the State Department began to pressure Pakistan's reluctant prime minister, Benazir Bhutto, to switch her country's support away from a Bridas pipeline in favor of Unocal's project. Behind the scenes, Unocal executives played on one of Bhutto's greatest vulnerabilities: rumors of her husband's corrupt business practices — fanned by Pakistan's powerful intelligence agency, Interservice Intelligence (ISI) — that had resulted in her downfall as Pakistan's prime minister back in 1990. Then, she had vigorously defended her husband and accused political operatives of using false allegations to discredit her. Now she was confronted with rumors that payoffs to her husband had assured her allegiance to the Argentine company. According to one Pakistani official, the message to Bhutto was to avoid more corruption charges by switching her allegiance to Unocal.[23]

When Bhutto refused to break Pakistan's contract with Bridas, which was still trying to stay in the game, US Ambassador Thomas Simons visited her in the spring of 1996. He had been informed that someone in her government had been paid off to support the Argentine company. He accused her of extortion and demanded that she go with Unocal. Furious over his extortion charge, she again refused and complained to the Clinton White House of the US ambassador's decidedly undiplomatic treatment of Pakistan's prime minister.[24]

Her remonstrations apparently had no impact, other than a letter of apology. This may have surprised her, given her good relations with the Clinton administration and strong support of the Taliban. The previous year, she had visited President Clinton and promoted the Taliban as a force that could help stabilize Afghanistan as well as open up new trade routes between Pakistan and Central Asia. Writes Coll: "She found a receptive audience among midlevel officials for her message about the Taliban's potential to bring peace. During her visit and for many months afterward Bhutto and her aides repeatedly lied to American government officials and members of Congress about the extent of Pakistani military and financial aid to the Taliban. . . . Bhutto had decided that it was more important to appease the Pakistani army and intelligence services than to level with her American friends."[25] She convinced Assistant Secretary of State Robin Raphel of the Taliban's value to the United States and Pakistan. Raphel, for her part, defended Bhutto against charges that Pakistan was the hidden force behind the Taliban's remarkable rise to power. Raphel and Clinton approved more economic aid to Pakistan, hoping it would strengthen the Bhutto government.

But when it came to choosing which oil company would control the route of the pipeline, Bhutto was no match against Unocal, which had firmly captured the allegiance of the Clinton administration. That became clear when Raphel, in the spring of 1996, announced at a press conference in Pakistan's capital of Islamabad that the Unocal pipeline project was "very good for Turkmenistan, for Pakistan and for Afghanistan as it will not only offer job opportunities but also energy in Afghanistan."[26] By the summer of 1996, an Islamist-fueled campaign against Bhutto's alleged corruption had begun, and by November 1996, Bhutto was put under house arrest. For a second time, her premiership ended.[27]

Bhutto, I believe, was a victim of pipeline politics and the ruthless Great Game. After her downfall, Nawaz Sharif took over as prime minister, and Sharif, his oil minister, ISI, and the army gave their full support to Unocal.

In the meantime, the Taliban captured Kabul in September 1996. A Unocal executive hailed the event, telling the press that the Unocal project would be easier to implement with the Taliban in control. He then quickly retracted the statement, but not in time to stop the spread of even more rumors about CIA support for the Taliban.* Just days after Kabul's capture, the US State Department stuck its foot deeper into the Taliban quagmire by declaring its willingness to establish diplomatic relations with the militant Islamists. The fact that the Taliban had imposed an extreme version of Islamic law on Afghanistan's citizens — and especially on its women — seemed of no consequence. Washington's "romancing of the Taliban" was in full swing.[28]

Notes Rashid, "Open U.S. support for the Unocal project" — in spite of the administration's insistence on not taking sides and devoting its energies to conflict resolution — "aroused an already suspicious Russia and Iran, which became even more convinced that the CIA was backing the Taliban."[29]

Pakistan's ISI also played a major covert role in the Taliban takeover. As longtime Afghanistan chroniclers Elizabeth Gould and Paul Fitzgerald explain, "The Taliban were actually a thinly disguised ISI strike-force paid for by a consortium of [Western] business interests." They claim that the Taliban also received help from Britain's high commissioner (similar to an ambassador) to Pakistan.[30] In an interview with me, Gould stated that Pakistan and Britain "wanted to make sure that Afghanistan did not rise to become a sovereign state. Pakistan was obsessed with gaining strategic depth in Afghanistan in its war with India." The Taliban, drawn from Afghan refugee camps in Pakistan on the border with Afghanistan, had been schooled in Saudi-funded madrassas teaching extremist Islamism whose main goal was the transformation of South and Central Asia. The British, seasoned veterans of the Great Game, had never given up their imperial aim of controlling the vast Central Asian land bridge. And now American oil interests were in on the game. It was a marriage of mutual interests, but

---

* In December 1996, a senior Iranian diplomat told Rashid that the CIA and Saudi Arabia had channeled $7 million in aid to the Taliban, but Rashid could not find hard evidence of this aid.

to the detriment of the Afghan people, who practiced a moderate Islam. In fact most had never heard of the Taliban until the mid-1990s.

The Taliban's Final Push to Victory — or Was It?

On May 25, 1997, the Taliban came closer than ever to unifying Afghanistan when they captured Mazar-e-Sharif, the home base of their biggest opponents — the Northern Alliance, formed in 1996 in response to the Taliban's capture of Kabul, and composed of various ethnic groups (among them Tajiks and Uzbeks) in northern Afghanistan. The alliance saw itself as the last holdout against the Taliban in a united effort for the sovereignty of Afghanistan. Steven Levine of the *New York Times* reported, "The World Bank and other international financial institutions consider [achieving] such nationwide authority [by the Taliban] — as well as peace — a prerequisite to loans for the trans-Afghan pipeline proposed in competing plans by Unocal and Bridas."[31] Some Western energy executives, Levine added, "allowed themselves a slim hope that the way was finally clear for [the] export pipeline from this energy-rich region to the growing markets of Asia."

But four days later, the Taliban were unexpectedly betrayed by the very northern warrior who had allowed them to enter the city. General Abdul Malik Pahlawan, today's leader of the Afghanistan Liberation Party, apparently became alarmed when the Taliban began to disarm his men. He decided to rejoin the anti-Taliban Northern Alliance from which he had recently defected.

Officially known as the United Islamic Front for the Salvation of Afghanistan, the Northern Alliance was backed by Russia and Iran. With their help, the rout of the Taliban from northern Afghanistan was about to begin. Suddenly, Unocal's prospects for achieving funding from commercial banks and international lending institutions, including the World Bank, seemed doomed. Everything hinged on establishing a recognized government in Kabul that could ensure peace and stability in the entire country before a pipeline project would be considered seriously.

Unocal President John Imle Jr. shrugged off the setback, insisting that oil companies were used to taking political risks and could ride out the turmoil. His company had taken risks in Thailand and Indonesia and could do the same in Afghanistan, he told the *New York Times*, adding that his industry wouldn't exist "if skepticism were a problem."[32]

Bridas, meanwhile, persevered. Back in February 1996, it had secured an agreement with Afghanistan to build its pipeline to Pakistan. That same month, smarting over Unocal's exclusive pipeline contract with Turk-menistan, Bridas filed a civil suit against Unocal and Delta Oil in Houston, charging the two companies with wrongfully interfering with Bridas's potential business relations and with stealing Bulgerhoni's idea.

Things turned really ugly as the lawsuit progressed and portions of pretrial depositions were leaked to the press. "The Americans came and wrecked our business," complained a Bridas official to the *Wall Street Journal*, which published an article on the rivalry, noting that charges of corruption between the two companies "were flying thick and fast." By now the international business community seemed to be looking at the pipeline wars with somewhat jaundiced eyes. As the *Wall Street Journal* rather snidely put it, both companies "are competing for the unlikely honor of building energy pipelines through war-torn Afghanistan." The two companies even resorted to "sending the modern-day equivalent of missionaries up and down a proposed route to sell their rival pipeline plans to tribal leaders. Westerners in the pay of oil companies in Afghanistan have taken to growing long beards, in the manner of some faithful Muslims, in an attempt to win the trust of Afghanistan's fundamentalist Taliban government."[33]

The Feminist Backlash

Meanwhile, back in the United States, the Taliban's reputation for abusing Afghan women had begun to stir anger and resentment among feminists, who in turn sought out powerful backers to help lead the charge. One of them was Madeleine Albright. In what has to be one of the great ironies of Bill Clinton's administration, his decision in January 1997 to appoint Albright as the first woman ever to become US secretary of state would soon boomerang back on Unocal, on Clinton's foreign policy toward Central Asia, and on US support for the Taliban.

Madeleine Albright came into the position with a stellar résumé (especially when compared to Trump-era appointees): an early career in journalism, an MA from Columbia University on the Soviet diplomatic corps, a PhD dissertation on the role of journalists during the 1968 reform movement in Czechoslovakia, a stint with none other than President Carter's National Security Council under Zbigniew Brzezinski, and another as the US ambassador to the United Nations. Perhaps most relevant to this discussion, in 1983 she directed Georgetown University's program on global women's studies. A graduate of the prestigious all-women Wellesley College and the mother of three daughters, she had a certain fondness for saying, "There is a special place in hell for women who don't help other women."

And so it occurred that on her first trip to Pakistan in November 1997, she visited a refugee camp along the border with Afghanistan and sat down with schoolgirls and their teachers in front of tents and mud huts, listening to harrowing stories of how they had fled the Taliban. One girl gave a particularly moving account of how her sister jumped out of a sixth-floor window to escape intruders whom she was certain were going to rape her. The girl died, and immediately after her family buried her, they fled to Pakistan. Albright nodded empathetically as she listened and explained that she, too, had been a refugee from terror, fleeing first the Nazis and later a communist takeover of Czechoslovakia. She told her young audience that the plight of women in Afghanistan was of great concern to her. Soon after, when she gave a formal press conference in Islamabad, she was even more blunt: "I think it is very clear that we are opposed to the Taliban because of their approach to human rights, their despicable treatment of women and children, and their lack of respect for human dignity."[34]

This was the first time a US official had publicly criticized the Taliban. Her comments were also aimed squarely at the government of Pakistan, which along with Saudi Arabia had supported the radical Islamists with arms and funding. Albright presumably got the go-ahead from Washington to make such harsh comments, which also reflected a growing concern back home over Pakistan's weak economy, its own susceptibility to Islamic fundamentalism, and the possible Talibanization of Afghanistan's neighboring countries.[35] But she also knew that Bill and Hillary Clinton had been coming under increasing pressure from feminist groups in the United States for supporting the Taliban, and the feminists, as a major part of Clinton's electoral base, were one group he could not afford to alienate.

Eleanor Smeal and the Feminist Majority Foundation had begun opposing the Taliban after it seized the city of Kabul in 1996 and began restricting the rights of women. It forbade girls and women from going to school, banned women from working outside the home, and ordered women to be covered from head to toe in burqas and accompanied by a male relative when they left the home. The Taliban also had denied women and girls access to hospitals unless there were female doctors or nurses in the hospitals to treat them — essentially denying them care altogether, as women were banned from working.

When women ventured outside in automobiles, they had to put drapes in the rear windows of their cars. "Even when they stayed indoors," said Smeal, "the Taliban ordered them to paint the windows on the ground floor black so no one could see out or in. These were draconian edicts that no one in civilized society could imagine."

The edicts came just one year after the United Nations held its fourth conference on women, declaring its goal "to advance the goals of equality, development and peace for all women everywhere in the interest of all humanity."[36] Yet, Smeal lamented, none of the participating countries spoke out against the Taliban when the Associated Press began running stories about the edicts. She and the foundation reached out to the State Department and the Clinton administration to confirm that the stories were true. "They affirmed," she said. "Now we were really agitated." They also reached out to Afghan women groups in the United States, and learned the United Nations and the United States were considering whether to recognize the Taliban.

That's when the Feminist Majority Foundation launched its Stop Gender Apartheid in Afghanistan campaign to protest that recognition. At the time, the internet was new as a means of communication. To the feminists' amazement, their email outreach generated hundreds of thousands of letters. "We were told by Secretary of State Madeleine Albright after she left office that she never saw such a huge response to a campaign," recalled Smeal. But the press didn't cover the campaign at the time. As a result, she said, "we couldn't get anywhere." Smeal reached out to human rights groups, who told her their plates were full.

Finally, in 1998 in honor of International Women's Day, President Clinton and Attorney General Janet Reno came out against recognition of the Taliban. The United Nations and European Union also came out against recognition. Still, Smeal kept puzzling over what was behind the Taliban's ability to take over Kabul and the Afghan government. "Why was this happening? I kept asking myself," she said. "It made no sense." The Taliban's abusive policies, she said, "were driving people out of Afghanistan. Anyone who could leave, left. After all, who would tolerate living under them? Millions of Afghans fled the country." There had to be an explanation to account for the Taliban's growing power, and the fact that no one seemed willing or able to stop their horrific policies.

Then she decided to adopt an old adage, "Follow the money."

A team of twenty Feminist Majority Foundation staff members went to refugee camps, asking, "Who are the Taliban?" The refugees responded, speaking in Urdu, "Pak, Pak, Pak." In other words, the Taliban were recruited out of refugee camps in Pakistan.

Foundation staff in Virginia also tried to figure out the money angle, said Smeal: "Two months later, they came back to me. 'We think we found it,' they said. 'It's about an oil pipeline. A royalty would go to the Taliban. And they would establish a religious dictatorship.'" Needless to say, there was a quid pro quo: Unocal would benefit from having the Taliban protect the pipeline and provide stability to the country in the eyes of financiers.

By then, the foundation was finally getting calls from the press about its campaign, including from reporters at the *Washington Post*. Smeal decided to ask them what they were doing in Turkmenistan. "They told me, 'There is a big discovery of oil and gas in the area around the Caspian Sea.' The challenge was how to get the oil to market."[37] For a landlocked country, the only way was through a pipeline.

Smeal realized the foundation's work was not over yet. "The Taliban were still in control. Now what do we do? We still couldn't get enough press [about Unocal's backing the Taliban] because we weren't viewed as experts. We were just 'women's rights people.'"

Observed Elizabeth Gould and Paul Fitzgerald, the Feminist Majority "was locked in an unprecedented battle with Unocal's team of well-connected lobbyists. It was hardly an even playing field." US Ambassador Robert Oakley and his team of veteran Afghanistan hands in the State Department, they reported, were "more than suited to controlling the debate from the inside out." (And Oakley's wife, Phyllis, at the time chief of the intelligence wing of the State Department, had far-ranging access to sensitive intelligence reporting throughout the US government.) In an interview "with a prominent member of the Afghanistan family long involved in the issue," the husband-and-wife team of Gould and Fitzgerald were given a stunning opinion on the Taliban's origins: "Robert Oakley was — along with the CIA — the *creators* of the Taliban."[38] Considering the role of Brzezinski in funding the mujahideen against the Soviets, this analysis is less far-fetched than would seem. And it would come up again when reporters began to explore the genesis of ISIS in Iraq.

Meanwhile, determined to get their concerns aired, Smeal and the foundation decided to turn to celebrities for help. Mavis Leno, wife of talk show host Jay Leno and a member of the foundation board, became chair of the

Stop Gender Apartheid in Afghanistan campaign. They started a petition campaign in behalf of Afghan women with slogans such as "You have blood on your hands" directed at Unocal and the US government. One particularly powerful poster showed someone pointing a gas-pump handle at a burqa-covered woman as if it were a gun. The poster's message: UNOCAL: STOP SACRIFICING WOMEN FOR OIL.

In 1999 the Clinton administration finally took heed. Hillary Clinton delivered a rousing speech denouncing the Taliban for physically beating women and destroying their spirit.

By then, all hopes were dashed that the Taliban could be reliable allies; not only was their control of Afghanistan in doubt, but their extreme social policies were also becoming well publicized and unjustifiable. The loud public backlash may have been an unexpected wrinkle for the government and Big Oil. As a pro-Taliban diplomat once explained to Rashid when comparing US support for the Taliban with its equally blind support of the Wahhabi extremism of the Saudi royal family, "There will be Aramco, pipelines, an emir, no parliament, and lots of sharia law. We can live with that."[39] After all, living with that had worked for half a century with the Saudis. But it was not working with the Taliban in 1998.

President Clinton, who was known to worry more about domestic concerns than foreign concerns, began to back off from the Taliban over the years 1998 and 1999. At the same time, shareholders in Unocal began to express their concerns over the Taliban's treatment of Afghan women. Yet it was neither the Clintons, nor the feminists, nor the Taliban, nor the rivalry between Unocal and Bridas that delivered the final coup de grâce to the lofty pipeline plans in Afghanistan. Instead, it was a wealthy Saudi and funder of Islamic extremists named Osama bin Laden.

OBL and the "Graveyard of Empires"

On August 7, 1998, between 10:30 a.m. and 10:40 a.m. local time, suicide bombers driving explosives-laden trucks simultaneously detonated their payloads outside the US embassies in the East African cities of Dar es Salaam, Tanzania, and Nairobi, Kenya, killing a total of 221 people. Of the thousands who were wounded in the joint attacks, most were civilians. Twelve Americans died, including two CIA agents.

A group calling itself the Liberation Army of the Islamic Sanctuaries took credit for the attacks, but US investigators concluded that the group was actually a front for the Egyptian Islamic Jihad, a core group of Al Qaeda that supported Afghan jihadists in their war against the Soviets. The planning of the attacks, it was surmised, was orchestrated by Osama bin Laden, who had founded Al Qaeda in 1988.[40]

There was good reason to suspect him. August 7, 1998 — the date of the two embassy bombings — was the eighth anniversary of a day of infamy in bin Laden's mind: the day when 540,000 US troops arrived in Saudi Arabia as part of George H. W. Bush's Gulf War against Iraq (1990–91). On February 23, 1998, six months before the two embassy bombings, bin Laden had put out a fatwa in the name of the World Islamic Front for Jihad against Jews and Crusaders. It read, in part, "For more than seven years the United States is occupying the lands of Islam in the holiest of its territories, Arabia, plundering its riches, overwhelming its rulers, humiliating its people, threatening its neighbors, and using its bases in the peninsula as a spearhead to fight against the neighboring Islamic peoples." The fatwa went on to declare it an "individual duty for every Muslim" to kill North Americans and their Israeli allies in order to liberate the Muslim holy places. Several months later, in an interview with ABC in Afghanistan, he elaborated that North Americans were "the worst terrorists. . . . We do not have to differentiate between military or civilian. As far as we are concerned, they are all targets."[41]

These were no idle threats. Bin Laden was by now an experienced warrior. He had used his prodigious wealth as the son of a Saudi contractor to help fund (along with the CIA) the jihadists in Afghanistan, who by 1989 had forced the Soviets to withdraw from that country. Bin Laden then returned to Saudi Arabia a hero. What the CIA had apparently not anticipated was the jihadists' belief that their success in defeating one major infidel power (the Soviets) could be replicated against another, should it prove hostile to the followers of Islam. To Osama bin Laden, the introduction of hundreds of thousands of American troops into Saudi Arabia was bad enough. That they were *invited by the Saudis' ruling elite* — ostensibly to protect them from Iraqi troops that had invaded neighboring Kuwait — was to him a travesty of the first order. His criticisms of the Saudi royal family intensified when President Bush broke his promise to withdraw all US troops after Kuwait had been liberated, instead leaving 20,000 troops behind in Saudi Arabia.[42]

The Saudi royal family did not take kindly to bin Laden's protestations and declared him persona non grata. He left for Sudan, where he found common cause with veterans of the anti-Soviet war in Afghanistan. They were equally disgusted by what they considered a US military penetration of Saudi Arabia.

Alarmed by bin Laden's widening anti-Saudi base, the Saudis renounced his citizenship in May 1996. He moved again, this time back to Afghanistan, where he reconnected with anti-Soviet jihadists. The following month the Taliban captured Kabul; shortly afterward, an emboldened bin Laden declared war on the United States for its military occupation of Saudi Arabia. "The walls of oppression and humiliation cannot be demolished except in a rain of bullets," he declared. "The 'evils' of the Middle East arose from America's attempt to take over the region and from its support for Israel. Saudi Arabia had been turned into 'an American colony.'"[43]

In 1997 he befriended the fiery Afghan leader of the Taliban, Mullah Omar. Now widely sought by the CIA, Osama bin Laden slipped into the city of Kandahar under the protection of the Taliban.[44]

The Clinton administration had already begun to back off from recognizing the regime as outrage over the Taliban's mistreatment of women influenced public opinion. Now, with the Taliban in support of and sheltering bin Laden, sworn enemy of the United States, any formal negotiations between the Taliban and the United States became unfeasible. As the *Washington Post* reported, "Without that U.S. imprimatur, banks and international financial institutions would not lend money to build the pipeline from Turkmenistan to Pakistan."[45]

Bin Laden's involvement in the two embassy bombings in Africa further eroded US-Taliban relations. The Clinton administration felt compelled to retaliate, launching missile strikes against Taliban camps in Afghanistan. Washington became obsessed with "getting bin Laden," who continued to make inroads with the Taliban leadership. Bin Laden's money and experience as a contractor in Saudi Arabia became useful in building his base, literally: He built a home for Mullah Omar and promised to build roads and badly needed infrastructure in Afghanistan. He funded other Taliban leaders and encouraged Arab-Afghan fighters to join the Taliban in their offensives in northern Afghanistan against the anti-Taliban Northern Alliance. The alliance's funders, Iran and Russia, were now convinced that Unocal was funded by the CIA and vowed to block construction of the pipeline.[46] The Russians were not going to succumb to what they saw as a naked power grab by the United States in their Central Asian backyard.

The Caspian region had been under their control for over a century, and now they saw the West conspiring to take the region and its vital resources away from them.

Russian President Boris Yeltsin had no doubts that the Great Game was in full force: "We cannot help seeing the uproar stirred up in some Western countries over the energy resources of the Caspian. Some seek to exclude Russia from the game and undermine its interests. The so-called pipeline war in the region is part of the game."[47]

Unocal, for its part, concluded that it could no longer rely on the Taliban to stabilize the pipeline route and unify the country by force. As long as there was continued instability in the region, international financing of its pipelines was impossible. In December 1998, Unocal pulled out of Afghanistan. The *New York Times* attributed the Unocal project's demise to low oil prices, pressure from feminist groups, and concern over the Taliban harboring suspected terrorist Osama bin Laden.[48]

And the Feminist Majority Foundation was ecstatic. It jubilantly announced the news in its December 1998 newsletter: "In a stunning victory for the Feminist Majority's 'Stop Gender Apartheid in Afghanistan!' campaign, Unocal Corporation has withdrawn its support from plans to build an $8 billion oil pipeline through Afghanistan. . . . The energy pipeline would have provided Afghanistan's repressive Taliban regime with $150 million in profits each year."

But the feminists ended their news on a sobering note: "While Unocal's abandonment of the pipeline project is good news, Afghan women are still being imprisoned in their homes and denied their basic human rights."

The prospects for peace in Afghanistan looked dimmer than ever. Robert Ebel of the Center for Strategic and International Studies had rightly predicted a year earlier, "The players in the game of pipeline politics must remind themselves that peace can bring a pipeline, but a pipeline cannot bring peace."[49]

The Clinton administration, though, did not give up on the dreams of a US-run pipeline in the Caspian region, reflecting a sentiment widely held in Washington. The stakes were simply too big. Noted one diplomat, "This is where we prove we're still the big boy on the block. China, Europe, Iran, Russia and all the others want to see if they can take us down. All of our so-called friends and all of our so-called enemies want control of this region."[50]

With Afghanistan out of the picture, the administration began to aggressively campaign for a pipeline running from Azerbaijan on the east shores of the Caspian Sea through Georgia to Turkey, a critical NATO ally. In 1999, the leaders of Azerbaijan, Georgia, and Turkey signed the Baku–Tbilisi–Ceyhan (BTC) Pipeline agreement. The BTC Company, a consortium of eleven energy companies operating the pipeline, was established in August 2002; the third-largest member was Unocal. As chapter 6 reveals, this new pipeline was predicted to be the linchpin of a shift in US energy policy away from the Middle East — but once again, pipeline politics would intervene, this time almost causing World War III.

Some oil company executives still pined for a pipeline running through Iran. The only obstacles were the sanctions imposed by Congress. Halliburton International, a Texas-based major supplier of oil and gas equipment, was an outspoken critic of the sanctions. Cecil Davidson, Halliburton's operations manager in Turkmenistan, bluntly told the *New York Times*, "Sanctions are a drag on our business position. The competition gains strength because . . . they can operate in Iran and we can't."[51]

Davidson was simply mirroring the views of Halliburton's CEO, who in 1998 was quietly courting the Taliban in his own search for secure pipeline routes. A man known for his steely resolve, he was determined to beat out any and all competition that thwarted Halliburton's goal of becoming a big winner in the Great Game for Oil. His name was Dick Cheney. In 2000 he was chosen by the Republican soon-to-be president candidate, George W. Bush, as his running mate. Together, the two oilmen would take the Great Game and pipeline politics to a new and dangerous level, one that would forever change the course of American foreign policy in Central Asia and the Middle East and, ironically, slowly erode America's standing in the world as a great world power.

CHAPTER FOUR

Bush's Oil and Pipeline Wars
The Most Censored Story

S eptember 11, 2001, that day of infamy, would forever change America and its impact on the world. Jerry and I watched it all on television from the safety of our living room in Burlington, Vermont. After our initial shock at seeing the Twin Towers of the World Trade Center collapse, first one, then the other, we were struck with the realization that the Twin Towers were monuments not only to free trade, but to the two men who had them built and financed in the 1960s: then governor Nelson Rockefeller and his brother David Rockefeller, chairman of Chase Manhattan Bank. Savvy New Yorkers had even wryly nicknamed the Twin Towers "Nelson" and "David." So while commentators like CBS news anchor Dan Rather called the 9/11 attack on the World Trade Center a major strike against the very symbol of American economic and international power, we couldn't help but wonder how David Rockefeller was reacting to an attack on the very symbol of his family's power.[1]

Within hours of the catastrophe, President George W. Bush was blaming Osama bin Laden and Al Qaeda terrorists for the attacks and vowed revenge. At 9 p.m., in a televised address from the Oval Office, a grim-faced Bush vowed, "We will make no distinction between the terrorists who committed these acts and those who harbor them." Soon, heavily armed and black-helmeted shock troops began prowling the streets of New York City looking for suspects, which invariably meant anyone who looked like an Arab or dressed like one . . . or harbored one. While the beefed-up security gave New Yorkers some confidence that they would be safe from further attacks, the day's optics were profoundly disturbing — the rapid descent of the towers into a pile of rubble, people screaming as they escaped the billowing smoke, howling fire engines and ambulances rushing to the scene, desperate and grieving relatives, and military deployments on the ground. The whole country seemed paralyzed by shock and grief.

The immediate impact of 9/11 on my life was comparatively minor, but deeply felt. The following morning, I reluctantly trudged off to the Burlington post office to mail an appeal to the CIA to turn over more documents about my father. I felt an overwhelming sense of foreboding. The enormity of the deaths of almost three thousand innocent Americans in the 9/11 attacks weighed heavily on all of us, and before we had even had a chance to process what had happened and why, President Bush was clearly preparing us for war. Since he targeted Osama bin Laden and Al Qaeda as the culprits, this meant war somewhere in the Middle East or Afghanistan. And that could only mean calamity of the first order.*

To a journalist who knew all too well that truth is the first casualty of war, it also meant a clampdown on the freedom of the press . . . and Freedom of Information Act (FOIA) requests. How, I brooded as I approached the post office, could I ever expect a prompt reply from the CIA to my appeal for more documents? It didn't help that my father had been a master spy operating in the tumultuous, terror-driven Middle East, even though that was five decades ago.

Overcome with feelings of gloom and doom, I was temporarily lifted out of my dark musings when a friend caught up with me.

---

* On September 14, just three days after 9/11, a frightened Congress passed the Authorization for Use of Military Force (AUMF), granting the president the power to use "all necessary and appropriate force against any nations, organizations or persons he determines planned, authorized, committed or aided the terrorist attacks that occurred on September 11, 2001, or harbored such organizations or persons." Barbara Lee, congresswoman from California, was the only representative to vote no on the AUMF, declaring (prophetically as it turned out) that it would give the government unlimited powers to wage war without a debate in Congress. Since then, it has been used to justify most US military actions in the Middle East, even though it was originally directed at the Taliban and Al Qaeda. President Obama used it as the legal basis for military airstrikes against ISIS in Syria, and the Trump administration in February 2019 first raised the AUMF as being a "legal rationale for striking Iranian territory or proxies." *Source:* Steve Vladeck and Tess Bridgeman, "About that Trial Balloon on Using the 9/11 AUMF to Authorize US Strikes on Iran," *Just Security*, February 21, 2019, https://www.justsecurity.org/62646/washington-times-aumf-iran/. See also, U.S. Congress, *Authorization for Use of Military Force*, S.J. Res. 23, 107th Cong., 1st sess., September 18, 2001, https://www.govinfo.gov/content/pkg/BILLS-107sjres23enr/pdf/BILLS-107sjres23enr.pdf.

"What do you make of yesterday?" he asked breathlessly.

"I don't know," I replied. "There's something about it that doesn't make sense." Like so many people, I couldn't understand why the 9/11 hijackers hadn't been intercepted by US warplanes in airspace as heavily protected as that above New York City and Washington, DC.

I showed my friend the envelope in my hand. He had known about my quest. "This is going to affect my FOIA request with the CIA," I confided. However much the world had changed the day before, September 12, 2001, was still my deadline for filing an appeal for more documents. "Now it's going to take me even longer to get the records I requested – if I get them at all – because everything will be explained away in terms of protecting national security."

Up until that day, I had been relatively successful in my search for information. I had first filed an administrative FOIA request with the CIA in 1999 at the suggestion of John Taylor, the legendary octogenarian military records specialist at the National Archives. The stoop-shouldered Taylor, much beloved to researchers, had been very interested in my quest. He was the custodian of the OSS records that had been declassified in 1985 on the order of Ronald Reagan's CIA director, William Casey, himself an OSS veteran. In a memo to all CIA employees, Casey explained his desire to make "significant historical information available without risking damage to national security." Huge volumes of OSS records were subsequently turned over to the National Archives and, with the help of researcher Timothy Naftali's tip, I had found roughly three years' worth of my father's reports.

Taylor encouraged me to file "in-house" requests to declassify records that had been withdrawn from my father's file, and while this effort had proved rewarding, I was still lacking information on the last three months of my father's life. The next step, Taylor had advised in 1999, was to file a FOIA request directly to the CIA.

After some delays, the CIA turned over some three hundred documents, a relatively large amount, which some of the archivists figured was out of courtesy to the daughter of "one of their own." Yet most of the documents were disappointing, covering routine personnel matters – salaries, airplane tickets, shipping of personnel effects, and the like. There was one document in the stack of three hundred, though, that made the entire effort worthwhile: a five-page "analysis of work" prepared by my father in early 1944 before his posting to Lebanon. Here was a recitation of his marching orders, including a recapitulation of everything he had learned during his training and indoctrination. Curiously, the last three pages of this nearly sixty-year-old document were almost completely blackened out. But the first few pages contained some surprising nuggets of information.

American prestige, Daniel Dennett stated, had grown steadily in the Middle East due in large part to "American educational, medical and scientific missions." However, up to 1939 and the start of World War II, "a deliberate effort was made by all great powers, Axis and Allied, to undermine our prestige." Frictions among allies, he continued, were likely to resume in the postwar period. His job was to protect and insulate US interests from these threats. And key among these interests was oil.

"We occupy a dominant position in [redacted]" — which I figured out was Saudi Arabia. The next sentence, which somehow escaped the CIA's black redacting pen, was startling in its simplicity: "The probable extent of these oil deposits is so great," Dennett wrote, "that we must control them at all costs."

This was a big breakthrough, a confirmation that Saudi oil was central to Carat's concerns, not just in 1947 but at the very outset of his mission to the Middle East in 1944. It caused me to wonder whether his job was to make Lebanon safe for the Trans-Arabian Pipeline. That's why I considered my appeal for more documents on September 12 to be so important . . . yet possibly doomed.

In the days and weeks after 9/11, I couldn't stop thinking about what oil might have to do with what clearly looked like an emerging war. Nor could I shake Carat's warning that engagement in the region would lead to utter chaos. But the "War on Terror" was unfolding amid a backdrop of patriotism so fierce that it squelched many questions — which is why I was relieved to find, three weeks after the 9/11 attacks, a *New York Times* piece by Frank Viviano with the tantalizing headline, "War Will Be Linked to Oil." At the time, I had yet to see anyone, not a single media pundit or government official, make this claim. And yet Viviano, whom I had never heard of, was writing with great confidence that war was coming, and it wasn't just about going after the 9/11 terrorists. He started his piece with this bold claim: "Beyond American determination to hit back against the perpetrators of the September 11 attacks, beyond the likelihood of longer, drawn-out battles producing more civilian casualties in the months and years ahead, the hidden stakes in the war against terrorism can be summed up in a single word: oil."[2]

Viviano described a map of terrorist outposts in the Middle East and Central Asia that, not coincidentally, corresponded to some of the main energy sources in the world. He continued, "The defense of these energy sources — rather than a simple confrontation between Islam and the West — will be the primary flash point of global conflict for decades to come, say observers in the region." His story had a great impact on me. As for the American public, who could know how many people had seen it? And there was little time for its message to sink in. One week after Viviano's piece appeared, President Bush announced that the United States and the United Kingdom had begun massive airstrikes on Taliban military outposts in Afghanistan. Operation Enduring Freedom had begun, and would indeed endure.

Some eighteen years later, with American troops still fighting the Taliban in Afghanistan, more people are examining the origins of the war and questioning its purpose. But back then, as revealed by Kristina Borjesson's *Feet to the Fire: The Media after 9/11*, hardly any mainstream journalist dared to counter the official narratives coming out of the Oval Office.[3] One who did was Marjorie Cohn, a law professor at the Thomas Jefferson School of Law in San Diego. By August 2000, halfway through the Bush-Cheney presidential campaign, Cohn was already hot on Dick Cheney's trail, warning readers in an opinion piece for the *Chicago Tribune* that "Cheney is ineluctably invested in keeping the world safe for his investments. Although he stepped down as CEO of Halliburton, he still owns shares of stock in the conglomerate and his financial interests in the Persian Gulf, the Caspian region and the Balkans will invariably continue." Cohn, even before Viviano, sniffed oil wars in the air: "Chosen by George W. Bush to bring foreign-policy expertise to the GOP presidential ticket, we can expect a Republican administration to increase U.S. intervention in regions when it suits Dick Cheney's oil and other corporate concerns." In sum, she stated, "War is big business and Dick Cheney is right in the middle of it."[4]

When I later asked Cohn how she had come to focus on Cheney so early on, she said it was actually the NATO bombing of Kosovo in 1999 that got her looking into Cheney's business interests in the Middle East. She had found a 1996 *New York Times* article (intriguingly titled "The Third American Empire") stating that the disintegration of the Soviet Union "prompted the United States to expand its zone of military hegemony into

Eastern Europe (through NATO) and into formerly neutral Yugoslavia. And — most important of all — the end of the cold war has permitted America to deepen its involvement in the Middle East."[5]

When, in 2000, George W. Bush selected Cheney as his running mate to bring foreign policy experience to the ticket, Cohn said she looked into Halliburton's oil interests in the Gulf and saw a parallel with the company's involvement in the Balkans. Halliburton's subsidiary Brown & Root had secured a lucrative contract to supply US forces in the Balkans in 1999. Cheney also had lobbied to lift sanctions against Iran in order to facilitate the transport of oil across Iran to the Persian Gulf.[6]

In other words, Cohn, by studying Cheney, had stumbled on a vast network of his oil interests that extended from the Balkans to the Middle East to the Caspian Sea. (Today, Halliburton is active in seventy countries, describing itself as "one of the world's largest providers of products and services to the energy industry.") When viewed in the context of the US/ NATO wars in Iraq and Kuwait (The Gulf War: 1990–91), Kosovo (1999), Afghanistan (2001–present), and Iraq (2003–2011), one could even conclude that the grand vision of Cheney and others in the oil sector was the equivalent to creating a new American empire.*

Looking back at this period, beginning with the war in Kosovo, I recall having been dubious about President Clinton's stated concern that the main reason for bombing Kosovo was to put an end to ethnic cleansing, but I was determined to stay focused on the Middle East. (I have since learned that there may have been a direct oil and pipeline connection to the NATO bombing of Kosovo, tied in with US interest in developing pipeline routes from the Caspian Sea that avoided not only Russia but also Serbia.[7] Today, I look at the region with new understanding as a vast continuum ripe for NATO intervention. The passage of time inevitably yields new insights.)

From 2001 to 2003, while waiting for a response to my FOIA appeal from the CIA, I delved into studying George W. Bush's wartime cabinet. Soon, I began giving my first public talks on the "War on Terror" and pipeline politics. My audiences were all ears — desperate for an explanation, a different perspective on 9/11 and its wartime aftermath. My talks often began with a quick recap of Bush and Cheney's pre–Oval Office lives.

---

* There were still 5,000 troops in Iraq as of July 2019, but the war is considered to have officially ended in 2011.

Killing Osama . . . or Making Afghanistan Safe for the Pipeline?

Dick Cheney, as CEO of Halliburton before becoming Bush's vice president, had certainly made it his business to know where the great oil and gas prospects of the world lay. He made a number of trips to Afghanistan to court the Taliban in 1998, knowing from firsthand experience that one of the greatest prospects in modern times lay in and around the Caspian Sea. According to Cohn, the Washington-based American Petroleum Institute had called the Caspian "the area of greatest resource potential outside of the Middle East," and Cheney readily concurred, telling a group of oil company executives in 1998, "I can't think of a time when we've had a region emerge as suddenly to become as strategically significant as the Caspian."[8] Even after Unocal withdrew from Afghanistan in 1999, Cheney kept a watchful eye on developments in the region, especially after Bush chose him as his running mate in 2000.

During his presidential campaign, Bush himself let the cat out of the bag about his priorities if elected president. He told a Boston audience during his first presidential debate on October 3, 2000: "I want to build pipelines to move natural gas. . . . It's an issue I know a lot about. I was a small oil person for a while."[9]

Indeed, compared to the Rockefeller-spawned ExxonMobil and Chevron giants that invariably cornered the most lucrative oil and gas markets in the world, Bush's Zapata Oil was small potatoes. His ascent to the presidency promised more open doors to the "small oil people" in the former Soviet republics in the Caspian Sea region, and in Iraq. Under Secretary of Defense Paul Wolfowitz even admitted to the *Guardian* in May 2003 that everyone in the oil business knew Iraq was rich in oil.[10]

Once in office, Bush appointed so many oil executives to his cabinet that the *Oil and Gas Journal* gushed, "From industry's perspective, the casting of the lead roles couldn't be better."[11] Besides Cheney as Bush's vice president, there was Condoleezza Rice, Bush's national security advisor, who had served on the board of Chevron and had once been honored by having a Chevron oil tanker named after her.[12] (The name was removed after she joined the Bush administration.) Bush's commerce secretary and former campaign manager, Don Evans, had been the CEO of a Colorado-based oil company and a director of TMBR/Sharp Drilling.[13]

The administration immediately explored rekindling relations with the Taliban, for the simple reason that the Taliban held out the most hope for stabilizing Afghanistan and enabling oil and gas pipelines to pass through the country. But by August 2001, the Taliban was balking at some of the conditions laid down by the Bush administration for moving forward, causing Washington to threaten the Taliban militarily if they did not cooperate: "Either you accept our offer of a carpet of gold," said US representatives, "or we bury you with a carpet of bombs," reported the French authors of *OBL: The Hidden Truth*.[14] Negotiations broke down when, after the 9/11 attacks, the Taliban refused to turn over Osama bin Laden. (Less known is the fact that the Taliban had sought proof that linked bin Laden to 9/11, and the Bush administration refused to supply it.)

The War in Afghanistan

It was just a month later, on October 7, 2001, that President Bush ordered the airstrikes against the Taliban, launching Operation Enduring Freedom. Within six months, American troops had soundly defeated the Taliban. Convinced by May 2002 that stability had been restored to the country, the leaders of Turkmenistan, Afghanistan, and Pakistan met to give the go-ahead for a natural gas pipeline, now called TAPI, for the countries it would traverse: Turkmenistan, Afghanistan, and Pakistan — and India, which was invited to join the project.

The economic benefits that would accrue to Afghanistan included millions of dollars in transit fees and thousands of jobs so desperately needed in the war-torn country. Reported the BBC, "It is also hoped such a project would boost regional economic ties and pave the way for further foreign investment." The Asian Development Bank began a feasibility study.[15] Everything seemed to be going according to plan.

But which plan? Was sending American troops to Afghanistan to avenge 9/11 and fight terrorism (and, little known to most people, to stabilize the country for secure pipeline transit) the makings of "a good war," as this "war of necessity" had been described? Or was it, as Australian journalist John Pilger declared after the initial relentless US and British bombing campaigns, a fraud? Pilger noted that "not a single terrorist implicated in the attacks on America has been caught or killed in Afghanistan." He charged that "one of the poorest, most stricken nations has been terrorised by the most powerful — to the point where American pilots have run out of dubious military targets and are now destroying mud houses, a hospital, Red Cross warehouses, lorries carrying refugees." Pilger questioned why the British Royal Air Force used cluster bombs that "spray hundreds of bomblets that have only one purpose; to kill and maim people."[16]

Two *New York Times* reporters, for their part, saw through the Bush administration's insistence that oil had nothing to do with the invasion of Afghanistan. In their December 2001 article, "As the War Shifts Alliances, Oil Deals Follow," Neela Banerjee and Sabrina Tavernise quoted a consultant with Cambridge Energy Research Associates: "Once we bomb the hell out of Afghanistan, we will have to cough up some projects there, and this [Unocal] pipeline is one of them."[17]

Since the 9/11 attacks, the two journalists reported, the United States saw Afghanistan as "a stable oil supplier," noting that the State Department was "exploring the potential for post-Taliban energy projects in the region, which has more than 6 percent of the world's proven oil reserves and almost 40 percent of its gas reserves." Muslims in Afghanistan and beyond, added Banerjee and Tavernise, harbored no illusions about Washington's ambitions: "Skeptics, especially in the Islamic world, contend that oil interests lie at the heart of the West's war in Afghanistan."

The authors cited a headline in a Pakistani newspaper as reflecting local sentiment: "The Pipeline of Greed," read the headline. The accompanying article went on to state, "The war on terrorism may well be a war for resources." Articles like this tended to be the exception in the West's coverage of the war. Canadians, however, got a rare dose of reality when, in 2009, a Canadian energy economist named John Foster declared in the *Toronto Star* that the war in Afghanistan was a pipeline-driven war.

Foster quoted a US State Department official revealing the purpose of the pipeline: "Richard Boucher, U.S. assistant secretary of state, said: 'One of our goals is to stabilize Afghanistan,' and to link South and Central Asia 'so that energy can flow to the south.' Oil and gas have motivated U.S. involvement in the Middle East for decades," Foster continued. "Unwittingly or wittingly, Canadian forces are supporting American goals."[18] In a scholarly report published earlier, Foster had shown that Canadian forces bore the brunt of the fighting in Kandahar Province along the pipeline route. "The impact of the TAPI pipeline on Canadian Forces must be assessed," he wrote, "given that the proposed pipeline route traverses the most conflict-ridden areas of Afghanistan, crossing through Kandahar province where Canadian Forces are attempting to provide security and defeat insurgents."[19]

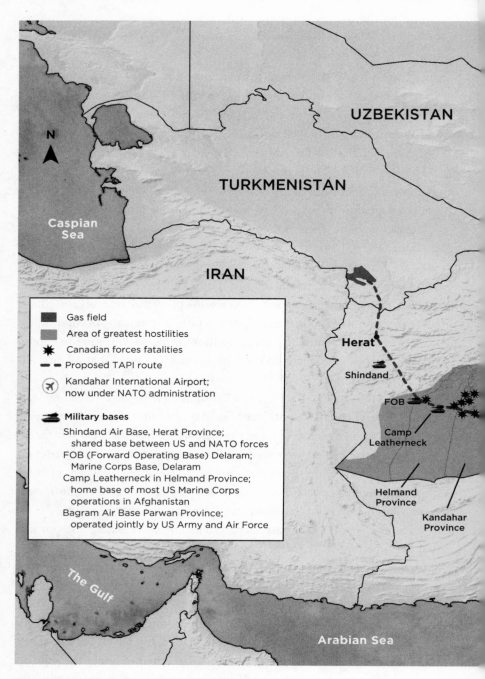

The War in Afghanistan and the TAPI Pipeline

Before and during the ongoing war in Afghanistan, a subterranean "pipeline war" has been waged to control and protect the route of the projected multibillion-dollar TAPI pipeline, which would travel from Turkmenistan, across Afghanistan, to Pakistan and India. An American oil company (Unocal) turned to Taliban warriors to protect the

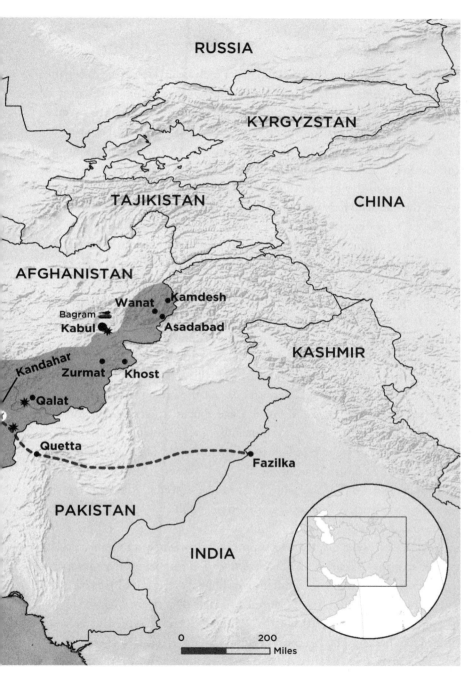

pipeline route and bring security to Afghanistan. After 9/11, US relations with the Taliban broke down, and the Bush administration ordered the invasion of Afghanistan. In 2006, Canadian forces were given responsibility for securing Afghanistan's flashpoint provinces of Helmand and Kandahar, key areas for the proposed TAPI pipeline route, along which major US and NATO military bases are located.[20]

Ten years after the war began, John Pilger took a hard look at the role of the media in describing — or ignoring — certain facts on the ground. He discovered a Pentagon media strategy that came straight out of the US Army's manual on counterinsurgency. It was none other than General David Petraeus, he explained, who described the war in Afghanistan as a "war of perception . . . conducted continuously using the news media. What really matters is not so much the day-to-day battles . . . as the way the adventure is sold in America where 'the media directly influence the attitude of key audiences.'"[21]

Never, Pilger concluded, "has so much official energy been expended in ensuring journalists collude with the makers of rapacious wars which, say the media-friendly generals, are now 'perpetual.'" Here was an early hint that the "good war" — going after the perpetrators of 9/11 — would become an endless war, possibly the very kind that Cheney had predicted when he spoke before the Los Angeles World Affairs Council in 2004 and warned that the "War on Terror" could last generations.[22]

General Tommy Franks, head of the US Central Command in Afghanistan, revealed in November 2001 during his first Pentagon briefing that "apprehending Osama bin Laden isn't one of the missions" of Operation Enduring Freedom. Added Colonel Dave Lapan, spokesperson for US Central Command, "If tomorrow morning someone told us Osama's dead, that doesn't mean we're through in Afghanistan."[23] The goal, explained Franks, was "the destruction of the al-Qa'eda network, as well as the . . . Taliban that provide harbor to bin Laden and al-Qa'eda." The stage was set for selling a relentless "War on Terror" to the public.

Eventually, the Pentagon's ubiquitous excuse that troops, followed by military bases, were needed to stamp out terrorism would come under greater scrutiny. As early as 2002, *Nightline's* Ted Koppel produced a documentary revealing that the installation of huge American military bases in the former Soviet republics of Central Asia had all happened "in the name of fighting terrorism," and that the "War on Terror" seemed to be best funded and best supplied in those regions with great reserves of oil. Yet extraordinary efforts to deceive the public still made their way into American news — a fact that pained me to the core. Even members of my own family could not understand my anguished outbursts when I watched disinformation being peddled as news on TV. When it came to comprehending the real motives for invading Afghanistan, most Americans were still experiencing the kind of "psychic numbness" that physician and antinuclear activist

Helen Caldicott blamed for public inaction on nuclear proliferation and that others have blamed for inaction on climate change.

By 2003, most Americans remained ignorant of the oil connection and pretty much accepted the official rationale for invading Afghanistan, but they were less inclined to support the other war emerging in Middle East: the Iraq War, which would commence in March 2003.

The War in Iraq

In the months leading up to the Iraq War, the US government and its allies, particularly the British government, began to proclaim ever more stridently that Saddam Hussein was building weapons of mass destruction (WMD) — and that he was ready to use them against the West. President Bush first officially enunciated these claims to the world at the United Nations in September 2002, and Secretary of State Colin Powell repeated them on February 5, 2003. Their claims were officially debunked by UN inspector Hans Blix on February 14. On February 15, protests against a war in Iraq erupted in six hundred cities around the world; it was the biggest antiwar protest in history. Some six to eleven million people in up to sixty countries participated. Among the chants that could be heard, whether in Switzerland, Norway, or Taiwan, was "No Blood for Oil!" Nevertheless, on March 20, 2003, President Bush declared war on Iraq, and allied forces began strikes against military targets in the country.

Robert Fisk, an award-winning British reporter who has covered the Middle East from 1976 onward, captured the world's pervasive scorn early on. Based mostly in Beirut, he had become a preeminent war correspondent, reporting extensively on the Lebanese civil war, the Soviet-Afghan war, the Iran-Iraq War, the Arab-Israeli conflict, the Gulf War, the invasion of Afghanistan, and the invasion of Iraq. His knowledge of Arabic gave him special access to prominent personalities in the Middle East, including Osama bin Laden, whom he interviewed three times between 1993 and 1997.

Over his long career as a war correspondent, his penchant for exposing uncomfortable truths and prescriptions for good journalism — "challenge authority, all authority, especially so when governments and politicians take us to war" — has won him widespread respect as well as condemnation.[24] On the same day that the worldwide protests erupted, Fisk's "Case Against War: A Conflict Driven by the Self-interest of America" appeared in the *Independent*, beginning with these brutally frank words: "In the end, I think we are just tired of being lied to. . . . We are sick of being insulted by Tony Blair and . . . the likes of George Bush and his cabal of neo-conservative henchmen who have plotted for years to change the map of the Middle East to their advantage."

In just a few sentences, Fisk took swipes at every rationale put forward by the Bush administration: that Saddam Hussein was another perpetrator of 9/11; that Saddam Hussein harbored weapons of mass destruction; that he posed a nuclear threat to the world. The British people, Fisk stated, "had no wish to embark on endless wars with a Texas governor-executioner who dodged the Vietnam draft and who, with his oil buddies, is now sending America's poor to destroy a Muslim nation that has nothing at all to do with the crimes against humanity of 11 September." Britain's foreign secretary, Jack Straw, he added, "brays at us about the dangers of nuclear weapons that Iraq does not have, of the torture and aggression of a dictatorship that America and Britain sustained when Saddam was 'one of ours.' . . . But he and Blair cannot discuss the dark political agenda behind George Bush's government, nor the 'sinister men' (the words of a very senior UN official) around the President."

In the United States, such a succinct analysis was not readily forthcoming, and to this day the "dark agenda" of the Bush administration "to change the map of the Middle East" is still not well known. For this reason, a slight digression is now necessary to highlight an important fact: Key members of Bush's wartime cabinet had plotted the invasion of *both* Afghanistan and Iraq *years before* Bush became president, beginning in 1989 and on through the 1990s and the Clinton administration.

The Neoconservative Agenda

Project Censored is a program based out of California's Sonoma State University that in every year since 1976 has identified the twenty-five most censored stories in the US press. In 2010, the project selected the "Neoconservative Plan for Global Dominance" as the most censored story of 2002–03. Its report began: "Rarely did the press, or, especially television, address the possibility that larger strategies might have driven the decision to invade Iraq." Drawing on the work of five journalists, the report takes the reader back to the 1970s, when the United States was reeling from an energy crisis and was embroiled in a "tug of war over oil" with the Middle East. American military presence in the Gulf was fairly insignificant, the report continues, "and the prospect of seizing control of Arab oil fields was pretty unattainable."[25]

Enter the neoconservatives.

In 1989, a small group of neoconservatives — both Democrats and Republicans — who had been influential strategists in the Defense Department during the Ford, Reagan, and George H. W. Bush administrations came together to produce the *Defense Planning Guidance* report, which advocated US military dominance around the world.* Key among the strategists was Dick Cheney (who would become George H. W. Bush's secretary of defense), Colin Powell (who would become George W. Bush's secretary of state), and Paul Wolfowitz (who would become Bush's deputy secretary of defense). Their plan called for the United States to grow in military superiority and prevent new rivals from rising up as challengers, particularly in the Middle East, where their goal was to preserve US access to the region's oil.[26]

Using aggressive concepts such as "preemptive" force and "forward military presence," the plan called for the United States to become absolutely powerful over both friends and foes.[27]

With the dissolution of the Soviet Union, however, Cheney and his fellow neoconservatives realized that they would no longer have the communist threat to justify large increases in military spending. They would have to come up with a new threat, one that would fill the void. The following year, on August 2, 1990, according to Project Censored, "President George H. W. Bush announced that the threat of global war had receded, but a new 'unforeseen threat to national security' loomed, one that 'could come from any angle, and from any power.'"[28] Coincidentally, that same day an "unforeseen threat" happened: Iraq invaded Kuwait, claiming that the bordering nation was slant-drilling to steal Iraq's oil. Bush responded

---

* There is considerable confusion over the terms *neoconservative* and *neoliberal*. Neoconservatives tend to favor military intervention to exercise their will in other countries, and neoliberals tend to employ economic means to commandeer the direction and weaken the sovereignty of other nations. I tend to identify neoliberals (or globalists) as those who fall into the David Rockefeller / Council on Foreign Relations / Trilateral Commission camp. Over a century of running an empire built on oil, neoliberals have learned through trial and error that more subtle ways of ruling are more effective than the military interventionist approach used by neoconservatives. Bush and Cheney, with strong neoconservative support, wanted to get in on the action of controlling resources before they were beaten out by the more sophisticated neoliberals, who inevitably got the best contracts due to their enormous wealth, power, and experience. Sometimes neoconservative and neoliberal interests coincide, or both approaches are used in tandem. Zbigniew Brzezinski, for instance, worked both sides in an effort to dominate Eurasia and undermine Russia.

with Operation Desert Storm, launched in August 1990 and concluded in February 1991. The Gulf War was a harbinger of the "War on Terror," which would come to replace the war on communism.

Working at the highest levels of power, an even bigger player in the New Great Game — Zbigniew Brzezinski — came up with his own strategy on how to deal with the purported end of the Cold War resulting from the demise of the Soviet Union. Brzezinski — national security advisor under President Jimmy Carter, a mentor to Madeleine Albright, and a close ally of banker David Rockefeller — prided himself on having been the mastermind behind the defeat of the Soviet Union in Afghanistan using CIA-funded Islamist jihadists (among them Osama bin Laden) to attack Soviet troops and expel them from the country. This further weakening of the Soviet Union in 1989 helped precipitate its dissolution in December 1991.

In 1997, when the riches of the Caspian Sea beckoned, Brzezinski authored a decisive report for a heavily Rockefeller-financed think tank, the Council on Foreign Relations. The report, which became a book — *The Grand Chessboard: American Primacy and Its Geostrategic Imperatives* — would become a blueprint for seizing and controlling Eurasia and establishing US hegemony against its biggest rivals, Russia and China. Brzezinski, like the neoconservatives, alluded to how the United States had become "the first and only true superpower" after the fall of the Soviet Union. He focused much of his grand strategy on the Eurasian countries bordering the Caspian Sea that were now freed from Soviet control.

Wrote Brzezinski: "The world's energy consumption is bound to vastly increase over the next two or three decades. . . . The momentum of Asia's economic development is already generating massive pressures for the exploration and exploitation of new sources of energy, and the Central Asian region and the Caspian Sea basin are known to contain reserves of natural gas and oil that dwarf those of Kuwait, the Gulf of Mexico, or the North Sea."

To be sure, energy demands were likely to explode, and with the increased demand, the importance of pipelines accelerated. Brzezinski chose to view pipeline development in positive terms: "Once pipelines to that area have been developed, Turkmenistan's truly vast natural gas reserves augur a prosperous future for the country's people. . . . In fact, an Islamic revival — already abetted from the outside not only by Iran but also by Saudi Arabia — is likely to become the mobilizing impulse for the increasingly pervasive new nationalisms, determined to oppose any reintegration under Russian — and hence infidel — control."[29]

In other words, an "Islamic revival" similar to the one he and the CIA helped create in Afghanistan could be a powerful counterforce against the Russians and their former sphere of influence around the Caspian Sea. Brzezinski did not anticipate jihadists later turning on the United States in the form of Al Qaeda. Much of his strategizing focused on the West fostering pipeline schemes in Central Asia that would necessarily bypass Russia, which no longer commanded the region as it did prior to the dissolution of the Soviet Union.[30]

Still, Brzezinski cautioned, there were "warning signs on the horizon" that would require putting "a premium on *maneuver and manipulation* in order to *prevent the emergence* of a hostile coalition that could eventually seek to challenge America's primacy in Eurasia." (emphasis added) Here, Brzezinski appeared to be arguing for the preemptive action and "forward military action" advocated earlier by the neoconservatives' 1989 *Defense Planning Guidance* report. He also anticipated that "as America becomes an increasingly multi-cultural society, it may find it more difficult to fashion a consensus on foreign policy issues, except in the circumstance of a truly massive and widely perceived direct external threat."[31] Observed journalist Nafeez Ahmed, Brzezinski "clearly envisaged that the establishment, consolidation and expansion of U.S. military hegemony over Eurasia through Central Asia would require the unprecedented, open-ended militarization of foreign policy, coupled with an unprecedented manufacture of domestic support and consensus on this militarization campaign."[32]

Yet this grand strategy went beyond Central Asia and included the Middle East. Iraq, in fact, had also been on the neoconservatives' drawing board long before George W. Bush became president. In 1997, complementing Brzezinski's grand chessboard, William Kristol, founder and editor of the conservative *Weekly Standard*, Robert Kagan, a neoconservative historian and political commentator, and Dick Cheney set up a think tank called the Project for the New American Century. On June 3, 1997, the project members published their "statement of principles," which called on the United States as "the world's pre-eminent power" to "shape a new century favorable to American principles and interests." This required increases in defense spending and "challenging regimes hostile to our interests and values."[33] Their prime target for regime change was Iraq under the presidency of Saddam Hussein.

The Biggest Prize of All

In January 1998, William Kristol and Robert Kagan set about creating the necessary threat to overthrow Saddam Hussein. In the aftermath of the first Gulf War, a cease-fire agreement had called for Iraq's elimination of all weapons of mass destruction, followed by continued monitoring by the United Nations. The two neoconservatives came up with a scheme to belittle the UN inspections. On January 1, 1998, Kagan and Kristol wrote an op-ed for the *New York Times* provocatively titled, "Bombing Iraq Is Not Enough," with these first four words: "Saddam Hussein must go."

The only way to remove Hussein's weapons of mass destruction, they argued, "is to remove him, and that means using air power and ground forces, and finishing the task left undone in 1991." They boldly proclaimed, "We can do this job. Mr. Hussein's army is much weaker than before the Persian Gulf War. He has no political support beyond his own bodyguards and generals. An effective military campaign combined with a political strategy to support the broad opposition forces in Iraq could well bring his regime down faster than many imagine."

The authors anticipated that President Clinton would have to "protect us and our allies from Iraqi biological and chemical weapons," creating a prelude to the "weapons of mass destruction" argument later used by the Bush administration for invading Iraq. They urged President Clinton to act by ordering ground forces into the Gulf.

It took a while, but on October 31, 1998, President Clinton signed the Iraq Liberation Act, which authorized funding for opposition groups in Iraq. The clear intention was regime change. In December 1998, just as impeachment hearings against President Clinton got under way, the United States and Great Britain launched missile attacks on some ninety-seven military targets in Iraq, ostensibly to degrade its ability to develop weapons of mass destruction. The pretext was Saddam Hussein's recent blocking of UN inspection teams. The chief UN inspector, Scott Ritter, would later insist that the regime had largely complied with their inspections as a matter of disarmament and that the buildup to war was based on lies and fear. As he told a *New York Times* reporter in September 2002, he would be "surprised if there is anything in Iraq worth finding," claiming that inspection efforts between 1991 and 1998 had resulted in the Iraqis giving up 90 to 95 percent of their most deadly weapons, rendering Saddam "fundamentally disarmed."[34]

Once Bush and Cheney won the 2000 election, they set into motion their ambition to "finish the job" in Iraq and seize the spoils of war. Iraq was said to have the second-largest oil reserves in the world, ranging from 112 billion to 300 billion barrels. The Russians, French, and Chinese were equally covetous and had already signed exploration contracts with the regime of Saddam Hussein, which were to go into effect when sanctions against Iraq were removed. Bush and Cheney, as oilmen, worried about getting beaten out by foreign competition. When Cheney set up the National Energy Policy Development Group in early 2001, his team drew up a map showing Iraqi oil fields, pipelines, refineries, and terminals, with an accompanying two-page list of "Foreign Suitors of Iraqi Oilfield Contracts."[35] Cheney fought the public release of these documents from his task force, but the Washington-based Judicial Watch was able to obtain a total of sixteen pages dated March 2001 through a Freedom of Information request. The emergence of these documents, noted Britain's *Daily Telegraph*, "could fuel claims that America's war in Iraq had as much to do with oil as national security."[36]

The serious plotting to get the oil of Iraq began as soon as Bush took office in January 2001, nine months before the tragedy of September 11. Just days after the inauguration, then treasury secretary Paul O'Neill learned that invading Iraq was "Topic A" at the first meeting of Bush's National Security Council. "It was all about finding a way to do it," O'Neill told Ron Suskind, author of *The Price of Loyalty*.[37]

"Finding a way" meant overcoming significant hurdles, both legal and political.[38] Saddam Hussein had not attacked or even threatened the United States, and America's intelligence agencies concluded in a classified report that he posed no threat to national security. Nonetheless, first President Bush and then Secretary of State Colin Powell told the UN that Saddam Hussein harbored weapons of mass destruction, and the rest is history.

Less known is the role played by an Iraqi then living in exile in a US-financed villa in Tehran. Ahmad Chalabi, a middle-aged banker known for his poker face when dealing with challenges, was considered the ideal candidate for replacing Hussein. Chalabi had formed the Iraqi National Congress back in 1992 with an aim to overthrow Saddam Hussein, receiving up to $100 million from the CIA between 1992 and 1996 in support of his efforts. He was a leading instigator of the invasion of Iraq, using *New York Times* reporter Judith Miller to perpetuate the cause in a series of articles about Iraq's WMD threat.[39] Chalabi was also a strong supporter of

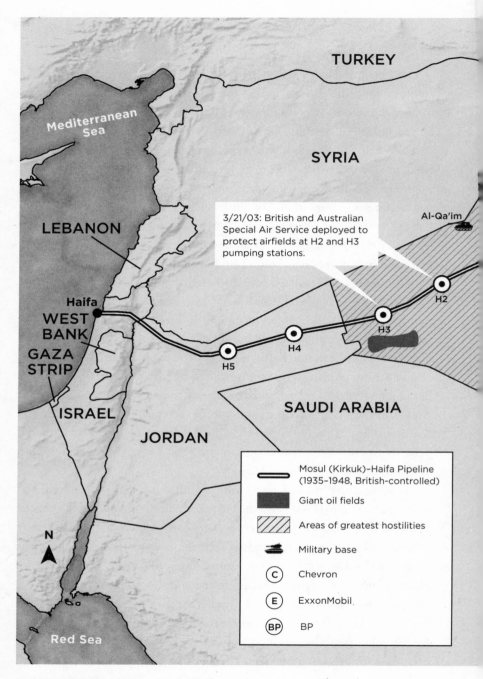

TURKEY

SYRIA

Mediterranean
Sea

LEBANON

3/21/03: British and Australian
Special Air Service deployed to
protect airfields at H2 and H3
pumping stations.

Al-Qa'im

Haifa
WEST
BANK

H2

GAZA
STRIP

H3

H4

ISRAEL

H5

SAUDI ARABIA

JORDAN

N

Mosul (Kirkuk)–Haifa Pipeline
(1935–1948, British-controlled)

Giant oil fields

Areas of greatest hostilities

Military base

C   Chevron

E   ExxonMobil

BP   BP

Red Sea

Military Priorities in the Iraq War:
Protecting Oil Installations and the Kirkuk–Haifa Pipeline Route

In 2003, at the start of the Iraq War, the first places coalition forces were deployed
were the oil fields of Kirkuk and Mosul and the airfields protecting the H2 and
H3 pumping stations along the old pipeline route carrying Iraqi oil to Israel. The

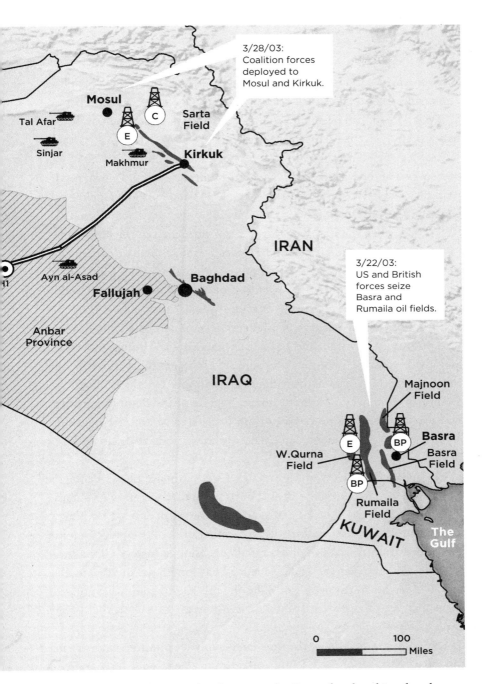

3/28/03:
Coalition forces deployed to Mosul and Kirkuk.

Mosul

Tal Afar

Sinjar

Makhmur

C

E

Sarta Field

Kirkuk

IRAN

3/22/03:
US and British forces seize Basra and Rumaila oil fields.

Ayn al-Asad

Fallujah

Baghdad

Anbar Province

IRAQ

Majnoon Field

E

BP

Basra

W.Qurna Field

Basra Field

BP

Rumaila Field

KUWAIT

The Gulf

0   100
          Miles

Kirkuk–Haifa pipeline was closed in 1948 after Iraq refused to ship oil to the new state of Israel. Benjamin Netanyahu and allies in the Bush administration hoped that a quick US victory in the Iraq War would install a new Iraqi leader friendly to Israel who, in turn, would reopen the pipeline to Haifa. Their dream never materialized, and the pipeline to Haifa has yet to be reconstructed.[40]

Israel and favored the reconstruction of the pipeline that originated in Iraq and terminated in the Israeli port of Haifa. The Kirkuk–Haifa pipeline, as it was named, had been built in the 1930s and supplied much of the Allied war effort in the Mediterranean during World War II. During Israel's War of Independence in 1948, the British constructed air force bases to protect two of the Kirkuk–Haifa pipeline pumping stations, shown on the "Military Priorities in the Iraq War" map as H2 and H3. The pipeline was closed in 1948 after Iraq refused to supply oil to the new state of Israel.

In 2003, when the Iraq War began, the resurrection of the pipeline became a viable aspiration, a fact underscored by the immediate deployment of troops to airfields protecting pumping stations along the Kirkuk–Haifa pipeline route and the oil fields of Kirkuk and Mosul. As the London *Observer* noted in the aftermath of the invasion, "To resurrect the pipeline would need the backing of whatever government the United States is to put in place in Iraq, and has been discussed — according to Western diplomatic sources — with the US-sponsored Iraqi National Congress and its leader Ahmed Chalabi, the former banker favored by the Pentagon for a powerful role in the war's aftermath. Sources at the State Department said that concluding a peace treaty with Israel is to be 'top of the agenda' for a new Iraqi government, and Chalabi is known to have discussed Iraq's recognition of the state of Israel."[41]

Key neocons with strong ties to Israel were in place in the Pentagon by the time the war began — Paul Wolfowitz, under secretary of defense under Dick Cheney; Douglas Feith, under secretary of defense for policy; and Richard Perle, past chairman and member of the Pentagon's Defense Policy Board. In April, a month after the invasion, a former CIA official told the *Observer* that the Haifa pipeline "has long been the dream of a powerful section of the people now driving this [Bush] administration and the war in Iraq to safeguard Israel's energy supply as well as that of the United States."[42]

Benjamin Netanyahu, at the time Israel's finance minister, exulted during the early stages of the US invasion of Iraq: "Soon you will see Iraqi oil flowing to Haifa. It's just a matter of time until the pipeline is reconstituted and Iraqi oil will flow to the Mediterranean. It is not a pipe dream."[43]

But, in fact, it was. Ahmad Chalabi, the designated replacement of Saddam Hussein, fell into disgrace (as did *New York Times* reporter Judith Miller) when it was revealed that he was the author of the fraudulent "weapons of mass destruction" pretext for the war. No other Iraqi leader could be found willing to make peace with Israel, and so the pipeline scheme fell through — at least for the next two decades.

What Charlotte *Could* Write

As the invasion of Iraq became imminent, I strongly suspected that there was an "oil and Israel" connection to the war, simply by virtue of my experience as a journalist in the Middle East and particularly because of my experience visiting Iraq in March 1975. That trip had shown me that Israel, along with the United States and Iran under Shah Reza Pahlavi, were actively trying to destabilize Iraq. Once again, oil was literally right in the middle of the intrigue and conflict — in this case, the so-called Kurdish rebellion against the Iraqi government in the mountains bordering Iran.

In a *Daily Star* article published on March 30, 1975, titled "The Kurdish War: A View from the Other Side," I wrote that most Western journalists covered the war by entering Kurd-held territories in the mountains of northeastern Iraq through Iran. (Journalists were banned from Iraq due to negative press coverage of the leftist Baathist regime.) I had been one of two Western journalists (the other was a reporter for *Time* magazine) who were allowed to get close to the war by going through Baghdad and then traveling up a steep mountainous road to the war zone near the Iran border. What I found was a story markedly different from the one portrayed in the Western press. The decades-old Kurdish rebellion, led by the aging Kurdish nationalist Mullah Mustafa Barzani, was hailed by the West as a valiant struggle for Kurdish autonomy and democracy in Iraq. In reality, Kurds who had defected from Barzani's mountain caves and moved into Baghdad to take up government jobs insisted that Barzani had become a reactionary old warlord using divide-and-rule tactics to hold on to his power over a traditionalist tribal society.

One of the defectors was Mullah Mustafa's own son, Obeidullah Barzani. From his government office in Baghdad, he told me that less than 25 percent of the 2.5 million Kurds living in Iraq supported his father. The Iraqi government had made significant strides in granting Kurdish autonomy, he explained. The Kurdish language was taught in all of Iraq's schools and a Kurdish university had been built in the autonomous region of Suleimaniya. There, self-rule was allowed — except in the areas of defense and foreign affairs, which were reserved for the state.

The one area of real contention between the Kurds and the Iraqi government, I discovered, was over control of the vast oil deposits located in Iraqi Kurdistan (including Kirkuk). The Baathist regime declared that the oil belonged to all Iraqis, while the Kurds claimed it for themselves.

According to one Kurdish fighter-turned-defector from Barzani, "Mullah Mustafa works in close collaboration with the Iranians, the Israelis, and the Americans." All three countries supplied money and arms to Barzani to keep Iraqi troops bogged down in fighting the rebels in the mountains bordering Iran. (This was later confirmed when Iraq and Iran signed a peace agreement shortly after I left Iraq, resulting in the collapse of the Kurdish rebellion.)[44] The "Kurdish war" drained Iraq's treasury and hampered the country's development as it strove to become a secular social-democratic mecca in the Middle East.

I will never forget walking down modern boulevards in Baghdad and seeing secular public art adorning the major town squares. I purchased a small wooden statue of a woman stretching her right arm skyward, as if to say, "I am free!" To me, this powerful symbol of women's liberation was just one sign that Iraq could be the future of the Middle East. What a sad delusion, as future events would prove.

What I did *not* know was that this disputed oil deposit in Iraqi Kurdistan once fed oil to Haifa, Israel, through the Kirkuk–Haifa pipeline — a fact I would discover only when I began to burrow into the causes of the US invasion of Iraq in 2003. It was then that I learned that energy-starved Israel had sought the pipeline's reopening for years, but the Baathist regime had remained steadfastly opposed. Only regime change in Iraq would change that equation, or so the planners of the 2003 Iraq War believed.

Fisking the War

Robert Fisk's piercing, controversial critiques of Western meddling in the Middle East drew such impassioned responses that a new word entered the English lexicon: *fisking*, something the *Cambridge Dictionary* describes as "the act of making an argument seem wrong or stupid by showing the mistakes in each of its points." A prime example was Fisk's February 2003 "Case against War" in the *Observer*, in which he took apart all the US and British rationales for the war. The British, he wrote, "have no love for Arabs but they smell injustice fast enough and are outraged at the colonial war being used to crush the Palestinians by a nation (Israel) that is now in effect running US policy in the Middle East. We are told that our invasion of Iraq has nothing to do with the Israeli-Palestinian conflict — a burning, fearsome wound to which Bush devoted just 18 words in his meretricious State of the Union speech — but even Blair can't get away with that one."

Pointing out that "the men driving Bush to war" were "mostly former or still active pro-Israeli lobbyists," he stated, "For years, they have advocated destroying the most powerful Arab nation. Richard Perle, one of Bush's most influential advisers, Douglas Feith, Paul Wolfowitz, John Bolton and Donald Rumsfeld were all campaigning for the overthrow of Iraq long before George W. Bush was elected — if he was elected — US President."[45] He then cited a 1996 report, *A Clean Break: A New Strategy for Securing the Realm*, that called for war on Iraq.[46] "It was written not for the US," wrote Fisk, "but for the incoming Israeli Likud prime minister Binyamin Netanyahu and produced by a group headed by — yes, Richard Perle."

In the United States at the time, as any journalist writing about the Middle East well knew, sentiments like those of Robert Fisk were verboten for fear of being labeled anti-Semitic. But rather than shy away from this reality, Fisk addressed it head-on: "No wonder, then, that any discussion of this topic must be censored, as Professor Eliot Cohen, of Johns Hopkins University, tried to do in the *Wall Street Journal* the day after Powell's UN speech. Cohen suggested that European nations' objections to the war might — yet again — be ascribed to 'anti-Semitism of a type long thought dead in the West, a loathing that ascribes to Jews a malignant intent.'"

Fisk had the audacity to call this line of reasoning "nonsense," pointing out that it was "opposed by many Israeli intellectuals who, like Uri Avnery, argue that an Iraq war will leave Israel with even more Arab enemies."

In closing, Fisk called the aims of Israel and the United States for the region "entwined, almost synonymous." The war, he stated bluntly, "is about oil and regional control. It is being cheer-led by a draft-dodger who is treacherously telling us that this is part of an eternal war against 'terror.' And the British and most Europeans don't believe him. It's not that Britons wouldn't fight for America. They just don't want to fight for Bush or his friends."

Final Reflections on Bush's Wars

At this writing, almost two decades have gone by since Bush launched wars in Iraq and Afghanistan, and the appalling death and instability continue in both countries. In November 2018, Brown University's Costs of War

Project released its latest statistics on the wars' casualties.[47] The number of American soldiers killed in the two countries was then 6,951 (4,550 in Iraq and 2,401 in Afghanistan). The impact on civilians has been devastating: between 182,272 and 204,575 civilians killed in Iraq and 38,480 in Afghanistan. Local military deaths had then climbed to 41,726 in Iraq and 58,596 in Afghanistan. "It is likely that many times more have died indirectly in these wars, due to malnutrition, damaged infrastructure, and environmental degradation," the report noted. Millions more have been driven from their homes. At the end of 2015, more than 4.4 million Iraqis and 1.2 million Afghans were displaced within their countries, and 264,100 Iraqis and 2.7 million Afghans were refugees abroad.

Among the project's other major findings: Both countries ranked "extremely low in global studies of political freedom"; women were "excluded from political power and experience high rates of unemployment and war widowhood"; and most of the US government funding for reconstruction efforts in Iraq and Afghanistan — which had totaled over $170 billion — had been spent to arm security forces. "Much of the money allocated to humanitarian relief and rebuilding civil society," it noted, "has been lost to fraud, waste, and abuse." Did this need to happen? "Compelling alternatives to war were scarcely considered in the aftermath of 9/11 or in the discussion about war against Iraq," the project reported. "Some of those alternatives are still available to the US."

The men and women sent to Iraq and Afghanistan to defend the region continue to be told that they are fighting a "War on Terror." But the people living in these hot spots have long recognized a different reality. As one Afghan warrior told German investigative journalist Lutz Kleveman, "We Afghans know very well the Americans did not come here to help us — they are here because they need Afghanistan to get access to the oil and gas of the Caspian Sea."[48]

The early days of the war in Afghanistan had opened the door to those who wanted to revive the pipeline route through Afghanistan. Wrote Kleveman in his 2003 book, *The New Great Game: Blood and Oil in Central Asia*, "The ties between politics and the petroleum business have become much easier to recognize. President Bush's special envoy to Afghanistan and member of the National Security Council, Zalmay Khalilzad, had previously worked for Unocal on an elaborate risk analysis for the Afghan pipeline."[49] The US-installed president of Afghanistan, Hamid Karzai, in power from 2003 to 2014, also had ties to Unocal, having represented the company in its 1997 pipeline negotiations with the Taliban.[50]

Such well-laid plans did not always end well, however. When President Karzai stepped down from power in 2014, he criticized the US role in the war. He could not understand why US soldiers were conducting raids on Afghan villages, inflicting heavy civilian casualties. Nor could he understand why the war had dragged on for so long (at the time, thirteen years). In his farewell address, he shocked the diplomatic community with some outspoken remarks. "Americans did not want peace because they had their own agenda and objectives," he said. According to a Reuters report of the event, "He did not elaborate, but in the past has suggested continued violence has been an excuse for the United States to keep bases in the country." What he did say was this: "The war in Afghanistan is not our war, but imposed on us and we are the victims."[51]

Bush's wars — and now Trump's wars — weren't just deceptive. They have backfired, a reality that Kleveman foresaw as early as 2003 after speaking to their victims: "The region's impoverished populaces," he wrote, were "disgusted with the United States' alliance with their corrupt and despotic rulers." Once again, the unintended consequence of the United States imposing its will on affected populations was their tendency to "increasingly embrace militant Islam and virulent anti-Americanism." The United States was no longer perceived as a beacon of democracy. It had used the 9/11 attacks, Kleveman added, "as an excuse to pursue policies seen by many outside the United States as arrogant, aggressive, and outright imperialist."

The nation had dramatically expanded its influence in Central Asia but was fighting an unwinnable war, both on the ground and in the hearts and minds of those living outside its borders. "Though military and intelligence action may be an effective short-term way to obliterate identified terrorist groups such as Al Qaeda and to discourage 'rogue states' from sheltering them," surmised Kleveman (even before ISIS became the latest reincarnation of previous terrorist groups), "it cannot eradicate terrorism as such and might instead make it easier for terrorist groups to recruit new fighters."[52]

The United States has yet to get what it came for in Afghanistan. The TAPI pipeline has still not been constructed due to ongoing violence. Noted a report by Radio Free Europe in February 2018, a big launch ceremony took place in Turkmenistan in December 2015 for construction of the 214-kilometer portion on Turkmen territory, and Turkmen officials have stated that there's been progress on construction since then. "But strangely," noted the broadcaster, "state media in Turkmenistan, which is obsessed with showing pictures and footage of the country's major projects, has not shown much proof of TAPI's construction." As for the Afghanistan section of the pipeline, a launching ceremony occurred in the city of Herat on February 23, 2018. "For what it's worth," Radio Free Europe rather cynically reported, "a spokesman for the Taliban and a Taliban splinter group" operating in northwestern Afghanistan "have both pledged to protect construction of TAPI through Afghan territory since it is a 'national project.'" However, Radio Free Europe continued, "there are other militant forces and warlords [in northern and western Afghanistan] as well." In short, Radio Free Europe seemed dubious about TAPI's success: "Given the government in Kabul's bold claims that TAPI would help bring prosperity and stability to Afghanistan, it is difficult to imagine any militant group in Afghanistan resisting the temptation to try to sabotage the project and keep the government from boosting its popularity and support in areas along the proposed TAPI route."[53]

Currently, American diplomat Zalmay Khalilzad, along with envoys from Iraq and the UN, are conducting secret "peace negotiations" with the Taliban in Qatar — without government involvement or any involvement of women leaders, notes Eleanor Smeal of the Feminist Majority Foundation, "despite a 2017 Peace and Security bill passed in the US that requires women's participation in peace negotiations." The foundation, meanwhile, along with Afghan women and members of the Afghan government are deeply worried about what is likely to happen if the Taliban are restored to power. It has launched another campaign to raise awareness about the considerable progress that has been achieved for Afghan women after a constitutional democracy was established in the aftermath of US invasion of Afghanistan and the collapse of the Taliban regime. Despite ongoing violence over the past eighteen years, the foundation reports that "Afghan women today are prominent members of civil society and have been serving their nation as nurses, doctors and teachers at all levels. As of 2019, approximately 9 million children attend 6,000 schools and . . . girls make up 39% of the students. . . . Currently 19% of the 8,744 doctors and 40% of the 19,743 nurses are women. Women are now actively serving as judges and attorneys, and 27% of the seats in parliament are held by women."[54]

The feminists are alarmed that the Taliban and their US supporters in the Trump administration are exaggerating the numbers of the Taliban in Afghanistan. Smeal says the foundation conducted a district-by-district analysis of the Taliban's presence in the country and found the Taliban control 3 percent of its territory, whereas the government controls 70 percent. Another 21 percent of Afghanistan is contested territory — attacked anywhere from twice a week to at least three times a month.

Which raises the questions: Why are peace negotiations going on with the Taliban? Could security for the TAPI pipeline be part of the negotiations?

Not surprisingly, the areas that are either most contested, or under Taliban control, are those areas nearest the pipeline route.

In fact, the fate of the TAPI pipeline is indeed central to the peace negotiations. In May 2019 the Indian think tank Observer Research Foundation, reported that "progress of the TAPI project [expected to bring 38 million metric standard cubic meters of gas per day to India] would largely depend on the outcome of negotiations between the US and the Taliban and the ability of different parties within Afghanistan to honour their side of the agreement."[55]

The report acknowledged the "uncertain security conditions," which were deemed likely to continue if the United States were to withdraw its forces, as Trump threatened to do. "It wouldn't be wrong to assume that international financial promoters would be reluctant to support such a project," the report continued. "On the other hand, construction of the TAPI project may become possible only in the scenario that the Taliban — which enjoys support from Pakistan's security establishment — shows political maturity and expresses its support to the project."

Will the treatment of Afghan's women be an issue? The Feminist Majority Foundation is gearing up again to make it one.

Smeal's claim that the Trump administration is hiding information about the Taliban's strength is borne out by a claim by John Sopko, the US special inspector general for Afghanistan reconstruction. He revealed in May 2019 to the *New York Times* editorial board that the Trump administration had stopped "releasing important metrics about the war — the size of the Taliban, for instance, or how many provinces they control." This, noted Sopko, was akin to "turning off the scoreboard at a football game and saying scoring a touchdown or field goal isn't important." Added the *Times* editorial board, "Put another way, the American people are being kept more in the dark about the dismal state of the United States' longest-running war, now in its 18th year."[56]

In Iraq, the United States continued to reveal its true motives when parliamentary elections were held in January 2005 prior to the drafting of a new Iraqi constitution. The United States relied on its tried-and-true method of "indirect rule" — an outgrowth of Britain's more onerous and colonial "direct rule" in dealing with imperial outposts: lending support for candidates loyal to the United States. The outcome was a parliament that reflected American interests. It did not represent Iraqi Sunnis (who had been ousted from government jobs and the military after the US invasion, and who boycotted the elections over the US destruction of the primarily Sunni city of Fallujah in November 2004), and it assured that there were few voices critical of the US occupation (even though most Iraqis favored US withdrawal from their country). Only a tiny minority in parliament represented national or secular attitudes. Missing from the subsequent negotiations over Iraq's new constitution was one very central issue: Would oil, which had dominated the Iraqi economy, remain in the public sector or would it be privatized?

According to Greg Muttitt, author of *Fuel on the Fire: Oil and Politics in Occupied Iraq*, "Provisions dealing with public ownership were not considered for removal or replacement; they were not discussed at all. Iraq's new politicians were far more interested in the question of which of them would control the country's oil wealth." Corruption flourished.[57] The constitution made vague references to the oil being owned by all Iraqis but did not specify how its wealth would be shared. To rectify this shortcoming, a new oil law began being drafted in 2007 that, according to oil expert Antonia Juhasz, "would transform Iraq's oil industry from a nationalized model closed to American oil companies except for limited (although highly lucrative) marketing contracts, into a commercial industry, all-but-privatized, that is fully open to all international oil companies." The state-owned Iraq National Oil Company, meanwhile, "would have exclusive control of just 17 of Iraq's 80 known oil fields, leaving two-thirds of known — and all of its as yet undiscovered — fields open to foreign control."[58] Since then, the draft law has been hotly contested and has yet to be ratified by parliament.

US forces were removed from Iraq by President Obama in 2011 but invited back in 2014 to fight ISIS. Throughout the Iraq War (2003–11) and in subsequent clashes with ISIS (2014–18), the deadliest conflicts have been in the northern half of Iraq, in Fallujah near the oil fields around Baghdad, in oil-rich Mosul, and in northwest Iraq in Anbar Province, which during the first four years of fighting was the region of deadliest conflicts, claiming one-third of US fatalities. As US-trained Iraqi forces routed ISIS, new US military bases were constructed in northern Iraq near the Kirkuk–Haifa pipeline route in Al Qa'im, Sinjar, Tal Afar, and Makhmur, and the Ayn al-Asad base was expanded. The Pentagon will no longer say how many forces are serving in Iraq, using an unchanging blanket number of "about 5,200 troops" when queried. Major US oil companies began negotiating deals with Iraq in 2011.[59] When President Trump announced in December 2018 that US troops should be withdrawn from Iraq and Afghanistan following his trip to Iraq (and following angry Iraqi demands, after he failed to meet with Iraq's head of state, that troops be removed), the US Senate voted against him, claiming that ISIS and Al Qaeda still posed a serious threat.[60]

Against this backdrop, one cannot fault journalist Lutz Kleveman for coming up with a new term to describe the endless wars in the world: energy imperialism. When those wars were still young, he wrote, "No matter how many soldiers and civilians have so far died in Iraq and other Great Game battlefields for the sake of brazen energy imperialism, they won't be the last. . . . The struggles over access and profits between countries and multinational corporations are fast becoming fiercer. . . . The fallout of energy imperialism will be felt in the United States and Europe in the shape of a flood of refugees."[61]

These dire predictions have all been borne out. Following the wars in Afghanistan and Iraq, the next battleground of the New Great Game would be Syria.

CHAPTER FIVE

Is the Syrian War
a Pipeline War?

Perhaps no other war in recent American history has been more confusing or more misunderstood than the war in Syria. The Western press has portrayed it as a civil war raging in a country with complex social, economic, and political problems and an ethnic and religious diversity that, as one CIA operative described it, includes "Alawites, Sunnis, Christian Arabs, Armenians, Assyrians, Druze, Kurds and Turks."[1] But in many ways, it's more like the Great Game on steroids, with various countries (including the United States, Russia, Britain, France, Iran, Saudi Arabia, Qatar, and Israel) all vying for geopolitical positioning in one of the most strategic parts of the world.

That positioning by outside forces was already becoming evident in my father's first letters home from Beirut in the 1930s, when he was trying to familiarize himself with the region before starting to teach English to mostly Arab students at the American University of Beirut. Shortly after his arrival there, he was given an unusual tour of Lebanon (then part of Syria) — and a history lesson about imperialism — from an old friend of his mother's, an Irish woman who had married an Arab prince, converted to Islam, and taken on the name Princess Fatma. Well connected to the Arab elite, she turned out to be an invaluable guide, exposing the young college graduate to the culture and politics of a region he knew little about, except that it was still under a post–World War I League of Nations mandate. The mandate had partitioned the former Ottoman Empire, which once controlled the entire Middle East, and put Syria and Lebanon under French mandatory control.*

---

* The French were supposed to act as trustees until the Syrians and Lebanese could stand on their own. The Syrians and Lebanese greatly resented what was actually French colonial

As the two drove through the mountains of Lebanon, Fatma pointed out signs of the French bombardment that had occurred six years before. Craters on the side of the road stared back like raw wounds left to fester on the very people who had started the 1925–27 Great Syrian Revolt against French colonial rule. The French had crushed the revolt but failed to extinguish a simmering nationalism that crept through rival ethnic clans and inspired them to forge a united front. This unifying, secular wave of nationalism was extending to other sectors of Syria and Lebanon previously victimized by colonial divide-and-rule tactics: rural peasants, urban elites in Damascus, Sunni and Shiite Muslims, Druse Muslims, Alouite tribesmen, and Christians. Fatma wanted her ward to see its signs with his own eyes.

On their way back to Beirut, Fatima pontificated on the intrigues and deceits of foreign powers in Syria. "She talked about American imperialism in the Philippines," young Daniel wrote home to his mother, "sniffed with contempt at all forms of American idealism which she saw only as a shallow hypocrisy, and then talked Syria with me. The French here, she said, have no use for the American influence which they fear and suspect, for the Americans come with their money, their heavily endowed colleges, Near East Relief, etc. and by giving employment and help to the people, turn them from French control which they compare unfavorably with Americans — and yet she says the Americans are not here for pure unselfishness and told many stories of business enterprises in the near east, and much of this is no doubt true."[2]

When Dennett returned to Lebanon in 1944 as Carat (with cover as a cultural attaché), he learned that the French were furious that Lebanon, their former colony, had become strongly Americanized upon gaining its independence in 1943. Worse yet, Lebanon had become a main contender to host the terminal point of the American-owned Trans-Arabian Pipeline. It was bad enough that the French had not been included in the pipeline concession with Saudi Arabia, as it had been with the Iraq Petroleum Company (IPC) concession with Iraq. They suspected, and rightly so (as Dennett later admitted in an OSS document), that both the British and the Americans were keen on removing French influence — and extricating French troops — from Lebanon, a land they had occupied since the end of World War I.[3]

---

control and eventually won their independence, the Lebanese in 1943 and the Syrians when the last remaining troops withdrew in April 1946.

In May 1945, while Dennett was on a brief furlough in the United States following the death of President Franklin Roosevelt, he received urgent orders to return immediately to Lebanon. A serious crisis (soon to be called "the Levant Crisis") was unfolding in neighboring Syria. With the armistice of April 1945 that ended World War II, French leader Charles de Gaulle strongly suspected that the British wanted to expel France from Syria. In a preemptive move, de Gaulle deployed French troops to protect the French pipeline terminating in Syria, which he viewed as vital to France's postwar security.[4] He also ordered French forces to bomb Damascus and shell the Syrian parliament.

Dennett was not surprised, having predicted a year earlier in his "Analysis of Work" that "the French can be depended upon to use every weapon in their power to recover their lost influence and prestige."[5]

Prime Minister Winston Churchill responded to de Gaulle's actions by sending British troops to Syria from British-controlled Jordan to restore order. Inter-allied war was narrowly averted.

Dennett's assessment of the Levant Crisis did not bode well for the French. "Events in Syria during May and particularly the bombardment of Damascus by the French on May 29-31," he wrote, "produced great indignation everywhere in Syria, including the leading towns of the Alouite region, and greatly strengthened the hands of the Syrian nationalist leaders, who in Lattaquia were almost exclusively Sunni Moslems. British military intervention, plus the activity of British political officers, and the fine show put on by the Syrian nationalists . . . convinced everyone except certain French officers that the French cause was lost."[6]

Indeed, under British and US pressure, the French withdrew in humiliation from Syria and Lebanon; the last of France's troops evacuated in 1946. De Gaulle accused the British of betrayal, seething that "the whole thing stank of oil."[7]

My own takeaway from this stark example of foreign interventionism is this: The Syrian people had both a long memory of foreign occupations and a long history of national pride (dating back to when they were living under occupation by the Roman Empire, even centuries before their resistance to European crusaders). They were unlikely to take a new occupation lightly.

How the Modern War in Syria Began

I was visiting Lebanon when, on April 26, 2011, the Beirut *Daily Star* ran the headline, "Syrian Army Storms Daraa: Thousands of Troops Backed by Tanks Storm Town, Killing at Least 20 People." Daraa is a city in southern

Syria that lies some 50 miles east of northern Israel and 100 miles southeast of Beirut. Witnesses reported seeing bodies lying on the ground and snipers posted on top of government buildings. The Syrian state news agency (SANA) explained that the troops had responded to "appeals for help" by residents who sought protection from "extremist terrorist groups."

The fact that this bloodshed was occurring next door had everyone, me included, concerned that the violence would spill over into Lebanon, which had already suffered fifteen years of civil war. It never occurred to me then that, instead, the violence in Daraa would soon spread throughout much of Syria, eventually costing the lives of hundreds of thousands of civilians and destroying whole sections of some of Syria's finest old cities and ancient archeological treasures.

The pandemonium had been sparked the previous month when Syrian president Bashar al-Assad's forces had arrested students from prominent families in Daraa. The students had written anti-Assad graffiti on walls in Daraa, proclaiming, "The People Want the Fall of the Regime" — a mantra that had been used in Arab Spring protests against authoritarian governments beginning in Tunisia, then Egypt, Libya, Bahrain, Yemen . . . and Syria.

After the arrests, anti-Assad protesters set fire to the headquarters of the ruling Baath party in Daraa. Assad then sent in troops, arresting scores of people and in one incident firing live ammunition that killed fifteen protesters. This only further inflamed the protesters, who, according to the *New York Times*, poured into the area around Daraa's Omari Mosque and shouted demands for "the release of all political prisoners; trials for those who shot and killed protesters; the abolition of Syria's 48-year emergency law; more freedoms; and an end to pervasive corruption."[8]

The Arab Spring had now erupted in Syria.

By late April 2011, antigovernment protests had spread to more cities and the Syrian military responded with heavy firepower, resulting in numerous civilian deaths. Some Syrian soldiers deserted and joined the protesters, while some of the protesters themselves took up arms. In July, a turning point occurred: A group of officers who had defected from Assad's army formed the Free Syrian Army (FSA). This event is widely accepted as the beginning of the Syrian Civil War. Over the next two years, foreign fighters joined the Syrian resistance, among them members of the Islamic State of Iraq and Syria (ISIS) and Al Qaeda. The Syrian regime responded by calling on its primary ally, Russia, for help.

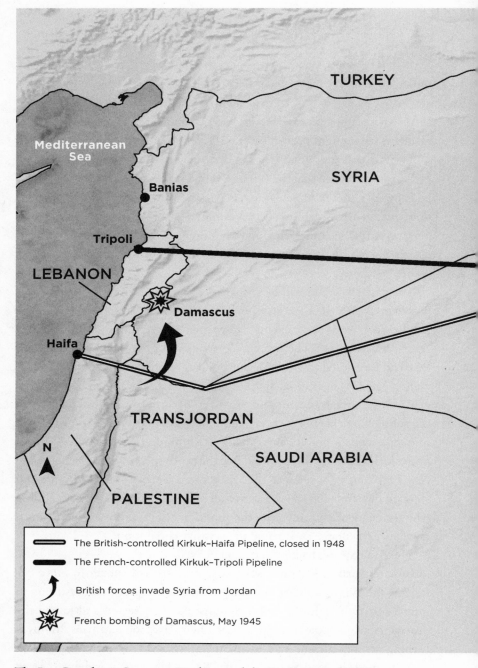

The Iraq Petroleum Company Pipelines and the Levant Crisis (1945)
The Levant Crisis of 1945 is one of the earliest examples of pipeline politics resulting in an armed intervention by a foreign power (France in Syria) to protect its pipeline, causing another foreign power (Great Britain) to retaliate. Pictured here are the two branches of the IPC oil pipeline, the northern branch controlled by the French, and

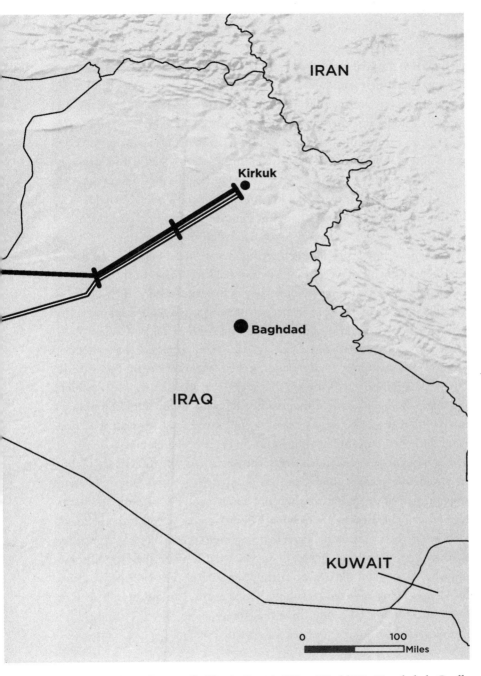

the southern branch controlled by the British. When World War II ended, de Gaulle suspected that the British wanted to expel France from Syria and deployed troops to Damascus to protect the French pipeline. Churchill responded by sending troops into Syria from British-controlled Jordan to restore order. War was averted. Oil stopped flowing through the Kirkuk–Tripoli pipeline in 1982 during the Iraq-Iran War.[9]

By 2015, the civil war looked more like a proxy war between superpowers and their surrogate fighters on the ground. On one side, the United States and its traditional European NATO partners sent military advisors to assist "moderate rebel groups" fighting the Assad regime. Saudi Arabia and Qatar, meanwhile, funded different Islamist rebels against the Syrian government. On the other side, Russia and its anti-US ally, Iran, provided financial and military assistance to Assad, with additional assistance coming from the Shiite, pro-Iranian Lebanese organization, Hezbollah.

The war dragged on, mostly out of sight for the rest of the world, as few journalists could get into Syria. This changed in the summer of 2013, when Western governments including the United States accused the Assad regime of dropping chemical weapons over rebel-held territories in the suburbs of Damascus. Syria's vehement denials triggered debates around the world as to whether these incidents were, in fact, false flag attacks designed as pretexts for full-scale Western military interventions and regime change.[10] When Western leaders called for military strikes against Syria in response to the chemical attacks, protesters cried foul, reminding their leaders of the Bush-era WMD falsehoods given to justify the war in Iraq. They insisted on proof.[11] President Obama, who once declared that his line in the sand for initiating military intervention would be Syria's use of chemical weapons, soon stepped back from the brink, postponing military action in favor of diplomacy.

Subsequent reports about chemical attacks by Assad's forces in 2017 only heightened suspicions among antiwar groups, triggering a flurry of articles suggesting that the Syrian war was not about a corrupt dictator and his alleged use of chemical weapons but about proxy wars for oil and pipelines.*

It was at this point that I began to do my own serious digging, compelled by the heart-wrenching images of children writhing on the ground spewing white foam, and the disturbing photographs of the historic Syrian city of Aleppo being reduced to rubble. Once again, I found myself seeking truth and finding oil. Only this time, some of the answers came from a most unexpected source: Robert F. Kennedy Jr.

---

* In June 2019, documents leaked from the Organization for the Prevention of Chemical Weapons showed that the 2018 chemical attack in Douma, Syria, was staged to undermine the Assad regime. According to MIT professor Ted Postol, UN reports on the attack a year earlier on Khan Shaykun were similarly compromised. RealNewsNetwork, June 10, 2019, https://www.youtube.com/watch?v=R6sgXY-n4LQ.

Kennedy's Mission

Robert F. Kennedy Jr., unlike his famous father and uncle, had eschewed politics for a career as an environmental attorney. Over the years, however, he took time off from his legal work to research the history of US involvement in the Middle East. As with me, he was motivated by a personal reason: the murder of his father — in his case, by a Palestinian Arab named Sirhan Sirhan.[12] It was the war in Syria that prompted him to dig deeper and share his findings, and even speak his mind.

Kennedy wrote up his findings in a piece for *Politico Magazine*. The article, published in February 2016, was remarkable for its frankness. His title, "Why the Arabs Don't Want Us in Syria," came with the provocative subtitle: "They don't hate 'our freedoms.' They hate that we've betrayed our ideals in their own countries — for oil."[13] The war in Syria, Kennedy contended, was not just an oil war — it was a war for pipelines.

I was stunned. Not only did Kennedy see a pipeline connection to a raging conflict in the Middle East, but his quest for answers converged with my own. We both looked back in time . . . back to 1947, when the Syrians rejected the Trans-Arabian Pipeline and soon suffered the consequences.

"In part because my father was murdered by an Arab," Kennedy wrote, "I've made an effort to understand the impact of U.S. policy in the Mideast and particularly the factors that sometimes motivate bloodthirsty responses from the Islamic world against our country." He suggested that a way to get at the root of the savagery employed by ISIS and other terrorist groups was to "look beyond the convenient explanations of religion and ideology." Instead, he offered, "we should examine the more complex rationales of history and oil — and how they often point the finger of blame back at our own shores."

What he provided was a much-needed and often missing historical context to today's energy wars, showing how US foreign policy toward the Middle East has seldom wavered from using covert actions, such as arming reactionary Islamist groups to undermine secular nationalist regimes that didn't go with the flow of American oil interests.

Kennedy reminded his readers of the little-known CIA-backed military coup in 1949 that had overthrown Syrian president Shukri al-Quwatli, who, Kennedy conveyed, "hesitated to approve the Trans-Arabian Pipeline, an American project intended to connect the oil fields of Saudi Arabia to the ports of Lebanon via Syria."

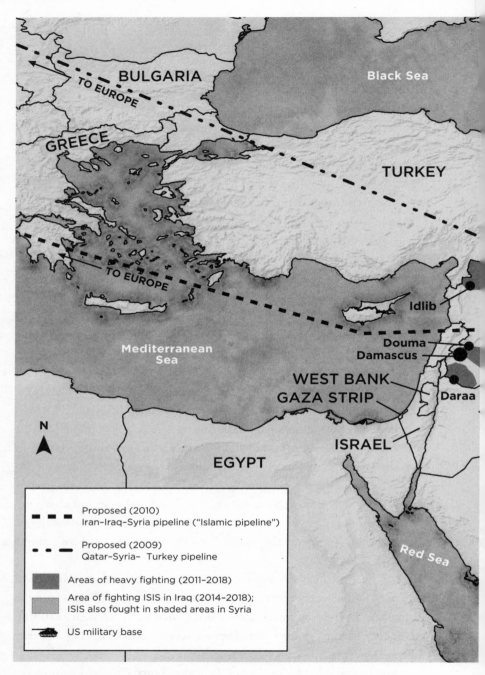

Two Competing Projected Pipelines through Syria: Prelude to the Civil War
In 2011, Syrian president Assad signed a deal for an Iran–Iraq–Syria gas pipeline to
supply markets in Europe. This so-called Islamic pipeline was viewed as a rebuke to
Qatar, which had proposed a Qatar–Syria–Turkey pipeline, also to supply markets
in Europe but allegedly rejected by Assad to avoid upsetting his Russian allies. In

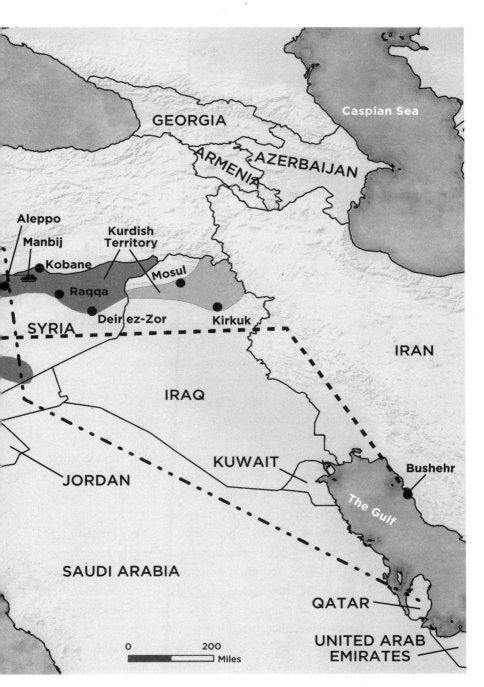

GEORGIA

Caspian Sea

ARMENIA AZERBAIJAN

Aleppo
Kurdish
Manbij Territory

Kobane
Mosul
Raqqa
Deir ez-Zor Kirkuk
SYRIA
IRAN

IRAQ

KUWAIT
Bushehr
JORDAN
The Gulf

SAUDI ARABIA

QATAR

0   200
Miles
UNITED ARAB
EMIRATES

2011, Qatar began to heavily fund the Syrian opposition against Assad. In 2012, Qatar called on Arab states to intervene against Syria, just as the West intensified covert actions against the Assad regime. Hence, many believe the Syrian war is a war over two competing pipelines — neither of which has been built. The final outcome of the war is likely to determine whether either of these projects is reactivated.[14]

What separated Kennedy's probes from those of other pipeline chroniclers was his determination to unravel historic events that directly involved his famous family and the Middle East. He described how a failed CIA coup attempt in Syria in 1957 prompted his uncle, John F. Kennedy, to give "a milestone speech endorsing the right of self-governance in the Arab world and an end to America's imperialist meddling in Arab countries," much to the chagrin of the Eisenhower White House. He mentioned the secret committee that his grandfather, Joseph P. Kennedy, former ambassador to Great Britain, sat on that was formed to investigate the CIA's clandestine activities in the Middle East. And he described how the now-declassified Bruce-Lovett Report of 1956, to which Joseph Kennedy was a signatory, detailed "CIA coup plots in Jordan, Syria, Iran, Iraq and Egypt, all common knowledge on the Arab street, but virtually unknown to the American people who believed, at face value, their government's denials." The report blamed the CIA for the rampant anti-Americanism that was then mysteriously taking root in many countries at the time.

What we are witnessing now, Robert Kennedy Jr. concluded in his *Politico* piece, is nothing less than an unintended and yet predictable blowback in the Arab world against a sordid legacy of CIA meddling. The most controversial aspect of Kennedy's story was his theory — which he claimed was shared by many Arabs — that the war in Syria was actually "just another proxy war over pipelines and geopolitics," one that started after President Assad resisted a scheme, proposed by the pro–United States emir of Qatar, to run a pipeline from gas-rich Qatar through Syria to Turkey.

If the CIA could overthrow a Syrian leader seventy years ago for resisting a foreign pipeline running through his territory, why couldn't the same thing happen again in Syria in 2011? According to Kennedy, "Secret cables and reports by the U.S., Saudi and Israeli intelligence agencies indicate that the moment Assad rejected the Qatari pipeline, military and intelligence planners quickly arrived at the consensus that fomenting a Sunni uprising in Syria to overthrow the uncooperative Bashar Assad was a feasible path to achieving the shared objective of completing the Qatar/Turkey gas link. In 2009, according to WikiLeaks, soon after Bashar Assad rejected the Qatari pipeline, the CIA began funding opposition groups in Syria. It is important to note that this was well before the Arab Spring–engendered uprising [in 2011] against Assad."

From 2009, Kennedy alleged, the United States stepped up its efforts to overthrow Assad, especially after Assad sought out an alternative pipeline scheme (proposed in 2010 and inked in 2011) that would ship gas from Iran, through Iraq and Syria, and on to Europe, dubbed the Islamic pipeline.

Dissenting Views

Kennedy's article was widely circulated, but soon some journalists and even other pipeline trackers began to raise concerns about it. Gareth Porter, writing for Truthout (a nonprofit news organization), argued that Kennedy had failed to get corroborating evidence that the Syrians had actually rejected the Qatari pipeline, other than a 2013 article by Agence France-Presse (AFP, an international news agency based out of Paris) that relied on an unnamed diplomat. Besides, Porter added, the Saudis were more likely than the Syrians to be the ones resistant to the pipeline because, quoting from a 2010 article in the *National* (a daily newspaper from the United Arab Emirates), they had a "track record of obstructing regional pipeline development" and "still had very bad relations with Qatar."[15]

Another critique of the "pipeline war" theory has come from pipeline tracker Nafeez Ahmed, the British journalist and historian. Ahmed had originally written a piece for the *Guardian* on August 13, 2013, titled "Syria Intervention Plan Fueled by Oil Interests, Not Chemical Weapon Concern." In this piece, he posited (as did Kennedy, relying on that 2013 AFP article) that Assad had refused to sign a pipeline deal with Qatar in 2009 in order "to protect the interests of [his] Russian ally, which is Europe's top supplier of natural gas." In 2010, Ahmed continued, Assad "pursued negotiations for an alternative $10 billion pipeline plan with Iran, across Iraq to Syria," which was "a direct slap in the face to Qatar." US intervention against Syria soon followed.

By 2018, though, Ahmed had discovered a number of State Department documents that had been released and posted on the WikiLeaks website. These documents caused him to come to a new conclusion. "It is a matter of record that US covert support to various opposition groups long preceded the 2011 uprising," he wrote. But, he added, "some commentators on the left, understandably traumatised by lies that preceded the 2003 Iraq War as well as the 2011 NATO war in Libya, have frequently misconstrued the details involved in this covert activity. It was not aimed at regime change, but at forcing the Syrian government to align with Western interests (many of which, as . . . State Department documents prove, revolve around Syria's potential as an energy supply route to Europe)."[16]

His 2018 report, titled *State Propaganda in Syria: From War Crimes to Pipelines*, reflected his concern that certain narratives around key issues in the Syrian Civil War had become polarized, making it difficult to sort fact from fiction. In an age of "fake news," he believed it was important to sort through explanations from all sides in the conflict so that the resulting narrative would be void of propaganda, whether generated by Russia or the United States.

As I read through Ahmed's heavily documented treatise and later spoke with him about it, I was curious to know his story — that is, how he had come to focus much of his writing on oil and pipelines. The war in Bosnia "awakened me as a young Muslim teenager," said Ahmed. He sensed that people around him "didn't understand what was going on over there and didn't really care." So, eventually, he took to studying empires and the British colonization of the Americas. He came to distinguish different types of violence and what created them. And along the way, he studied the intersection of resources, energy, and the structures of society, which also led him to want to understand conflicts.

He began to understand the problems that occur when leaders fail to see things systematically, often resulting in dysfunction — for example, he noted, "Trump with his wall, Britain with Brexit." He also began to see journalists and politicians "trained in silos" failing to see certain intersections, so their tendency was to oversimplify things. And in the case of Syria and its depiction as a pipeline war, that's exactly what he felt had happened in many cases: oversimplification.

To be clear, Ahmed says that pipelines play a "surprisingly prominent role in decisions that great powers are making." So, too, "when you shine the light on pipelines, you discover things that no one else had seen." But, he cautions, it is important to avoid speculation, especially if it's about pipeline schemes that never leave the drawing board, as is the case so far with Syria's two competing pipelines.

All good advice. I melded it with my own experience as a journalist in the Middle East, having learned that every news account of war or conflict in that part of the world had to be viewed with a large degree of skepticism because of the huge financial stakes in the region. There was so much secrecy, and so many different power plays under way to exploit the region's prodigious energy riches, that one could not be certain what the truth was at any given time. Plus, government strategies that were put forward at one time could change rapidly as things changed on the ground — a point that Ahmed made during our discussion. The truth would eventually emerge, but it would take time.

To use an old adage, one has to "peel the onion" to get at the core. The war in Syria required a lot of peeling.

In this case, the best tool for peeling away layers is to go back in time to the George W. Bush administration and then to trace forward events through a timeline leading up to the outbreak of the war. Although events never proceed along a straight line (especially in the fractious Middle East!), I find this method to be an effective way of discovering contradictions and omissions in official histories. Fortunately, in the course of the eight-year Syrian Civil War, some whistleblowers have come forward, some FOIA requests have yielded new insights, and some uncontested official documents have been released to the press by WikiLeaks. Predictably, the affected officialdoms have struck back by trying to discredit the whistleblowers, making the journalist's task all the more difficult. With this in mind, I have exerted my best efforts to provide, as veteran *Washington Post* reporter Carl Bernstein is wont to say, "the best approximation of the truth" that can be arrived at.

The Bush Administration's Redirection (2007–2009)

In March 2007, four years before the Syrian Civil War started, seasoned investigative reporter Seymour Hersh described, in a piece for the *New Yorker*, how the George W. Bush administration had dramatically redirected its Middle East strategy after painfully acknowledging that "the most profound — and unintended — strategic consequence of the Iraq war is the empowerment of Iran."[17]

Iran's long-term rivalry with Saudi Arabia for supremacy in the Gulf, its hatred of both Israel and the United States (frequently derided by Iranians, since the 1978 revolution, as the "Great Satan"), and its growing power, both militarily and as a major provider of oil and gas, had Bush administration officials running to the drawing board to see how they could curb its influence. As a result, Iran's growing influence in the region affected the Bush administration's plans for all of its neighbors — including Syria.

Hersh, relying on a wide range of sources including government insiders, former ambassadors, and Middle East experts, learned that the Bush administration had ignored intelligence warnings that Iraqi Shiite leaders living in exile in Iran were forming ties with leaders in Iran, where the majority of the population is Shiite. "Now, to the distress of the White House," wrote Hersh, "Iran has forged a close relationship with the Shiite-dominated government of [Iraq's] Prime Minister Nuri al Maliki." The impact on Iraq's neighbor to the west, Syria, could disrupt all the Bush administration's long-held plans for reshaping the Middle East.

On January 10, 2007, Hersh continued, President Bush gave a speech declaring that Iran and Syria were "allowing terrorists and insurgents to use their territory to move in and out of Iraq." Rather than acknowledge his administration's ongoing bungling in Iraq, he put the blame for the chaos there on Iran's alleged interference in the Iraq War. Consequently, Saudi Arabia and Israel had joined in a "strategic embrace, largely because both countries see Iran as an existential threat." (Iran's president, Mahmoud Ahmadinejad, had frequently fulminated over the need to destroy Israel and to develop Iran's nuclear program; Saudi Arabia, while ruled by a Sunni royal family, feared its large Shiite majority within its eastern provinces, where its major oil fields could be found and sectarian tensions were the greatest.)

Vice President Cheney weighed in on January 14, 2007, stating that a "nuclear-armed Iran, astride the world's supply of oil, [would be] able to affect adversely the global economy, [and] prepared to use terrorist organizations and/or their nuclear weapons to threaten their neighbors and others around the world. . . . If you go and talk with the Gulf states or if you talk with the Saudis or if you talk with the Israelis or the Jordanians, the entire region is worried. . . . The threat Iran represents is growing." The result of these pronouncements, Hersh added, was a series of informal agreements between the Saudis, the Israelis, and the Bush administration that included Saudi Arabia's covert supply of "funds and logistical aid to weaken the government of President Bashar al Assad of Syria."

Keep in mind the word *weaken*. Chroniclers of the civil war to this day differ over whether Washington's goal was just to weaken Assad to force him to come around to Western initiatives in the region (Ahmed's view) or to overthrow him (the view stated by Kennedy). Regime change, many believed, especially during the Obama administration, posed a huge risk if Islamic fundamentalists allied with Iran were to fill the vacuum left by an overthrow of Assad. There is in fact strong evidence that these two options fluctuated back and forth as facts on the ground changed in the course of what became a highly chaotic situation. One thing was clear: The Bush administration's strategic redirection was based largely on ways to contain Iran, which was considered by 2007 to be the major existential threat to Western corporate and strategic interests in the region.

Still, there is evidence that suggests that the Bush administration wanted regime change in Syria.

Seven Countries in Five Years?
General Clark's Surprising Statement (2007)

Also in 2007, retired NATO commander Wesley Clark made some shocking revelations while touring the United States following the publication of his memoir, *A Time to Lead*. On October 3, 2007, in a speech before San Francisco's elite Commonwealth Club, he declared that Syria, along with Iraq and five other countries, had long been a target for regime change — since 2001, in the weeks following 9/11. He said that an official with Donald Rumsfeld's Department of Defense had disclosed to him the Pentagon's plans to "attack and destroy the governments in seven countries in five years," starting with Iraq and moving on to Syria, Lebanon, Libya, Somalia, Sudan, and Iran.[18]

Clark was subsequently criticized for not substantiating his claims by showing an actual Pentagon document outlining this plan, and he did indeed confirm that he did not *see* any documented proof of this claim. In his memoir Clark described two visits with that unnamed Pentagon official, who allegedly told him, two weeks after 9/11, that the administration was planning to attack Iraq and six weeks later held up a memo on his desk and stated, "Oh, it's worse than that! Here's the paper from the Office of the Secretary of Defense [then Donald Rumsfeld] outlining the strategy. We're going to take out seven countries in five years.' And he named them, starting with Iraq and Syria and ending with Iran."[19]

Joe Conason, writing for *Salon*, which covered the controversy, pointed out that "Clark says he didn't read the memo from Rumsfeld's office. When the general first held it up, he remembers asking, 'Is it classified?' Receiving an affirmative answer, he said, 'Well, don't show it to me.' He also says that when he saw the same general last year and reminded him of their conversation, the officer said, 'Sir, I didn't show you that memo! I didn't show it to you!'" Conason also mentioned a subsequent interview with CNN's Wolf Blitzer in which Clark "backed off slightly, conceding that the memo 'wasn't [necessarily] a plan. Maybe it was a think piece. Maybe it was a sort of notional concept, but what it was, was the kind of indication of dialogue around this town in official circles.'"[20]

Clearly, there is a big difference between a "think piece" and "a plan." And until the document is declassified, we don't know exactly what was said and by whom. The question arises: Would a former NATO commander of Clark's stature risk his reputation by rashly making unwarranted claims? Of course it is possible, but it is also possible that Clark had struck a raw nerve, prompting the questioning. And in the eighteen years since 9/11, it would appear that serious efforts by the United States to undermine the governments of Iraq, Syria, Lebanon, Libya, Somalia, Sudan, and Iran took place (although over a longer period of time than five years) in order to gain geopolitical influence, much of it shaped around oil.[21]

During his book tour, Clark openly stated that the Bush strategy was shaped around gaining control of the Middle East's vast oil and gas resources, and that its impetus came from the neoconservatives who quietly schemed during the Clinton administration over what they could do should George W. Bush become president in the year 2000.[22]

The neocons' aim, Clark explained in another interview, was to "spread lots of money abroad, ultimately requir[ing] us to use U.S. troops to secure access to these energy supplies abroad." Of course, he added, "that's exactly what happened. This led then to the creation of al Qaeda, 9/11, our invasion of Afghanistan, the Bush administration decision to invade Iraq. It's led to expenditures of a couple of trillion dollars and more, much more to follow. And we're not done yet."[23]

Still another question arises: Why would Syria figure into the Bush administration's oil calculation when Syria is not a major oil producer? The answer, I believe (to quote a favorite real estate mantra), is "location, location, location." Syria — along with Israel, Gaza, and Lebanon — shares both the blessing and, some would say, the curse of lying astride the Eastern Mediterranean, now being coveted as a major energy corridor for pipelines.

In fact, in April 2003, when the US war in Iraq was one month old and looked like it would meet the CIA's prediction of "a slam dunk," Israel's infrastructure minister Joseph Paritzky openly declared his vision of Israel's port of Haifa becoming a major energy transshipment hub, a "new Rotterdam," but only on one condition: "the day after a new regime begins operating in Iraq." Four days after Paritzky's statement, James Akins, a former US ambassador to Saudi Arabia, made another startling declaration about Israel's energy plans, with Syria in the calculus: "There would be a fee for transit rights through Jordan," he told the *Guardian*, "just as there would be fees for Israel from those using what would be the Haifa terminal." After all, he added, "this is a new world order now. This is what things look like particularly *if we wipe out Syria*. It just goes to show that it is all about oil, for the United States and its ally."[24] (emphasis added)

That's unusually blunt talk for a diplomat. If we accept his statement as true (and I can find no other corroboration), it raises the question: What would "wiping out Syria" accomplish for Israel, especially in the context of a new world order based on oil and gas?

One needs only look at a map to understand the geographical significance of Syria (see the figure on page 102). If in an ideal world (for Israel, at least) powerful forces could simply "wipe Syria off the map," there would be no geographic impediment (other than 139.8 miles of Lebanon's coastline) obstructing Israel's desire to become an energy corridor along the Eastern Mediterranean coast connecting Israel — as a recipient or, eventually, as a supplier of gas and oil.

Six years after Akins made this comment, the RAND Corporation in 2009 produced a study, titled *Natural Gas and Israel's Energy Future: A Strategic Analysis under Conditions of Deep Uncertainty*. Energy-hungry Israel might, the study posited, be supplied with natural gas from Russia, "or from a source in the Caucasus or central Asia, via a pipeline routed through the existing Turkish terminus at Ceyhan on the eastern Mediterranean." However, RAND cautioned, "given the present and prospective [hostile] political relations with Israel's northern neighbors, Lebanon and Syria, this would have to be an underwater pipeline, probably to Haifa."[25]

In addition, though not widely known outside of Israel, the discovery of a large gas field off the coast of Israel and Gaza in 2000 and the even more massive Tamar and Leviathan natural gas fields in 2009 and 2010 (see chapter 8) undoubtedly triggered consideration of how that natural gas would be transported to markets abroad. The easiest route, through Syria, was not possible as long as Syria remained Israel's avowed enemy.

On the basis of Syria's location and Assad's enmity with Israel, it stands to reason that a regime change in Syria, along the same lines as the regime change in Iraq, replacing an enemy with a friend of Israel, would bring about a hoped-for new economic reality to the region, in which all countries bordering the Eastern Mediterranean would enjoy a peaceful energy renaissance. But so far, the evidence of "a plan" comes up short.

Bush Administration Financing for Syrian Opposition Groups (Begun in 2005, Revealed in 2011)

As so often happens with "filling in the facts," evidence that the Bush administration began financing Syrian opposition groups in 2005 came well after the financing itself. In April 2011, relying on "previously undisclosed diplomatic cables" (via WikiLeaks), the *Washington Post* reported that the State Department had "secretly financed Syrian political opposition groups and related projects."[26]

When the money began flowing to the opposition in 2005, the Bush administration "effectively froze political ties with Damascus," the *Post* reported, without further explanation. The United States, in fact, withdrew its ambassador from Syria in February 2005 (over allegations that Syria was responsible for the assassination of former prime minister Rafik Hariri in Lebanon) and in 2004 had imposed sanctions against US firms doing business in Syria (as Syria had been listed as a country supporting terrorism).

In 2006, as much as $6 million was transferred to the London-based Barada TV, a "satellite TV channel that beams anti-government programming into [Syria]." The Barada group, the *Post* continued, also funded "other activities" in Syria.

A State Department cable dated December 2006 and released to the public by WikiLeaks analyzed different vulnerabilities within the Assad regime and ways to exploit them. One possible action was to "play on Syrian fears of Iranian influence"; as the cable noted, "There are fears in Syria that the Iranians are active in both Shia proselytizing and conversion of, mostly poor, Sunnis." Another possible action was to "highlight Kurdish complaints against the regime," as "there are few threats that loom larger in Bashar's mind than unrest with the Kurds." Other possibilities: to "publicize Syrian efforts against extremist groups in a way that suggests weakness, signs of instability, and uncontrolled blowback" and to "highlight failures of reform, especially in the run-up to the 2007 Presidential elections," a move "that Bashar would find highly embarrassing and de-legitimizing."[27]

Despite the administration's seeming desire for destabilizing the Asssad regime, if not accomplishing out-and-out regime change, things did not turn out as hoped. Assad won another seven-year term in a 2007 election that, according to the *Washington Post,* "gave voters just one choice: a green circle to approve Assad or a gray one to oppose his second term. In his first referendum, he received 97.29 percent approval."[28] Emboldened by the results, Assad began to entertain the idea of opening up Syria to international oil companies. That year, he contracted with the British-Dutch major, Royal Dutch Shell (commonly known as Shell), to develop a Syrian oil and gas master plan.*

Bashar al-Assad's Energy Plans (2007–2012)

As first impressions go, Bashar al-Assad hardly fit the image of a thuggish dictator. A tall, thin, rather meek-looking man, he had trained in London in his postgraduate years to become an ophthalmologist. He was known during that time as a "geeky I.T. guy."[29] He married a Londoner of Syrian descent, Asma, in 2000 and began to raise a family. He had not aspired to power. But when his elder brother died, he was groomed to succeed his father, the steely Hafez al-Assad, who presided over the country for nearly thirty years. When the elder al-Assad died in 2000, Bashar al-Assad became the new president. He relied heavily on his military and the much-dreaded secret police, the Mukhabarat, to keep order.

In the immediate post–9/11 period, Assad cooperated with the Bush administration in hunting down suspected terrorists and torturing them in secret Syrian prisons. He also entertained the idea of bringing in oil companies to survey Syria's potential for upgrading its domestic oil production, especially later, after his 2007 reelection. Until the Obama administration took over, however, no American majors got involved and the only American oil company to operate in Syria, ConocoPhillips, sold its natural gas plant (built in 1999) to Syria at the end of its contract in 2005.[30] According to a November 2005 State Department memo, this did not stop the US Embassy in Damascus from citing an assessment by the general manager of ConocoPhillips before he left that international oil interest in Syria was "frothing," particularly among "medium and small companies that are unable to get their foot in the door in other markets."[31] That same State Department memo indicated that the British-Dutch Shell Oil was

---

* Royal Dutch Shell is headquartered in the Netherlands and incorporated in the United Kingdom. Shell Oil is the US-based subsidiary of Royal Dutch Shell, based in Houston, Texas, yet owned by Royal Dutch Shell.

frustrated with the Syrian government's alleged ineptitude in running its energy sector. Shell was also reported to be skeptical about the caliber of oil companies seeking concessions. According to Shell's general manager, Campbell Keir, the companies interested in Syria were "not to be taken seriously" and "even Shell was undecided whether it would actually submit a bid or not, given the unstable political situation, even though there were blocks that were of significant potential."

Still, by 2007, according to another State Department cable published by WikiLeaks, Shell had contracted with the Syrian government to develop a master plan for developing its gas potential and linking it and other Arab countries "with gas markets to Turkey and Europe."[32] According to this document, "collaboration with Iraq, particularly the development of the Iraqi gas field near Iraq's border with Syria," figured largely in Syria's plans. The cable revealed that senior managers of both Shell and Petro-Canada, which was also operating in Syria, admitted to the US Embassy that "their presence in Syria is due in part to its strategic location next to Iraq. They view Syria as a platform to move into Iraq." It also revealed that Shell "presented a plan to SARG [Syrian Arab Republic Government] managers, and subsequently to the Iraqis, to export natural gas from the Akkas field [in western Iraq near the border with Syria] . . . through Syria to either the Arab Gas Pipeline [which carries natural gas from Egypt to Syria] or an LNG plant to be constructed in Syria's oil port of Banyias." In this way, Syria could "act as a conduit for gas, oil and other commodities transiting from the Gulf and Iraq to Europe."

The hope among these companies was that Syrian cooperation with the West would be further enhanced. "Though economic considerations rarely, if ever, trump political interests in Syria," the 2007 cable stated, "achieving its stated goals for developing its gas sector will require greater SARG cooperation with both Iraq and the West." Here, then, was a plan — generated not by an American company, but instead by a British-Dutch oil company — to develop Syria as a transit hub for gas "from the Gulf and Iraq." Such a plan, once put into action, would strengthen Syria's position with its neighbors, particularly Iraq, and would position Syria as a major energy hub. Yet according to Seymour Hersh's investigation into the Bush administration's strategic redirection, the last thing that administration wanted was a strong Syria allied with both Iraq and Iran, the latter having drawn closer to Syria after the Iraq War. As a Lebanese political leader told Hersh about advice he had given to Vice President Cheney, "To weaken Iran you need to open the door to effective Syrian opposition."[33] And that, Hersh explained, was happening clandestinely by funding the opposition with Saudi money.

It will be remembered that when the Obama administration took power in January 2009, hope was in the air, mixed with relief that the warmongering neocons in the Bush-Cheney administration were a thing of the past. Obama clearly wanted to signal a clean break from the past vis-à-vis the Middle East, declaring in a historic speech in Cairo that he sought "a new beginning." His speech stunned his audience. He mentioned his Muslim roots through his father, peppered his speech with quotations from the Koran, and acknowledged the wrongs of colonialism and globalization:

> *The relationship between Islam and the West includes centuries of co-existence and cooperation, but also conflict and religious wars. More recently, tension has been fed by colonialism that denied rights and opportunities to many Muslims, and a Cold War in which Muslim-majority countries were too often treated as proxies without regard to their own aspirations.*[34]

Here, in Cairo, was an American "president of color," an American-born son of a Kenyan Muslim and an American Christian woman, addressing a roomful of hopeful Arabs with eloquent language and an understanding of their grievances. The world responded favorably: If anyone could restore the United States' deteriorated relations with the Middle East, they thought, it was Barack Hussein Obama. Small wonder that former Secretary of State Henry Kissinger, a protégé of Nelson Rockefeller, had crooned before Obama's inauguration that the African American president could "give new impetus to American foreign policy, partly because the reception to him is so extraordinary around the world. . . . Really, a new world order can be created. It's a great opportunity. It isn't just a crisis."[35]

But what did the "new world order" portend for Syria? And what did the Rockefellers, America's richest and most powerful oil family, and their allies expect of Obama?

As noted previously, few families in the world have accumulated more knowledge about the Middle East than the Rockefellers. Through trial and error over more than a century of negotiating lucrative oil deals and bank loans with foreign governments around the world, they have learned what works and what does not work in the grand scheme of conquering markets, resources, governments, and goodwill. Going into Iraq with a sledgehammer, as Bush and his neoconservative allies did, displayed a profound ignorance of the region's sensibilities. Obama, it was clearly hoped, would correct the United States' eroding standing in the Middle East . . . and the world.

Coming into 2009 on the heels of the Iraq War, and another war in Afghanistan that was escalating, along with a crippling economic crash, Americans might easily find themselves feeling cynical.

Not Obama. He chose to play the hope card.

"I know there are many — Muslim and non-Muslim — who question whether we can forge this new beginning," he said in his Cairo speech. "There is so much fear, so much mistrust. But if we choose to be bound by the past, we will never move forward."

Beyond the spellbinding words was Obama's desire to more firmly realign Syria with the West. It would happen largely by creating a stable energy market in the Eastern Mediterranean dominated by Western oil companies.

The Crucial Year: 2009

In April 2009, a secret State Department cable sent to the CIA, the National Security Council, and the White House indicated that the Obama administration had clearly stepped away from the strategy of regime change: "US policy may aim less at fostering 'regime change' and more toward encouraging 'behavior reform,'" it stated.[36] The key word here was *may*, but it seemed to jibe with President Obama's own calculations on how to deal with Syria in particular, and the Middle East in general. Put differently, the Obama administration appeared to be adopting a strategy of "coercive threats" short of regime change.[37]

By June 2009, Assad's ambitions for developing Syria as an energy hub took on even greater significance. He took advantage of deteriorating relations between Turkey and Israel over Israel's war in Gaza by luring Turkey into what he called the "four seas" strategy. Assad proposed a regional alliance between Turkey, Iran, Iraq, Jordan, Armenia, Azerbaijan, and Syria, the countries that lie at the shores of the Mediterranean Sea, the Red Sea, the Black Sea, and the Persian Gulf. Yoav Stern of Israel's *Haaretz* newspaper noted that key Syrian figures had been promoting this strategy "as a main pillar of Syria's Foreign Policy."[38] The idea was to break Syria out of its isolation and improve its investment opportunities. It was also, according to Nafeez Ahmed, a "strategy to consolidate Syria's role as a major oil and gas transport hub to supply regional supplies to Europe." As he notes, State Department cables from this time show that "the plans were pushed forward because they were strongly believed to be feasible — with the right mix of investment and geopolitical alignment. The British-Dutch firm Shell was in the driver's seat, crafting the 'masterplan' to maximize Syria's domestic production and identify the most promising pipeline routes."[39]

Assad's ambitious energy schemes soon attracted the attention of Qatar. A tiny peninsula jutting out from the southeastern flank of the Arabian Peninsula into the Gulf, it possesses the third-largest natural gas field in the world, totaling about 900 trillion cubic feet, much of it lying in the Gulf. The field lies adjacent to Iran's equally huge gas field in the Gulf. In August 2009, the emir of Qatar floated his plan for a pipeline to run from Qatar through Syria to Turkey.

"We are eager to have a gas pipeline from Qatar to Turkey," Sheikh Hamad bin Khalifa al-Thani, emir of Qatar, announced. He had just completed talks with Turkish President Abdullah Gül and Turkish Prime Minister Recep Tayyip Erdoğan, who were equally eager for the project to go through. "A working group will be set up that will come up with concrete results in the shortest possible time," said Erdoğan.[40] The leaders discussed "the possibility of Qatar supplying gas to the [proposed] strategic Nabucco pipeline project, which would [start in eastern Turkey and] transport Central Asian and Middle Eastern gas to Europe, bypassing Russia." (See chapter 6.)

As things turned out, as they often do with pipeline politics, the "shortest possible time" for setting up a working group apparently never materialized. President Assad rejected the pipeline project proposed by Qatar and Turkey, claiming, according to an AFP news item, that he did so to "protect the interests of our Russian ally." Russia, which carefully guards its naval base and only access to the Mediterranean Sea's coast at the Syrian port of Tartus, allegedly viewed the pipeline as an existential threat because it "would supply copious amounts of natural gas to Europe at the expense of Russia, which sells 70 per cent of its gas exports to Europe."[41]

The exact date when Assad allegedly rejected the pipeline project has not come to light. But a number of pipeline chroniclers have conjectured that the stepping up of covert actions against Syria began after Assad's rejection.

To be sure, US relations with Syria hit a snag in April 2009. According to the *Washington Post*, relying on a leaked cable from the top-ranking US diplomat in Damascus, Syrian intelligence agents had gotten wind of the fact that the State Department was funding Barada TV programs, which began broadcasting shows against the regime that month. The intelligence agents started asking questions of US embassy officials, which prompted officials to suggest "that the State Department reconsider its involvement, arguing that it could put the Obama administration's rapprochement with Damascus at risk." Syrian authorities, the *Post* reported, "would undoubtedly view any U.S. funds going to illegal political groups as tantamount to supporting regime change."[42]

The *Post* article, written in April 2011, then affirmed that the "financial backing of opposition groups continued under President Obama, even as his administration sought to rebuild relations with Assad."

The Iran–Iraq–Syria Pipeline Is Announced (2010)

Whatever Assad thought — or knew — about clandestine efforts to fund opposition to his regime, he barreled ahead with yet another energy scheme, announcing in 2010 a $10 billion Iran–Iraq–Syria pipeline scheme, the so-called Islamic pipeline that would run from Iran's South Pars field toward Europe via Iran, Iraq, Syria, and Lebanon. Many viewed it as repudiation of the Qatari pipeline scheme, including, initially, Nafeez Ahmed. But on closer examination, Ahmed realized that there had been no memorandum of agreement or feasibility study of the Qatari pipeline. He concluded it inconsequential, as so often happens with pipeline schemes: "They come and they go," he explained to me.

Possibly to keep all his options open, however, Qatar's ruler continued to maintain relations with Assad up through April 2011, when the first protests erupted in Syria. The emir then sent his foreign minister to Damascus to deliver a message of support, according to Syrian state media. But by July, relations had sharply deteriorated. On July 18, Qatar withdrew its ambassador from Syria. The Qatar-based Al Jazeera news service ramped up its coverage of the civil war, showing eyewitness accounts that countered Syrian claims that the protests were stirred by Islamist forces backed by the West. Syrian media, for its part, went so far as to blame Qatar for the unrest.[43]

What accounted for Qatar's sudden turnaround against Assad and support for the opposition? Could pipeline politics, possibly accompanied by pressure on Qatar from NATO forces, have played a role?* It appears so, and that Qatar's Gulf neighbor and natural gas competitor, Iran, may have been a trigger.

To understand why, we can look to early July 2011, when Iran's first vice president took a momentous step that would consolidate relations between Iraq and Iran (George W. Bush's "axis of evil" for allegedly "harboring terrorists") and now Syria, and paid a visit to Baghdad to discuss the transfer of Iranian gas through Iraq and Syria to markets in Europe via the Iran–Iraq–Syria (Islamic) pipeline. By July 25, the oil ministers of Iran, Iraq, and Syria had made the Islamic pipeline official by signing a preliminary memorandum of understanding.

The Iraqi ambassador to Iran, Mohammad Majeed al-Sheikh, had stated on July 5 that the gas deal would allow Baghdad to use Iran's natural gas supplies. The implications were huge. If the project went through (it was estimated that it would take three to five years to construct the pipeline once funding came through), Iran would become a major supplier of natural gas to Iraq, Syria, and Europe.[44] And in becoming so, Iran would greatly strengthen its influence in the Middle East and abroad, something that successive US administrations had tried to thwart ever since the Iranian revolution of 1978 booted Shah Reza Pahlavi out of Iran. The Islamic pipeline — an alternative to the Qatari pipeline — could thwart tiny Qatar's very big ambitions to become a major regional player by virtue of its command over some of the greatest natural gas reserves in the world.

At the September 2012 session of the UN General Assembly, the emir of Qatar made a direct appeal to the Arab states to intervene against Syria. The Obama administration, however, was still not willing to go that far. According to the *Washington Post*, the emir's appeal received a "cool response" from Washington: "U.S. officials have made clear that they do not support a military solution to the crisis in Syria and that they are unlikely to provide military backing for an Arab force. U.S. officials still assess the Syrian opposition as scattered and Assad's government is strong enough to

---

* Qatar, which hosts a large US military base, had already become a willing partner in NATO's operation against the regime of Muammar Gaddafi in Libya in the spring of 2011. According to *Foreign Affairs*, in March 2011, Qatar "supplied six Mirage Jet fighters to join in NATO's air operations" and in April began arming the anti-Gaddafi rebels. See David Roberts, "Behind Qatar's Intervention in Libya," *Foreign Affairs*, September 28, 2011, http://www.foreignaffairs.com/articles/libya/2011-09-28/behind-qatars-intervention-libya.

hold onto power for some time. The official, who spoke on the condition of anonymity to describe closed-door diplomacy, said the Qatari proposal may be part of an emerging 'Plan B' for international involvement." No options, the official said, were off the table, but "in our view military intervention from the outside right now would do more harm than good."[45]

This did not mean that Qatar abandoned its plan to get rid of Assad. Nor did it mean that Qatar had shelved its plans for its pipeline. In October 2012, investment strategist Felix Imonti, reporting for Oilprice.com, bluntly explained the situation:

> The kingdom [of Qatar] is a geographic prisoner in a small enclave on the Persian Gulf coast. It relies upon the export of [liquid natural gas] because it is restricted by Saudi Arabia from building pipelines to distant markets. In 2009, the proposal of a pipeline to Europe through Saudi Arabia and Turkey . . . was considered, but Saudi Arabia that is angered by its smaller and much louder brother has blocked any overland expansion. . . . The discovery in 2009 of a new gas field near Israel, Lebanon, Cyprus, and Syria opened new possibilities to bypass the Saudi Barrier and to secure a new source of income [for Qatar]. Pipelines are in place already in Turkey to receive the gas. Only Al-Assad is in the way.[46]

He went on to explain what may very well have been Qatar's Plan B: Qatar and Turkey, he speculated, wanted to remove Assad and install the Syrian chapter of the Muslim Brotherhood. "It is the best organized political movement in the chaotic society and can block Saudi Arabia's efforts to install a more fanatical Wahhabi based regime. Once the Brotherhood is in power, the emir's broad connections with Brotherhood groups throughout the region should make it easy for him to find a friendly ear and an open hand in Damascus.

"The fighting is likely to continue for many more months," Imonti concluded, "but Qatar is in for the long term."

Once again, hard documentation is missing from this report. Imonti did not quote any Qatari officials affirming that getting rid of Assad was on the agenda. Yet Oilprice.com is widely read by energy insiders.

The *Post*, for its part, reported that the Obama administration had not ruled out regime change. Indeed, the *Post* went on to report that Secretary of State Hillary Clinton "is likely to pledge additional U.S. aid for Syrian opposition groups during a meeting Friday with activists and diplomats from several other countries that support a move to democracy in Syria. The 'Friends of Syria' session will focus on unifying the political opposition inside and outside the country."[47]

As the fighting between Syrian government forces and rebel groups escalated throughout 2012, the Obama administration increasingly distanced itself from Assad and threw greater support to the opposition groups. Simultaneously, Assad cemented his ties to Iran and Russia.[48] Realizing that Assad was likely to remain in power for the foreseeable future, the United States began to focus on containing Iranian encroachment in Syria. This is borne out by a report by the US Marine Corps Intelligence Department, which stated:

> *The Syrian Alawite-Baathist regime led by Syrian President Bashar al Assad will weaken significantly over the next three years, but its break point is unlikely to be imminent. . . . The potential for the regime to collapse cannot be ruled out, but the road to regime change will be a long and bloody one. . . . None of the major stakeholders in the region, including Israel, Turkey, Saudi Arabia and the United States, appear interested in dealing with the destabilizing effects of regime change in Syria in the region. However, [they] have a common interest in trying to severely undermine Iran's foothold in the Levant, and dial back Hezbollah's political and military influence in Lebanon. Turkey, in particular, is the country with the most leverage over Syria in the long term and has an interest in seeing this territory return to Sunni rule. . . . The sectarian dynamics are far too complex for the United States to afford becoming embroiled in. Instead, this will be a regional crisis for Turkey to manage.[49]*

The bottom line: US military intervention was deemed far too risky, with the potential to cause even greater instability. The Obama administration did not want to go to war with Russia over Syria. Turkey, one of the few Islamic countries to maintain good ties with the West, would have to step up to the plate and play regional policeman. Meanwhile, the rebel forces would need beefing up, if only to further weaken Assad without overthrowing him.

Another Turning Point (2013)

Meanwhile, as the civil war raged into its third year, the Iran–Iraq–Syria pipeline came closer to realization. In February 2013, the Iraqi cabinet announced final approval of the plan, with the expectation that the pipeline would reinforce energy and diplomatic ties between Iran and Iraq. Israel National News was quick to see the ramifications of the agreement: "The move . . . may prove to be a game-changer in Syrian President Bashar al-Assad's two-year-long savage civil war against opposition fighters," it reported, adding portentously, "It also extends and strengthens Iran's grip on the region."[50]

This was the type of game changer that Israel could not ignore. Neither could its allies, the United States and Saudi Arabia. The pipeline scheme, if allowed to proceed, would likely strengthen the Assad regime and consolidate a deepening alliance between Syria, Iran, and Iraq — and Russia. Something had to be done.

In May 2013, the *Financial Times* reported that "the gas-rich state of Qatar has spent as much as $3bn over the past two years supporting the rebellion in Syria, far exceeding any other government," citing dozens of interviews with "rebel leaders both abroad and within Syria as well as regional and western officials."[51] That would confirm Qatar's involvement in the escalation of the civil war in 2011, and would even confirm Assad's claim early on that the war was being bankrolled by Qatar.

Clearly, the Qatar–Syria–Turkey pipeline was still on the drawing board.

In early August 2013, Prince Bandar bin Sultan al-Saud, Saudi Arabia's intelligence chief (the famous "Bandar Bush," so nicknamed because of his close ties to the Bush family), traveled to Moscow to try to convince Russian president Vladimir Putin to back off from his support of Assad. He also wanted Russia to refrain from vetoing future UN Security Council resolutions against Syria. In return, Bandar pledged $10 billion in arms purchases from Russia and a promise not to interfere with Russia's preeminent position as the major gas supplier to Europe. According to a senior Syrian opposition figure quoted in the *Times of Israel*, "Bandar sought to allay two main Russian fears: that Islamist extremists will replace Assad, and that Syria would become a conduit for Gulf, mainly Qatari, gas at the expense of Russia. Bandar offered to intensify energy, military and economic cooperation with Moscow."* However, the article continued,

---

* This report from the *Times of Israel* offers further corroboration of the AFP article of the same date, reporting that Russia feared the Qatar–Syria–Turkey pipeline. See Agence France-Presse, "Moscow Rejects Saudi Offer to Drop Assad for Arms Deal," August 8, 2013.

"an unnamed Western diplomat was pessimistic about the likelihood that Russia would give up its influential position in the region in return for even such a lucrative arms deal."[52]

According to a transcript of the meeting that was leaked to the press, Bandar said, "We understand Russia's great interest in the oil and gas in the Mediterranean from Israel to Cyprus. And we understand the importance of the Russian gas pipeline to Europe. We are not interested in competing with that. We can cooperate in this area," he added, claiming to have the full backing of the United States.

Russia's military base in Syria, he continued, would not be affected if the Russians allowed the Syrian regime to crumble. However — if Putin declined the offer — Saudi-financed Chechen rebels could be unleashed on Russia's Winter Olympics in Sochi. Conversely, they would no longer be a problem in Syria if Putin went along with the Saudi proposal. "We control them," Bandar said. "They could be turned on or off." But if Putin rejected the Saudi olive branch, "there can be no escape from the military option."[53]

Putin rejected the Saudi proposal. The Saudi threat of a "military option" apparently did not faze the wily ex-KGB officer, who by now was a seasoned player of the Great Game. But there would be consequences to his decision.

Within two weeks, a major chemical attack on rebel-held territories in the Damascus suburb of Ghouta prompted US, British, and French warships to head toward Syria, threatening to launch missiles. President Obama came close to intervening but then stepped back from the brink. Nevertheless, behind the scenes, Turkey and Qatar began pouring in armaments to support the rebels.

ISIS Goes on the Offensive (2014)

One of the most sinister of the jihadist forces to fight in Syria was ISIS (Islamic State of Iraq and Syria), otherwise known as ISIL (Islamic State of Iraq and the Levant). Best known for its videotaped beheadings, violence against women, insistence on sharia law, and destruction of holy sites, ISIS dictates a fundamentalist Salafist version of Sunni Islam. Said to have originated in Iraq in opposition to the US invasion of that country, it first attracted widespread attention when its leader, Abu Bakr al-Baghdadi, delivered a sermon from the pulpit of the Great Mosque of al-Nuri in Mosul in July 2014, declaring himself as caliph with the authority to declare jihad and purify the world of infidels.

Earlier, during the US occupation of Iraq, Baghdadi had been arrested in the Iraqi city of Fallujah and held in the notorious Abu Ghraib prison. He was released in 2005, and in 2010 he was declared the leader of ISI, the Islamic State of Iraq, also known as Al Qaeda in Iraq. In 2013, he led his followers to northern Syria, where they took over the cities of Raqqa and Deir ez-Zor. It was in Syria that he declared the formation of ISIS.

Interestingly, the US Defense Intelligence Agency (DIA) had already anticipated the creation of ISIS in August 2012, when it produced a report predicting that rebel forces taking control in eastern Syria might result in "a declared or undeclared Salafist Principality in eastern Syria," which is "exactly what the supporting powers want, in order to isolate the Syrian regime." The supporting powers, Nafeez Ahmed noted, are identified in the report as the West, the Gulf countries, and Turkey, and the point, he concluded, was to not only isolate the Syrian regime but also weaken the Shiite influence from Iraq and Iran. There might even be a parallel consolidation of Al Qaeda in parts of Iraq, the report forecast, leading to the declaration of "an Islamic State through its union with other terrorist organisations in Iraq and Syria."[54]

In 2014, a year after funding began pouring into ISIS and other rebel groups, and after Vladimir Putin refused Saudi Prince Bandar's offer, Hillary Clinton sent a secret memo to John Podesta, then an advisor to President Obama, describing how both the Saudi and Qatari governments "are providing clandestine financial and logistic support to ISIL [the Islamic State] and other radical Sunni groups in the region."[55] The memo went on, "With all of its tragic aspects, the advance of ISIL through Iraq gives the US Government an opportunity to change the way it deals with the chaotic security situation in North Africa and the Middle East."[56] (This was among the infamous Clinton emails released to the world in October 2016 by WikiLeaks. Not surprisingly, its contents were not widely shared by the mainstream media.)

The "tragic aspect" Clinton referred to was likely a reference to the brutalization of the Syrian and Iraqi people subjected to the occupying forces of the Islamic State, most notably the massacres of the Yezidi people in northern Iraq, which would soon turn into a full-fledged genocide. The "advance of ISIL through Iraq" undoubtedly referred to the extremists' lightning-fast seizure of Iraq's oil-rich city of Mosul in June 2014; by nightfall on the day Mosul fell, they were already advancing on nearby Kirkuk.

According to the *Guardian*, the United States described the situation as "extremely serious," calling for a "strong, coordinated response to push back against the attack" — a response that ultimately created an opportunity for President Obama to deploy more troops to Iraq.[57]

As I watched this development carefully, I was reminded of the fact that Kirkuk, in the province of Mosul, was the originating point of the IPC Kirkuk–Haifa pipeline that Israel had so desperately wanted to rebuild. During the first days of the US invasion in 2003, US troops had been sent first to Mosul, Iraq's second-largest city, and to Kirkuk. With Obama's withdrawal of troops in 2011, followed later by the unanticipated Shiite alliance between Iraq's prime minister Nuri al-Maliki and the Iranians, alarms were undoubtedly ringing in Washington that this crucial territory could once again become vulnerable to anti-Western forces.

What was striking about the ISIS conquest of Mosul was the ease with which the city fell. Iraqi soldiers were said to have simply abandoned their posts as the ISIS fighters advanced. Said a Mosul businessman, "The city fell like a plane without an engine. They were firing their weapons into the air, but no one was shooting at them."[58]

In retrospect, the attack seems somehow contrived. The rapidity of the conquest was reminiscent of how suddenly the Taliban seized Kabul in 1994, with the assistance of the CIA and Unocal.

"The rapid organisation and mobility of ISIS has shocked leaders across the region," wrote *Guardian* reporter Martin Chulov. Even Iraqi prime minister Nuri al-Maliki was "caught completely off guard."[59] The Iraqi government called for a state of emergency and entertained the idea of calling back the US military. In late 2014, President Obama obliged, ordering a deployment of special forces to help coalition forces uproot ISIS from Mosul. The "Battle of Mosul" lasted from 2014 to 2017 and would be described as "one of the most brutal urban warfare campaigns in modern history." US-led coalition warplanes dropped bombs that leveled building after building. Iraqi troops are believed to have endured casualty rates not seen since World War II.[60] Over the three-year period, 100,000 coalition troops were deployed to Mosul to oust ISIS, comprising the world's largest military operation in fifteen years.[61]

Meanwhile, across the border in northern Syria, ISIS began to focus its efforts on seizing large portions of Syria's largest city, Aleppo. This was yet another horrific tragedy in the making, lasting four years and described as one of the longest sieges in modern warfare, as well as one of the bloodiest battles of the Syrian Civil War. By the time pro-government forces, aided by Russia, finally succeeded in ousting the rebel groups, an estimated 33,500 buildings had been either damaged or destroyed and at least 31,000 civilians killed. Once again comparisons were made to damage inflicted on European cities in World War II. The city's once vibrant industrial center was flattened.[62]

The *Independent*'s Robert Fisk managed to tour the industrial zone in June 2014 and interviewed residents who had survived the onslaught. When he asked them to identify the nationalities of the foreign fighters, he was told, "Chechens . . . and Afghans and Egyptians, Saudis, Qataris, Algerians." He commented, "Only rarely do they admit to the Syrians who also fought here against the government army." The rebel forces had spent two years mining buildings, digging underground tunnels, cutting out snipers' nests, and reducing the modern industrial showcase of factories, chemical plants, and homes to "a city of death."[63]

The ISIS forces, meanwhile, were not entirely defeated by the unrelenting bombing. In their retreat from Aleppo, they succeeded in holding on to a section of cross-border territory that spread east from Aleppo, through the Syrian desert, and on into Iraq's Anbar Province.[64]

The Russian Stake, and the Road from Here (2015–Present)

The Russians used the presence of Western-backed jihadists in Syria to justify their 2015 military intervention to support the Syrian government. They have used the same excuse to justify their support of the Syrian air force's brutal bombing of rebel-held strongholds in Syrian cities. But Russian self-interest also plays a role. The country refuses to give up its only naval base in the Mediterranean, located at the Syrian port of Tartus. Established in 1971, it underwent modernization in 2007; as of 2014, it can accommodate eleven Russian warships, including nuclear vessels. And oil and gas interests have determined Vladimir Putin's calculations in the region, just as they have determined the West's foreign policies there. Russia has vested interests in Syria's offshore oil and gas resources, having concluded deals worth a billion dollars with the Assad regime to develop fields.

There is some disagreement, though, about just how much the opposing pipeline schemes have motivated Russia's actions in Syria.

Nafeez Ahmed, for instance, notes that a 2014 report from the Russian International Affairs Council, with an office located in Damascus and, according to Ahmed, supportive of the Assad regime, assessed potential Syrian transport corridors and concluded that an Iran–Iraq–Syria pipeline would pose "a potential threat to Russia, as it would serve as an alternative source of gas delivery to European markets and could undermine Gazprom's monopoly position." (Gazprom, you will remember, is Russia's huge state-owned gas company.) The way Ahmed sees it, "Russia has carefully exploited Syria's invitation to militarily intervene in the conflict to scupper any prospect of Assad challenging Russia's goal of dominating regional energy markets and undermining Gazprom's hegemony in Europe."[65]

Others see a more direct link to the competing pipelines. According to Yuri Shvets, a former KGB officer quoted in Britain's *Spectator* in March 2018, Russia's first priority is to prevent Qatar from building a gas pipeline across Syria if the rebels win. "It would be a mortal threat to Gazprom," he said. "Gazprom is the financial backbone of the Putin state . . . the major provider to the state budget. Putin needs to bribe the bureaucracy, he needs to pay pensions, he needs to get people to vote for him."[66]

Steve Austin, managing editor of Oil-Price.net, noted that the Iran–Iraq–Syria pipeline "pleased Russia's Putin, because he already had long standing agreements in place with Iran," which was "more amenable to gas price coordination with Russia."[67] Russia, he explained, had built up influence within the Iranian administration and armed forces over the years. And Russia's military base in Tartus "would strategically allow Putin to control a second gas pipeline to Europe." Without offering any evidence of his views, Austin concluded, "Naturally this Iranian pipeline to Syria quickly became a top priority for Moscow. Assad and Russians worked their contacts to dissuade the Qatar deal and promote the Iranian plan."

The passage of years will show which, if either, of the two pipelines comes to fruition. Meanwhile, noted Ahmed, Syria's own oil and gas resources were described as early as 2011 by the French oil services company CGG Veritas as "a truly frontier area of exploration" based on initial discoveries that could "represent billion-barrel/multi-TCF [trillion cubic feet] of drilling targets."[68] In May 2016, Russian Energy Minister Alexander Novak announced that Syria had invited Russian oil majors Lukoil, Gazprom Neft, and Zarubezhneft to rebuild Syria's oil and gas infrastructure and begin pipeline construction. (He apparently did not go into details as to where the pipelines were to be located.)[69] Iranian companies have also been invited to help rebuild the country's badly damaged refineries and power grid.[70]

The rebuilding will be a daunting task. Al Jazeera, in its 2015 assessment of war damage in Syria, painted a grim picture. After four years of fighting, at least 210,000 people had been killed and 5 million civilians seriously wounded. At least half of all Syrian physicians had fled the country.[71] The war had already produced 3.8 million refugees, and 7.1 million Syrians were internally displaced.[72] Those numbers have since swelled. The destruction, too, was massive: Gone were 1.2 million homes, 9,000 industrial facilities, 36 percent of Syria's hospitals, 4,000 schools, close to 50 percent of Syria's major cities, 1,549 places of worship, and 290 heritage sites. All destroyed. According to a 2019 report using satellite data collected for UN use, "overall conditions in Syria remain extremely challenging, due to the ongoing security situation, poor socio-economic conditions, and large-scale damage. In addition to the 5.7 million refugees outside of Syria, over six million people remain displaced inside Syria."[73]

Putting It All Together

Was the Syrian Civil War a pipeline war? I believe it was. Nafeez Ahmed is more cautious in his assessment: "Pipeline geopolitics is . . . only a subset of wider competition to dominate global energy markets," he wrote in his 2018 *State Propaganda* report. "This was not about one specific project. It was about Syria's unique geographical location, offering a range of potential routes to transport Mediterranean oil and gas to Europe. Whoever Syria decided to align with would determine the future energy map of the region."[74]

Ahmed is right that broad geopolitical tensions simmering in the region came to bear on Syria due to its unique location. But in Syria, as elsewhere in the Middle East, the moment that war becomes a reality it oftentimes coincides with critical decisions or disagreements over a more concise concern — pipelines, the arteries that chart the course of the region's lifeblood. Big-power efforts to undermine the Syrian regime at the very time that two competing pipeline projects were being considered underlay much of the political maneuvering in the region. The escalating war in 2015 made all pipeline schemes involving Syria unfeasible. But once the fighting stops, the covert pipeline wars between the West (seeking to bypass Russia) and Russia (seeking to consolidate its hold over pipeline routes to Europe) will no doubt resume.

Not coincidentally, as US-trained forces have routed ISIS from Iraq and Syria, new US military bases are being constructed in Iraq near the Syrian border, as well as in Manbij, a Syrian city on the border with Turkey. This is the very region that the proposed (and now on hold?) Qatar–Syria–Turkey pipeline would have traversed.

In many instances, we would not have known about the bloody "games" being played in Syria by the West, the Gulf States, and Turkey on the one hand and Syria, Russia, and Iran on the other had it not been for journalists piecing together the facts from classified documents produced from successful Freedom of Information Act requests and WikiLeaks.

To be sure, during the early years of the Obama administration, there were covert efforts to pressure the Assad regime to ally with Western oil interests, even after Assad purportedly rejected the Qatar–Syria–Turkey pipeline. But when the oil ministers of Syria, Iraq, and Iran signed their $10 billion pipeline deal (bypassing Qatar and Turkey) on July 25, 2011, that may have been the proverbial last straw, triggering the formation of the Free Syrian Army the same month. The fighting escalated sharply thereafter into "civil war." The Obama administration, through Secretary of State John Kerry, continued to apply diplomatic pressure on Syria, while allowing Saudi Arabia, Qatar, and Turkey to secretly fund outside mercenaries to further destabilize the regime.

The involvement of the CIA in the war has been harder to assess, and as most investigative journalists know, the CIA often acts independently of the State Department, with little or no oversight except by the president and his top national security advisors. The one certain indication of its involvement was revealed when CIA officer Douglas Laux "broke cover and spilled secrets" in a book about how he spent much of 2012 in the Middle East "examining options for how the CIA could overthrow the Bashar al-Assad regime, helping craft a covert plan to arm rebels and pressure Assad."[75] As he recounts in his book, "Our task was to find ways to remove President Assad from office. . . . My ops plan laid them out in black and white. But political leadership [redacted] hadn't given us the go-ahead to implement a single one."[76] He resigned in frustration.

Meanwhile, the Obama administration resorted to diplomacy. The visit of US ally Prince Bandar with Putin in August 2013 was designed to put further pressure on Russia to abandon Syria. When this did not succeed, the United States allowed its proxies, Saudi Arabia, Qatar, and Turkey, to fund jihadists to weaken Assad to the point of collapse.

Arguably, it was the *combined* threat (to the West) of Assad's rejection of the Qatar–Syria–Turkey pipeline plan and his promotion of the

Iran–Iraq–Syria pipeline plan that triggered intensified covert actions to destabilize Syria. The latter Islamic pipeline scheme, notes journalist Pepe Escobar, "bypasses the two nations which are absolutely keen on regime change in Syria: Turkey and Qatar,"[77] both countries being heavy funders of the rebels in Syria. Observes analyst F. William Engdahl, "That refusal [of the Qatari pipeline] combined with the Iran-Iraq-Syria gas pipeline agreement in 2011 ignited the full-scale Saudi and Qatari assault on Assad's power, financing al Qaeda terrorists, recruits of Jihadist fanatics willing to kill Alawite and Shi'ite 'infidels' for $100 a month and a Kalishnikov."[78]

As for ISIS, there are many in the Middle East who believe not only that the Islamic State was used to justify military intervention in Syria, but that it was actually the *creation* of US and British intelligence agencies. One of the first reporters to raise this widely held suspicion was Thomas Erdbrink, writing for the *New York Times* in 2014: "ISIS, Iranian leaders have been saying for a long time, is made-in-the-U.S.A., a tool of terror intended by the world's superpower to divide and conquer the energy-rich Middle East and to counter the growing influence of Iran in the region. Iran's supreme leader, Ayatollah Ali Khamenei, has often said that he believes ISIS was created by the United States as a way to regain a foothold in Iraq and to fight President Bashar al-Assad of Syria, an ally of Iran."[79]

Two weeks later, Anne Barnard reported in the *New York Times* that Syrian Kurds also believed ISIS was a Western creation and that NATO ally Turkey was involved in "creating the extremist group to kill Kurds and stop them from using the chaos in Syria to establish autonomy there." A Turkish Kurd involved in refugee relief told Barnard, "It's a lie that the USA and the Turks are bombing ISIS; they are the ones who made ISIS to fight Kurds and weaken us." Turkey, he added, had been allowing ISIS fighters to cross the border into Syria so they could fight the Kurds, which have long struggled — against fierce Turkish resistance — to set up an autonomous state along the border between Turkey and Syria.[80]

Whether ISIS was created or simply used by Hillary Clinton's State Department to justify the deployment of US troops to Iraq and Syria in 2014 and 2015, its "holdout" location in eastern Syria on the border with Iraq tells a bigger story. When the United Nations issued a report on ISIS enclaves in July 2018, it caused a flurry of news articles variously interpreting its finding that ISIS had been given "breathing space" in the eastern region.[81] The UN report described "a loss of momentum" in 2018 "by forces fighting ISIS in the east of the Syrian Arab Republic," which gave ISIS "prolonged access . . . to resources and gave it breathing space to prepare for the next phase of its evolution into a global covert network."

The rather oblique mention of "resources" could be a reference to more funding and arms supplied by Qatar, Turkey, and Saudi Arabia. But as the world learned in October 2019, most of Syria's oil and gas resources are located in northeastern Syria. Whitney Webb, an investigative reporter with MintPress News, had already reported, in April 2018, that "this area contains 95 percent of all Syrian oil and gas potential — including al-Omar, the country's largest oil field. Prior to the war, these resources produced some 387,000 barrels of oil per day and 7.8 billion cubic meters of natural gas annually, and were of great economic importance to the Syrian government. However, more significantly, nearly all the existing Syrian oil reserves — estimated at around 2.5 billion barrels — are located in the area currently occupied by the U.S. government."[82]

ISIS's lingering positions in eastern Syria stand in marked contrast to their near elimination in the rest of Syria in 2017, where Russian and Syrian forces subjected the rebels to unrelenting bombings. There have been reports that in the east, US bombing attacks against ISIS were announced ahead of time, allowing ISIS fighters to escape. Some ISIS fighters have even been recruited into security forces that the United States is training to guard the border between Iraq and Syria. Attempts by the Syrian government and pro-regime forces to rout ISIS out of the eastern region were thwarted by the United States, which managed to take control of the area and kept the pro-regime forces out . . . hence the "loss of momentum" in defeating ISIS by the Syrians, and the need for the continued presence of US forces.[83]*

Notably located in the region is a Conoco gas plant, the largest in the country, capable of producing nearly 40 million cubic feet of gas per day. Conoco and Shell left Syria in 2005 due to Bush-era sanctions against Syria, but US troops remain in the region.

---

* A protracted US-supported bombing campaign to dislodge ISIS from its last holdouts in northeastern Syria took place in March 2019. In northwestern Syria, Syrian forces waged an unrelenting campaign during the summer of 2019 to dislodge the last rebel forces from Idlib, near the border of Turkey. With Russian help, they succeeded in reclaiming most of the Syrian territory after American troops withdrew in late 2019.

When former US ambassador to the UN Nikki Haley announced in April 2018 that American forces would remain in Syria until "US goals are accomplished," she described those goals as ensuring that chemical weapons would not be used, that ISIS was defeated, and that a "good vantage point" enabled the United States to watch what Iran was doing.[84] Those goals have long been the pretext for US involvement in this war. Yet in reality, protecting US oil interests in both Syria and Iraq has been the primary goal since the days when President Obama tried to work with Assad in behalf of Shell (and its master plan for Syria's energy sector), and it will be until the day when, possibly, Assad is replaced by a more pro-West ruler. Russia's ever-increasing influence over Syria, allowing it to "win the war" except for a few pockets of ISIS, suggests that day may be a long way off.

Donald Trump's initial vow in January 2019 to withdraw US troops from Syria drew a predictable — at least to pipeline trackers like myself — pushback from defense officials and politicians. The reason became clear — this time to everyone — nine months later, when Trump ordered US troops to withdraw from Syria while giving Turkey the green light to invade northern Syria to attack the Kurds. More pushback occurred, forcing Trump to openly acknowledge that some troops would return to "protect the oilfields," ostensibly to prevent ISIS from getting access to them. Days later, he declared the oilfields "belonged to America. We're keeping the oil. . . . Forty-five million dollars a month? Keep the oil!" Outrage followed, with much international handwringing over Trump's violation of international law. Russia called Trump's claim on Syria's oil "state banditry," pointing out the hypocrisy of US claims to be fighting terrorism when in fact it seemed bent on seizing a nation's territory and resources.[85]

As for the Syrian people, "they know this is not a struggle for democracy," Robert F. Kennedy Jr. said in an interview with Thom Hartmann that focused on Syrian refugees who had fled the war-torn country. Instead, Kennedy opined, they saw it as "a war between two superpowers over their sovereign nation, and they will have nothing to do with picking what government they're going to have. Someone else will pick it for them. And that's why so many are leaving. No one wants to die for a pipeline war."[86]

CHAPTER SIX

The Turkish Cauldron

O ne of the most perplexing enigmas in the mystery of my father's death has been the role of Turkey. How, I wondered, could Turkey have helped determine his fate during his final months? I knew that in the late 1940s it was a viper's nest of spies; one need only consider its location to see why. It controlled the Bosporus Straits, a vital passageway taking all commercial traffic from the Black Sea to an eventual outlet on the Mediterranean. A World War II map showed it as a buffer between Soviet Russia to its north and the Mediterranean Sea to its south. No wonder it was a focal point for the Truman Doctrine — the United States' all-out effort to contain Soviet expansionism, particularly in the Middle East, announced just weeks before my father's plane crash.

Carat's last major mission, before traveling to Saudi Arabia, was to explore the situation of minorities in northern Syria and along its border with Turkey.[1] Reading through his reports, I had gathered that the "Kurdish problem" was for Carat his most pressing "Soviet problem" in northern Syria. In the fall of 1946, he and his top agent, the Lebanese historian and scholar Asad Rustum, spent two weeks meeting with tribal leaders in the region.

The Soviets, Carat had been informed before making the trip, planned on turning the region into a Soviet-influenced autonomous Kurdish state, allied with Kurds in Kurdish Iraq and northern Iran. "Under cover of a bid for real democracy," Carat's source (a businessman from Syria) confided, "the Kurdish Democratic Party plans to stage a revolution in the spring of 1947 with the help of the Soviets."[2]

Carat and Rustum traveled throughout northern Syria, meeting with different Kurdish leaders to determine the extent of Soviet influence among the Kurds. His twelve-page single-spaced report read like a primer on the history of Kurdish relations with the Turks, the Syrians, the Iraqis, and the Iranians, peppered with anecdotes and pungent declarations of nationalism from some of the leaders.[3]

"The Soviet Government has granted the Kurds living within the USSR a high degree of autonomy," Badr Khan, a leading spokesman of Kurdish nationalism, told him, "and the most cherished of all privileges — the right to teach in the Kurdish language. The Soviet regime is indeed the principal sponsor of the Kurdish cultural renaissance."

Ahmed Nafiz, a medical doctor who served as a spokesman for the Kurds in the Jazireh region of northern Syrian, made a distinction between Kurds who had been born on the frontiers of Syria, and were on the whole well satisfied with their treatment by the Syrian regime, and Kurds who fled to escape Turkish massacres and found asylum in Syria. The latter, Nafiz explained, "very naturally wished to be revenged and they saw an independent Kurdistan carved out of Turkish territory as a forward step toward obtaining such revenge."

Nafiz impressed upon Carat that any attempt by any government to force the Kurds to assimilate would be doomed. "The Turks had tried, and had failed. The Iraqis had tried, and had failed. The Syrians were trying, and would fail." Nafiz added bitterly that any attempt by Western powers to "compel the Turks to grant the Kurds full rights of citizenship while permitting them to develop their own culture and language unmolested," would also inevitably fail "the minute the pressure was off" from the West. The Turks, he insisted, "would seize the opportunity to return to their practice of coercion and massacre. There was thus no solution but an independent Kurdistan."

Carat then explored what the Kurds would accept as borders for an independent Kurdistan. Nafiz spread out a map of Kurdish territories and explained that their minimum demand was for territory whose population was 80 percent Kurdish, and included all of eastern Anatolia that was west of Lake Van, a portion of northern Iraq, and a portion of Azerbaijan and western Iran.

They would not ask for an inch of Syrian territory.

Carat indicated that he was pleasantly surprised, that this demand seemed reasonable, and then asked Nafiz "to define frankly" his position on the Soviet Union.

Nafiz smiled, and replied, "We Kurds are like a man lost in the desert in a dark night. He looks in all directions for help and a guiding light and finds none. Finally, he catches a glimpse of a faint light faraway to the east. He goes in that direction." Lest the American were to miss his meaning, he elaborated. "It would appear that neither the British nor the Americans are concerned with our issue, whereas something has come to us from Russia. So it should not be surprising if we continue in this direction."

Carat would end up reporting that "there is growing interest among Syrian Kurds of Jazireh in the project of an independent Kurdish State," but he found no evidence, "that the Kurdish leaders of the Jazireh have been in direct, or indirect touch with Soviet government" or that "Soviet, or other foreign agents, have been operating in the Jazireh within recent months."

Nafiz's allegory about the man lost in the dark of night seeing a light "faraway to the east" presumably was enough of a fair warning to Washington to take Kurdish nationalism seriously and to act on it before it was too late. Carat was also supposed to gather information on the security of the Syrian-Turkish border. "While the Turks are extremely strict about Syrians crossing into Turkey and remaining there," he wrote on October 28, 1946, "the Syrians are rather more lax. Kurdish and Christian villagers on the Syrian side of the frontier have relatives and kinsmen on the Turkish side." Still, despite the Turks posting gendarmes every 5 kilometers on the Turkish side of the frontier, he learned that it was "extremely simple for anyone to walk across at night."[4] I had to wonder if this was a tip-off to any future agent wanting to cross into Turkey.

The cities that Carat had visited and listed in his reports — Qamishli, Hassatche, Deir ez-Zor, and Raqqa, among them — had a familiar ring to me; in recent years, they had all figured prominently in the last stages of the Syrian Civil War, as Kurdish forces battled against the last remnants of ISIS. But Carat, in late 1946, wouldn't be visiting them again. Soon after his trip, the Syrian government closed all the regions he had visited to all consular and diplomatic personnel of all foreign legations. "I got in my Jazireh trip just in the nick of time," he wrote to Washington. "This means that I cannot go to Lattaquia again, or to Deir ez-Zor, or to other places in the areas defined."[5]

The oil that was known to exist in the northeastern Kurdish region of Syria, also mentioned in declassified State Department reports, undoubtedly explained Washington's interest in the border region. It likely also explained the Syrian government's obvious alarm over my father prowling around in the region. But why was Turkey more stringent in protecting its border with Syria? For that matter, what did I *really* know about Turkey? Surprisingly little, despite the fact that my grandmother had taught biology to Armenian girls in Istanbul (then Constantinople) in 1900. My father had also visited Turkey in 1931 on his way to Beirut and described visiting his mother's old haunts in vivid detail. I sensed that the day would come when I would have to see for myself what they had experienced, if only through a modern lens. Meanwhile, my focus on pipeline politics continued, and as it did I discovered that Turkey figured largely in the Great Game for Oil and the battles between Russia and the West over pipeline routes in Central Asia.

The Miracle of the Baku–Tbilisi–Ceyhan Pipeline

It was the reporting of Ted Koppel on *Nightline* that alerted me to the Baku–Tbilisi–Ceyhan pipeline that connected the Caspian Sea to the Turkish port of Ceyhan on the Mediterranean Sea. The BTC pipeline, as it is called, became "the anchor of national security interests of the United States in central Asia and the Caucasus," according to Koppel, "because that goes to the heart of an American policy goal, that is, the uninterrupted transport of Caspian oil."[6]

Uninterrupted is the watchword in Koppel's 2002 report. At the time, the Bush administration eyed Turkey as a potential major energy corridor for the West after the dissolution of the Soviet Union, one that would facilitate the shipment of oil from the Caspian Sea westward (instead of eastward, as in the TAPI pipeline), thus shutting out the Russians. The BTC pipeline was central to this strategy, provided it could avoid major ethnic hostilities along its route. Right from the outset of its construction, beginning in 2003, its planners braced for attacks on the pipeline because it was to traverse some of the most volatile regions in the world.

The BTC pipeline would start in Baku on the western shores of the Caspian Sea in the former Soviet republic of Azerbaijan, pass through Tbilisi in Georgia, and terminate in the Turkish port town of Ceyhan. From there, it would pipe oil to Europe, bypassing Russia. In preparation (one has to assume), the United States poured money into Turkey to train Turkish military officers who in turn trained officers in Azerbaijan between 1989 and 1999, so much so that Turkey became the world's largest recipient of US military training, according to the Arms Control Monitor.[7] With the necessary military presence in place, the BTC pipeline agreement was signed by

Azerbaijan, Georgia, and Turkey in November 1999. The BTC Company, a consortium of eleven energy companies, was established in August 2002.[8] Construction of the pipeline began in 2003 and was completed in 2005.

The stakes for BTC's successful completion were significant. The newsletter *Energy Security* predicted that it "could provide a livelihood for many people in Azerbaijan, Georgia and Armenia as well as stimulate economic activity in eastern Turkey, and it will make a contribution to enhancing world energy security by developing a non-OPEC oil source." In other words, it was viewed as the "linchpin of the shift in U.S. energy policy away from the Middle East." With so much riding on its success, warned *Energy Security*, "failure of the countries involved to ensure the security of the project will have severe implications on the future of the region as well as global energy markets at large."[9] Ensuring that security, of course, meant cooperating with the United States' demands for *providing* the security.

In 2004, the Institute for the Analysis of Global Security was reporting that the pipeline was "not yet finished and already threatened with new terrorist campaigns."[10] Its largest opponent, predictably, was Russia. The pipeline originated in Baku, Azerbaijan, a major oil port on the Caspian Sea where Stalin once organized oil workers in his rise to power. Azerbaijan was incorporated into the Soviet Union in 1920 as the Azerbaijan Soviet Socialist Republic. In 1991, it declared its independence. Russia viewed the BTC pipeline as a US-backed project taking place in Russia's backyard and designed to decrease the Kremlin's economic and political influence in the Caucasus. Or, as *Energy Security* characterized it, the BTC project was seen as an effort "to redraw the geography of the Caucasus on an anti-Russian map."[11] When the "contract of the century" between Azerbaijan and Turkey was signed in 1994, the capitals of Azerbaijan and Georgia were beset by internal coups and political assassinations, all reportedly having links to Moscow.[12] The newsletter *Energy Security* did not finger Russia directly but hinted that "Russia will not shed tears if BTC is sabotaged. It might even clandestinely lend its hand to groups that might do just that. Russia might also team up with Iran in an effort to promote the alternative route southward out of the Caspian to the Persian Gulf."[13]

Azerbaijan, now allied with the West thanks to heavy courting by Zbigniew Brzezinski, welcomed the pipeline as a means to decrease its dependence on Russia and solidify its political, economic, and security links with Turkey (an ally) and western Europe. Boasting that the BTC was to be "the

The Baku–Tbilisi–Ceyhan Gas Pipeline

The BTC pipeline passes through some of the most volatile parts of the world, causing the United States to pour millions of military-assistance dollars into Azerbaijan and Georgia to protect the pipeline. It was completed in 2005. The Russians saw it as a threat to their gas interests and an effort "to redraw the geography of the Caucasus

RUSSIA

SOUTH OSSETIA

Caucasus Mountains

GEORGIA

Tbilisi

AZERBAIJAN

Caspian Sea

Baku

Sangachal

ARMENIA

Mosul

Tehran

Baghdad

IRAN

IRAQ

Pipeline

Military bases

Flashpoints of Russia-Georgia War, 2008

Pipeline sabotage in Turkey, 2009

Region of conflicts between Azerbaijan and Armenia

SAUDI ARABIA

The Gulf

on an anti-Russian map." In 2008, Georgia (aligned with the West) and Russia came to blows near the route of the pipeline, causing many to fear the start of a world war. War was averted, but a year later, the pipeline was attacked by saboteurs — most likely Russian — in Turkey. Russia continues to keep a watchful eye on the BTC pipeline from Abkhazia and South Ossetia, which are aligned with Russia.[14]

most secure pipeline in the world," Azerbaijan promised "constant safety surveillance" along its route. (The BTC pipeline is, in fact, entirely underground, with only pumping stations visible.) In the aftermath of 9/11, Azerbaijan pledged its cooperation with the United States, sent troops to Afghanistan and Iraq, and fully cooperated with NATO and the United States in border security. Secretary of Defense Donald Rumsfeld visited Azerbaijan in August 2004 and signed an agreement with the government to deploy US forces to the region.* Nonetheless, Azerbaijan anticipated ongoing terrorist attacks from Armenian and Chechen groups and threats to blow up the pipeline from the Kurdistan Workers' Party (PKK), which had already bombed oil pipelines in Turkey.[15]

Georgia was yet another potential flashpoint of tension due to disagreements with Russia over Georgia's two "breakaway regions" — South Ossetia and Abkhazia — which were more aligned with Russia and wanted to be independent from Georgia after the fall of the Soviet Union. In August 2004, Georgian president Mikheil Saakashvili warned, "If war begins it will be a war between Georgia and Russia, not between the Georgians and Ossetians."[16] That same month, troops from Turkey, Azerbaijan, and Georgia came together in Baku for six days of joint military exercises, ostensibly to prepare for possible terrorist attacks against the pipeline. But not coincidentally, there were larger security concerns at play.

Meanwhile, the United States beefed up Georgia's security, supplying it with hundreds of millions of dollars' worth of military aid. According to energy expert Michael Klare, this aid made Georgia "the leading recipient of US arms and equipment in the former Soviet space."[17] The United States also established two joint (US-Turkish) military air bases in Georgia.

In July 2006, Turkish Prime Minister Recep Tayyip Erdoğan proudly stood with the presidents of Georgia and Azerbaijan in front of a giant map of the BTC pipeline. They had converged at the Turkish port of Ceyhan to celebrate the completion of the last stretch of the BTC pipeline. President Saakashvili of Georgia was particularly effusive, declaring that the $3.9 billion pipeline

---

* Tensions remain in Azerbaijan, which has received millions of dollars in US military aid as well as Israeli missiles, over its border disputes with Russian-backed Armenia. Thirty thousand people died due to the Azerbaijan-Armenia conflict in the 1990s, and skirmishes continue. The Azerbaijan military built a new base in the Tartar region, near the disputed border territories, in 2016.

was "not only about energy independence or economic independence. This project is about independence — about real independence for our countries."[18] Real independence, in other words, from the former Soviet Union.

The chief executive of BP, the pipeline's major investor, declared that the newly inaugurated BTC "changes the energy map of the world."[19] But within two years, such celebratory sentiment would fade with the realization that Russia was not about to abandon its own ambitions for the region.

Erdoğan, for his part, understood Russian ambitions all too well and was more circumspect. Back in November 2005, he had been pictured shaking hands with Russian president Vladimir Putin to celebrate the inauguration of the Blue Stream pipeline, which carried natural gas from southern Russia and under the Black Sea to the Turkish city of Samsun and from there on to Ankara. It had been conceived before Erdoğan's time, in 1997, with Russia's Gazprom and Italy's giant Eni as the main investors. Putin, by now a master of Great Game manipulations, audaciously suggested during the Blue Stream inauguration that a second Black Sea pipeline be constructed. Erdoğan, therefore, was playing all sides to achieve his dream of turning Turkey into a major energy hub, a crucial bridge that could transfer oil and gas from the Caspian and Black Seas to the West.

Still, thanks to the millions of US dollars already poured into protecting the BTC pipeline — now the world's largest — the establishment of an East–West corridor had finally been achieved. Geopolitically, it was believed to be a brilliant accomplishment. The pipeline bypassed Iran, the politically unstable northern Caucasus (including Chechnya), and Armenian-occupied parts of Azerbaijan. While the BTC pipeline supplied only 1 percent of the world's oil and, contrary to predictions, did not significantly lessen US reliance on Middle East oil and gas, it was a serious challenge to the Russians, who, until this moment, had been the masters of energy distribution to Europe.

But in the summer of 2008, everyone who had worried about the security of the pipeline route saw their worst fears realized in what has come to be known as the first war in Europe in the twenty-first century.

The Russo-Georgia War

For a few tense weeks in August 2008, fighting broke out between Georgia and Russia in South Ossetia, and the world held its breath as it braced for serious escalation. The *Wall Street Journal* reported that "the fighting began in the craggy mountains of separatist South Ossetia province when ethnic fighting that has long plagued the area abruptly got much worse."[20] Georgia tried to retake the capital of South Ossetia. The *New York Times* reported that Georgian forces had shot down at least two Russian jets over South Ossetia and that in retaliation, "Russia's Black Sea fleet, warplanes and tanks [were] bearing down on the small mountainous country. Georgian officials acknowledged they were taken by surprise by the intensity of the Russian response."[21]

I remember this well, having noticed that the conflict was occurring close to the BTC pipeline, for which the Vermont-based firm Northern Power was a contractor. I visited the firm during the hostilities and asked one of its engineers what he thought. He showed me a map of the various ethnic groups in the region and alluded to the possibility of World War III. I was shocked. Surely the war could not be this serious?

Fortunately, a major war was averted with the signing of a peace agreement on August 25, 2008. Georgia's president apparently had expected NATO to intervene, but it did not. Much to the annoyance of the United States, Russia used the peace agreement to formally recognize the independence of the two breakaway republics.

Al Jazeera, reporting on the war's tenth anniversary, called the war a victory for Russia and a humiliation for Georgia.[22] Energy expert Michael Klare wrote, "The Russians are sending a message to the rest of the world that they intend to keep their hands on the Caspian Sea energy spigot, come what may. This doesn't mean occupying Georgia outright. But they will certainly retain their strategic positions in Abkhazia and South Ossetia — for all practical purposes, daggers aimed at the BTC jugular."[23]

Geopolitical strategist George Friedman released an analysis of the Russo-Georgia War a month after it ended with some sobering conclusions for the United States. The war, his report stated, occurred at a time when "U.S. ground forces were stretched to the limits." American military commitments in the Islamic world, principally in Iraq and Afghanistan, meant that "it had no forces to spare." The Russians took advantage of this "window of opportunity" by invading Georgia following Georgia's attack on South Ossetia. At the war's end, Russia emerged as a power to be reckoned with. Friedman likened the Russian impudence to that of the pirate ships of the eighteenth century: Russia "ran up the Jolly Roger."[24]

Russia's president at the time, Dmitry Medvedev, took the opportunity to drive home a message to the West. Russia's foreign policy, he stated, was governed by five points. (Over time, these five points came to be known as the Medvedev Doctrine.) Chief among them was that Russia "does not accept the primacy of the United States in the international system," and that "as with other countries, there are regions in which Russia has privileged interests." In other words, Friedman commented, "the Russians have special interests in the former Soviet Union," where it had friendly relations, and "intrusions by others into these regions that undermine pro-Russian regimes will be regarded as threat to Russia's 'special interests.'" It was no accident, Friedman's report concluded, that "the first world leader [the Russians] met with after invading Georgia was Syrian President Bashar al Assad. This was a clear signal that if the U.S. responded aggressively to Russia's actions in Georgia, Moscow would ship a range of weapons to Syria — and far worse, to Iran."

For Georgia, Turkey, and other countries scattered around the Black and Caspian Seas, pipeline politics seem to be erupting in new and ever more volatile ways — all amid the continual presence of superpowers, and the inevitable conflicts and shifting alliances that presence guaranteed.

I've often wondered whether such a volatile future could have even been imagined way back in the 1940s, between the two world wars and the Cold War, when my father was dispatched to decipher the emerging confluences of geopolitics and oil. But how long before that did oil interests begin to write the future of the region? That's a story that would unfold as I inevitably began to investigate how my grandmother got caught up in the Great Game for Oil in Turkey and, like her master-spy son, delivered intelligence — wittingly or not — that helped shape US foreign policy in the region.*

The Lure of Wickedness

It was in the summer of 2004 that Turkey lured Jerry and me to its shores. Erdoğan did not enter into our thinking at the time, although that same summer the fiery prime minister had announced his candidacy for the

---

* At the time of my grandmother's arrival in 1900, Turkey was the political and financial epicenter of a dwindling Ottoman Empire, which by then comprised only today's Turkey, Syria, Lebanon, Jordan, Israel, Palestine, Iraq, and the western territories of Saudi Arabia. World War I would further "carve up the Turkey," as the victorious Great Powers were wont to say after defeating Turkey and Germany in the war. They proceeded to partition former Ottoman territories, with the League of Nations establishing a French mandate over Syria and Lebanon, and a British mandate over Iraq, Jordan, and Palestine.

presidency. Our reason for the trip was a personal one. After years of researching my father's adventures and misadventures as Carat, Turkey had
begun to loom large in my quest for more answers about his life and death.
Jerry kept telling me, "You need to know more about your grandmother!"
I agreed, but neither of us realized that I would end up spending many
months delving into the events surrounding Elisabeth Redfern's three
years in Turkey, from 1900 to 1903. Nor could I have guessed that my
grandmother's posting to Turkey — as a missionary educator, no less — coincided with the United States' first significant commercial penetration of
the Middle East.[25]

Once again, my quest back in time was about to unlock secrets for me,
and, once again, that little-known history would have a lot to do with the
search for oil. In preparation for my trip to Turkey, I visited the archives
of my grandmother's alma mater, Smith College, in Northampton, Massachusetts. The archivists there were able to dig out her yearbook from
1897. I turned to the Rs, and there was her photo with a brief caption
underneath. She was the very picture of a Victorian-era woman: her head
held high, her hair neatly parted and pulled back from her face in a bun,
her blouse closed and gathered into a prim turtleneck, no jewelry. And yet
the wisp of a smile was on her face. Below her picture were these words:
"Elisabeth Redfern is in a constant struggle between a puritan conscience
and a desire to be wicked."

Oh, Grandma! If only I had known thee! What better place, I mused,
to work out your struggle than in the land of the sultans and their mighty
City of the World's Desires, Constantinople (today's Istanbul)?

I remembered my grandmother from my childhood years as a sweet old
lady — not, as I imagined her now, as an adventuress trapped in Puritan
clothes. She would welcome me to sit on her plump lap so she could read
to me. Those were special moments, but I knew nothing about her or her
son's adventures in Turkey, Syria, and Lebanon. Maybe she was trying to
protect me from the horrors of war in the Middle East. (But she did leave all
those wonderful scrapbooks in the steamer trunk for someone — perhaps a
grandchild turned adult — to read.)

In her 1907 tenth-reunion yearbook from Smith, her comments suggested that her three years in Turkey had been the most exciting of her life.
She had taught biology and other subjects at the American College for Girls
in Constantinople, had met Armenians, Bulgarians, Turks, Greeks, Jews,

Austrians, Germans, and Serbians, and had been irreversibly charmed by the country. "If one has lived there, one can never set aside its spell," she wrote.

She must have passed on her enthusiasm to her son. My father was twenty-one when he visited Constantinople on his way to Beirut in 1931, and he wrote copious letters about seeing some of her old haunts and about sailing through the Bosporus, one of the world's most strategic waterways that cuts the city in two (the "European side" and the "Asian side") and links the Black Sea to the Mediterranean. He described the Bosporus to a friend as "no wider than the Charles [River] at Harvard bridge." To each side, he wrote, were "ruined fortresses whose walls, crumbling with age, go back to the victorious Turkish years that followed 1453, and as the boat approaches the city, one suddenly gets the feeling that here at last is a foreign country and a new architecture. What a sensation one feels on seeing for the first time the genuine Byzantine arches, domes and columns, but most wonderful of all was the vision of the first mosques with the minarets dazzling white in the sun."[26]

He called it "the experience of a lifetime." I had always wondered, on reading this passage in his letter, what I myself might find in going there, and there's no denying that modern Istanbul cast a spell on me, too. The sultans' palaces — Topkapi, the most famous one — the mosques and minarets and mighty Hagia Sophia, the endless covered bazaars, and, more than anything, the Bosporus — it is a beautiful city, and it was here that I found an unexpected epiphany.

It happened while I was visiting the grounds of the former American College for Girls. Its location had moved from the Asian to the European side of Istanbul after a mysterious fire in 1910 gutted the old buildings where my grandmother had taught. (A boys' school now occupies the original space, and I noticed a plaque on the wall of one of its buildings: "The third floor of Martin Hall was contributed to the school by Mobil Oil Turk A.S. 1992.")

The college's newer campus lay high on a plateau overlooking the Bosporus. It seemed like the perfect location for an American outpost that strove to be taken seriously as an up-and-coming power in the Middle East. Three large, imposing buildings rose high above its gardens and bore the name of the wealthy families who financed them following the fire: Gould Hall (donated by Helen Gould Shepard, daughter of the nineteenth-century Wall Street financier and railroad developer Jay Gould); Russell Sage Hall (donated by Margaret Sage, widow of Russell Sage, another financier and railroad developer and associate of Jay Gould); and Mitchell Hall (donated by Olivia Phelps Stokes, heiress to the Phelps Stokes copper and banking fortune, who renamed the hall after a friend, Sarah Mitchell).

From this impressive hilltop location, I gazed out upon the boats traveling back and forth on the waterway — mostly large tankers carrying cargo that in Grandma's day was just beginning to capture the imagination of the world: oil. Only in her day, the boats were laden with barrels of kerosene, used in lamps to light up homes before electricity became prevalent. Railroads carried the emerging fuel of the twentieth century — the oil that powered engines — and when Grandma arrived in Turkey the race was on to build railroads across Europe and Turkey. One that directly affected Turkey was the Berlin to Baghdad railway, with which the women at Grandma's college would become intimately familiar.

I knew that Constantinople had for centuries been a capital of world commerce. Now, as I reflected on what the marine traffic on the Bosporus must have been like in 1900, I realized that it would have meant different things to different people, depending on how well informed — and powerful — they were. To Elisabeth Redfern, the boats and their barrels may have been mere tourist curiosities. She may not have known that the wealthy families chartering them — the Nobels of Sweden and Russia, the Rothschilds of France, and the Rockefellers of North America — were tracking their progress in the same way they followed all their vessels, whether boats or railroads: with the zeal of ruthless players caught up in a competition for power and control of what soon became the most precious resource of the new twentieth century.

What Elisabeth, like most people, most definitely knew was that kerosene would soon revolutionize the world, bringing light — and hope — to the twentieth century. Oil, the emerging fuel of industrialization and transportation (both civilian and military), was being carried overland by railroads financed by the famous "robber barons" of the nineteenth century. By 1900, pipelines began to replace railroad tank cars in the United States. America's premier oil baron, John D. Rockefeller, would come to be known as the "King of Pipelines."[27]

Between 1884 and 1915, the battle for oil markets abroad had become so intense that it was actually being called the great Russo-American war.[28] The Nobel brothers developed huge tanker fleets in the Caspian Sea, Black Sea, and Mediterranean Sea, allowing Russia to market oil throughout

Europe and the Near East. American consuls reporting from Europe and the Middle East sent dire warnings to the US State Department about Russian competition and declining sales of American kerosene.

In 1894, Rockefeller's Standard Oil was supplying 90 percent of Germany's oil, 77 percent of France's oil, and 69 percent of England's oil. Meanwhile, Russian oil dominated the markets of Austria-Hungary, the Balkans, and Turkey. Standard's own agents reported that the Russo-American war boiled down to a contest between the southern and northern ports of Europe.[29] The Great Game for Oil was now in full swing.

The turn of the century proved to be a turning point for the United States' richest men. It heralded their arrival on the world stage as new players in a big thrust toward economic empire, with newfound access to markets and resources, and a barely disguised quest for political and cultural domination. My grandmother was there to see it all, whether or not she understood its ramifications.

The scouting for new oil properties abroad required not only secrecy but also its proactive counterpart: intelligence gathering. Or, in a word, espionage. Standard Oil employees became skilled at obtaining information on the most minute subjects dealing with the competitive sales of oil, while keeping mum on their own work.[30] When Standard began to expand overseas, its agents frequently used covers, posing as agricultural technicians or rubber gatherers, or even carrying the official title of US diplomatic agent.[31]

Making the Connections

It was not until I returned to the United States that I fully understood the connection between my grandmother's missionary experience, the missionaries' role as natural intelligence gatherers (no cover needed; they were in place in foreign lands and utilized their powers of observation), and the importance of the American College for Girls to America's early aspirations to control the oil of the Middle East. Up until this time, all my focus on missionary activity had been centered on Latin America — and those were evangelical missionaries, mostly from America's heartland, not "modernist" missionaries from East Coast colleges who eschewed Bible-thumping proselytizing (which was found to alienate "the natives") in favor of providing modern secular education as a means of winning over hearts and minds.[32]

The archives of the American College for Girls, I had been told during my Istanbul visit, had been moved to safety in New York City because of the college's early history in educating Armenian girls. Any connection to Armenians was still viewed with great suspicion by the Turks.

As happened so many times during my quest, one visit to this newest set of archives reaped reams of extraordinary revelations.[33] Not only was there correspondence describing Elisabeth as a young teacher whose "numerous gifts" and enthusiasm had made her "the life of the College," but there was evidence that she played a major role in fund-raising for the school when she returned to her hometown of Winchester, Massachusetts.[34] I was surprised to find that she had approached Winchester's leading citizen, textbook publisher Edwin Ginn, and his associate in New York, George Plimpton, about the college's financial needs, which eventually brought the situation to the attention of John D. Rockefeller.[35] Rockefeller's offer of $100,000 to help the school with a new power house was initially rejected by the Congregational church, which ran the college, as "tainted money," Rockefeller's ruthless business practices having outraged many in the congregation.[36] But his gift was eventually accepted and celebrated by the time the US ambassador to Turkey, Henry Morgenthau, helped inaugurate the new campus in 1914.

As the guest speaker to an audience of Turkish notables, church dignitaries, and relatives of the students, Morgenthau spoke with utter conviction of the great prospects that lay ahead for the United States to espouse modern, American-styled education in Turkey — and the Middle East. And in many respects, he was right. The heavily endowed, formerly Protestant-turned-secular American universities that arose in Istanbul, Cairo, Beirut, and Jerusalem during the late nineteenth and early twentieth centuries did wonders in building solid pro-American relations with the elites in the Middle East, many of whom sent their sons and daughters to be educated in these Western schools. The British, I would later discover, had relied on more heavy-handed "direct rule" in their colonies and by World War II seethed with envy over the success of these American colleges in engendering local support for the "American way of life."

The Berlin-to-Baghdad Railroad

By far my greatest find at the college's archives was a book sitting inconspicuously on a bookshelf wedged between histories of the Congregational church and its foreign missions. It immediately caught my attention because of its decidedly secular title: *The Berlin to Baghdad Express*. What, I wondered, did this have to do with a Protestant women's college in Turkey? The answer, for my purposes, was: everything. It answered my questions about what American oil and railroad barons were doing in Turkey at the turn of the century, why they threw millions of dollars into the American College for Girls, and why my grandmother's father, a Massachusetts lumber merchant who sold white pine from Maine (presumably for railroad ties) to Germany, decided that it would be a good thing for his daughter to be his eyes and ears in Turkey as the United States entered the Great Game.[37]

Prior to discovering this book, I had found only hints and hypotheses from family friends and relatives about why my grandmother went to Constantinople in 1900. They concurred that her parents wanted to separate her from a suitor. But there were clearly other reasons. Elisabeth Redfern's well-off parents had early imbued her with a sense of mission at the Congregational church in her hometown of Winchester. From the family's favorite pew she could gaze up at the Redfern stained-glass window, the only one in the church that honored a pilgrim rather than a biblical figure, suggesting that the Redferns identified more with modern-day religious pioneers than with heroes from ancient history, thus expressing a "missionary spirit." Her upbringing, at least by Winchester standards, was the epitome of high culture. She played the piano and attended the Boston Symphony and the theater. She read avidly and belonged to the local Shakespeare club. She took citizenship seriously and became an advocate for women's right to vote.

My hunch is that Elisabeth wanted adventure, independence, and an opportunity to use her brains beyond intelligent conversation in drawing rooms. Teaching abroad was one of the few avenues open to her. Though she was deeply religious, Elisabeth was not inclined to wear the missionary label conspicuously. Rather, she considered herself an educator, a "modernist" missionary who had been schooled in the secular sciences at one of the best colleges in the East. She had completed postgraduate studies in biology at the Massachusetts Institute of Technology in 1899 as one of three women in a class of 169 men. She was in Turkey to teach biology at the American College for Girls. But I still didn't have an answer to my question: Why Turkey?

My father's boyhood friend, Sherman Russell, had told me that my grandmother's presence in Turkey had something to do with "a

German-Caliphate connection," and my great-aunts had told me Grandma and her father were overheard talking about "the land between two rivers" — that is, Mesopotamia, today's Iraq. Now the two clues connected as I discovered that this fertile stretch of land between the Tigris and Euphrates Rivers was to be the ultimate destination of the fabled Berlin-to-Baghdad railroad that the Germans planned to build through Turkey in order to link Germany directly to the Middle East.

Kaiser Wilhelm II, emperor of Germany and cousin of England's King Edward VII, had already made two well-publicized trips to Turkey to secure the railroad concession, the latest time in 1898, two years before my grandmother's arrival. Kaiser Wilhelm was a flamboyant ruler who tried to mask his own insecurities with a giant handlebar mustache and much fanfare. He feted the wary Hamid II, sultan of the Ottoman Empire, with parades and promises. The single rail line, he vowed, would secure Hamid II's hold over all his subjects and serve as a rapid troop carrier if the need arose to quell disturbances in the far-flung but rapidly disintegrating empire.[38] Germany, the kaiser insisted, had no designs on Ottoman territory, as the other European powers had.

Kaiser Wilhelm promised an economic boon as well. He had sent out a German technical commission to confirm rumors of vast riches in the Ottoman Empire. The reports that came back were more than promising. Besides a treasure trove of minerals such as iron ore and copper, the fabled Fertile Crescent, which included Mesopotamia, was just that: a vast land ripe for great agricultural development. But even more important was the region's oil potential. The German survey described Mesopotamia as a veritable "sea of petroleum."

And what did the Germans get in return? The sultan promised them oil concessions along either side of the railroad. In short, the Berlin-to-Baghdad railroad was a win-win deal for both countries. For Turkey, whose rulers distrusted Europe's encroaching colonial powers, the railroad and the oil-rich lands it traversed meant a new source of revenues free of usurious foreign loans; for Germany, the railroad offered a rare chance to dominate world trade in a highly strategic region, beginning with Turkey as the gateway to the Middle East, then beyond all the way to the Gulf and Bombay, India.

It was as if this single stretch of track could bind the destinies and overcome the weaknesses of two great empires, restoring unity to an Ottoman empire humiliated by territorial losses to the Europeans, and bringing power and dignity to a German empire that until now had felt unappreciated by the older colonial powers of Europe. By getting control over the oil of the Middle East — oil that was rapidly gaining appreciation as an alternative fuel source to coal — Kaiser Wilhelm envisioned a boon to his country militarily as well as economically. "All the long years of my reign," the kaiser confided to the king of Italy, "my colleagues, the monarchs of Europe, have paid no attention to what I have to say. Soon, with my Navy to endorse my words, they will be more respectful."[39]

When Elisabeth Redfern arrived in Turkey, negotiations on the German-Caliphate railroad concession were reaching their final stages. Now all the great powers of Europe began to take notice. Britain, for the past century considered the ruler of the seas, was particularly attentive. In London, observers correctly interpreted Germany's overland rail route as a "shortcut to India." India was then Britain's most prized colonial possession, and His Majesty's government had jealously protected the sea routes to India, including the Suez Canal and Red Sea. Now the Germans' overland railroad seemed to be encroaching not only on British interests in India, but also on Persia, where legendary oil seeps were attracting the interest of the British, the French, and the Russians. The Americans, still in the junior league among world powers, played a more subtle role of watching and listening.

The American missionaries at the American College for Girls did their part in informally gathering and passing on intelligence to the school's wealthy trustees.[40] While on their daily horseback rides on the outskirts of the city, the missionaries would pass by a German railway station near the school and examine — skeptically at first — the German railway cars found there brandishing, in large letters, the promise "Constantinople to Baghdad."

"We knew very well that those pretentious cars really went a very short way into the interior," Mary Mills Patrick, the college's president, commented. But that did not stop rumors about German penetration of the Middle East from constantly reaching the missionaries' ears via Austrian, Russian, English, and French sources. Patrick later mused in her memoirs about "how great an influence the potential control of Asia Minor by Germany had in creating conditions that made the World War possible."[41] Whether they understood it or not, Elisabeth and all her colleagues at the college were living in a pivotal time. The fate of Turkey, the command center of the far-flung Ottoman Empire that encompassed so much of the Middle East's oil, had seized everyone's imagination.

Completed railroad line

- - - Projected railroad line

Major battles near the route of the railroad

Austria-Hungary attack on Serbia in 1914

Failed British offensive in 1915 against Gallipoli, Turkey, in an effort to seize Istanbul from the Ottomans

British-Turkish hostilities in 1915 in area of proposed route of the railroad, which became effectively useless to the Germans that year

Adana, the site of Turko-German genocidal attacks against Armenias in 1905; Germans relied on Armenian prisoners to build the railroad—after the war Germany lost all rights to the railroad

The Berlin-to-Baghdad Railway:
How Railroad Politics Led to World War I

Railroads played the same geopolitical role in the nineteenth and early twenti-eth centuries as pipelines did after World War II, often sparking bitter rivalries over resources that ended in war. The Berlin-to-Baghdad railroad, constructed

RUSSIAN EMPIRE

ROMANIA

Black Sea

TURKEY

Adana

Aleppo

Mosul

IRAN

Mediterranean Sea

Haifa

Baghdad

Basra

IRAQ

The Gulf

0   300
Miles

by the Germans and Turks between 1903 and 1915, was key to Germany's "Drive to the East" and is now widely regarded as a major cause of World War I. The British in particular viewed it as a threat to their oil holdings in the Gulf (Iran) and their plans to seize the oil of Iraq, which they considered a "first-class war aim."[42]

In 1908, Turkey's Sultan Abdul Hamid was seriously considering offering another railroad concession, this time to the Americans, that would run north of the Berlin to Baghdad railroad and would also offer oil and mineral rights on either side of the railroad. His dreams of establishing a mighty Islamic caliphate enhanced through railroad and oil development suddenly came crashing down, however, when several army officers turned against him in an insurrection that spread rapidly through the realm, culminating in the end of the Sultanate and the beginning of the Turkish Republic. The "Young Turk" revolution was greeted with widespread rejoicing throughout the former empire.

Back in the United States, Elisabeth celebrated with her new husband, Daniel Dennett, a physician who had once served as a former editor of Maine's *Portland Daily Express*, and with her father-in-law, Liberty Dennett, who enthused in a letter to the *Express* that "the absolutism of the Sultan of Turkey is over" and that this was "the most significant revolution of modern times," hinting strongly that two American colleges — Robert College and a "female college close at hand" (in other words, the American College for Girls) had a role to play in the revolution. "Long may these and all other free colleges in the Orient prosper so that liberty may enlighten the world," he exulted.[43]

On the very day the Young Turks came to power, large donations to the college began to pour in, including $150,000 from railroad heiress Helen Gould, $100,000 from Miss Olivia Phelps Stokes of the copper fortune, and another $100,000 from Mrs. Russell Sage, another railroad heiress.[44]

The British were pleased as well with the revolution, acting as a guiding hand for the new government. They placed a British admiral to head up the Ottoman navy and a British financier to become Minister of Finance. The Young Turks, who originally derided the Baghdad Railway Convention as a monstrous drain on Turkey's finances, came around soon enough and reopened negotiations with the Germans on the terms of the railway concession, realizing that the Baghdad railway, and railways in general, promised great economic and political importance.[45]

Winston Churchill, meanwhile, had already begun to fret, as First Lord of the Admiralty, over how he was going to supply the British navy with fuel after making the momentous decision in 1911 to convert its fuel from coal to the more efficient and economical oil (which Great Britain lacked). "The whole fortunes of our race and Empire would perish . . . if our naval supremacy were to be impaired," he confessed. And naval supremacy meant greater speed and efficiency through oil. "The use of oil made it possible in every type of vessel to have more gun-power and more speed for less size or less cost." The problem for him — and for Great Britain as it warily monitored the German buildup of its own naval power — was where to find the oil. Churchill had been the first to admit that "oil was not found in appreciable quantities in our islands. . . . To commit the Navy irrevocably to oil was indeed 'to take arms against a sea of troubles.'" Small wonder, then, that gaining control over oil supplies in Persia and Mesopotamia would become "a first-class British war aim."[46]

Given the emerging importance of oil as the main fuel of militaries — not just for the British, but for all European militaries (which followed suit and converted to oil) — big-power concerns over the fate of the Berlin-to-Baghdad railroad intensified as its construction pushed eastward toward Iraq and Persia.[47] The British, in particular, viewed it as a threat to their oil holdings in the Gulf (Iran). They calculated that Serbia was "the first line of defense of our eastern possessions. If she were . . . enticed into the Berlin-Baghdad system, then our vast . . . empire would soon have felt the cost of Germany's eastward thrust."[48]

On June 28, 1914, when the Berlin-to-Baghdad line was well under construction but still hundreds of kilometers short of its destination, a Serbian nationalist shot and killed Archduke Franz Ferdinand of Austria, heir to the Austro-Hungarian throne, and his wife. The fallout from that assassination sparked the beginning of World War I. Austria-Hungary, Germany, and the Ottoman Empire, among other nations, joined forces as the Central Powers against the Allied Powers, which included Britain, Russia, France, Serbia, and (eventually) the United States, as well as Arab allies that wished to break free from Ottoman rule. The subsequent Allied-Arab attacks (involving "Lawrence of Arabia") against the Turks in Palestine led to the British and French mandates, freeing the Levant for the Iraq Petroleum Company (IPC) pipelines and setting the stage for the Balfour Declaration of 1917 that promised a Jewish homeland in Palestine.

Germany's former ambassador to Great Britain, Prince Lichnowsky, would privately admit to friends during World War I that Germany's *Drang nach Osten* (Drive to the East) was its greatest blunder.[49] The push by Germany crystallized an alliance among the British, the Russians, and the French, all of whom were busily trying to stake out their own claims in

Mesopotamia, the land between two rivers. Within a year, it would become very clear that the Great Game was a driving force behind the Great War, that oil was a coveted prize, and that anyone who stood in the way would be brutally eliminated. Today, the Berlin-to-Baghdad railroad is finally being credited as a contributing cause to World War I.

Armenian Lives versus American Properties: The Great Dilemma

In my research into Turkey during this period, I was struck — indeed, amazed — over the important role of the American College for Girls in the conduct of US foreign policy before, during, and after World War I. It had never been discussed in my grandparents' home. Nor had the fate of the Armenians who lived in Turkey. I learned from the archives that my grandmother sewed clothes for the Armenian orphans who had survived the first wave of Turkish attacks against the Armenians in the 1890s. I did know that in 1947, after my father's death, my mother brought her Armenian maid, Mary Bedoian, back to the United States to help care for my siblings and me. My mother and my grandmother made contacts with the large Armenian community in the Boston suburb of Watertown by visiting Oriental rug stores. Their goal was to find an Armenian husband so that Mary could remain in the United States. She found her man and married him, and in gratitude she and her husband, Johnny Mekjian, invited our family every year to an "Arabic feast" featuring hummus, baba ghanoush, kibbe, and tabbouleh.

These fabulous feasts were my first introduction to Middle Eastern culture, and a big reason why I happily agreed to go to Beirut with my mother in 1963. Mother had dearly missed Beirut, and she was able to secure a job as a librarian at the American Community School, where I attended my last two years of high school. Those two years changed my life. I became deeply interested in US policy in the Middle East and discovered an array of books that presented an interpretation of the Middle East that was entirely different from anything I'd seen in the United States. My neighbor, a well-known Beirut publisher and bookstore owner named Paul Khayyat, told me a story of how a set of volumes on Arab culture and history that he had lovingly published with an American audience in mind never made it into the bookstores. "They were seized off the boat and dumped into the East River," he told me with great emotion. I could never confirm this, but his tale only reinforced in me a growing realization that the American people were not getting the full truth on this part of the world.

While in Beirut, my experience with Armenians was decidedly different from our family's joyous annual feasts with the Mekjian family. I often drove past a high cement wall concealing the interior of an Armenian refugee camp, except for the tops of corrugated tin roofs. Women dressed in white scarves and multicolored dresses appeared and disappeared through the camp's only gate, often carrying jugs of water on their heads. The stench coming from the camp was overpowering, a sign of appalling living conditions inside. I wondered then: How can this be? No one talked about it.

Years later, I would finally learn about the genocide of Armenians during World War I — an event, I would discover with horror, that would become one of the world's first examples of an oil-genocide connection.

The Horror

On June 28, 1914, the very day that Archduke Ferdinand was assassinated, the grand vizier of Turkey — the de facto prime minister of the sultan — had penned a diplomatic message promising an oil concession in Mesopotamia to the Turkish Petroleum Company (TPC). The TPC was largely foreign owned, with the British Anglo-Persian Group owning 50 percent of the company, the German-owned Deutsche Bank and Royal Dutch Shell each owning 22.5 percent, and an Armenian oilman and banker named Calouste Gulbenkian — who regularly talked with German railway engineers about the progress of the Berlin-to-Baghdad railroad — owning 5 percent. The outbreak of war left the grand vizier's pledge up in the air and put Anglo-German cooperation on hold.[50]

In October 1914, the head of the American College for Girls, Mary Mills Patrick, wrote the trustees about her faith in US Ambassador Morgenthau, who was "extremely wise and able and will probably succeed in protecting the college against undue influence."[51] She hoped that the Turks would stay out of the war, and if anyone could convince them to stay out, she was certain it would be the American ambassador. The Turks liked him, she wrote, and they appreciated the American educators who had opened their schools to the Turks. But she also knew that the Turks liked the Germans. "There are thousands of Germans in the country who are constantly stirring up the Turks in different ways," she wrote to Grace Dodge, the board of trustees president and an heir to the famous Phelps Dodge copper fortune. "German officers drill the troops, and German sailors man the fleet. . . . Their methods of mobilization have been very cruel."

When Turkey did join the war on the side of the Germans in November 1914, Patrick sent a worried note to trustee George Plimpton. "Our policy at present must be, I should think, as great a degree of obedience to the government as possible," she wrote. A year later she wrote Plimpton that the school's property, with its new buildings, had been saved on account of the helpful intercessions of Ambassador Morgenthau with the Turks. "If we save our buildings to the end of the war . . . we shall owe him a great debt of gratitude."[52]

There was, however, a problem keenly felt by the missionaries and Morgenthau: vicious Turkish attacks on Armenians. The Turks, humiliated over the rout of their troops from the Russian front in the winter of 1914–15, blamed their defeat on Armenians in Russia for having provoked the Turkish offensive. Within a month, Turkish authorities had ordered all Armenians in the army to be disarmed, disbanded, and forced into labor camps. Soon Turkish soldiers were leading Armenian soldiers on forced marches into remote areas. In the spring of 1915, the Ottoman government ordered the expulsion of all Armenians from their homes. Tens of thousands of men, women, and children were forced to walk in convoys toward the Syrian Desert. Thousands perished along the way in the Armenian death march.[53] The landing of British and French troops at Gallipoli on the Dardanelles in April 1915 only intensified Turkish hatred of Christian Armenians and Christian foreigners, unleashing a killing frenzy that sent the Europeans into a retreat (costing Winston Churchill the admiralty) and the Armenians running for cover. Death squads now roamed Turkey's eastern province of Anatolia, spreading a wave of terror whose aim was to cause the massive deportation of Armenians out of Turkey proper into Russia and Iran to the north and into what is now Iraq, Syria, Lebanon, and Palestine in the south.

Reports of massacres and deportations poured into the offices of Ambassador Morgenthau from missionaries, regional American consuls, and ordinary citizens from all over Turkey. In August 1915, an American diplomat stationed in the Syrian town of Aleppo informed Morgenthau that over the course of just more than two weeks, the "German Baghdad railway" had brought five thousand Armenians deported from Turkish cities, bringing the total number of Armenians arrived from the north to twenty thousand. "They all relate harrowing tales of hardship, abuse, robbery and atrocities committed en route," he reported.[54] By mid-August,

Morgenthau declared, the number of dead exceeded 500,000, with most of the Armenian provinces decimated and their populations exterminated.

During this summer, Morgenthau urged the Wilson administration to weigh in against the Turks. On September 3, he sent an urgent cable to the State Department reporting that the "destruction of the Armenian race in Turkey is progressing rapidly." His plea quickly circulated around his friends and associates connected with the American College for Girls. First, it reached James Barton, the foreign secretary of the American Board of Commissioners for Foreign Missions. Barton immediately contacted their mutual friend, Cleveland Dodge, whose sister Grace, recently deceased, had been replaced by Charles Crane as president of the American College for Girls. Within days, a meeting was held at Dodge's office. Out of it was born the Committee on Armenian Atrocities. Charles Crane served as treasurer, American College for Girls trustee and donor George Plimpton joined the committee as a board member. A media blitz followed, beginning with a lengthy press release by Charles Crane headlined "Entire Race, One of the Most Ancient and Honorable in History, Undergoing a Process of Complete Extermination in Turkey." After the first year of fund-raising, Crane's committee raised $290,000 from the Rockefeller Foundation, and by the end of 1917, some $610,00 into Armenian and Syrian relief.

As news of the atrocities spread and *Armenia, race extermination*, and *Terrible Turks* became household words, debate intensified over whether the United States should enter the war. Former president Teddy Roosevelt wrote an angry letter to the Committee on Armenian Atrocities in the fall of 1915, noting, "Mass meetings on behalf of the Armenians amount to nothing" if not followed by action. But it was not until April 1917 — some two years after the loss of a hundred American lives when a German U-boat sank the RMS *Lusitania*, and after nonstop news coverage of the Armenian massacres in the American press — that the US Congress declared war on Germany and Austria-Hungary.

Despite all the clamor over the Armenian genocide, Woodrow Wilson could not bring himself to declare war on Turkey. The high-level missionaries in Turkey, torn as they were, understood why.

Mary Mills Patrick, who would spend most of 1917 in New York fund-raising for the American College for Girls, admitted to Plimpton, the school's treasurer and trustee, that her "first consideration as long as the war lasts" continued to be "the protection of the Arnaoutkeuy property."[55]

That fall, she accepted Plimpton's invitation to take up quarters in his sumptuous Park Avenue apartment in New York. There she would share the benefit of her years of wisdom acquired at the helm of the college with President Wilson's inner circle: Charles Crane and Cleveland Dodge, along with former ambassador Morgenthau, who had resigned his position in disgust in 1916 over the Ottoman government's genocide of Armenians. James Barton had already written in his 1909 book, *Missionaries and Their Critics*, of "the superior knowledge necessarily possessed by the older missionaries." If American missionary property, he said, were to be "injured or destroyed without fear of retribution, it would at once be interpreted that our government is too weak to protect the property of its citizens, and all American property would be jeopardized." All four men, in their many conferences with the president, spoke of keeping the Turks at a stern — but not overly hostile — distance when war broke out. In February 1917, Barton prepared a statement for the State Department that carried the official blessings of Dodge, Morgenthau, and Crane. He gave five reasons why the United States should maintain harmonious relations with the Turks:

- The United States alone, among the world's great nations, harbored no designs on Ottoman territory.
- German demands on Turkey would become more vocal if Turkey lost "friendship with the United States."
- "Millions of dollars have gone from the United States to [help] Turkey," without "even the suggestion that Turkish sovereignty should thereby be weakened or that American national control should be increased."
- Constantinople needed the support of America's "great colleges and universities."
- After the peace, the United States would be in a better position than Germany to serve the Ottoman Empire, without imposing on the latter "conditions that will impair sovereignty."[56]

Nowhere did Barton and his backers mention a major underlying concern of US policy toward Turkey: getting a foothold in the oil of the Ottoman Empire.

During the postwar Paris Peace Conference in 1919, President Wilson tried to reassure Armenians that he cared about their plight by recommending a federated American mandate under the League of Nations over "Armenia." It would extend from the Eastern Mediterranean port of Mersin in the south through eastern Anatolia and the Caucuses, including the oil ports of Batum (today known as Batumi) and Baku on the Caspian Sea. He, like all Allied leaders, had expected that the communist regime in Russia would collapse after the 1917 revolution under the weight of assaults by Western-funded "White" armies on order to, as Churchill put it, "crush the infant in its crib." But they miscalculated. In April 1920, Bolshevik troops occupied Baku and then promptly nationalized the oil fields that had been contemplated in the proposed Armenian mandate. The United States then shifted gears, abandoning the Armenian cause, and successfully focused on gaining a foothold for two Standard Oil companies in Iraq's oil.

Mark Bristol, the US high commissioner to Turkey, never wavered on the subject of oil or the importance of maintaining friendly relations with the Turks.[57] Bristol urged his assistant, a young lawyer named Allen Dulles (the future CIA director), to try to pressure the American press to back off on its sympathetic coverage of the Armenians. Dulles replied, "Confidentially, the State Department is in a bind. Our task would be simple if the reports of the atrocities could be declared untrue or even exaggerated [as the Turks were alleging], but the evidence is, alas, irrefutable." Dulles admitted that "I've been kept busy trying to ward off congressional resolutions of sympathy for these groups."[58]

With the election of Republican Warren Harding as president in 1920, the betrayal of the Armenians seemed certain. Harding, a decidedly "pro-oil" president, had chosen former Standard Oil lawyer Charles Evans Hughes as his secretary of state. The State Department, in turn, told American oil companies to "go out and get it," using the nation's time-honored Open Door policy to force their way into the former Ottoman territories and effectively compete with the French and the British to gain access to the oil of the Middle East.*

---

* The Open Door policy, first advanced by the United States at the turn of the century (1900) to ensure it had equal access with other nations to the markets of China, was actively pursued by the United States after World War I to allow its corporations to have equal political and economic opportunities in the post-Ottoman Middle East, including American access to petroleum resources.

In 1923, the warring parties (excluding the United States) signed a peace treaty, the Treaty of Lausanne, that settled Turkey's borders. At the Turks' insistence, no mention was made of Armenia. The United States signed a similar commercial treaty with Turkey that guaranteed an open-door policy for US businesses, especially the oil business. A Turkish-Armenian attorney named Vahan Cardashian expressed his indignation, noting that "the Department of State became a concession-hunting agency for the Standard Oil Company."[59]

E. H. Bierstadt, author of *The Great Betrayal*, blasted High Commissioner Bristol and the State Department as tools of economic imperialism. The treaty, he said, "was signed in oil, and sealed with the blood of the . . . Armenians who were sacrificed to make the signings possible."[60]

Peter Balakian, a major chronicler of the Armenian genocide, notes in his book *The Burning Tigris* that Mark Bristol and Charles Evan Hughes "agreed that Turkey's treatment of its minorities was now less important than American business interests and the vast real estate holdings of the American missionaries."[61]

Having learned this, I had to ask myself: How did my grandmother come to terms with what must have been a terrible conflict in her life? Did she value the survival of the college she loved more than the Armenians whom she aided? What did she tell my father about the Armenians? Did she hope I would stumble on the scrapbooks that contained so many letters and photographs, some of which mentioned Armenians? I would never know. But one thing I *did* know from giving talks about World War I and by soliciting feedback from members of the audience is this: The unrivaled death and destruction from that supposed "war to end all wars" — including the Armenian genocide — were so horrific that the people, including vets, who survived the war did not wish to talk about it. The memories were just too painful, and in some cases, too shameful.

The Time between Two Wars

When the war ended, the former Ottoman Empire was served up on a platter at the Paris Peace Conference in early 1919 to see who would get the biggest "slice of the Turkey." Behind the scenes, all the major players in the Great Game for Oil sharpened their diplomatic knives and maneuvered against one another. The oilmen engaged through diplomats and secret agents, through proxies and puppets. They preferred to keep their names out of the sordid quest for power that was engulfing the peace talks and threatening to make a mockery of President Woodrow Wilson's assertion that the war was about "making the world safe for democracy."

It would take another eight years of intense wrangling over who would control the land bridge, or "rectangle," that connected the oil fields of Mesopotamia with the Mediterranean coastline of Syria and Palestine. Even though the United States was not party to final treaty negotiations with the Turks because it had never declared war on Turkey, it managed through some deft maneuvering to secure a 23.75 percent holding in the Turkish Petroleum Company, later to be known as the Iraq Petroleum Company. How this happened reads like an early primer of pipeline politics; see chapter 8 for details. Great Britain and France divided up the land bridge into French and British mandates, with the borders defined by the two branches of the IPC pipeline, one ending in French-controlled Syria and the other in British-controlled Palestine. The Arabs, promised independence during the war in return for allying with the British to rout out the Ottoman Turks, saw their dreams betrayed. The British took control of Iraq, Jordan, and Palestine and honored their 1917 promise to the Jews (the Balfour Declaration) by favoring a Jewish national home in Palestine. This, too, would have an oil dimension to it, as did the West's betrayal of the Jews two decades later, when, as we'll see, it failed to rescue Jews from the Holocaust in favor of protecting American oil interests in Saudi Arabia.

As for the Turks, they emerged from World War I with their far-flung empire in the Middle East wrested out from under them by the European powers. But their commitment to democratic and cultural reforms and modernization enhanced their prestige in the West. Writing about "The New Turkey (1927–1932)," former US ambassador to Turkey (1927–1932) Joseph Grew acknowledged that the Turks had to face up to a pressing reality in a "short space of time": that achieving parity with European nations required their having to "adopt western civilization and western culture." He was impressed with what he found. "This amazing revolution," he wrote, "is due to a keen and forceful nationalistic spirit . . . due in greatest measure to Mustafa Kemal," the first president of the Turkish republic, who "set about to cure the 'Sick man of Europe' and to make him permanently well and strong."[62] Mustafa Kemal Ataturk made Ankara the new capital and seat of government, signifying a break from the old Ottoman Empire. He abolished the caliphate (which had governed Turkey by applying the sacred laws of Islam), Latinized their alphabet, and emancipated their women. Turkey would go on to be a key defender of NATO and acted as a crucial buffer state between Russia and the Middle East.

In the immediate postwar years, some notable Turkish women who had graduated from the American College for Girls played a major role in instigating the reforms. Among them was Halide Edib, the first Turkish woman to receive a bachelor of arts degree and the college's most famous graduate, who worked with her husband, Adnan Adivar, to help organize the new republic.

The Turks had lost the war by virtue of siding with the Germans, a bitter lesson. But the friendship they had forged with the Americans and the American missionaries proved a wise decision, at least for the near future. Their genocidal attacks on the Armenians would always be a stain on their image in the eyes of world public opinion. And by the time Recep Tayyip Erdoğan became president of Turkey, Turkey's place in the world would undergo another radical transformation, away from being a secular republic, with a modicum of democracy, to an increasingly authoritarian regime determined to play another winning hand in the Great Game.

Erdoğan Switches Sides

If ever there were an example of how Western meddling in the Middle East — or even perceived Western meddling — can go awry, it would be found in Turkey under the rule of Recep Tayyip Erdoğan. Turkey's burly prime minister for eleven years before becoming president in 2014, Erdoğan allowed American forces to use Turkey as a staging area during the 2003 invasion of Iraq. Not long before, Turkey had become a candidate for full membership in the European Union, something that would be granted only if Erdoğan carried out certain democratic reforms. He seemed amenable, especially since Turkey was fast becoming a major transit hub for Western gas pipeline schemes after the successful completion of the BTC pipeline to Turkey. But when he stood with Vladimir Putin for the inauguration of the Russian-Turkish Blue Stream Pipeline in 2005 — just months after the Western-backed BTC pipeline to Turkey was completed — the United States watched nervously. Not only had Putin suggested at the ceremony that another pipeline beneath the Black Sea to Turkey might be in the works, but "hawks in the Turkish military were said to favor strengthened ties with Russia."[63]

Then, in 2013, what started as a small sit-in to protect an Istanbul green space from development morphed into protests against Erodğan's increased authoritarianism, triggering an overreaction (much as in Syria) by government forces. Erdoğan accused the United States and Israel of plotting against him, and in the ensuing three years his paranoia grew. When he foiled a coup attempt in 2016, he accused a former ally living in the United States — exiled cleric Fethullah Gulen — of orchestrating it and began cracking down, arresting 149 generals, more than 200 journalists, and hundreds of academics.

Between 2013 and 2016, Erdoğan drew closer to Russia, despite tense past relations. As the Brookings Institution explained it, "Erdogan and Putin see the West's instruments of democracy promotion as targeted directly at their own regimes." Just as Erdoğan considered the United States to be harboring Gulen, "Putin sees American support for civil society actors and democracy activists in Russia and in surrounding countries as pitted against his power. As democratic leaders in the West grow increasingly wary of Erdoğan's authoritarian order and Putin's brazen acts of aggression, the two leaders have cozied up to one another."[64]

The fruits of this new alignment would shock the very core of NATO: the creation of a mammoth new Russian-Turkish pipeline project called TurkStream — and a military deal to protect it.

As Offshore Technology, a news and market analysis company, reported in February 2016, "The Black Sea holds vast volumes of oil and gas, much of it in deep water."[65] The Black Sea is bordered by Romania, Bulgaria, Turkey, Ukraine, Georgia, and Russia, and all of these countries have commenced exploration in its waters. Exxon, Shell, and Total are among the Western oil majors currently involved. But Russia has the edge on pipeline development.

The TurkStream Pipeline, beginning on the Russian side of the Black Sea, and thanks to advances in underwater pipeline technology, carries Russian gas beneath the Black Sea, coming ashore in the Thrace region of Turkey. The Russian energy giant Gazprom completed construction of the pipeline in March 2019. Running more than 900 kilometers and delivering up to 15.75 billion cubic meters of gas, it should amply meet Turkey's growing energy needs and serve additional markets in eastern Europe. Putin announced the project during a state visit to Turkey in 2014, but it was put on hold after Turkey shot down a Russian airplane over Syria. The two countries soon reconciled — for obvious reasons — and Putin and

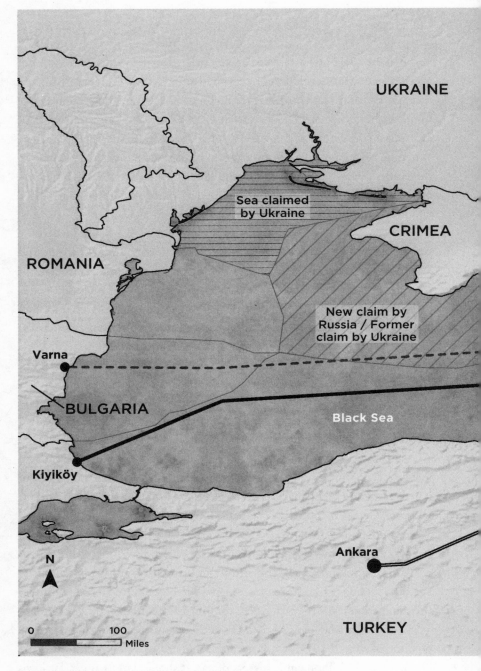

The Blue Stream and TurkStream Pipelines Bypass Ukraine
The Black Sea is known to hold enormous volumes of oil and gas, which puts the recent conflicts in Crimea and Ukraine in a new light. Russia's annexation of Crimea in 2014 afforded Russia access to vast underwater gas reserves in the Black Sea previously claimed by Ukraine. For example, the shaded area below Crimea and

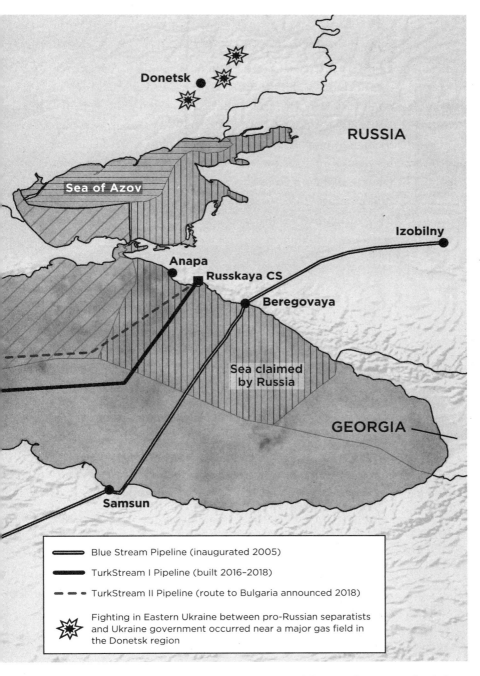

Donetsk

RUSSIA

Sea of Azov

Izobilny

Anapa

Russkaya CS

Beregovaya

Sea claimed
by Russia

GEORGIA

Samsun

━━━━ Blue Stream Pipeline (inaugurated 2005)

━━━━ TurkStream I Pipeline (built 2016–2018)

- - - TurkStream II Pipeline (route to Bulgaria announced 2018)

✺ Fighting in Eastern Ukraine between pro-Russian separatists
and Ukraine government occurred near a major gas field in
the Donetsk region

surrounding it on all sides (including a portion of the Sea of Azov) used to belong
to Ukraine and is now held by Russia. In 2014 Vladimir Putin announced the Turk-
Stream Pipeline to Turkey, making it the second Russian-Turkish pipeline under
the Black Sea. (The first was the Blue Stream.) In November 2018 Putin announced
TurkStream II, and Ukraine and the United States announced plans to stop it.[66]

Erdoğan signed the TurkStream agreement in October 2016. A year later, the two leaders concluded a military pact in which Russia would sell to Turkey a $2.5 billion state-of-the-art missile defense system.

Suffice it to say, this project did not fit into the West's long-range plan to break the Russian monopoly over natural gas to Europe. As I contemplated what this all meant for the future of US foreign policy in the region, I couldn't help but think how Kim Philby, Soviet spy par excellence, would be clapping from his grave. I also concluded that he was a key to unraveling how, in 1947, Turkey fit into my father's death. First, though, I had to unravel the mystery of Kim Philby.

CHAPTER SEVEN

Mare Nostrum

The Militarization of the Eastern Mediterranean

"The case name is *Dennett v. the CIA*," I hurriedly told the information desk on the ground floor. A man next to me muttered, "Wow, you're suing the CIA?" After finding out which of forty-four courtrooms I was headed to, I took the elevator to the fourth floor of Manhattan's towering, twenty-seven-story Daniel P. Moynihan federal courthouse. On this October morning in 2007, I was focused only on the task before me: convincing a panel of three judges that my case against the CIA was important, not only for me personally, but also for an American public that deserved to know the truth about a secretized history of the Middle East.

Just as I had predicted back in September 2001, the CIA had done everything it could to impede and delay my Freedom of Information Act requests, even though the records I sought predated the Eisenhower administration and most of the people named in them were dead. After four years, I took the next step and reluctantly sued the CIA, having been advised that the CIA would take me seriously when the matter was in federal court. That 2005 FOIA lawsuit had yielded some more documents and removed some redactions but ceded nothing on the last three months of my father's life. Why? I wondered. What was so sensitive that documents over seven decades old could not be turned over?

There was one document in my father's records that continued to intrigue and annoy me. It was a cover sheet to a document titled "British Intelligence" that headquarters had sent to my father in December 1946. Despite all sorts of cross-reference notations on the cover sheet, I could not find the document that was supposed to be attached to it. Archivists at the National Archives were equally perplexed. I had to wonder: Was Washington giving Carat some information about Kim Philby, who had just been posted to Turkey as Britain's head of counterintelligence for the Middle East?

When a federal judge in Vermont dismissed my case on a technicality, I appealed it to the US Court of Appeals in the Second Circuit (New York), where I now was ready to present my case in oral arguments.

The elevators opened to a pair of heavy doors, which in turn revealed a most unexpected scene. There, filling row after row in a huge, oak-lined courtroom, more than a hundred other people sat, waiting. They were all nicely dressed for the occasion, of all ages and ethnicities, some sitting alone, others clustered in groups of two or three, apparently all there for the same reason I was: to get their allotted *five minutes* to present their case before the three black-robed, grim-faced judges presiding over this ornate courtroom.

I was a practicing lawyer by then, but the personal significance of the outcome made me so nervous that when I stepped up to the podium, I still clutched my pocketbook around my left arm, a little detail picked up by a *Village Voice* reporter who happened to be sitting in the same room. Graham Rayman, an experienced court reporter, was there on another assignment, but when he heard "CIA," he turned his attention to my presentation. Later, in a *Voice* article on my case, he described the "prim Vermont woman uneasily holding her handbag [as she] stood up in federal court in Manhattan to try yet again to pry the . . . secrets about her father's death from the U.S. government."[1]

Prim? *Me?* Did I really seem so uptight? He was likely detecting my sheer terror of screwing up. As I would soon learn, a reporter for the *New York Times* was also sitting in the courtroom, and his ears also pricked up upon hearing I was appealing a case against the CIA.

"I am appealing to you to consider my personal story as part of the relevant circumstances of this case," I told the three judges. "I want to know why that plane went down the way it did, taking my father's life and the lives of five other Americans loyally serving their country. The CIA is holding back documents. I want this court to examine the documents and decide whether they are a threat to national security or of sufficient public interest and historical value to be released."

When a bell indicated that my five minutes were up, I made one last appeal for the release of documents that could shed light on my father's last three months — documents, I added, that would also contain vital information for historians and the American public, who had been sorely deprived of the full history of how this country became fatefully involved in the Middle East. Then, as the judges shuffled papers and prepared to move on to the next case, I turned around and walked out of the courtroom. I wondered: Was this an act of futility?

Up to this point, the CIA had refused to turn over any substantive documents covering the crucial period from January 1 to March 20, 1947 (the day of the plane crash), which of course were the most important to me. So I had decided to devise a list of my father's purported enemies in late 1946 and early 1947, picking up clues from his earlier reports and consulting a multitude of books on espionage during World War II. That's when I began to zero in on Kim Philby, who had become an acute embarrassment to both the British and the Americans for having moled his way into the highest levels of British intelligence on behalf of the Soviets, and in the process had sent many Western operatives to their deaths.

The Philby Enigma

Philby had been assigned to Istanbul in December 1946 as head of British counterintelligence for the entire Middle East, and that made him my father's exact counterpart. As the top Allied intelligence officers in the field, they were surely aware of each other's existence, if not sharing highly sensitive information about a highly sensitive part of the world. Yet I had found no evidence in the heavily redacted records the CIA turned over to me that Philby even existed. The omission of someone that important — and so controversial — was astonishing.

Philby's posting to Turkey came at a critical time, about six weeks before President Truman announced his famed Truman Doctrine on March 12, 1947, to contain Soviet expansion. Though Truman pledged resistance to communist expansion everywhere in the world, his real concern was Soviet expansion in the oil-rich Middle East. (Significantly, mention of oil was deliberately deleted from his address before Congress at the suggestion of Under Secretary of State Dean Acheson.)[2] Explained one of Philby's biographers, *Treason in the Blood* author Anthony Cave Brown: "If Greece should fall to the communist element in the civil war that racked the country, the effect on Turkey, its neighbor, would be immediate and serious. Free institutions everywhere would collapse, including in the Middle East, with its oil so needed by Western industry. Congress allocated $225 million in military assistance to the Graeco-Turkish armed forces, and . . . Turkey became a hot Russian intelligence target. Thus vanished Kim's prospects of a paid holiday beside the Bosphorus at the expense of the British government."[3]

Kim had landed in a country swarming with spies. As a double agent, he had to be nimble, supplying important information to the British to convince them of his worth, while providing information on both the British and the Americans to his Soviet handlers to prove his true allegiances. What, I had to wonder, might he have revealed to the Soviets — and the British — about my father's activities in the Eastern Mediterranean and the Middle East?

Although I had found no proof that they ever met or were aware of each other's existence, their missions, if not their paths, surely must have crossed. By the time Philby arrived in Istanbul, Carat was well aware that Beirut was a center for financing Soviet penetration of the Middle East and had been focusing most of his efforts on tracking Soviet activities in the Levant and northern Syria near the border of Turkey. After all, some port on the Eastern Mediterranean was to be the terminal point for the biggest pipeline ever built, the Trans-Arabian Pipeline. Like my father, Philby well knew its importance. In January 1947, an article in *Izvestia* noted that "American oil concessions in Arabia and the Trans-Arabian Pipeline appear as enterprises whose position goes far beyond the limits of economics. They may be called auxiliary enterprises of the American system of world-wide military bases."[4]

That same month, while Americans were discussing with the Saudis setting up a military base in eastern Arabia near the Dhahran headquarters of the Arabian American Oil Company (Aramco), Kim Philby was paying a visit to his father, Harry St. John Philby, in the Saudi capital of Riyadh. The elder Philby had been a longtime advisor to Ibn Saud, Saudi Arabia's founder and first monarch, and in that position had passed on intelligence to both the British and the Americans. He also wrote letters to his wife and Kim every week, starting in 1945 and continuing on for eight years. In one letter, he wrote: "The Americans are out to dominate everything here and at present they are having it all their own way."[5] From this (and based on the father and son's subsequent travel plans), we can assume that Kim Philby learned from his father that the Americans wanted to beef up their military presence in Saudi Arabia, including western Saudi Arabia near the major Red Sea port of Jidda.[6] During Kim's January 1947 visit to Saudi Arabia, he and his father boarded a Saudi royal aircraft and flew to the British military base in Taif, above Jidda — the same place my father would visit two months later. In Taif, Kim spent thirty-six hours with the head of the British military mission. Then he returned to Istanbul, soon to grapple with Truman's announcement of his doctrine.[7]

What transpired during Kim's visit to Taif in January and Dennett's visit in March was not known to me when I sued the CIA, but both visits fell within the time frame of the last three months of my father's life. I did know from my father's last letter to my mother, dated March 10, that he had "hooked a ride" on a British RAF (Royal Air Force) plane to visit Taif, "Mecca's summer resort, 5000 feet up in the mountains." The following day, he added, the US military attaché, Colonel McNown, was due to land in Jidda and "is then going on to Asmara, Eritrea and then to Ethiopia (Addis Ababa)." If McNown had room on his plane, he wrote, he hoped to go with him to Ethiopia. As it turned out McNown got off the plane in Jidda, so his seat became available for Dennett.

The Accident Report

On one of my many visits to the National Archives, I consulted with an archivist specializing in army aircraft matters during World War II. I asked how I might find the accident report on my father's plane crash. He knew just where to look, and within thirty minutes, I was sitting at a desk in front of a large folder, about three inches thick, devoted entirely to the crash of the C-47 army aircraft plane in Ethiopia. I carefully surveyed its contents and then zeroed in on the photographs of the plane wreckage. To my relief, there were no close-up pictures of bodies. They had been removed from the wreckage by Ethiopian locals before the investigators arrived. One photo showed them transporting large duffel bags (with bodies presumably inside) on muleback to the nearby town of Dessie.

McNown, who immediately left Jidda for Ethiopia on news of the crash, had been assigned to be the chief accident investigator, and he was hard-pressed to come up with a definitive explanation for the crash in his report. McNown concluded that pilot error could have been the cause, though the pilot knew the route well and was highly trusted. Wrote McNown: "It is extremely difficult to believe a pilot of Lt. Smith's ability and experience could have had an accident of this type."* Weather reports indicated clear skies upon takeoff, but in any event, McNown wrote, they "cannot be trusted." Rainy weather, he added, "in this area is very rarely a flying hazard." He noted that because the passengers did not have their seat belts fastened, nor did any of them get into parachutes, "it is believed the pilot did not think he was in any trouble." McNown held out the possibility of sabotage and vowed further investigation.

I also found detailed radio communications between the pilot and the air towers of Asmara, Eritrea (where the Americans had spent the night before proceeding to Ethiopia the next day), Addis Ababa, and Jidda, as well as weather reports and summaries of plane flights in the past month by the military attaché. A preliminary report had been written by a Swedish air force officer who was in Ethiopia training Haile Selassie's air force at the time and had proceeded on the emperor's orders to the crash site. He was the first official investigator to arrive on the scene. Colonel McNown arrived several days later. Both wrote reports, though McNown's was the more substantive.

From the accident reports I was able to determine the C-47's flight pattern after it left Cairo. Flight 3804 arrived in Jidda on March 19, nine days after my father's March 10 letter and eight days after he had anticipated its arrival. I also learned Colonel McNown had decided to stay in Jidda "for the purpose of meeting Prince Mansour, Minister of War for the Saudi-Arabian government to discuss military equipment given to that Government and to discuss the possibility of future visits of the U.S. Military Attaché personnel to the Saudi Arabian Military headquarters at Taif."[8] McNown did, however, allow Dennett to get on the plane to join another civilian, Cairo-based US petroleum attaché Donald Sullivan, on the flight to Asmara and Addis Ababa.[9]

With this information, I wondered why McNown's flight had been delayed, and why he got off the plane at the last minute. His change of

---

* I was able to track down the pilot's surviving relatives, who told me they had always been haunted by the understanding that Smith had been the cause of the crash. I was sad to hear that, and I assured them that the chief investigator, who knew Lieutenant Smith and his excellent flying record, had found it hard to believe that pilot error was the cause.

plans was so last minute, in fact, that a cable from the Asmara airport to Addis Ababa on March 20 (the day of the crash) states that "USATC C47 DEPARTED FOR ADDIS 06:15. ETA: 0900. US MILITARY ATTACHE ON BOARD." Perhaps the passenger list was not revised in time to delete McNown's name. Perhaps there was not enough room on the plane for Dennett, so McNown gave up his seat and stayed in Jidda. Perhaps the British officer who had accompanied McNown from Cairo to Jidda, Captain M. F. Cubitt of the Royal British Army, convinced McNown to stay longer in Jidda.

Having copied and combed through the report many times, at one point I decided to scrutinize it through a different lens: Did it harbor any clues about what Philby might have known about McNown's trip? My father's papers made it clear that he knew that foreign powers were on to him, and I wanted to know who they were. Philby's name had come up in connection with the airplane crash in 1943 that had killed Polish premier Wladyslaw Sikorski shortly after he took off from Gibraltar en route to the Middle East. At the time, Philby was in charge of Britain's Iberian desk (while working simultaneously for the Soviets). Before then, in 1941, he had worked as a trainer in Special Operations Executive, a British organization that specialized in sabotage. More than seventy years after Sikorski's death, the plane crash remains under investigation. Among those suspected of having been involved in sabotaging his plane are the Soviets and the British.* Both the former Polish ambassador to Washington, Romuald Spasowski, and Sikorski's biographer, Polish general Marian Kukiel, believed that Philby had a hand in the alleged assassination, at the very least by providing the Soviets a detailed itinerary of Sikorski's journey.

I wondered whether Philby could have known about McNown's travel plans from the British captain who had accompanied him on the plane to Jidda, Captain Cubitt. Or perhaps he had learned about it even earlier,

---

* The Soviets have been accused of Sikorski's death because Sikorski questioned their explanations that the Germans were responsible for the massacre of 12,000 Polish officers at Russia's Katyn Forest in 1943. (The Soviets finally admitted responsibility in 1990.) The British have been implicated on the basis that Churchill was angry at Sikorski for straining British-Soviet relations in 1943. A memorial plaque to Sikorski at Gibraltar notes that "the cause of this mysterious accident has never been ascertained; a fact which has given rise to many speculations, doubts and rumours."

when Philby and his father stayed in Taif in January. The monthly operations report indicated that the military attaché made several trips to Saudi Arabia between January and March.* Or could Philby have learned about the flight from Carat, or from the British, as Carat spent those nine days in Jidda and Taif waiting for McNown to arrive?

Another mystery: Why was no overdue action taken immediately when the plane did not arrive as scheduled? And why was there no follow-up report on any subsequent investigations, since sabotage was not ruled out? These were just some of the questions I wanted answered when I appealed my case before the Second Circuit Court of Appeals in New York City.

To my surprise, the *Village Voice* and *New York Times* journalists who had sat in the room and heard my arguments came rushing after me. They wanted to know more. They sensed that I did not consider my father's death an accident, and they were curious why the CIA would not turn over documents over half a century old. They knew, as journalists, how hard it was to break through the wall of secrecy that the CIA had put around everything concerning the Middle East since the attacks of 9/11. They wondered whether the CIA had something to hide, and whether the lower court had killed my chances for a successful appeal on a technicality.[10] In short, they suspected there was more to the story. And they were right.

They asked for interviews. Initially, I hesitated. If I talked to them, how much should I reveal? Would I hurt my chances on appeal? How would the CIA react? What would the judges think? This was, after all, the administration of George W. Bush, which put such a premium on protecting information for the sake of national security. Hadn't the lower court judge accepted the CIA's zealous claim that these documents, despite being so many decades old, had to be protected for this reason?

In the end, responding to my own instincts not as a lawyer but as a journalist, I took a calculated risk — out of respect for the reporters, the

---

* Official logs of McNown, the military attaché, indicate that he made several visits to both Saudi Arabia and Ethiopia. On January 30, 1947 (following the Saudi trip), he traveled to Ethiopia, presumably to get accredited as a military attaché; on February 6, he left again for Ethiopia. On February 17, he was off to Tripoli (Libya) and Turkey, after having been in "Naples, Rome, Bahrain, Saudi Arabia, Yemen, Jidda, Addis Ababa, Kartoum, Asmara, Eritrea." On February 28, he was off again to Jidda. His final trip was on March 19, 1947.

public, and the Freedom of Information Act, whose very intent is to curb government secrecy and encourage transparency. I was worried about the secretizing of our history in the Middle East. And, above all, I wanted to get the word out that whatever accounted for my father's death by plane crash in 1947, this much I knew: He and the other five Americans on that plane were victims of the Great Game for Oil, and that Great Game has continued right on up to the twenty-first century, America's wars in Iraq and Afghanistan, and the deep unrest in Syria and elsewhere. When I sat down with Alan Feuer of the *New York Times* in a Manhattan café, it was clear that he understood that the story had dimensions beyond a daughter's David-versus-Goliath search for her father. It was, he commented, indeed that, but also "a hidden history of the Middle East conflict."

A lot happened after my court appearance — some bad, some good. The appeals court rejected my appeal to keep the case going, as did the US Supreme Court when I took the case to them. But the two reporters had given my story some credibility, and months after their stories came out, the CIA did something quite unexpected, something that amazes me to this day: It paid tribute to my father, if not on its Memorial Wall at CIA headquarters in Langley, Virginia, at least on its website, calling Daniel C. Dennett the "CIA's forgotten first star." Wrote CIA historian Nicholas Dujmovic about my father:

> *Contemporary scholars of the Mideast considered him unusually insightful, even brilliant. . . . Because Dennett died before CIA legally came into being, his case was automatically disallowed in early 1974 when CIA's Honor and Merit Board considered death cases to be represented by the first stars to be carved onto the Memorial Wall. Although he had been an OSS officer, he died well after World War II ended. Daniel Dennett is represented neither on the OSS memorial on one side of the OHB lobby nor on the CIA Memorial Wall on the other — as a CIG officer he almost literally falls in between, and he has fallen therefore from institutional memory. . . . There is a compelling argument that this highly praised and deeply respected US intelligence officer should be considered CIA's forgotten first star and should be commemorated on CIA's Memorial Wall. . . . Certainly the Agency's leadership considered that CIA was simply a continuation of CIG.*[11]

I vowed that the day would come when my siblings would join me at the CIA's headquarters in Langley, Virginia, to stand before the Memorial Wall while Daniel Dennett, the Forgotten First Star, became recognized as such and appropriately commemorated.

Meanwhile, I contented myself with doing more archival research and giving talks at colleges and community gatherings about pipeline politics and how they related to the wars in Afghanistan and Iraq. I had not yet realized that the Great Game for Oil was becoming militarized along the *entire coast* of the Eastern Mediterranean. Nor had I understood that this militarization began in March 1947 with President Truman's opening salvo of the Cold War, the Truman Doctrine. The clues had been staring at me from the printed pages of Anthony Cave Brown's *Treason in the Blood*, which said that Truman believed the Soviets wanted to break up the British Empire "starting with a bid to dominate the eastern Mediterranean" and then to "transform the Mediterranean from a British into a Russian lake."[12]

Yet because the "Eastern Mediterranean" seldom appeared in press accounts during the second half of the twentieth century, it effectively slipped into obscurity as a subject matter of geopolitical concern.

But that would change. Four years after my court appearance, I would come face-to-face with the Eastern Mediterranean.

Lebanon Beckons

In March 2011, when the Arab Spring was spreading across the Middle East, I got a surprising invitation by email.

"Would you like to come to Beirut in late April and join us for about a week?"

I hit "reply" without thinking. "YES YES YES!"

The sender was my brother, Dan, who was teaching a graduate philosophy course on Darwinian evolution during the spring semester at the American University of Beirut. He had been sending photographs and descriptions of Beirut, and now suddenly and unexpectedly came this invitation to me and my sister, Cynthia, to join him and his wife in Beirut some 5,000 miles away.

Beirut was my birthplace, something like a second home to me. A place where I had come of age, learned about politics, and became a journalist.

I would never turn down an invitation to Beirut.

Or would I?

It took a day or two for the exhilaration to wear off and some trepidation to sink in. The Middle East was roiling with revolts as the Arab Spring spread from one country to the next: first Tunisia, then Egypt, then Libya, Yemen, and Syria. Would Lebanon be next, and did I want to be there when it did? Lebanon was a fierce player in the Middle East during certain moments of crisis, "attracting an international attention disproportionate to its size," as veteran journalist David Hirst wrote in his latest book, *Beware of Small States.*

I did not relish a repeat of the violence I had witnessed in Lebanon thirty years ago, just before full-scale civil war broke out. After being shot at, I had spent days hunkered down in my apartment listening to bursts of shrapnel and gunfire all around me. After that experience, I could never again enjoy the big bangs that accompanied Fourth of July fireworks back home.

The US State Department had issued an advisory warning Americans not to travel to Syria. No such advisory had been issued for Lebanon, but on March 24, seven Estonian tourists had been kidnapped by unknown forces in Lebanon's Bekaa Valley, prompting the Beirut *Daily Star* to report that the kidnapping triggered old fears — dating back to the civil war in the 1980s when nearly 100 foreigners, mostly Americans, were held hostage by militant factions — causing mounting concerns that Lebanon would again lapse into a state of lawlessness.[13]

Whatever fears I held were trumped by something that would place all three Dennett siblings in Beirut in late April 2011: the need to honor the memory of our father. We all sensed that this reunion might become our first collectively conscious search for meaning in his death, and its relevance to today's current events, especially since we knew him to be a true (if quite naïve) believer in bringing democracy to the Middle East. It was this same yearning that had ignited the Arab Spring.

Mare Nostrum: NATO-izing the Eastern Mediterranean

Ten minutes before touching down into Lebanon, I had an epiphany. I'd flown over the Mediterranean before, as a high school student during the mid-1960s and later as a journalist in the mid-1970s, but this time I was experiencing it as a different person, someone who had spent hours and hours poring over maps of the Middle East while searching for clues to my father's death. Looking out the window this time, I could see nothing but a vast stretch of blue. The Mediterranean. Its sheer size overwhelmed me.

Until this day, I had been studying *the lands* encompassing Israel, Palestine, Lebanon, and Syria. They all bordered on the "Eastern Mediterranean." The French colonialists called the entire region the Levant, French for "rising," as in the sun rising in the East. I had been trying to look at this region as oil company executives did in my father's time — as a prime piece of real estate serving as a strategic terminal point for three pipelines, the two IPC pipelines carrying oil from Iraq and TAPLINE carrying oil from Saudi Arabia.

Now, flying above, I was graced with a new vantage point. From this time on, I began to look at the entire Mediterranean, not just the eastern end of it. I was aware that oil had been found off the coast of Israel, though the American press had been pretty much silent on the subject. And during the flight I had read an article, "The Libyan War and the Control of the Mediterranean," explaining that control over the Mediterranean had been the unfulfilled dream of empires for thousands of years. It was the only sea bordered by three continents: Europe, Asia (including the Middle East), and Africa. The Romans had coveted it as *mare nostrum*, "our sea," a desire subsequently shared by the Ottoman Turks, the British, the French, the Russians, and the Americans. Now, according to this article, the leaders of the European Union were seriously toying with the idea of NATO-izing the entire Mediterranean, turning it into the new *mare nostrum* of the twenty-first century.[14]

There was only one problem: Muammar Gaddafi. He wouldn't buy in, claiming the scheme would divide Africa and the Arab world. "We shall have another Roman empire and imperialist design," he was quoted in Britain's *Daily Telegraph* on July 10, 2008. "There are imperialist maps and designs that we have already rolled up. We should not have them again."[15]

I took out my own map, one that had appeared in an April 2011 article in the *Wall Street Journal* titled "As Arab Spring Turns Violent, Democracy Advocates Face Big Challenges." Sure enough, I noticed that four of the five countries in revolt — Tunisia, Libya, Egypt, and Syria — all bordered on the Mediterranean. Libya, the only major oil exporter among them, had come under attack by NATO warplanes. Was this a coincidence, or was Gaddafi simply more deserving of being pummeled with bombs? This got me thinking about Gaddafi.

When I was a novice journalist in Lebanon, many Arabs revered the dashing young colonel as a revolutionary, a genuine people's hero who had overthrown a corrupt monarchy and vowed to rid the Middle East of imperialist schemes. He knew — and was even now still stating with vehemence — that oil was at the *core* of the West's imperial designs. Not democracy. Not charity. Not education or "nation building." Oil. But oil had severely corrupted him, as it had corrupted Saddam Hussein of Iraq and most of the old dictators in the region. These strongmen had served a strategic purpose for almost half a century: They enforced stability so the oil would flow unhampered to Europe and the United States. Now, in the wake of a global recession, millions of educated yet jobless young people in the cities of Egypt, Tunisia, Libya, and Syria yearned for a better life, for meaningful employment *and* democratic reform.

The protests in Libya had begun in February 2011, two months before my trip to Lebanon. Soon Gaddafi was charged with sending in foreign mercenaries to terrorize the Libyan protesters and with ordering his air force to fire on them from the air.[16] In March, NATO forces intervened under the aegis of UN Security Council Resolution 1973 in order to protect civilians under attack from the Gaddafi government. Shortly after the campaign began, missiles launched by a British destroyer in the Mediterranean hit a compound close to Gaddafi's residence, barely missing him but raising questions about whether he was the target of the attack and whether the real mission was regime change. President Obama insisted that the purpose of the mission was humanitarian and that "broadening our mission into regime change would be a mistake."[17]

On April 29, three days after the Beirut *Daily Star* had reported on Syrian troops firing on protesters in the Syrian town of Daraa, the US ambassador to the UN, Susan Rice, accused Gaddafi forces of distributing Viagra to his troops as part of a campaign to rape women.[18] (She also assailed the Assad regime for "not listening to his own people" and "blaming outsiders" for the violence in Syria.)

Hearing the Viagra rape story, I couldn't help but recall the (false) charges made during the first Iraq War, under the administration of George H. W. Bush, that Iraqi soldiers had dragged Kuwaiti babies from their incubators, killing them all. This NATO intervention didn't smell right, and within months, my concerns would be vindicated as reporters began to question the rape stories and other pretexts for "humanitarian intervention."[19] But as usual, it would take another five years before the full story was revealed — in Secretary of State Hillary Clinton's emails, compliments of a FOIA request to the US State Department and WikiLeaks.*

Clinton's emails spared me from having to "follow the money" to get to the bottom of the war in Libya. (Back in the 1980s, it had taken Jerry and me over a decade of following the money to figure out what was really going on in the Amazon.) In an email "for Hillary from Sid," dated April 2, 2011, journalist and long-term Clinton confidant Sidney Blumenthal explained France's concern about "Gaddafi's gold." The Gaddafi government, he explained, "holds 143 tons of gold, and a similar amount in silver. This gold "was accumulated prior to the current rebellion and was intended to be used to establish a pan-African currency based on the Libyan golden Dinar. This plan was designed to provide the Francophone African countries with an alternative to the French franc." The gold and silver were "valued at more than $7 billion" and became "one of the factors that influenced President Nicolas Sarkozy's decision to commit France to the attack on Libya." Among Sarkozy's goals was "to gain a greater share of Libya's oil production," to "increase French influence in North Africa," and to "provide the French military with an opportunity to reassert its position in the world."[20]

So the French, who had never gotten over the loss of their colonies in Africa and the Levant, were at it again!

More in-flight googling helped me put pieces of my earlier research into perspective, revealing that the United States clearly had its own set of interests in the Libyan intervention — namely, increasing its control of Africa and the continent's resources. To this end, it had set up the African Command (AFRICOM) in 2008, blandly describing its mission as "assisting African

---

* In January 2016, the *Foreign Policy Journal* published an online article with links to some of Hillary Clinton's emails with her advisor, Sid Blumenthal. They were a shocking refutation of all the claims that the NATO intervention was for humanitarian reasons, revealing "admissions of rebel war crimes, special ops trainers inside Libya from nearly the start of protests, Al Qaeda embedded in the U.S. backed opposition, Western nations jockeying for access to Libyan oil, the nefarious origins of the absurd Viagra mass rape claim, and concern over Gaddafi's gold and silver reserves threatening European currency." See Brad Hoff, "Hillary Emails Reveal True Motive for Libya Intervention," *Foreign Policy Journal*, January 6, 2016, https://www.foreignpolicyjournal.com/2016/01/06/new-hillary-emails-reveal-true-motive-for-libya-intervention/.

Emails linked to in the article include a March 27, 2011, email from Blumenthal to Clinton "re: Rumor, Q's rape policy" and an April 2, 2011, email from Sidney to Hillary re: "France's client & Qaddafi's gold."

states and regional organizations to strengthen their defense capabilities."[21] The Chinese, in contrast, who have also been getting heavily involved in Africa, described AFRICOM's role as one that "facilitates the United States advancing on the African continent, taking control of the Eurasian continent and proceeding to take the helm of the entire globe."[22]

As I returned to reading the article on Libya's war and the battle for the Mediterranean, it became clear to me that Africa, a major continent bordering the Mediterranean, was quickly emerging as another new arena for the Great Game, with China seen as the primary foe to the United States, much as Russia was viewed as the United States' main rival in the Middle East following World War II.

I felt a twinge of uneasiness as my plane approached Beirut for a landing. The sea below me looked deceptively calm. I knew that less than 100 miles away, to the east in Syria or to the south in Israel, violence was threatening to spill over into Lebanon.

Beirut, the City That Would Not Die

The Dennett family reunion began at the arrivals terminal of the Beirut International Airport. Almost fifty years had passed since we were all in Beirut at the same time. As our taxi sped down into the city's cluttered and chaotic streets, we could see scars from the fifteen-year civil war all around us.

Beirut had changed. That war had ended in 1990, having claimed some 120,000 lives, injured nearly 300,000, displaced tens of thousands within the nation, and caused nearly a million people to flee the country's borders entirely. At its inception in 1975, it had looked — at least to outsiders — like a religious war between Christian and Muslim factions, but its political roots were soon exposed as it morphed into conflicts within those factions and drew in Syria, Israel, a UN peacekeeping force, and a multinational force comprising American, French, Italian, and British troops.[23]

The multinational force was to oversee the withdrawal of Palestinian forces from Lebanon, which occurred in 1982, during the first phase of the civil war. In hindsight, that withdrawal appears to have been the goal all along of the conservative Christian Maronites and their ally, Israel, when the war erupted in 1975.

The pro-Western Maronite Christians in Lebanon had clung to power ever since a parliamentary formula had been created in the 1940s that accorded the presidency to a Christian, the premiership to a Sunni Muslim, and the speakership of Parliament to a Shia Muslim. But with the huge influx of several hundred thousand Palestinian (mostly Muslim) refugees after Israel's War of Independence in 1948 and the Arab-Israeli War of 1967, the Maronite Christians worried about becoming outnumbered by Muslims, who in turn were being radicalized by leftist Palestinian groups. As Pierre Gemayel, leader of the Lebanese Front (a coalition of right-wing Maronite parties, dominated by his Phalangist party), declared, "The Muslim majority is oppressive, and a danger for the sheer existence of the Christians in all of Lebanon."[24]

On April 13, 1975, Phalangist gunmen fired upon a busload of Palestinian refugees, killing twenty-seven unarmed passengers, including women and children. That was the spark that started the civil war.

Following the evacuation of Palestinian forces, more chaos descended on Lebanon. In June 1982, Israeli forces invaded Lebanon. In September, Lebanon's President-elect Bachir Gemayel, the son of Pierre Gemayel, was assassinated. The following day Israeli soldiers allowed Phalangist forces to encircle and then enter the Palestinian refugee camps of Sabra and Shatila, where they massacred hundreds of men, women, and children.

In October 1983, suicide bombers attacked the barracks of US marines, killing 241 US military personnel. Once multinational forces began to withdraw from Lebanon in 1983 and Israeli forces withdrew to southern Lebanon, infighting ensued between (pro-Syrian) Shiite and (pro-Palestinian) Sunni militias in and around Beirut's refugee camps. Between 20,000 and 40,000 Syrian forces intervened in Lebanon, and at one point they sided with the Maronites against the Palestinians out of fear, writes author David Hirst, "that together, Palestinians and Muslim/leftists might turn Lebanon . . . into a hotbed of revolutionary militancy . . . and an avenue of subversion against [Syrian president Hafez al-Assad]."[25] When a peace agreement was finally signed in 1989 in Taif, Saudi Arabia, Syria and Lebanon signed their own Treaty of Brotherhood, Cooperation, and Coordination, which legitimized Syria's military presence in Lebanon to protect Lebanon against external threats. Eventually, the Lebanese public turned against the Syrian occupation, which ended in 2005.

Now, six years later, the Beirut that had championed itself as the "City That Would Not Die" in posters at the airport was also the City of Prolonged Uncertainty. All we had to do was look up. Rising above all the other buildings was the white pockmarked carcass of Beirut's tallest and long-vacant building, the Holiday Inn. During the civil war it had been seized by different militias as a prime lookout point over the embattled city. Palestinian leader Yasir Arafat had holed up there for months. Then the Israelis took it over. Then the Syrians. And finally, in 2005, the Lebanese army occupied it and guards it to this day. Much to the annoyance of Beirut's developers and promoters, the building's owner, the oil-rich emir of Kuwait, has refused to rebuild it until he is convinced that true and lasting stability has returned to Lebanon. Until then, the Holiday Inn stands as a constant reminder of the horrific viciousness of the civil war that tore Beirut apart — and the possibility that it could return.

Now, with the Arab Spring threatening to unravel Lebanon, the emir's caution did not seem unwarranted. During the next week, I found a sense of wariness pervading all discussions, whether in the press or over dinner among friends. "You think the Arab Spring is a big event? You ain't seen nothing yet!" joked a university professor over dinner at a near-empty restaurant in Beirut's fashionable Hamra section. She was an intense, dark-haired woman, part Jewish, part Palestinian, and her dark eyes lit up with emotion. "If and when the Arab Spring comes here, we will outdo everything that has gone before it."*

At the time, I sensed she was right. The slightest trigger could ignite a conflagration. That's how the civil war had started. After fifteen years of bloodshed and destruction, what had it accomplished? The Palestinian leadership and its followers had been expelled from Lebanon, and a Lebanese public, which had once shown considerable sympathy for Palestinian refugees, had hardened toward them, concluding that they were the reason the civil war had erupted in the first place. Part of this hardening of attitude developed after the Israelis invaded Lebanon in 1982 to evict the Palestine Liberation Organization; one of the unforeseen consequences of the invasion was the formation of Hezbollah, a Shiite-based military force formed to expel the Israelis from southern Lebanon. Their success won widespread

---

* As it turned out, it was not Lebanon, wearied from fifteen years of civil war, that would erupt once again in sectarian violence as part of the Arab Spring, but its neighbor, Syria. Lebanon, instead, in an eerie throwback to 1948, when it had accepted 100,000 Palestinian refugees driven from their home in what would become Israel, would once again become host to refugees. By 2018, 1.5 million Syrian refugees fleeing from the civil war in Syria would arrive in Lebanon.

political support, both within and outside Lebanon, including from Iran, which dispatched Iranian Shiite forces and money to strengthen Hezbollah's appeal. Here was yet another unintended consequence from war: the emergence of a paramilitary/political force whose ties to Iran would place Israel on a constant war footing. Next to seeing the United States as the Great Satan, Iranians saw Israel as their mortal enemy. Israel responded by launching campaigns to weaken Iran's political and military influence in Lebanon and Syria.

The Legacy of an Assassination

It was not until halfway through our reunion, during a trip through downtown Beirut and then up the coast to northern Lebanon, that Lebanon's need to avoid a maelstrom became even clearer.

As our taxi headed north along the Corniche, Beirut's famed promenade aside the Mediterranean Sea, we came upon the scarred façade of the St. George Hotel. This was once the watering hole of diplomats, dignitaries, journalists, and spies. Like the Holiday Inn, it, too, was vacant, but for another reason. The road in front of it was still partly cordoned off, for here was the site of a gigantic explosion that in 2005 ripped apart the motorcade of Lebanon's former Prime Minister Rafik Hariri and sent him and five of his bodyguards flying into the air. The site was Lebanon's equivalent to Dealey Plaza, where President John F. Kennedy was killed in Dallas, a constant reminder that the assassination of a widely revered leader had never been solved, nor had the perpetrators been brought to justice.

A few feet from the hotel, we spotted a statue of Hariri elevated above the hole in the road where his motorcade came to grief. Farther up the road, in the heart of Lebanon's Martyrs' Square, a large, tentlike structure flanked by armed guards seemed to be some kind of memorial to him. Posters of a smiling Hariri, with his wavy salt-and-pepper hair, graying mustache, and black bushy eyebrows, adorned the entrance to the tent.

"Unduk hon, min fudluck," I said to our driver. (Please stop, I want to go inside.) How could I not? I felt I owed it to Hariri and those who suffered from his loss to at least pay a visit to . . . whatever was inside.

Inside the huge tent, something akin to a large wedding reception tent, I was taken aback by the somberness of the scene. A group of schoolchildren gathered quietly behind Hariri's roped-off grave, which was simply a large engraved granite slab sunk in the ground and profusely adorned with fresh flowers. Pictures of him covered the wall, including those taken in his last few minutes alive. Hariri had risen from humble origins to become a billionaire contractor in Saudi Arabia, and he had financed the rebuilding of Beirut's shattered downtown with his own and Saudi money. I had seen the results back in 2004, when I had visited Lebanon for the first time in thirty years with my husband. From the rubble of shattered buildings, Hariri had achieved what seemed like a miracle: resurrecting downtown Beirut into a stylish recombination of French and Ottoman architecture, relying wherever possible on original masonry and design. How sad, I now thought, that the man dedicated to restoring Beirut's cosmopolitan charm and grace would be repaid for his efforts with an assassination that threatened to plunge Lebanon into another civil war, with different factions accusing one another with responsibility for his death.

Clearly the ghost of Rafik Hariri lingered over Lebanon like a restless soul crying for closure. His posters were everywhere, in shops, on street corners, on apartment walls and balconies. Debates about who had killed Hariri were as heated now as they had been six years ago, when the assassination took place. And for good reason. Since January, the Lebanese government had been paralyzed over how to handle some expected indictments from a UN-created tribunal set up to investigate his death. Rumors were that Hezbollah — the Iranian-backed guerrilla forces that had since formed a political party and were now members of parliament — were implicated, something they fiercely rejected. It was like waiting for the Warren Commission to publish its findings on JFK, knowing that a large segment of the population would still not believe them. What would happen if those rumors about Hariri's assassination proved true?

It was hard to believe that more violence would benefit Hezbollah, particularly after it had gained political power in parliament, or anyone else in Lebanon, but it seemed that Hezbollah could easily be provoked if a sealed indictment were finally, officially released naming some of its leaders as the culprits behind Hariri's assassination.

At the time that Hariri was assassinated, Syrian forces still occupied Lebanon. Hariri, who considered himself an Arab nationalist but also a pragmatist, had just reluctantly given in to demands from the young Syrian president Bashar al-Assad to extend for three years the presidency of Emile Lahoud, a former Lebanese army commander who became president of Lebanon in 1998 and was widely loathed as a Syrian puppet. Although

Hariri resented Syria's ultimatums, he relented. Nor did he agree with disarming the pro-Syrian forces of Hezbollah, something the Israelis wanted and Lebanon's Christians were demanding as well. As a result, their neoconservative allies in the Bush administration sponsored UN Security Council Resolution 1559 calling for the removal of all foreign forces in Lebanon and the disarming of all paramilitary organizations.*

In the aftermath of Hariri's assassination, the Bush administration got its way: Syrian troops withdrew from Lebanon after tens of thousands of people marched in the streets, crying, "Syria out! Syria out!" President Bush praised the people of Lebanon and assured them that "millions across the earth are on your side."

A UN Commission was promptly set up to investigate the assassination. Initially, it blamed the Syrians. But the Syrians were later exonerated and the blame shifted to Hezbollah, whose popularity had only increased after its forces defeated Israeli ground forces that invaded Lebanon in the summer of 2006. By 2008 Hezbollah had won eleven out of thirty cabinet seats in the Lebanese parliament. It was now a force to be reckoned with inside Lebanon.

Meanwhile, the head of that first UN investigation resigned in disgrace and three pro-Syrian Lebanese generals he had imprisoned were released after their lawyers proved he had relied on false witnesses. So a new commissioner was appointed, the investigation proceeded, and then, in January 2011, a Canadian journalist leaked the news that leaders of Hezbollah were expected to be indicted. Whereupon Hezbollah's ministers walked out of parliament in protest, and the government collapsed.

By the time we were heading out to Lebanon three months later, the country's cabinet had still not met. In short, Lebanon's government was paralyzed and the country was running on sheer willpower.

One thing seemed clear: The indictments were being held up by whatever powers-that-be deemed it necessary, certainly until things settled down in Syria. But eventually the lid would have to come off.

---

* As described by David Hirst, author of *Beware of Small States* (New York: Nation Books, 2010), UN Security Council Resolution 1559, sponsored by France and the United States and adopted on September 2, 2004, demanded a "free and fair electoral process . . . without foreign [i.e., Syrian] interference or influence," for "all remaining foreign [i.e., Syrian] forces to withdraw from Lebanon," and for the "disarmament of all Lebanese [i.e., Hezbollah] and non-Lebanese [i.e., Palestinian] militias." (page 302)

The Pain of Not Knowing

"Who do *you* think assassinated Hariri?" I asked our driver as I got back into our taxi and we headed up the coast to northern Lebanon.

"I don't know," he responded. "We may never know."

I knew the feeling. For a few minutes, I got lost in a muse over what a top CIA officer had told me about my father at a cocktail party for former spooks at Fort Myer, Virginia: "We always thought it was sabotage, but we could never prove it." That affirmation kept me going for years.

Some suggested that Hariri was killed because he had refused to go along with the building of a large US military base in northern Lebanon near the border with Syria. This is, in fact, a widely held belief in Lebanon, but due to the usual problem — secrecy — it has been hard to confirm.

According to some sources, the engineering firm of Bechtel Jacobs was contracted to build the base. The company, which does work for the US Department of Energy, has no confirmation on its website of any work done in Lebanon. However, the *New York Times* reported in 1991 — after the Taif peace agreement — that the Bechtel Group planned to do "a $6.9 million study ordered by the Government of Lebanon to determine how to rebuild Beirut's downtown, wrecked by 16 years of civil war." Citing the head of Lebanon's Council for Development and Reconstruction, the study by Bechtel would "consist of a four-month phase for infrastructure planning, an eight-month phase for reconstruction planning and, finally, a 10-year economic plan." But there was no mention of a military base.

There was, however, an eyewitness report from an American lawyer visiting Lebanon in 2007 suggesting that a US air base was in the making in northern Lebanon near the border of Syria. Franklin Lamb, a former assistant counsel of the US House Judiciary Committee and professor of international law at Northwestern College in Oregon, sent a dispatch to *CounterPunch* magazine in May 2007 about his observations in northern Lebanon, where the United States was allegedly trying to reopen an abandoned air base. Lamb, relying on interviews with residents of nearby Bibnin (located two miles from the site), and on reports in the Lebanese daily newspaper *Ad-Diyar*, shared their speculation that "construction of a US airbase on the grounds of the largely abandoned airbase at Klieaat in northern Lebanon may begin late this year. To make the project more palpable, it is being promoted as a 'US/NATO' base that will serve as the headquarters of a NATO rapid deployment force, helicopter squadrons, and Special Forces units."[26]

The air base is located near the Nahr al-Bared Palestinian refugee camp, which in May 2007 came under unrelenting attacks by the Lebanese army — the worst violence since the end of the civil war — to rout out a group calling itself Fatah al-Islam. Noted Lamb, citing a Lebanese journalist, "The Bush administration has been warning Lebanon about the presence of Al Qaeda teams in northern Lebanon. And the base is needed to deal with this threat. [Lo] and behold, a new 'terrorist group' called Fatah al-Islam appears near Kleiaat at al-Bared camp."[27]

Nicholas Blanford, a reporter for the Christian Science Monitor, was able to speak to residents of the camp about Fatah al-Islam during a cease-fire. "They're all extremely angry and upset with Fatah al-Islam," he told Amy Goodman of *Democracy Now!* "They say that they're not Palestinians, that they're foreigners, and they have nothing to do with them."[28]

Zaki Chehab, the political editor of the London-based *Al-Hayat* newspaper, concurred, telling Goodman: "It's so easy for someone who have the money and the arms just to take a corner of the camp, hijack it, and just fight with the others. It's a gang. It shouldn't really use the Palestinian name."

The prolonged bombing of the Nahr al-Bared camp had upset me greatly. At the time, in 2007, it made no sense, and I wondered what the Palestinians had done to deserve yet another military onslaught. Today, with the benefit of hindsight, I look back on the assault on Nahr al-Bared and make note of the fact that it occurred after the 2005 assassination of Hariri, the West's blaming of Syria for the assassination, and the forced evacuation of Syrian troops from Lebanon later that year. This is mere conjecture, but it seems to me that the US military wanted a base in northern Lebanon near the border of Syria. After all, wasn't Lebanon on the list of seven countries to be taken out by the Bush administration, as explained to NATO commander Wesley Clark? Hariri may have foiled those plans. His assassination forced the Syrians out of Lebanon and weakened Syria diplomatically, because Syria was blamed for the assassination. The bombing of Nahr al-Bared to uproot a new, supposedly Al Qaeda–affiliated group provided the usual pretext for setting up a military base near the camp on the border of Syria, possibly also as a prelude to bringing about regime change in Syria. But the base never materialized. This plan, if this truly was a plan, had not succeeded. Lebanon had survived fifteen years of bloody civil war (1975–90), the internal turmoil following the Hariri assassination of 2005, the Israeli invasion of Lebanon in 2006, and the bombing attacks in northern Lebanon in 2007.

As far as I can determine, no NATO military base exists in Lebanon. But according to a 2015 report relying on some sleuthing by IHS Jane's, a British company specializing in intelligence development and analysis, Hezbollah set up a drone base in northern Lebanon near the border with Syria — and it has regularly sent recruits into Syria to assist the Assad regime, which now appears to have won the war.[29] Talk about unintended consequences.

A New Lens on Old Conflicts

Once again, the United States (and its allies in the region — Israel, Lebanon's Christian Maronites, and the Arab Gulf states of Saudi Arabia, Bahrain, and the UAE) has played its hand badly in the Great Game for Oil in its bid to control the Middle East and the Eastern Mediterranean. The dreams of the neoconservatives in the Bush administration have yet to be realized, but one day there will be an accounting in the form of lives lost and trillions spent in the seemingly never-ending mission to "control the oil at all costs."

Meanwhile, discoveries of vast offshore oil and gas reserves in the Levant have experts looking at the Eastern Mediterranean as the emerging hot spot of the Middle East. But wasn't that the real hot spot all along?

Even in 1947, both Philby and Carat understood the Eastern Mediterranean as the key chessboard on which major powers would vie for the region's oil riches. President Truman surely agreed. His issuance of the Truman Doctrine in March 1947 — two weeks before Carat's death — was an unmistakable signal to the Soviet Union that its intrusion into the Eastern Mediterranean would not be tolerated by the United States.

In the intelligence community, the dance of the post–World War II allies — cooperative on some counts, competitive on others — played out intensely on the region's shores. They had already learned to look at the Middle East the way oilmen did — and the way I finally came to see it, through maps and my bird's-eye, plane-seat view. What they saw sheds light on the origins of conflicts we thought we knew well, like the one in Israel and Palestine.

It also sheds light on what might really have happened to Carat.

CHAPTER EIGHT

The Hidden History of Pipeline Politics in Palestine and Israel

O ne of my missions during the 2011 Dennett family reunion in Lebanon was to take my family members on two trips along the Mediterranean coast, one south to the old Phoenician town of Sidon, and the other north to the ancient Lebanese port of Tripoli (not to be confused with Libya's Tripoli). "I want us to see, with our own eyes, where the pipelines terminated," I told them. They obliged, although our driver was less than happy about the adventure.

The Trans-Arabian Pipeline, the multimillion-dollar project that had consumed the final days of my father's life, had ended up where he wanted it: not in Haifa, Palestine, at the time racked by violence between Arabs, Jews, and British colonial authorities, but near the tranquil port of Sidon, some 40 miles south of Beirut. In 1976, at the height of Lebanon's civil war, TAPLINE was closed. It has never reopened.

When we approached Sidon, I could understand why our driver was becoming nervous. The entire oil complex — giant drums of oil refineries hidden behind barbed wire fences — had been taken over by the Lebanese army. There was no pipeline terminal in sight. The closest we could get to it was an army checkpoint. Armed guards sporting automatic pistols on their hips sternly ordered us to leave immediately.

Another day, we traveled north in search of the terminal point of the Iraq Petroleum Company (IPC) pipeline near Tripoli. The Kirkuk–Tripoli pipeline (as distinguished from the southern IPC branch, the Kirkuk–Haifa pipeline) had been constructed by the French in 1935 and connected the oil fields of Kirkuk in Iraq with the Mediterranean. This trip was even less successful. Yes, we could see giant oil tankers parked close to the port, and yes, we could see the large steel drums of oil refineries, but nothing remotely resembling the terminal point of a pipeline.

The more I urged our driver to go farther north in search of the pipeline — "Dugre, dugre!" (Go straight, go straight!) — the more uncomfortable he became. I gave up, only to learn later that the terminal point of the (closed) IPC pipeline was very close to the border with Syria, and (understandably) that was one place we did not want to go.

Toward the end of our stay, as we sat eating breakfast in the apartment where my brother, Dan, and his wife, Susan, lived in downtown Beirut, I spread out on the coffee table a copy of a post–World War II pipeline map of the Middle East I had acquired from the National Archives. I wanted to imprint on my family's mind that following the pipelines was the secret to unraveling many of the mysteries of the Middle East, including the death of Carat.

The map showed several routes for the projected Trans-Arabian Pipeline: one route to Syria, another to Lebanon, yet another to Egypt, even one to Gaza, and finally, the then-preferred route to Israel and the port of Haifa. Deliberations at the time (1945) included terrain, the political situation in each country, the projected cost, and the most secure route. I later returned to that map while trying to figure out the location of various military bases in the Middle East and how they correlated to proposed pipeline routes. Where, I asked myself, was the military base that would protect the Trans-Arabian Pipeline?

It wasn't in Lebanon. It wasn't in Syria. And then it hit me. It wasn't *in* Israel. It *was* Israel.

Tracing Back

That realization got me to thinking about the old IPC pipeline route from Kirkuk, in Iraq, to Haifa, in Israel. It also reminded me of a comment made in the *Observer* in April 2003, shortly after the US invasion of Iraq: "It has long been a dream of a powerful section of the people now driving this administration [of President George W. Bush] and the war in Iraq to safeguard Israel's energy supply as well as that of the United States. . . .

The Haifa pipeline was something that existed [up until Israel's War of Independence in 1948], was resurrected as a dream and is now a viable project — albeit with a lot of building to do."[1]*

It also led me to another line of inquiry: How far back did this connection between the oil of Iraq and the port of Haifa go, especially in the minds — and dreams — of Western oilmen and war planners?

Digging up the past had continually proved to be a rewarding exercise in my quest to understand the region, so I employed it once again. Where was my journey back in time going to take me?

I knew that the *construction* of the IPC pipeline dated back to the early 1930s, but as usual, the *planning* for the pipeline had to precede its construction. And the planning could not take place until the oil was seized and controlled. That takes us back to World War I and the period from 1917 to 1918, when seizing the oil of Iraq had become "a first-class war aim" for the British due to wartime petroleum shortages and Winston Churchill's long-term calculation that the British navy, now relying on oil instead of coal as its fuel, had to find new sources of oil.

Britain's Secretary of the War Cabinet, Sir Maurice Hankey, wrote to Foreign Secretary Arthur Balfour that "oil in the next war will occupy the place of coal in the present war, or at least in a parallel place to coal. The only big potential supply that we can get under British control is the Persian and Mesopotamian supply."[2]

Balfour, for his part, fretted that declaring the oil of Mesopotamia (now Iraq) a "war aim" sounded too imperialistic. It would be better, he wrote to Britain's prime minister of the dominions, to call Britain the "guiding spirit" in Mesopotamia, since Mesopotamian oil was the one resource that Britain did not have. "I do not care under what system we keep the oil,"

---

* According to a *New York Times* article by Robert Mackey on February 25, 2015 ("Kerry Reminds Congress Netanyahu Advised U.S. to Invade Iraq"), "Secretary of State John Kerry reminded Americans on Wednesday that Prime Minister Benjamin Netanyahu of Israel, who is expected to denounce a potential nuclear deal with Iran during an address to Congress next week, also visited Washington in late 2002 to lobby for the invasion of Iraq. . . . Apparently referring to testimony on the Middle East that Mr. Netanyahu delivered to Congress on Sept. 12, 2002, when he was a private citizen, Mr. Kerry told the House Foreign Affairs Committee, 'The prime minister, as you will recall, was profoundly forward-leaning and outspoken about the importance of invading Iraq under George W. Bush, and we all know what happened with that decision.'"

Balfour declared. "But I am quite clear it is all-important for us that this oil should be available." Britain's capture of Iraq's oil-rich region of Mosul in 1918 achieved Churchill's "first-class war aim."[3] But that, of course, was only half the equation. Once seized, where would the oil be piped?

Enter the Balfour Declaration, best known for documenting the British government's support for the establishment of a Jewish homeland in Palestine. The declaration, written on November 2, 1917, begins: "His Majesty's government view with favour the establishment in Palestine of a national home for the Jewish people, and will use their best endeavours to facilitate the achievement of this object . . ."

The second half of the declaration has been endlessly debated: ". . . it being clearly understood that nothing shall be done which may prejudice the civil and religious rights of existing non-Jewish communities in Palestine, or the rights and political status enjoyed by Jews in any other country."

But what has been almost entirely lost from the many analyses of the declaration's intent is the significance of the two men who were party to it. The declaration was in fact a letter from the same Lord Balfour, British foreign secretary, conveyed to Lionel Walter Rothschild, otherwise known as the second Baron de Rothschild. We know that Lord Balfour was concerned about seizing the oil of Mesopotamia. What about the second Baron de Rothschild? He was not only a London banker (of N. M. Rothschild and Sons), politician (a member of Parliament), and scion of the Rothschild family, but also a scion of one of the most powerful oil dynasties of Europe and an ardent Zionist who knew Theodor Herzl, the father of Zionism, and Zionist leader Chaim Weizmann, who would later become the first president of Israel.*

---

* Another close friend of Chaim Weizmann was Baron Edmond de Rothschild, who was heir to the French branch of the European banking colossus. (Baron Lionel Walter de Rothschild was part of the London branch.) Baron Edmond de Rothschild promoted huge colonization schemes in Palestine in the late nineteenth century. The Paris Rothschilds were focused on developing their oil monopoly in Russia around the Caspian Sea. They financed the construction of the Baku–Batum railroad, otherwise known as the Transcaucasus railroad. In 1866 they formed the Caspian and Black Sea Petroleum Company. They contracted with British businessman, oil trader, and founder of Shell Oil Marcus Samuel to sell their Caspian oil east of the Suez Canal. With Samuel's ingenuity, they had gone on to outwit their chief competitor, Rockefeller's Standard Oil, in ordering the construction of the only oil tanker that could pass the safety standards of the Suez Oil Company. The Paris Rothschilds kept in frequent touch with the London Rothschilds. See Daniel Yergin, *The Prize: The Epic Quest for Oil, Money and Power* (New York: Touchstone, 1992), 61–72.

Out of concern over growing anti-Semitism in Europe, Herzl had written a pamphlet, *Der Judenstaat* (The Jewish State), in 1896. In advocating for such a state in Palestine, Herzl knew how to appeal to Rothschild's — and Britain's — imperial interests. Writing to Lord Lionel Walter Rothschild on July 12, 1902, Herzl stated that his motives in advocating for a Jewish state in Palestine went beyond the humanitarian. "In addition to this human interest, I have a political motive. A great Jewish settlement in the East Mediterranean would strengthen our own efforts for Palestine."[4]

By mentioning the Eastern Mediterranean, Herzl was appealing to British colonial ambitions in Cyprus, Egypt, and Palestine.

It has been openly acknowledged that Zionist leaders, in order to win British support for their cause, advocated for a Jewish state in Palestine as a European outpost to protect the Red Sea and Britain's vital trade route to India. On the one hundredth anniversary of the Balfour Declaration in 2017, a few chroniclers went further in describing the declaration's larger geopolitical purpose, one that was related to British "imperial interests" in Mesopotamia and Palestine. Notes Bernard Avishai, author of *The Tragedy of Zionism*, "Haifa was an ideal port — and the natural place for a pipeline terminal bringing oil from the east."

Avishai is one of the few chroniclers to bring up the oil connection to the Balfour Declaration. He describes how Britain's high commissioner to Egypt, Sir Henry McMahon, promised independence to the Arabs in 1915 (in appreciation for their fighting the Turks) *provided that* "Britain would protect the holy places [in Jerusalem] and have special interests in Baghdad and Basra, where oil had been discovered." Not a year later, he continues, "in May, 1916, Sir Mark Sykes and François Georges-Picot, diplomats secretly negotiating on behalf of the British and French governments, signed an agreement carving up this same territory in a very different manner. France asserted 'a sphere of influence' over Syria and Lebanon, and Britain over most everything to the south, including direct rule over Palestine [and its port in Haifa]."[5]

Following the Russian Revolution in 1917, the new Soviet government (whose predecessor, under the now-deposed czar, had also been a party to the secretly negotiated agreement) released the Sykes-Picot Agreement to the press to discredit the British, in what today could be equated to a WikiLeaks event, causing acute dismay among the Arabs, who felt betrayed,

and causing considerable embarrassment for the British. The British nonetheless managed to assuage Arab fears, and by 1920 they had solidified
their hold over the land bridge that connects Palestine with Mesopotamia,
through the San Remo Agreement (described on page 198).[6]

The Americans, meanwhile, were feverishly gathering intelligence
about British prospecting for oil in Mesopotamia and Palestine. The State
Department's William Yale, who had worked for Standard Oil in Egypt,
wrote in 1919 that 25 percent of the Turkish Petroleum Company was
owned by British petroleum interests "controlled in a large measure by the
Rothschilds."* Yale further reported that the Turkish Petroleum Company
had "field deposits in Palestine and Syria in August, 1914."[7] Yale was regarded in Washington as someone "familiar with oil business conditions
in Palestine and Mesopotamia" and was often on the lookout for "the possibility of acquisitions by American oil interests."[8]

It would take another year for the United States to discover precisely
what the British were doing in Palestine, especially Major James Rothschild,
son of Baron Edmond de Rothschild, a shareholder in a Zionist enterprise
called the Dead Sea Undertaking Company that was prospecting for oil
near Palestine's Dead Sea. According to a memo from the US consulate in
Jerusalem to the US secretary of state, "The Zionist connection with the
Dead Sea Undertaking Company has been concealed as much as possible
[from the local populace] but in addition to the general local understanding
that such direct connection exists this Consulate has learned that a minor
representative of the company . . . has been receiving his monthly pay from
the treasurer of the local Zionist Commission."[9]

By February and March of 1920, more ominous reports began to arrive in Washington, suggesting that the British and French were working
out a deal for the oil-rich Baku region of the new Soviet Union and for
Mesopotamia. The US trade advisor in Turkey sent a long report emphasizing how imperative that area was for "access by American companies to
supplies of oil" in all the Near East. "In this region," he argued, "there is no
economic matter more important than oil. . . . The Standard Oil Company
has two concessions in Palestine, and there is a possibility of an American

---

* Yale was undoubtedly referring to the Rothschilds' large share in Shell Oil, which
  had a 25 percent share in the Turkish Petroleum company before Gulbenkian got his
  percentage of the company.

concession in North Persia." Then came more confirmation that the British government was "refusing to allow any exploratory work by any [Standard Oil] geologists in Palestine or Mesopotamia, although it is suspected that representatives of British oil companies are in the country wearing British military uniforms or serving as British government officials."[10]

At this point, the British and French were winning the game. In April, the Allies' Supreme Council (minus the United States, which, it will be recalled, had remained neutral in the war against the Turks) hastily arranged a meeting in San Remo, Italy. The French and the British put two years of bickering over the terms of the Sykes-Picot Agreement behind them and settled on a formula for divvying up the rectangle of former Ottoman land stretching from Syria and Palestine through Mesopotamia. Their compromise agreement would come to be known as the San Remo Agreement. In those days, however, State Department documents more accurately termed it the San Remo Agreement on Oil.* Over time, the word *oil* disappeared from descriptions of the agreement in history books, just as it would disappear from public discourse over US foreign policy, which in the 1920s was known as "oleaginous diplomacy," until the term *oleaginous* also disappeared.

God forbid if the American people came to realize that World War I was fought, in large part, not to make the world safe for democracy but to help robber barons reap enormous profits and establish spheres of influence in resource-rich parts of the world, including the Middle East.

Under the 1920 San Remo Agreement, Britain proclaimed Mesopotamia and Palestine to be under British control and reaffirmed the terms of the Balfour Declaration favoring the creation of a Jewish national home in Palestine. (In 1921, Mesopotamia became the Hashemite Kingdom of Iraq under British administration; Iraq assumed full independence in 1932.) The agreement also gave Syria (including Lebanon) to France under French mandatory control. In the United States, American newspapers

---

* The importance of oil in the post-WWI period was certainly well known to the people of France, as evidenced in an article appearing in Paris's *Le Liberte* on June 4, 1920: "In the economic struggle which is also a struggle for existence, petroleum will henceforth play the dominating part. It plays a very important part in warfare. 'Gasoline is the blood of war,' Mr Clemenceau, the French Prime Minister, exclaimed one day. 'A drop of oil is worth a drop of blood.' . . . A country can no longer consider itself secure unless it is master of its gasoline supplies."

went wild with indignation, denouncing the San Remo Agreement as a stark example of European imperialism.

The reaction in the Arab world went from disbelief to despair to anger. Historian George Antonius wrote later in his classic work, *The Arab Awakening*, "The fact that the [decisions] had violated a compact sealed in blood made the betrayal more hateful and despicable." Over the next two years, Syrians rose up against the French in Syria and Palestinians rioted against the Jews and the British. Iraqis, furious over the denial of their independence and subjugation to British rule, staged the deadliest revolt of all, suffering 10,000 casualties from British troops and Allied bombing between June and October.

The entire rectangle seethed with anger as Arab nationalists declared 1920 to be *Am al Nakba*, the Year of the Catastrophe.

But for American oilmen, with the US State Department at their beck and call, 1920 was just the beginning of an all-out concerted campaign to beat the British and the French at their own game.

A Special Relationship

Standard Oil Company of New York (Socony, later rebranded as Mobil) first began to explore for oil in Palestine in 1913. It had concessions to seven plots throughout Palestine and was negotiating for sixty more when World War I interrupted its explorations. After the war, as William Yale conveyed to the State Department, Standard Oil encountered strong resistance from the British. But in the end, the Americans turned British competition to their own advantage. Knowing that their exploration had turned up dry, they shrewdly cut a deal with the British: In return for giving Britain their concession in Palestine (which, they secretly knew, was worthless),[11] Britain granted them a 23.75 percent stake in the Turkish Petroleum Company (soon to become the Iraq Petroleum Company).[12]

American interest in Palestine did not stop there, however. John D. Rockefeller Jr. ended up paying a goodwill visit to Jerusalem's holy places in 1924. In 1927 he pledged $12 million for the construction and endowment of the Palestine Archaeological Museum, which would become one of the most massive buildings in the Near East. He also went on to fund the Hebrew University of Jerusalem. Thus began a strong Rockefeller interest in Palestine that would endure through the tumultuous 1930s and more Arab revolts, right up to the 1948 Israeli War of Independence. The person most credited for helping Israel become a state under the auspices of the United Nations was Junior's son, Nelson Rockefeller.*

The "special relationship" between the United States and Israel is usually presented in the context of the United States recognizing the dire need of Holocaust survivors to have a state of their own, one that would ensure that the Jewish people would never again be subjected to the kind of genocidal horrors inflicted on them by the Nazis. It is certainly true that Jewish survivors and their supporters in Europe, the United States, and Israel believed this, and for good reason. The Jews had been persecuted in Europe for centuries by Christians and subjected to anti-Semitism throughout the West, with Hitler's Final Solution as the ultimate evil. Who could blame them for wanting a state of their own where they could protect themselves from more evil?

Yet there is an irony to this special relationship that has seldom come to light. As chroniclers of the Rockefeller oil empire around the world, Jerry and I — the Colby-Dennett team — inevitably began to focus on Rockefeller ambitions in the Middle East, particularly as these ambitions revolved around securing the oil of Saudi Arabia. Jerry, who has German heritage through his father's side, had always been haunted by the Holocaust and the failure of the West to rescue the Jews during World War II. And through our joint investigation into the intrigues around the routing of the Trans-Arabian Pipeline, we found an answer to the question of why the United States failed to stop the genocide: protecting the oil of Saudi Arabia "at all costs."

At the very time that the full extent of the genocide became known to US officials in 1943, President Roosevelt was desperately trying to find a way to

---

* As former Assistant Secretary of State for Latin America, Nelson Rockefeller played a key role in securing votes for the November 1947 UN Resolution 181, favoring the partitioning of Palestine that would lead to the founding of the state of Israel. See John Loftus and Mark Aarons, *The Secret War Against the Jews: How Western Espionage Betrayed the Jewish People* (New York: St. Martin's Press, 1994), 166–67. The authors cite unnamed British and American intelligence sources as having compromising information on the Rockefellers' "early financial support for Third Reich industrialists," allowing Zionists to "blackmail the hell out of Rockefeller" and getting him to corral the Latin American votes needed for UN endorsement of the partition plan. See also Ignacio Klich, "Latin America, the United States and the Birth of Israel: The Case of Somoza's Nicaragua," *Journal of Latin American Studies* 20, no. 2 (November 1988): 389–432, https://www.jstor.org/stable/156720.

convince Ibn Saud to agree to admit tens of thousands of Jewish survivors into Palestine, even offering to make Ibn Saud the head of state of Palestine. Ibn Saud refused to back the plan and threatened to end the United States' exclusive oil concession in Saudi Arabia if increased Jewish immigration to Palestine were allowed. The Saudi king's warning, transmitted in 1943, coincided with deliberations over whether or not to bomb Auschwitz-Birkenau to shut down the huge killing machine, where up to 10,000 people were killed every day. Everything came to a head in the summer of 1944, when the World Jewish Congress (followed in the fall by the War Refugee Board) forwarded requests to bomb Auschwitz to the US War Department.*

The United States decided against bombing Auschwitz, with the excuse being offered by John J. McCloy, assistant secretary of war, on August 14, 1944, that "such an operation could be executed only by the diversion of considerable air support . . . now engaged in decisive operations elsewhere and would in any case be of such doubtful efficacy that it would not warrant the use of our resources."[13] It mattered not that the I. G. Farben synthetic oil and rubber works, which US warplanes bombarded within a week after McCloy made his statement, lay just five miles from Auschwitz, in such close proximity that warplanes would not have needed to be diverted to hit the camp.[14] Instead, the Auschwitz concentration camp was the target of aerial photographs.

Ironically, prisoners in the camp had cheered when the bombers flew overhead and many hoped that Auschwitz would be next. One survivor told Jerry and me that he and his fellow prisoners shouted and gesticulated to the planes flying overhead, "Bomb us! Bomb us!" Stopping the genocidal machine of mass murder was to them more important than being killed by bombs. His recollection has been confirmed by the US Holocaust Memorial Museum, which on the subject of bombing Auschwitz quoted another survivor, Elie Wiesel, as saying, "we were no longer afraid of death; at any rate not of that death. Every bomb that exploded filled us with joy and gave us new confidence in life."[15]

---

* President Roosevelt by executive decree created the War Refugee Board in early 1944 after being told of "the State Department's incompetence, delay, and even obstruction of a variety of rescue efforts." (FDR Library, "FDR and the Holocaust," citing *Diaries of Henry Morgenthau, Jr.*, book 694, pages 190–92, http://www.fdrlibrary.marist.edu/archives/pdfs/holocaust.pdf.)

The consequences of saving Jews from the Holocaust had been considered at the highest level in the US State Department. Adolf Berle, in charge of the intelligence division of the State Department in 1943 and a longtime advisor to Nelson Rockefeller, considered where rescued Jews might end up. "We all know the consequences [of Jews escaping to Palestine] are too terrible to bear," he mused.[16] His comments were made at the very time that the State Department — to its everlasting shame, in my opinion — was suppressing reports of the genocide, while playing close attention to Ibn Saud's warnings against further Jewish immigration to Palestine.[17] As the primary beneficiaries of the Saudi oil concession by virtue of their holdings in Aramco and Standard Oil of California (now Chevron-Texaco), the modern-day heirs to the huge fortune, most notably the Rockefellers, might conceivably feel a measure of guilt for not helping to stop the crime of the century — a guilt that Israeli leaders were most certainly aware of and could hang over the heads of US policymakers should their support for the state of Israel seem to waver. Sadly, what has occurred is one tragedy in Europe (a horrific genocide over the course of a decade) begetting another tragedy in the Middle East (repeated wars, death, and destruction over seven decades), the latter largely concealed from view in deference to the victims of the earlier genocide, just as the Holocaust itself was largely concealed, even after millions had been murdered. When viewed from this vantage point, the accountability for so much death and suffering of Jews and Arabs (and Armenians, Kurds, Turks, Iranians, and other ethnic groups) lies at the highest levels.

American Support for the Militarization of Israel

American Zionists and their supporters (Nelson Rockefeller key among them) heavily lobbied the UN General Assembly for the passage of UN Resolution 181 recommending the partition of Palestine into Jewish and Arab states. The resolution was officially adopted by the United Nations in 1947. After Israel declared its independence in 1948, President Truman became the first world leader to recognize the new state.

The earliest known discussions about the need to militarily protect the Trans-Arabian Pipeline had occurred in the spring of 1944. In fact, it became a hotly debated issue after the Roosevelt administration formally announced plans for TAPLINE to the world. At the time, the Trans-Arabian Pipeline was projected to terminate in the port of Haifa, which already had the largest refinery in the Middle East and a well-developed infrastructure serving the IPC pipeline.

Hearings were held before the Senate Oil Policy Committee in April 1944 about the pipeline and the Saudi concession, and in the course of the hearings, questions arose from senators as to whether the pipeline was vulnerable to sabotage, as the IPC pipeline from Kirkuk to Haifa had been during the 1936–39 Arab revolt in Palestine. When Aramco's Terry Duce testified before the committee on April 19, 1944, he was confronted with harsh questioning by Maine's Senator Owen Brewster. According to Duce, Senator Brewster complained that "the Government of the United States might have to send troops to protect the pipeline." Brewster later qualified his concern, suggesting that Aramco was trying to get "special protection" and that it "might involve dispatching troops to Saudi Arabia."[18] At the time, Brewster was worried about alleged Russian designs on Saudi Arabia.

But by 1946, when Palestine was racked by violence as both Arabs and Jews fought the British (and each other), State Department officials worried more about the pipeline's potential vulnerability in Haifa. Warned George Wadsworth, the US minister to Lebanon, in July 1946, "It doesn't seem to make good political sense that the terminal of an Arabian-America pipeline be built in what may for at least another generation be a land of bitter Arab-Jewish conflict."[19]

These concerns were borne out as Arabs and Zionists continued to battle in the run-up to partition and, afterward, in the 1948 Israeli War of Independence. The State Department, and ultimately Aramco, rejected Haifa as a terminal point due to increased violence in the area.

Equally persuasive were King Ibn Saud's repeated statements that he did not want to see TAPLINE going through Palestine.[20] When President Truman had publicly endorsed the creation of a Jewish state on the eve of the November 1946 elections, Aramco's Terry Duce had informed the State Department "if the present American policy continued it would result in the destruction of the US and political and economic position in the Middle East, including inevitably the loss of the oil concession in Saudi Arabia."[21]

The main point is this: Protection of the Saudi oil concession and the Saudi pipeline "at all costs" trumped all other considerations, whether the protection was at the point of origin in Saudi Arabia or at its terminal point on the Mediterranean.

Brewster's concern about the United States giving "special protection" to Aramco in Saudi Arabia was prescient. Today, the nations most heavily armed and financed by the United States are Israel and Saudi Arabia. Even though Haifa was rejected as the terminal point in favor of Lebanon, the US-Israel special relationship ensured that no Arab nation in the region would easily challenge that relationship without suffering dire consequences. In short, a strong militarized Israel could serve as the key regional protector of the Saudi pipeline, whether it terminated in Israel or Lebanon, two countries with strong ties to the United States and headed respectively by pro-American Jews (in Israel) and Christians (in Lebanon).

The port of Haifa, meanwhile, regained its strategic importance during the mid-1980s when the US Sixth Fleet began to send forty to fifty of its ships a year to the port. Visits declined during the 1990s as US military deployments focused on Yugoslavia and the Gulf War, and they ceased in 2000 with the Second Intifada uprising in Palestine. In 2008, Haifa once again became a regular port of call for the Sixth Fleet, marking "a renewed connection between Israel and the American navy," according to the mayor of Haifa.[22]

Israel also provides other logistical support to US forces in the Middle East. As noted historian and Middle East expert Joel Beinin wrote in a 2003 essay, "The single most important factor shaping the US-Israel relationship over the last 30 years has been the geo-strategic interest of the United States as perceived by Washington policy makers. Israel has protected the flank of the Persian Gulf — the repository of two-thirds of the world's known petroleum reserves — and threatened to topple or punish any Arab regime that undermined the secure supply of oil at a reasonable price."[23]

While Israel frequently appeals to its supporters in the United States for funds and arms with reminders that it is a small state surrounded by "a sea of Arabs," the leaders of its Arab neighbors have long known they are no match for Israel's military might (including its possession of at least eighty nuclear warheads) and have traditionally gone along with US policies to keep their people in line through authoritarian rule.[24]

Meanwhile, Israel, according to Beinin, "has been willing to do Washington's bidding in a wide range of foreign adventures. No Arab state can reliably serve as a replacement for these functions. . . . [Today] a powerful coalition comprised of the Zionist lobby, evangelical Protestants and arms makers now constitutes a significant domestic constraint on those who might seek to alter U.S. policy toward Israel."*

Since World War II, Israel has received more military aid from the United States than any other country. Between 1949 and 1991 alone, the United States contributed more than $50 billion in economic aid to Israel, with arms sales accounting for most of it.[25] This symbiotic relationship has only intensified over the years. Beginning in 1999, the United States and Israel developed memorandums of understanding guaranteeing Israel a steady supply of armaments over ten-year periods. The most recent one, signed in 2016 under the Obama administration, pledged $38 billion in military assistance, with payments again spanning a decade. It was the biggest military aid deal in US history. Obama's former secretary of defense, Robert Gates, originally appointed by George W. Bush, described the relationship in 2011 in terms of fighting terrorism and nuclear proliferation:

> *The U.S. and Israel are cooperating closely in areas such as missile defense technology, the Joint Strike Fighter, and in training exercises such as Juniper Stallion. . . . Our bilateral relationship and this dialogue is so critical because Israel lives at the focal point of some of the biggest security challenges facing the free world: violent extremism, the proliferation of nuclear technologies, and the dilemmas posed by adversarial and failed states. And I think it important, especially at a time of such dramatic change in the region, to reaffirm once more America's unshakable commitment to Israel's security.*[26]

Gates apparently decided to suppress his previous vocal concerns about Israel's nuclear capabilities, which he famously "outed" in 2006, telling a Senate committee during his confirmation hearing that Israel possessed nuclear weapons, which in turn explained why Iran was motivated to acquire nuclear weapons: "They are surrounded by powers with nuclear weapons — Pakistan to their east, the Russians to the north, the Israelis to the west and us in the Persian Gulf."[27] (It has been Israel's consistent policy to be "ambiguous" about the size of its nuclear arsenal, although such secrecy has obviously failed to curb Iran's nuclear ambitions.)

---

* Many American fundamentalist Christians see the rebirth of Israel as a sign of an impending "Second Coming of the Lord Jesus."

Israel has also been an endless source of profits for US armaments makers, plus it has acted as a testing ground for new weapons.[28] And as long as there is no peace with the Palestinians, the need for armaments continues on the grounds of fighting terrorism. Small wonder, then, that the United States and Israel signed that $38 billion military aid deal. And as early as January 2018, Republican members of Congress were calling that amount inadequate, given the security threats to Israel posed by the Syrian war, not to mention the ongoing war in Gaza.[29]

Leviathan: The Sea Monster of the Eastern Mediterranean

Adding to the further militarization of the region are massive oil and gas fields waiting to be developed off the coast of Israel, including 1.4 trillion cubic feet of natural gas discovered in 2000 off the coast of Gaza, valued at $4 billion. They require pipelines, and pipelines will need military protection.

Before the offshore discovery, Israeli prime minister Benjamin Netanyahu, and prime minister Golda Meir before him, would often joke to visiting dignitaries about how Moses led his people through the desert for forty years to the only place in the Middle East without any oil. This seemed to be Israel's fate since its founding in 1948 — much exploration and drilling producing little results. In 2002–2003, when Israel was facing a severe energy crisis and Netanyahu was Israel's foreign minister, he pinned his hopes on gaining access to Iraq's oil following the Bush administration's invasion of Iraq.

Of course, by then, he should have had additional reasons for being optimistic, since the huge gas fields off the coast of Israel and Gaza were discovered in 2000. And yet, for Netanyahu, the gift that had long eluded Israel also posed a problem. Part of the immense gas field lay in close proximity to the Gaza Strip, the heavily populated, slender piece of land ruled by Palestinians that runs twenty-five miles along the Eastern Mediterranean shore and borders Egypt in the south and Israel in the north. The Palestinians claimed that the gas field, known as Gaza Marine, belonged to them. That meant Netanyahu would have to deal with Israel's archenemy, Yasir Arafat, who exclaimed upon announcing the Gaza find, "This is a Gift of God for our people and a strong foundation for a Palestinian state."[30]

The Palestinians based their claim on authority they had been granted when Israel and the Palestine Liberation Organization (PLO) signed the

Oslo Accords to end their conflict in 1993. The accords had established a new entity — the Palestinian Authority, first led by the PLO's Yasir Arafat — that was granted authority over the Gaza Strip and West Bank.

Notes author and sociologist Michael Schwartz, "Back in 1993 . . . nobody was thinking much about Gaza's coastline." Israel, he adds, even agreed that "the newly created [Palestinian Authority] would fully control its territorial waters, even though the Israeli navy was still patrolling the area. Rumored natural gas deposits there mattered little to anyone, because prices were then so low and supplies so plentiful. No wonder that the Palestinians took their time recruiting BG — a major player in the global natural gas sweepstakes — to find out what was actually there."[31]

When British Gas (BG) confirmed large quantities of gas in 2000, the Palestinians signed a contract with the company that gave Palestine a meager but nonetheless welcome 10 percent of the revenues, potentially worth billions of dollars.[32]

For Israel's Netanyahu and then prime minister Ehud Barak, surrendering this massive gas bonanza to the Gazans was unthinkable. Barak canceled the deal with BG, ordered Israeli naval vessels to patrol the waters off Gaza, and declared that the Palestinians had no right to revenues from the reserves, which, he argued, would be used to fund terror campaigns.[33]

The Israeli government then took control of all commerce in Gaza, curtailed its food imports, and eliminated its fishing industry, while boasting of putting Gazans on "a diet." Predictably, the Palestinians resisted in every way they could. They tried diplomacy and politics. They engaged in border demonstrations that were fired upon by Israeli soldiers. And they retaliated by firing rockets into Israel.

Another complication developed after Hamas, a Palestinian militant movement, won a majority of seats in the 2006 Palestinian elections, which gave it control of the Gaza Strip, leaving a weakened Palestinian Authority to control the West Bank. In 2007, Israel went on the offensive, embarking on a campaign to eliminate Hamas's control over the Gaza Strip while bolstering the position of the Palestinian Authority on the West Bank.* This was a classic divide-and-rule tactic, with its primary motivation derived from concerns about Israel's gas supplies.

---

* Hamas is considered the more radical — and therefore more dangerous to Israel — of the two political groups representing the Palestinians.

Oil and Gas Fields in the Eastern Mediterranean: A Tinderbox Ready to Explode
The countries bordering the Eastern Mediterranean are vying for control of the huge offshore gas fields in the Levantine Basin. Initially, gas discoveries in 1999 and 2000 fueled hope for regional cooperation and peace. Sadly, new discoveries in 2010 and 2011 and claims that oil lies beneath Israeli-occupied Golan Heights have instead

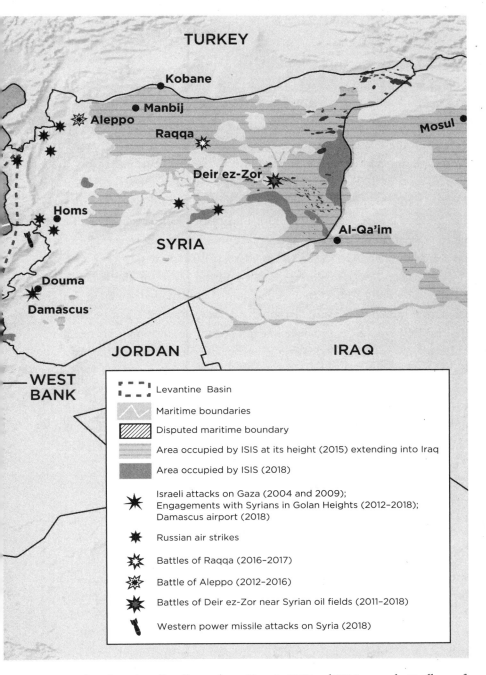

TURKEY

Kobane

Manbij

Aleppo

Raqqa

Mosul

Deir ez-Zor

Homs

Al-Qa'im

SYRIA

Douma

Damascus

JORDAN

IRAQ

WEST
BANK

Levantine Basin

Maritime boundaries

Disputed maritime boundary

Area occupied by ISIS at its height (2015) extending into Iraq

Area occupied by ISIS (2018)

Israeli attacks on Gaza (2004 and 2009);
Engagements with Syrians in Golan Heights (2012–2018);
Damascus airport (2018)

Russian air strikes

Battles of Raqqa (2016–2017)

Battle of Aleppo (2012–2016)

Battles of Deir ez-Zor near Syrian oil fields (2011–2018)

Western power missile attacks on Syria (2018)

exacerbated tensions. Israel's attacks on Gaza in 2009 and 2014 were admittedly an effort to keep gas development out of Palestinian hands. Syria, with Russian backing and Iranian assistance, remains an obstacle to the creation of a pro-Western energy corridor for Levant gas pipelines to Europe. ISIS, routed from oil regions in northeastern Syria and Iraq, has been replaced by US troops. The potential for conflict is ever present.[34]

Ya'alon on the Warpath

A leading protagonist for subjugating Gaza is the balding, bespectacled Moshe Ya'alon, Israel's defense minister from 2013 to 2016. A military hardliner whose philosophies belie his intellectual appearance, he once compared the "Palestinian threat" to cancer. "Some say it's necessary to amputate organs but at the moment I am applying chemotherapy," he told *Haaretz* in 2002, when he was serving as head of the Israel Defense Forces."[35] In 2009 he came up with a new medical metaphor to describe an Israeli peace group, Peace Now, calling it "a virus."[36] His oft-stated determination to crush Hamas has an economic underpinning, however: Hamas's perceived threat to what he considered Israel's offshore gas.

In October 2007, Ya'alon wrote an opinion piece for the Jerusalem Center for Public Affairs that eviscerated claims made by former British prime minister Tony Blair that the development of Gaza's offshore gas, by BG, would bring badly needed economic development for the Palestinians. (Blair, upon leaving the office of prime minister, had taken on the role of a "peacemaker" to the Middle East.) Proceeds of a Palestinian gas sale to Israel, Ya'alon said, could amount to up to $1 billion yet "would likely not trickle down to help an impoverished Palestinian public." Like Netanyahu and Barak, he insisted that the proceeds would "likely serve to fund further terror attacks against Israel." It is clear, he added, that, without an overall military operation to uproot Hamas control of Gaza, no drilling work can take place without the consent of the radical Islamic movement."[37]

What followed was his declaration of war against Hamas.

Ya'alon got his way one year later.

On December 27, 2008, Israeli forces launched Operation Cast Lead with the aim, according to its commanding general, Yoav Galant, of sending Gaza "decades into the past."[38] The operation, which ended on January 18, 2009, pummeled Gaza, killing nearly 1,400 Palestinians (over 700 of whom were civilians) and 13 Israelis (3 of whom were civilians).[39] But it still did not result in Israel's gaining sovereignty over the Gazan gas fields.[40]

Within a year, Israel also had to contend with its neighbor to the north, Lebanon, which disputed Israel's exclusive claims to another gas field located off the coast of Israel about 50 miles west of Haifa. Lebanon eventually resolved its maritime border through the United Nations and in August 2010 ceded its claim to Israel — though it indicated that other prospective fields in the region could very well be within Lebanese territory, a prognosis that turned out to be true.[41]

Netanyahu, who was reelected as Israeli's prime minister in 2009, was cautiously optimistic about Israel's energy future. In December 2010, prospectors had discovered the much larger Leviathan gas field in the Levantine Basin, estimated to hold enough energy to supply Israel's energy needs for the next forty years. Celebrations were short-lived, however. While Leviathan opened up more opportunities for solving Israel's energy woes, it also presaged more conflicts with Israel's neighbors. Soon Palestinians and Cypriots followed Lebanon in laying claims to the giant offshore field, with Israelis insisting that it had sovereignty over most of it. In the end, Israel prevailed over its ownership of the Leviathan field, although Lebanon still disputes another offshore area it claims are within its maritime boundaries.[42] Efforts to develop the Gaza Marine have encountered considerable setbacks.

According to a 2009 report by the *Journal of Energy Security*, the so-called Gaza War "highlighted many security, economic and diplomatic challenges for Israel. . . . With the war's outbreak in December 2008, major population centers in the south like Ashdod and Be'er Sheva were, for the first time since Israel's establishment 60 years ago, under rocket fire." At risk, *Energy Security* continued, were "some of Israel's strategic and energy infrastructure facilities, among them the port of Ashdod, the Ashkelon power station, and even the nuclear reactor in Damona."[43]

Israel's decision to shift its power generation from oil and coal to "cleaner burning natural gas" was controversial, the 2009 *Energy Security* article explained, due to the waning supply of its only existing offshore gas field, Yam Tethis, and increasing reliance on the import of natural gas from Egypt.[44] In addition, much of the natural gas infrastructure that Israel was building lay within Hamas's ever-increasing range of fire.

The discovery of 36 trillion cubic feet of high-quality natural gas in the Tamar and Leviathan gas fields off the coast of Israel in 2009 and 2010, respectively, offered "unprecedented energy security" for Israel, according to the Hazar Strategy Institute. "But the discovery has also presented Israel with one of its greatest military challenges yet: protecting its new offshore gas infrastructure in the Eastern Mediterranean, which is vital to its energy security, and therefore to its economic security."[45]

On November 12, 2012, the Israeli government seemed primed and ready for another invasion of Gaza. As usual, its official rationale was the need to fight terrorism, and specifically to retaliate against Hamas, which had just fired long-range rockets that landed on the outskirts of Jerusalem. This was certainly a first: Never before had Palestinians fired long-range missiles that could reach Jerusalem. Widespread panic ensued in Jerusalem as residents heard sirens wail, warning of impending danger. No Israelis were killed in these rocket attacks, which Hamas claimed it launched in response to Israeli bombardments of Gaza over the previous three days, in which thirty Palestinians had been killed. On November 14, Israel launched Operation Pillar of Defense, which ultimately claimed the lives of 167 Palestinians (87 of them civilians) and 6 Israelis (4 of them civilians), according to the Israeli human rights group B'Tselem.[46]

When critics accused Israel of a disproportionate response, Prime Minister Netanyahu was unfazed, claiming that the Israeli army was "continuing to hit hard and is ready to expand the operation in Gaza." Hamas, for its part, was defiant, boldly declaring, "The time in which the Israeli occupation does whatever it wants in Gaza is gone." Reported the *New York Times*, "The combination of longer-range and deadlier rockets in the hands of more radicalized Palestinians, the arrival in Gaza and Sinai from North Africa of other militants pressuring Hamas to fight more, and the growing tide of anti-Israel fury in a region where authoritarian rulers have been replaced by Islamists means that Israel is engaging in this conflict with a different set of challenges."[47]

As I read with sadness the news reports from the *New York Times*, I was struck by the paper's attempt to be even-handed in covering both sides of the growing conflict — something that in my days at Beirut's *Daily Star*, in the mid-1970s, was a rarity. The massacres of Palestinians in the Lebanese refugee camps of Sabra and Shatila in September 1982 by far-right, Lebanese Christian militias allied with Israel had been a turning point in worldwide media coverage and marked a gradual shift in public opinion on the "Arab-Israeli conflict." Now the *Times* was giving space to the opinions of former *Daily Star* editor Rami Khouri, a professor at the American University of Beirut, who declared that "as long as the crime of dispossession and refugeehood that was committed against the Palestinian people in 1947–48 is not redressed through a peaceful and just negotiation that satisfied the legitimate rights of both sides, we will continue to see enhancements in both the determination and the capabilities of Palestinian fighters — as has been the case since the 1930s."[48] There had been many years before that 1982 turning point when the dispossession of Palestinians in 1948 from their homes, through scare tactics and at gunpoint, was not acknowledged in Israel or the Western press.

In 2012, the political climate in Israel was unsettling, to say the least. The Israelis were becoming increasingly defiant; a former air force commander warned that they would advance on Gaza again.[49] Seen in retrospect, this period of escalating tensions revealed a hardening of resolve on both sides that would inevitably lead to Israel's massive attack on Gaza in 2014. President Obama could see it coming and formally expressed his concerns to Netanyahu by phone in an effort to deescalate the growing crisis. As the *New York Times* reported in November 2012, the Obama administration believed "that a ground incursion by Israel there could lead to increased casualties, play into the hands of the militant Palestinian group Hamas and inflict further damage to Israel's standing in the region at an already tumultuous time."[50]

But his warnings were for naught.

Prime Minister Netanyahu ordered Israeli forces to launch Operation Protective Edge in the summer of 2014, with the renewed aim of uprooting Hamas and ensuring Israeli monopoly over the Gazan gas fields. The ensuing conflict was more protracted than the 2008 war, lasting fifty days. It was also even more brutal, triggering international condemnation and sharp criticism within Israel, especially after four Palestinian boys playing innocently on a Gaza beach were struck down by Israeli airstrikes. According to the United Nations Human Rights Council, more than 2,100 Palestinians were killed, three-quarters of them civilians.[51] To get ahead of a complaint that Palestinians intended to file with the International Criminal Court, which takes cases only when the country involved is unwilling or unable to investigate itself, Israel announced in September 2014 that it would undertake a criminal investigation into "possible military misconduct."

Still, with all the international and domestic outrage, the underlying purpose of this invasion was still missing from most mainstream news reports.

The inveterate Nafeez Ahmed once again proved to be an exception, writing an extensive piece in the *Guardian* titled "IDF's Gaza Assault Is to Control Palestinian Gas, Avert Israeli Energy Crisis." Since the discovery of oil and gas in the Occupied Territories, he observed, "resource competition has increasingly been at the heart of the conflict [in Gaza] motivated largely by Israel's increasing domestic energy woes." Those woes, he indicated, are significant. A 2012 letter by two Israeli government chief scientists, he reported, "warned the government that Israel still had insufficient gas resources to sustain exports despite all the stupendous discoveries."

Ahmed's article concluded, "The Israel-Palestine conflict is clearly not all about resources. But in an age of expensive energy, competition to dominate regional fossil fuels are increasingly influencing the critical decisions that can inflame war."[52]

Meanwhile, the Israeli government has succeeded in effectively destroying Gaza, as planned. A fall 2018 World Bank report concluded that the Gazan economy was in a free fall. Ravaged by unemployment, which approached 70 percent, the potential for increasing unrest was growing. Nazareth-based journalist Jonathan Cook reported, "Israeli Prime Minister Benjamin Netanyahu has ignored repeated warnings of a threatened explosion in Gaza from his own military." Instead, Netanyahu was determined to uphold a blockade of Gaza, preventing goods from entering the besieged enclave and radically restricting local fishing zones. Worse yet, the Trump administration cut all food, education, and health assistance provided by the United Nations' relief agency for Palestinians.[53] To Gazans, it seemed as though the Israelis wanted to starve them into submission.

When tens of thousands of Gazans gathered every Friday beginning in March 2018 to protest the blockade, Israeli forces opened fire, killing 189 and injuring more than 9,000. According to a twenty-five-page report released on February 28, 2019, by the UN Human Rights Council, Israel may have committed war crimes yet showed no interest in prosecuting those responsible. "The Israeli security forces killed and maimed Palestinian demonstrators who did not pose an imminent threat of death or serious injury to others when they were shot, nor were they directly participating in hostilities," the report stated. "Less lethal alternatives remained available and substantial defenses were in place, rendering the use of lethal force neither necessary nor proportionate, and therefore impermissible."[54] The Israeli government dismissed the report as the work of "three individuals that lack any understanding in security matters" and blamed Hamas, the governing body of Gaza, for provoking violence.[55] The United Nations has since accepted the findings of its Human Rights Council claiming that Israeli forces committed war crimes.

What is certain, regardless of a tremendous humanitarian crisis in Gaza, is that Israel is proceeding in earnest to determine how it will pipe its vast natural gas resources — and that the United States has not retrenched on its support.

In May 2018, the Trump administration announced that it would recognize the contested city of Jerusalem as Israel's capital and move its embassy there, causing 40,000 Palestinian protesters to gather at the Gaza-Israel border. Israeli troops responded with fire, killing 60. The Palestinians soon asked the International Criminal Court (ICC) to launch an investigation into Israeli war crimes and crimes against humanity.[56] The Trump administration, in turn, threatened actions against the ICC. National Security Advisor John Bolton told the conservative Federalist Society, "The United States will use any means necessary to protect our citizens and those of our allies from unjust prosecution by this illegitimate court."[57]

A year later, in the spring of 2019, renewed fighting occurred between Gazans and Israelis, killing at least 27 people (23 of them Palestinians, 4 of them Israelis) and injuring hundreds. According to NBC reporters, the fighting broke out after Palestinians accused Israelis of failing to live up to a cease-fire deal agreed to in March, and fired on soldiers near the border. The situation immediately escalated, as Israel targeted 350 sites in Gaza and Hamas fired nearly 700 rockets toward Israel, according to Israeli military sources.[58]

President Trump's envoy to Israel, son-in-law Jared Kushner, had to once again shelve his long-awaited peace plan. That plan, which proposes economic investments as an avenue to peace, was soundly rejected by the Palestinians, who see it as an attempt to bribe the Palestinians into submission while avoiding their political demands for a free and independent Palestinian state.[59] The Palestinians do not consider the United States an honest broker in negotiating peace, a point raised by *Axios* reporter Jonathan Swan in a televised interview with Kushner.[60] Reminding Kushner that the Trump administration had moved its embassy from Tel Aviv to Jerusalem and cut millions in humanitarian aid to the Palestinians, he asked the purported peace advocate point-blank: "Can you not see why [Palestinians] might not want to talk to you and that they might not trust you?" Kushner, stony-faced and seemingly unrattled by the question, hedged on Swan's reference to the cutback of aid, saying it was up to the Palestinians whether they wanted "a better life or not." But the most embarrassing part of the widely circulated interview regarding the peace plan came when Kushner suggested that the Palestinians were not capable of governing themselves without Israeli interference, provoking cries of outrage — including in Israel.[61]

Pipeline Perplexities

The Eastern Mediterranean has always been a focal point of competing oil powers throughout the twentieth century, but historically as a terminal point for pipelines from the interior of the Middle East, not as a production zone. In this new age, with billions of dollars' worth of revenues at stake (not mere transit fees), the Eastern Mediterranean becomes doubly burdened with pipeline politics and worries that a single spark could ignite a conflagration.

"Suddenly," notes a report from the University of Pennsylvania's Wharton School, "it's all happening in the Eastern Mediterranean," underscoring a new geographic reality for Middle East oil production that has continued to be missed by the mainstream media.[62]

The report, focusing on the extreme complexities of developing Israel's Leviathan gas field, was published in 2017, when the most likely candidate to receive Leviathan's gas was deemed to be Turkey, which already fancied itself a major energy hub. According to Bulent Gultekin, a professor of finance at Wharton who served as governor of the Turkish central bank in the 1990s, Turkey was the second-largest buyer of gas from Russia (after Germany). Economically, though, it would be cheaper for Turkey to buy gas from Israel than from Russia.

The challenge to this route was, predictably, Syria. The "pipeline from Leviathan to Turkey would have to traverse the EEZ [exclusive economic zone] of either Syria or Lebanon — which is a non-starter for Israel-sourced gas — or the EEZ of Cyprus," noted the Wharton report. "The latter presents no political problem from the Israeli side, but Cyprus is itself a divided country so that, from a legal and practical perspective, piping Leviathan gas through Cypriot waters — let alone via a facility on Cyprus itself — would require resolving the decades-long Cyprus dispute between Turkey and Greece."[63]

It's as if all the imperial intrigues of the twentieth century that contributed to the Middle East conflict had returned to wreak their vengeance on the region once again.

As for Turkey, despite President Erdoğan's frequently expressed sympathies for the Palestinians, he would likely put the commercial advantages to both countries of gas sales to Turkey above any political differences, according to Turkish professor Gultekin. Israeli economics professor Zvi Eckstein agreed: "As soon as the pipeline is constructed and the gas flowing, Erdoğan will be able to say whatever he wants about Israel and/or Netanyahu — it won't make any difference."[64]

But that was in 2017. In January 2018, Erdoğan — always ready to show his Islamist colors — accused the United States and Israel of meddling in Iranian affairs during recent protests in Iran. Talking to reporters before heading to Paris, Erdoğan bitterly complained about problems in Syria, Palestine, Egypt, Libya, and Tunisia and accused the West of playing a "game" in these countries, all of which are Muslim-majority nations. Like everyone else who lives in the Middle East, Erdoğan held strong opinions as to who was responsible for the instability in those countries, alluding to foreign powers "taking steps towards making the plentiful underground riches in all these countries their own resources."[65]

For now, regardless of the state of Israeli-Turkish affairs, building a pipeline across Syria to Turkey is an unrealistic prospect as long as Bashar al-Assad, with Russia's help, remains in power. The Assad regime, having faced unrelenting attacks from foreign jihadists, survived in part by negotiating massive military support from Russia in exchange for a twenty-five-year contract to develop Syria's claims to that Levantine gas field. Included in the deal was a major expansion of the Russian naval base at the port city of Tartus, ensuring a far larger Russian naval presence in the Levantine Basin.[66]

The feasibility of constructing underwater pipelines has been explored, but there are still technical problems with that approach. Roee Zass, an Israeli energy consultant, has cautioned that "there are significant technical problems involved in building a pipeline over 500 km long deep beneath the sea." In addition, Zass forecast a huge investment of billions of dollars and questioned whether any financier would be willing to invest given the "risk profile" in the area. Lastly (and here's an implied reference to pipeline politics), "Both the financiers and the users of this projected pipeline will demand that the Turkish and Israeli governments sign a bilateral agreement that effectively 'ring-fences' the pipeline from any future diplomatic or political spats between them."[67]

The Wharton School report considered another alternative: piping the Leviathan gas to Egypt. Geographically, the report explained, Egypt was much closer, hence reducing expenses. Politically, relations between Israel and Egypt were more stable, especially in the realm of shared security policies against terrorist groups on the Sinai Peninsula. On the downside, the Arab Spring–related upheavals in Egypt in 2011–13 produced delays in negotiations and political uncertainty (something that investors dread). But then came a new game changer that had nothing to do with security or politics: the discovery in 2015 of a giant gas field (with an estimated 30 trillion cubic feet) off the Mediterranean shores of Egypt. Named Zohr, it had the potential of meeting Egypt's domestic demands for several years.[68] Why deal with Israel when Egypt had its own supply of natural gas?

Egypt and Israel put all speculation to rest on February 19, 2018, when Prime Minister Netanyahu jubilantly announced a ten-year, $15 billion pipeline deal to pipe Leviathan gas to Egypt, emphasizing its benefits to the "education, health and welfare of Israeli citizens."[69] The deal, he added, will "strengthen our security, strengthen our economy, strengthen regional relationships, and most importantly, it will strengthen the citizens of Israel."

The official reaction in Egypt has been more circumspect. Egyptian President Abdel Fattah el-Sisi lauded the deal as "a victory," saying it would "help transform Egypt into a regional energy hub," but quickly added that the government was not involved in the deal. It had been worked out by privately owned companies.[70]

The Egyptian public, known for its hostility to Israel, predictably erupted in anger, insisting that the giant Zohr field was enough to meet Egypt's energy needs. The head of the parliamentary bloc of the Egyptian National Movement Party, Mohamed Badrawy, promised an investigation. "Just three weeks ago," he told a reporter, "we were celebrating the opening of the Zohr gas field and had rejoiced at the prospect of achieving energy self-sufficiency — and now this. Do we even know who our friends and who our enemies are anymore? At a time when Egyptians are struggling because of the ailing economy and the country is facing a foreign currency shortage, is it acceptable for Egypt to pay $15 billion to Israel?" he asked indignantly.[71]

Even Israeli commentators were wary. "Why Isn't Egypt Joining Israel's Natural Gas Deal Party?" ran the headline in *Haaretz* on February 2018. "The contrast between how Israel and Egypt reacted to Monday's agreement," wrote correspondent David Rosenberg, "should serve as a warning to anyone looking forward to a grand new era of energy cooperation."[72]

On paper, he observed, the deal looked promising:

> *The eastern part of the Mediterranean Sea is sitting on top of a huge reservoir of natural gas. Israel has the Leviathan and Tamar offshore fields, Cyprus its Aphrodite and Egypt the giant Zohr field — altogether some 1.89 trillion cubic meters of gas. And there's almost certainly more to be found, including in Lebanon and Gaza. The Middle East doesn't need all that energy, but Europe is only a pipeline*

*away. If all of these emerging gas powers could team up, the economics
of exporting the gas look reasonably good.*

His reservations? Pipeline politics as usual. Analogizing the situation to
a horse race, he averred that the winners might be the optimists who "can
at least point to it as a sign of Cairo's willingness to do business with Israel."
But, he wondered, "would a bookie bet on that nag?" After analyzing all the
variables in shipping the gas overland to Turkey or by undersea pipeline to
Cyprus, he saw "that old nag of politics pulling ahead: Turkey is doing its
utmost to block any deal with Cyprus, and the chilly reception Israel got
in Egypt this week doesn't bode well for a future of energy cooperation."[73]

There are two routes for Leviathan gas that are likely to be secure: pipelines to Israel and Jordan. By September 2018, engineers were finishing
up a pipeline that is located between Tel Aviv and Haifa and will connect
to a pipeline carrying gas from the smaller offshore field, Tamar. From
there, it will supply gas to power stations and industrial plants throughout
Israel. Another pipeline is under construction that will carry Leviathan gas
to Jordan, which, it is predicted by energy expert Simon Henderson, will
"generate most of the kingdom's electricity from 2020." This pipeline will
use the right-of-way established by the old Kirkuk–Haifa pipeline that had
fueled the dreams of Benjamin Netanyahu at the outset of the Iraq War
and has yet to be rebuilt.[74] Still, cautioned Henderson, "Israel's ongoing
tension with Hamas and Hezbollah could likewise erupt in a fresh round
of hostilities at any time." Noting that "Hamas rockets landed near Dor
[where the Leviathan pipeline will commence over land] during the 2014
Gaza war, and Hezbollah's huge arsenal of missiles in Lebanon is even
closer," he added with some confidence, "Israeli missile defenses have been
able to stave off major infrastructure in previous rounds, but they could be
overwhelmed in future conflicts by more (or more accurate) projectiles."

No Man's Water

The development of the Gaza Marine continues to look bleak. British Gas
gave up on negotiating any deals with Israel in 2007. Compounding the
situation was a lawsuit brought by an Israeli natural gas company, Yam
Thetis, challenging BG's concession. Although the court ruled in favor of
BG, it also declared the Gaza Marine as a "no man's water," thus putting its
legal standing in question.[75]

In 2016, Royal Dutch Shell paid BG $58 billion for its holding in Gaza Marine. Yet by 2018, Shell had unloaded its shares as part of a major divestment strategy during a time of sagging oil prices. But many suspected that politics played a role, too; Tareq Baconi, a visiting fellow at the European Council on Foreign Relations, accepted in part Shell's "divestment strategy" rationale but told a reporter for *Egypt Oil and Gas* that he also believed that "Shell has reached the same conclusion as BG before it, which is that the field will not be politically viable in the near or medium term."[76] A Reuters report was more explicit. Shell pulled out, it said, "due to internal Palestinian rivalry and conflict with Israel as well as economic reasons."[77]

A small or medium-size company might be more willing to take a risk in investing in Gaza Marine, Baconi theorized, but its future rested on Israeli decision-making.

After Shell divested, the Palestine Investment Fund became the sole owner of the field and began looking for a company to invest 45 percent. A Greek company, Energean Oil and Gas, announced in July 2018 that it was willing to take up that stake in the field "if Israel and the Palestinians agree." The Energean deal has, however, been delayed due largely to "Palestinian political disputes and conflict with Israel."[78] Israel has stated that it agrees with the development of the field, provided the natural gas goes to Israel's natural gas processor in Ashkelon, and from there to Jenin on the West Bank.

Sadly, some of the worst violence since 2014 erupted in Gaza in March 2019 while Israel's president Benjamin Netanyahu was visiting the Trump White House. After a rocket attack hit a house in Tel Aviv, injuring seven people, Israel responded by hitting multiple Hamas targets in Gaza. At the same time, President Trump proclaimed the Israeli-occupied Syrian territory of the Golan Heights to be part of Israel, in violation of international law and UN resolutions. Trump claimed that the Golan Heights were needed for Israeli security, citing the rocket attack from Gaza. This, he said, was an example of "the significant security challenges that Israel faces every single day."[79]

If securing oil in the Golan Heights was on anyone's mind, no one was letting on.[80] Nor did the prospect of an all-out war on Gaza come up — a scenario that had been secretly promoted by Saudi Crown Prince Mohammed bin Salman in 2018 to divert attention away from the murder of Saudi journalist Jamal Khashoggi by Saudi forces in the Saudi consulate in Turkey (see chapter 9) and to reemphasize the strategic importance of Saudi

Arabia to Israel's security.[81] At the time of this writing, rumors were rife that President Trump planned to call for war to support Israel and remove Syrian President Bashar al-Assad once and for all.

So it goes with the Great Game, pipeline politics, and endless wars in the Middle East. The sufferings of the affected peoples, like the causes of the wars themselves, are largely ignored by the game players, who undoubtedly convince themselves that the ends — in this case, supplying cheap energy to both domestic populations and the world, and reaping huge profits in the meantime — justify the means. Adolf Hitler once famously asked, in defense of his Final Solution, "Who remembers the Armenians?"

Indeed, the United States bears a heavy burden for its failure to rescue the Jews during the Holocaust, as does the State Department. Scores of books have been written addressing the central question of *why* they turned a blind eye. I daresay that few, if any, have fully come to terms with a central motivating factor, beyond traditional explanations of bureaucratic bumbling, callousness, and anti-Semitism within our government's blue-blood ranks. To be sure, there was plenty of evidence of that. But as we consider what has happened in the Middle East over the past seven decades, and what is happening today in Syria, Iraq, Gaza, and now Yemen, we have to question whether the timeworn quest for oil — to be pursued and protected "at all costs" — lies at the heart of many of these tragedies.

I had to wonder, did my father know or even care about what was happening to the Jews of Europe when he strove to make Lebanon safe for the Trans-Arabian Pipeline? How carefully was he following events in Palestine, as Jews fought against British colonialists determined to hold on to their mandate?

As happened before, it happened again: The recent declassification of documents was about to answer some questions. This time they concerned British MI5 intelligence documents pertaining to Palestine at the British archives.* Better still, some of them came straight from the hand of the ever-wily Kim Philby, who, the summer before he was posted to Turkey in December 1946 and took his trip with his father in Saudi Arabia, was meddling in Palestine . . . and Lebanon.

---

* MI5 stands for Military Intelligence, Section V, which involves Great Britain's domestic counterintelligence and security services. MI5's range also covered British colonies and, for this reason, pertained to Palestine under British rule.

CHAPTER NINE

Pipeline Politics, Assassinations, and the West's War on Yemen

S ometimes, in the land of secrets, a cataclysmic event can suddenly burst open decades of hidden deals and relationships and expose them for all to see.

I was deep into my father's papers at the National Archives when, on October 5, 2018, the news broke that a Saudi columnist for the *Washington Post* had gone missing after he entered the Saudi Embassy in Istanbul, Turkey. I paid close attention, devouring every breaking article in the *Washington Post*, which of course had a vested interest in finding out what had happened to their man, journalist Jamal Khashoggi. His disappearance — followed by confirmation of his murder — were soon to cause a huge diplomatic and political crisis for Saudi Arabia, the United States (its traditional closest ally), and many other countries that had benefited over the years from Saudi largesse. The rundown of events following his disappearance was a fascinating indulgence in doublespeak from the Saudis . . . and the Trump administration.

First, Khashoggi was declared missing. Turkish Prime Minister Erdoğan, his personal friend, immediately ordered "all measures to be taken" to find him. Turkish police scoured the streets of Istanbul and began to review hours of security camera footage taken from the city's massive surveillance system. They concluded that Khashoggi never left the embassy, despite claims by the Saudis to the contrary.

Turkish authorities then focused on fifteen Saudis who had arrived by plane earlier that day. It didn't take long for their identities to become known. Twelve of them had ties to Saudi security forces, only strengthening charges that Crown Prince Mohammed bin Salman had to have been involved.[1] According to Turkish authorities, the Saudi nationals "removed the security cameras and surveillance footage from the consulate building prior to Khashoggi's arrival."[2]

As information began trickling out from the Turkish government, revelation by revelation, the Saudis were forced to shift their official position. When it was no longer possible to state that the sixty-year-old journalist had left the building alive, as they initially had, they declared that he had died accidentally in a brawl with Saudi officials. That explanation was trounced, too, though, when photographs from Turkish surveillance cameras showed a Khashoggi impersonator with a fake beard leaving the embassy through a back door . . . wearing the wrong shoes. Why, the world asked, would the Saudis go to such great lengths to cover up an "accidental" death?

As international indignation grew and Saudi explanations fell flat, the Turks became bolder in their release of information, divulging finally that they had audiotapes revealing that the journalist had been beaten, drugged, and killed shortly after he entered the consulate. The killer-in-chief, identified as Salah Muhammad al-Tubaigy, the head of forensic evidence in the Saudi general security department, reportedly played music to drown out Khashoggi's screams as he dismembered the journalist's body, while he was still alive, with a bone saw.[3]

As most of the world recoiled in horror over this latest revelation, social media erupted with snarky comments referring to the Crown Prince Mohammed bin Salman, widely known as MBS, as "Mohammed Bone Saw," a sobriquet that was likely to endure and have lasting consequences.

It was quite a story: A murder in an embassy . . . of a Saudi who worked for the *Washington Post*. His alleged killer was the crown prince of Saudi Arabia, who resented Khashoggi's written attacks on the kingdom and on him as its leader.[4] And the crown prince was very close to President Trump.

This undoubtedly was why President Trump kept prevaricating over holding MBS responsible for Khashoggi's murder, continually repeating that it was probably a rogue operation. When pressed by the media, Trump insisted that Saudi Arabia had been "a very strong ally" of the United States. Especially now, in its role as counterweight to Iranian ambitions in the Middle East. And particularly in Yemen, where Saudi Arabia was engaged in a brutal two-year war against Houthi tribal rebels said to be allied with the Iranians.[5]

As the *Wall Street Journal* elaborated on the president's professed dilemma: "Trump has stressed Saudi Arabia's huge investment in U.S. weaponry and worries it could instead purchase arms from China or Russia. He has fretted about the oil-rich desert kingdom cutting off its supply of petroleum to the United States. He has warned against losing a key partner countering Iran's influence in the Middle East. He has argued that even if the United States tried to isolate the Saudis the kingdom is too wealthy to ever be truly isolated." National Security Advisor John Bolton even chimed in with a short history lesson, emphasizing that Saudi Arabia's special relationship with the United States "goes back to Franklin Roosevelt's time. It's very, very important. It's been a lasting relationship and certainly something we want to preserve."[6]

How true, I thought. And how uncanny that while this story was unfolding, I was pursuing another unfolding story in my long quest, one that had brought me back to the archives to dive once again into my father's OSS records covering Saudi Arabia, Palestine, and a world of intrigue and assassinations. The person who drew me there, of course, was the world's craftiest double agent, Kim Philby. Just as I knew that there was more to the story about Philby's machinations in the Middle East in the time of FDR and Truman, I knew that there was more to the story about Khashoggi's murder. Maybe my historical explorations would shed even more light on this huge story as it kept changing in the fall of 2018.

I was particularly interested in Kim's relationship to Palestine. I knew he had a special connection to Zionism. His first marriage was to a young Zionist and fellow communist, Alice Friedman, whom he had met as a young man in Vienna. According to Philby biographer Anthony Cave Brown, Kim married Alice on "chivalric and sexual impulse," the chivalry relating to Kim's being able to "provide her with the protection of his British passport."[7] The fact that he had to protect her, as both a communist and a Jew, from Austrian fascists made him sympathetic to the Zionist cause. Teddy Kollek, the future mayor of Jerusalem, attended their Vienna wedding, and although they subsequently divorced (her communist sympathies could possibly arouse suspicions about her spouse and put him in danger), they maintained their friendship.

Most of Philby's Soviet controllers during his first ten years (1934–44) of spying for the Soviet Union were Jews from Eastern Europe who believed that the communist cause could help facilitate the Jewish cause, namely a Jewish state in Palestine.[8]

During this period, Kim Philby began to spy on his father, Harry St. John Philby, who had built a career as an advisor to King Ibn Saud and, as a businessman in Saudi Arabia, came up with a plan to bring peace between Arabs and Jews. It proposed recognizing the Balfour Declaration and allowing continued immigration of Jews to Palestine in return for a Zionist pledge not to politically dominate Palestine. His so-called Philby plan (first presented in 1929 to the president of Hebrew University, who tried in vain to get the plan accepted by Zionists and Arabs and resuscitated by President Roosevelt in 1943) failed, but it made the elder Philby a major player in Zionist and Western diplomatic circles.[9] Philby was also instrumental in getting Standard Oil of California's oil concession in Saudi Arabia. As such, he was intimately familiar with the origins of the West's two special relationships in the Middle East: with the Saudis and the Israelis.

Now I had new leads that indicated that Kim got involved in Palestine during the summer of 1946, just weeks before the sensational bombing of the British military headquarters at the King David Hotel and subsequent bomb attacks against the British and American Legations in Beirut. Equally important, I was curious to see how the British handled Kim, and whether there was any communication between them and my father in Beirut, or for that matter, between Kim and my father.

Piercing the Philby Enigma

The British at this very time were struggling to hold on to their mandatory control over Palestine. Interestingly, they were particularly concerned about security around the port of Haifa, as it had been beset with terrorist attacks by the Irgun paramilitary organization fighting for an independent Jewish state. Author and terrorism expert Bruce Hoffman, in his groundbreaking book, *Anonymous Soldiers*, describes how, on the night of January 2, 1947, Irgun fighters struck in a dozen places throughout the country and that evening attacked a military camp near Haifa. The following day Britain's *Daily Telegraph* ran the headline "Palestine. Full Scale Terror; Irgun Attacks with all Resources."

On January 12, Zionist Lehi fighters (known to the British as the Stern Gang) sent a stolen car full of explosives into the police headquarters covering the district of Haifa.* In February 1947, the Irgun bombed the the Kirkuk–Haifa pipeline, which brought oil from Iraq to Palestine, in two places.

Hoffman and others who have gained access to recently declassified MI5 documents on Palestine make it clear that the Irgun and Stern Gang went to great lengths to fight against anyone who stood in their way of achieving an independent state of Israel. Their resolve included assassinating British colonial officials (including the British minister for the Middle East, Lord Moyne, in 1944), bombing British military headquarters at the King David Hotel in July 1946 (considered one of the worst terror attacks on the British in the twentieth century), sabotaging railroads and pipelines, and bombing the British Embassy in Rome in October 1946. According to Hoffman, they also plotted to kill high-ranking British officials in London, including Britain's foreign secretary, Lord Ernest Bevin.[10]

This part of the Zionist struggle for Palestine may not be well known to most Americans, but it was of pressing concern to both British and American counterintelligence officers in the region because it was their job to know, and to protect their countries' economic interests and human capital against terrorist attacks. By the same token, perhaps because they were so caught up with their ongoing security concerns, they showed little humanitarian appreciation for the human tragedy of the Holocaust that fired the Irgun and Stern Gang's determination to rid Palestine of the British and achieve a Jewish home where Jews could feel safe.†

---

* Hoffman, who is a senior fellow at the US Military Academy's Combating Terrorism Center, noted in his book the centrality of Palestine and the Kirkuk–Haifa pipeline to Britain's imperial security in the Middle East. US intelligence reported in July 1945 that some major British construction projects were under way, including a military base near Haifa, "reported to be the largest British military installation in the Near and Middle East . . . Obviously the military authorities plan for permanence in Palestine." The fact that the OSS was reporting on Britain's desire for "permanence in Palestine" is significant for the simple reason that the United States aspired to replace Britain in Palestine, and the British knew it. Foreign Secretary Ernest Bevin warned the US ambassador to Britain in August 1947 that "the Palestine situation was poisoning relations between the U.S. and Britain." See Bruce Hoffman, *Anonymous Soldiers: The Struggle for Israel, 1917–1947* (New York: Knopf, 2015), 464.

† According to author Calder Walton, who also wrote about the declassified MI5 documents, some MI5 officers in Palestine in their reports on Zionist matters ("which they never thought

What role did Kim Philby play in Palestine during this time? According to these same recently declassified British MI5 documents, Philby, then a senior officer in Britain's Secret Intelligence Service (SIS) in London, sent a report to the British Foreign Office on July 9, 1946, warning of an imminent "Irgun plot to attack British diplomatic personnel and facilities in Beirut." Some of Philby's chroniclers have interpreted this as a ploy by Philby's Soviet handlers to divert senior British Intelligence officers away from Palestine to Lebanon at the very time when the Irgun's plot to bomb the British King David Hotel in Jerusalem was about to happen. According to author Bruce Hoffman, "the British already knew that the Irgun had operatives in Beirut." For that reason, they took the threat seriously and sent Britain's highest intelligence officers in Palestine — Sir Gyles Isham, a lieutenant colonel with the Defense Security Office, and Sir Arthur Giles, head of the Criminal Investigation Department (CID) — to Lebanon. But then came Hoffman's astonishing conclusion: "The threatened attacks never materialized, and nothing more was ever heard of the alleged plot. Isham was convinced that it was a deliberate Irgun ploy to ensure that the country's two most senior intelligence officers would not be present in Palestine when the attack on the King David occurred."[11]

This information is intriguing for several reasons. It shows that Philby, from his perch in London, was receiving intelligence reports from both the British and the Soviets in the Middle East that enabled him to keep an eye on events in the Levant — before he was transferred to Turkey in December 1946. In other words, he didn't have to be physically present in Palestine or Lebanon in order to gather and generate intelligence on those countries. More important, unbeknownst to Hoffman and others who have seized on this information and accepted Isham's theory, bombings of the British Embassy and the American Embassy did in fact take place in Beirut on August 9. My father, who was having dinner in his summer mountain retreat at Chemlan when the bombings took place, raced down to inspect the scene and found minimal damage to the British Embassy and much greater damage to the American Legation.

---

would be declassified and read by outsiders"), showed "a degree of the mild anti-Semitism that infected much of Britain's ruling classes at the time." But MI5 "was always careful to separate the activities of the overwhelming majority of Jews and Zionists from the tiny minority who posed a security threat to Britain." See Calder Walton, *Empire of Secrets: British Intelligence, The Cold War, and the Twilight of Empire* (New York: Overlook Press, 2013), 87.

Carat subsequently headed up the US investigation, writing several reports. Carat's secretary — Ruth Dennett, his wife and my mother — wrote home in some detail about the bombing. "The British think the Jews did it," she wrote, "but our people think the Arabs did it." Carat's investigation indicated that the types of explosives found were not as sophisticated as the Irgun's and the materials used in the bombings could not compare in sophistication to "the King David Hotel outrage," which happened on July 22, 1946. "All very amateurish," Ruth added, "with little planning."[12] Carat concluded that the Beirut bombings were the acts of Arab nationalists upset over the Truman administration's support for a Jewish state. The culprits — young radicalized Arabs — were found, and Minister Wadsworth used the event to issue stern warnings to Lebanese officials not to tolerate such acts of violence even if the Arabs supported their cause.[13]

Out of Carat's investigation came a response from CIG headquarters in Washington, DC, wondering why the British were not assisting in the investigation — and why had the British Embassy suffered much less damage than the American Embassy?

This is another intriguing question for which I have no answers. But it heightened my suspicions that the British were not always on the "up and up" with the Americans, including my father. The passage from Hoffman, meanwhile, is a prime example of how an author's theories can emerge only from the facts that were known or discovered at a certain time — in his case 2013. It was thanks to declassified documents in my father's OSS reports (which, though they were declassified much earlier, were apparently unknown to Hoffman) that we now know that Philby's warning was apparently genuine, as the bombings did take place, albeit against the Americans as well as the British. For now, I can only conclude that Philby may have tipped off the British about the planned attack in Beirut to keep him in good stead with his British handlers. If he did not deliver with timely intelligence (in this case, an impending plot against the embassy), his British handlers might begin to suspect him of being the double agent that he was. Meanwhile, on behalf of the Soviets, he was assisting the Irgun to undermine Britain's power in Palestine.

I wonder why the information Carat was getting from the British after the Beirut Embassy attacks ("The British think the Jews did it") was not known to (or perhaps not acknowledged by) Isham, one of Britain's highest intelligence officers in Palestine, who claimed that he was diverted to

Beirut on a false alarm. Was he making this argument to assuage his guilt over his failure to protect the King David Hotel?

I hunted through Carat's declassified reports at the National Archives again to see if I could find any answers. Oddly, there was no mention of any warning from British intelligence—which likely would have come through Philby—about a possible terrorist attack in Lebanon. Were all Philby memos purged from the files, or were they never shared with Carat? Since Dennett and Philby were exact counterparts in counterintelligence, why wouldn't Philby have passed on his warning to Dennett?

For that matter, what did Philby know about Dennett, and vice versa? Philby, from his headquarters in a London suburb, had trained all the new OSS recruits in the dark arts of espionage and counterespionage.[14] He must have trained my father. He trained James Jesus Angleton, who would go on to be the OSS chief of station in Italy and later head of counterintelligence for the CIA. The two became close friends. Did my father know of their friendship? Did he have any inkling at all that Philby was a double agent working for the Soviets? Once again, I enlisted the help of archivists in the search for the missing December 1946 document on "British Intelligence." It was nowhere to be found—or, if found, it was not turned over to me. Philby must have been playing a masterful game with the British, the Americans, and the Soviets, supplying all three of them some valuable information, but cherry-picking who would get what. Because he was famous for his treachery, I had to at least consider him as a deadly adversary to Carat, especially since both the British and the Soviets had become wary of the growing power of the United States in the Middle East.[15]

As the reader can by now surmise, getting at the truth behind murder, violence, and assassinations in the Middle East is extremely difficult, especially when secret intelligence services are involved. I discussed this with author Liz Gould, who, in the course of investigating the secret history of US and British involvement in Afghanistan, spent decades with her coauthor husband, Paul Fitzgerald, trying to figure out who was behind the assassination of US Ambassador Adolph Dubs in Afghanistan—an event that immediately preceded the Soviet invasion of Afghanistan. Dubs, Gould explained, was tasked with moderating, if not neutralizing, growing Soviet power in Afghanistan and its influence over a purportedly "reckless" Afghan reformer, President Hafizullah Amin. In fact, Gould explained, the goal of President Carter's national security advisor, Zbigniew Brzezinski, was to get rid of Amin altogether and then, as we previously learned, to draw the Soviet Union into its own Vietnam. The assassination of Ambassador Dubs, her book argues, "ended any meaningful diplomatic effort by the U.S. to prevent a Soviet invasion of Afghanistan. The death was employed however from that day forward by President Carter's National Security Advisor Zbigniew Brzezinski as the opportunity to increase the level of provocation for luring the Soviets into their own Vietnam quagmire."[16]

Gould and I specifically discussed the Khashoggi assassination, and she opined that the elites involved in high-level assassinations are highly talented in throwing out false leads and decoys in order to confuse investigators. "We couldn't believe the Saudis would be so stupid as to kill a high-end *Washington Post* journalist in their embassy," she said. But then again, she added, sometimes "high-level elites don't care about looking stupid as long as they get the job done."

Especially, I figured, if "matters of national security" were at stake. Back at the National Archives, it hit me that the United States and Britain were today supplying arms to the Saudis for the same reason they were struggling to hold on to their respective strategic interests in Palestine and Lebanon in those post–World War II years. Back then, according to author Hoffman, British authorities decided that martial law would have to be declared in Palestine to protect their refinery and pipeline terminal in Haifa. British foreign secretary Ernest Bevin believed that it was impossible "to separate Palestine's immediate security needs from the government's ultimate determination of the mandate's future. In the meantime, however, British prestige in the region was crumbling." This was very dangerous, he warned, because Britain's prosperity and stature as a world power depended on its continuing access to Middle Eastern oil. Palestine was thus "strategically essential to British interests in the region and any settlement of Arab and Jewish claims must take account of this."[17]

Harold Beeley, the British Foreign Office's principal advisor on Palestine, remarked that same month to Foreign Secretary Bevin, "Abdication of Palestine would be regarded in the [Middle East] as symptomatic of our abdication as a Great Power, and might set in motion a process which would result in the crumbling away of our influence throughout the region."[18]

Great Britain, in fact, had to abandon Palestine after the Israeli War of Independence in 1948, and the United States happily took over as the new state of Israel's main protector. The special relationship between the United

States and Israel was fortified. But the United States and Great Britain, once they overcame their subterranean wartime and Cold War rivalries, also reinforced their own "special relationship" to protect their oil interests in the region. In this respect, it seems as though nothing has changed in seven decades. Then, as now, the two countries seemed willing to both overlook and fund the unthinkable to keep their oil connections alive.

The Dark Side of a Special Relationship

The Khashoggi affair has forced a different special relationship into the open as perhaps never before — the one with Saudi Arabia. This one, though, has key differences, as a *Wall Street Journal* editorial pointed out: Saudi Arabia "lacks the deep emotional support that Israel has among the U.S. public." Still, the conservative editorial page could not come down as hard as might be expected given the severity of the crime, further editorializing that the "U.S. goal should be to preserve the U.S.-Saudi alliance while making clear that murdering journalists is unacceptable and that MBS's erratic judgment and willful use of power are problems for the bilateral relationship." The editorial called sanctions of individual Saudis "inevitable and warranted" but warned that a "moratorium on arms sales is probably counterproductive since MBS could turn to Russia and China. But the U.S. could work with the Saudis to reduce their bombing in Yemen, which is killing civilians, in return for U.S. interdiction of Iranian arms deliveries to Saudi enemies in Yemen."[19]

Some would say the Khashoggi murder could not have come at a worse time, at least for MBS and his powerful Western backer, Donald Trump. In late October 2018, the crown prince was about to convene a major conference in Riyadh intended to induce Western countries to make massive investments in Saudi Arabia. The conference, nicknamed "Davos in the Desert," was intended to herald the crown prince as a player on the world stage. Instead, as the appalling details of Khashoggi's disappearance and suspected murder came to light, many businesses and major news organizations began to bail out of the conference. Not all did, though, and the conference opened on October 24 to standing-room-only crowds.

The prince arrived, all smiles, to flashing cameras and exuberant applause, especially when he denounced the Khashoggi murder and promised cooperation with Turkey in the investigation.[20] But, in reality, the crown prince's image as a bold reformer intent on modernizing Saudi Arabia and weaning the country off its oil reliance was in serious jeopardy. The *New*

York Times reported that "he is now regarded as an impulsive, unreliable autocrat who falls back on crude tactics to crush dissent." Many financiers and technology executives worried about their multibillion-dollar investments in Saudi Arabia, while others fretted over their management of billions of dollars of Saudi money in the United States and elsewhere. "They want to keep the money flowing," the *Times* reported, "even if they cringe at lending their names or prestige to Crown Prince Mohammed's gathering."[21]

President Trump, who had approved billions in arms sales to Saudi Arabia and was encouraging more, found himself in a particularly dicey position. He had made Saudi Arabia his first foreign visit after he assumed the presidency, made memorable by the TV images of his happy sword dance with white-robed Saudi officials after concluding some serious dealmaking in March 2017, having negotiated $350 billion in US aid, including $100 billion in arms sales to the kingdom.[22] Small wonder that Trump, then secretary of state Rex Tillerson, and their Saudi hosts were seen holding hands and dancing for joy.

Trump's son-in-law, Jared Kushner, had played a major role in elevating MBS's position in the West and making the relationship a centerpiece of the Trump Administration's Middle East policy. That included securing a Saudi pledge of $230 million to "stabilize Syria," according to the *Washington Post*.[23] Part of Kushner's Middle East peace plan, according to investigative journalist Vicky Ward, author of *Kushner, Inc.*, included "plans for an oil pipeline from Saudi Arabia to Gaza, where refineries and a shipping terminal could be built."*[24] I had always wondered whether the Trans-Arabian Pipeline would be reopened. I knew that Gaza was once viewed as a possible terminal point for the pipeline. Would this new proposed pipeline follow much of the same route, including through the Golan Heights, which President Trump had recently declared belonged to Israel?

The assassination of Jamal Khashoggi, at the very least, had the potential of throwing to the wind Kushner's peace plan and Trump's budding relationship with MBS.

---

* Kushner "kind of got played by MBS," Vicky Ward, author of *Kushner, Inc.*, told CNN. "He pushed for Trump to hold ... the first official American visit ... not to a country with shared Democratic values, but to the Kingdom of Saudi Arabia, this brutal regime." See Jason Lemon, "Saudi Arabia 'Made a Mockery' of the US after Trump's Visit, and Jared 'Got Played,' Author Says," *Newsweek*, March 20, 2019.

It was clear that President Trump was doing a different dance while waiting for all the facts to come out on the Khashoggi murder. Initially, he adopted a hard line, threatening "severe punishment" for Saudi Arabia if the kingdom were shown to be complicit in the murder, but also expressing support for the Saudi explanation that a "rogue killer" may have been involved. Trump seemed to be doing everything in his power to avoid implicating the crown prince.

Trump eventually had to acknowledge that the murder was probably premeditated after debriefing CIA head Gina Haspel, who had gone to Turkey to see Prime Minister Erdoğan's evidence of the murder and to hear the audiotapes he claimed to have recording Khashoggi's screams as he was being dismembered. Meanwhile, even members of Trump's own party expressed indignation over the gruesome assassination, with Republican senator Lindsey Graham telling Fox News that the crown prince was "toxic" and "has to go," adding his plans to "sanction the hell out of Saudi Arabia."[25]

MBS, for his part, was reportedly perplexed by the developing international outrage and expressed his surprise in a phone call to Jared Kushner, according to the *Washington Post*. Said one royal family insider, "He was really shocked that there was such a big reaction to it. He feels betrayed by the West."[26]

The Yemen Debacle

The Saudi war in Yemen has made the Saudi-US relationship particularly vulnerable to international criticism. So, too, has it rested criticism upon Britain, especially since, according to *Independent*'s Richard Hall, the British government continued to pursue arms deals with Saudi Arabia "in the weeks after the killing of journalist Jamal Khashoggi, even as it publicly condemned the murder."[27] US assistance for the war has outweighed British assistance by far. "Britain and the US," wrote international relations expert Anna Stavrianakis in the *Guardian*, "have been the key supporters of the Saudi-led coalition, providing arms, intelligence, logistics, military training and diplomatic cover."[28]

Yemen is the least developed Arab country in the Middle East, and its civilian population, already battered by poverty, malnutrition, and disease, has borne the brunt of the Saudi bombing that began in 2015. Over 100,000 have been killed since the war began. On September 11,

2018, Jamal Khashoggi himself penned a searing critique of Saudi Arabia's conduct in the war for the *Washington Post*: "Saudi Arabia must face the damage from the past three-plus years of war in Yemen. The conflict has soured the kingdom's relations with the international community, affected regional security dynamics and harmed its reputation in the Islamic world." He concluded, "The longer this cruel war lasts in Yemen, the more permanent the damage will be. The people of Yemen will be busy fighting poverty, cholera and water scarcity and rebuilding their country. The crown prince must bring an end to the violence and restore the dignity of the birthplace of Islam."[29]

Were his articles the proverbial straws that broke the camel's back for MBS?* "We [Muslims] should not need to be reminded of the value of human life," Khashoggi argued, undoubtedly irritating the purported leader of the Muslim world and guardian of the holy sites of Mecca and Medina.

But was MBS so threatened by Khashoggi's outspokenness that he ordered the hit? *Washington Post* columnist David Ignatius pointed out that the crown prince had already ordered officials to lure Khashoggi back to Saudi Arabia — something Saudi Arabia had been doing with other dissidents, often imprisoning them upon their return, a fact hitherto not widely reported while MBS was on a charm offensive in the United States. Surmised Ignatius, "My guess is that Khashoggi was seen as dangerous for the simple reason that he couldn't be intimidated or controlled. He was an uncensored mind. He didn't observe the kingdom's 'red lines.' He was an insistent, defiant journalist."[30]

Left Unsaid

Other reasons have been advanced for why the Saudis wanted Khashoggi dead. Some journalists who are familiar with Khashoggi or his work point to his affiliation with the Muslim Brotherhood, which has vied with Saudi

---

* Khashoggi's previous columns in the *Washington Post* decried the hypocrisy of the Saudi regime's self-portrayal of its policies as reformist when it was arresting the reformers. His May 21, 2018, column read: "It is appalling to see 60- and 70-year-old icons of reform being branded as 'traitors' on the front pages of Saudi newspapers. Women and men who championed many of the same social freedoms — including women driving — that Crown Prince Mohammed bin Salman is now advancing were arrested in Saudi Arabia last week. The crackdown has shocked even the government's most stalwart defenders."

Arabia for domination of the Muslim world.* The *New York Times*, in a lengthy profile on Khashoggi, interviewed friends who said he joined the Brotherhood when he returned from college to become a journalist in Saudi Arabia. "Although he later stopped attending meetings of the Brotherhood," these friends told the *Times*, "he remained conversant in its conservative, Islamist and often anti-Western rhetoric, which he could deploy or hide depending on whom he was seeking to befriend."[31]

Australia's former foreign minister, Alexander Downer, contended that Khashoggi "wasn't some Western-oriented liberal brutally murdered because of his passion for freedom. This man was a player." He had deep ties to the royal family and to Saudi intelligence. At the time of his murder, Downer pointed out in an opinion piece for the *Financial Review*, Khashoggi "was in the process of setting up a centre to promote the ideology of the [Muslim Brotherhood]. He was setting it up in Turkey with Qatari money. The Saudis wanted to stop him. In September they offered him $9 million to return to Saudi Arabia and to live there unhindered. They wanted him out of play. Khashoggi refused and the rest you know. The Saudis killed him."[32]

Turkey's Erdoğan is an avid supporter of the Muslim Brotherhood in his bid to replace Saudi Arabia as the supreme power in the Muslim world, which largely explains his aggressive role in exposing Saudi Arabia's MBS as the perpetrator behind the death of his friend Khashoggi.

According to Felix Imonti of Oilprice.com, the political ambitions of the Muslim Brotherhood, in alliance with Turkey and Qatar, are far-ranging, including a sustained effort to establish a branch of the Muslim Brotherhood in Syria to replace Bashar al-Assad.

So the murder of Jamal Khashoggi has arguably blown open a power struggle for the domination of the Middle East and the Gulf, pitting the Saudis, the Egyptians, and the United Arab Emirates against Turkey and Qatar. Both sides vied for power in Syria, backing different rebel groups to achieve their ends.

---

* The Muslim Brotherhood, founded in Egypt in 1928, regards itself as a transnational organization (as opposed to a political party) of Sunni Muslims who follow a conservative interpretation of Islam. It came to power briefly in Egypt following the Arab Spring but was overthrown in 2013. It had backers in Saudi Arabia — including, in his early years, Jamal Khashoggi — but since 2015 has been branded a terrorist organization by Saudi Arabia, Egypt, Bahrain, Russia, and the United Arab Emirates. Today its main supporters are Turkey and Qatar.

Australia's Downer insists that the Saudi role in the power struggle is "not about oil. . . . And it's not about arms sales. It's about maintaining a power balance in the Middle East and in particular in the Persian Gulf." Yet power and oil are so intertwined in the Middle East that it is hard to separate the two factors. At times political machinations dominate events; at other times economic intrigues around oil dominate. But all too often, as author Matthieu Auzanneau shows in *Oil, Power, and War: A Dark History*, the power of oil in shaping modern society cannot be dismissed as a conspiracy theory; instead it has been a driving force, and most certainly when it comes to the Middle East.

Nowhere is this clearer than in the war in Yemen, which has caused a great deal of handwringing inside Washington's Beltway but (as usual) seldom gets discussed in the context of oil.

The Pipeline Factor in the Yemeni War

The Brookings Institution's Center for Middle East Policy, for example, held a panel on Yemen in the midst of the Khashoggi crisis, with panelists admitting that the war was a "strategic disaster."[33] Yet there was not one mention of Saudi Arabia's scheming to protect its oil while trying to control the oil of Yemen — factors that lie at the heart of the war. Nor was there any mention of oil in the lengthy congressional report *Congress and the War in Yemen: Oversight and Legislation, 2015–2019*.[34] To understand those factors, we need to once again confront the deadly role of pipeline politics.

Like most conflicts in the Middle East, the war in Yemen has been portrayed as a "war on terror" — a battle between Sunnis and Shiites, between Saudi-backed government forces and Iranian-backed Houthi tribal rebels. Never before have the Saudis become so directly engaged in a war beyond their borders. This would seem to raise the question: What is in it for the Saudis? Is there anything in it for their American backers?

In simplest terms, the war in Yemen can be summarized in one paragraph: It began in 2014, when Shia rebels from the country's north, the Houthis, gained control over the nation's capital in Sanaa and deposed the Saudi-backed ruler, Abdu Rabbu Mansour Hadi. The ousted leader fled to Saudi Arabia. In response, a Saudi-led Arab coalition began bombing Yemen in 2015 in order to restore the exiled government to power.

Geography and a map of the Arabian Peninsula tell the rest of the story. The Saudi royal family has always known that the Arabian Peninsula, for all its enormous oil wealth, carries with it the danger of potential choke holds on both its eastern and western shores that could close off oil tanker shipments to the rest of the world if the peninsula fell into the "wrong hands." On the western side of the peninsula lies the Bab el Mandeb Strait, a narrow sea channel that separates Djibouti, in East Africa, from Yemen. It is one of the world's major oil shipping corridors, connecting to the Red Sea, the Suez Canal, and the Mediterranean Sea. On the east, there's the Strait of Hormuz, an equally vital oil shipping channel in the Gulf that separates the United Arab Emirates and Oman from Iran. Its importance would become world news in the summer of 2019 when the Trump administration nearly went to war with Iran after accusing Iran of planting a mine on a foreign oil tanker in the strait. It turned out the tanker's Japanese owner contradicted US claims, citing reports from crew members who said it was hit with a flying object. "They say something came flying toward them, then there was an explosion, then there was a hole in the vessel," the owner told the *Washington Post*.[35]

Sunni Saudi Arabia and Shiite Iran have been rivals for supremacy of the Gulf for decades. Though they have not directly clashed, Saudi Arabia has put in place some contingency plans should Iran manage to close off the Strait of Hormuz, which would stop all Saudi tanker traffic from passing through it. Saudi Arabia also has cast a wary eye on its neighbor, Oman, which controls the Gulf of Oman adjacent to the Strait of Hormuz.

As far back as 2008, Saudi Arabia began plans to build a pipeline from its oil fields in eastern Arabia directly south, traversing Yemen to the Gulf of Aden on the Arabian Sea. The pipeline would avoid the Strait of Hormuz and give Saudi Arabian oil ready access to Asian markets, including India and Pakistan.

In 2014, this projected "trans-Yemen" pipeline attracted further attention when Iran signed a deal with Oman to construct an underwater gas pipeline to Oman, with an eye to transshipping the gas to the same Asian markets.*

---

* In December 2017, the Russian energy giant Gazprom announced its interest in helping to construct the underwater Iranian pipeline. Ali Kardor, director of the National Iranian Oil Company (NIOC), announced, "There has been huge interest in the prospects of the joint construction of Iran-Pakistan-India and Iran-Oman gas pipelines" and that Gazprom and NIOC were committed to cooperating in developing Iran's "gas fields, gas transportation, and monetization." See "Iran Ready to Develop Onshore Section of Gas Pipeline to Oman," *Financial Tribune*, January 14, 2018, https://financialtribune.com/articles/energy/80050/iran-ready-to-develop-onshore-section-of-gas-pipeline-to-oman.

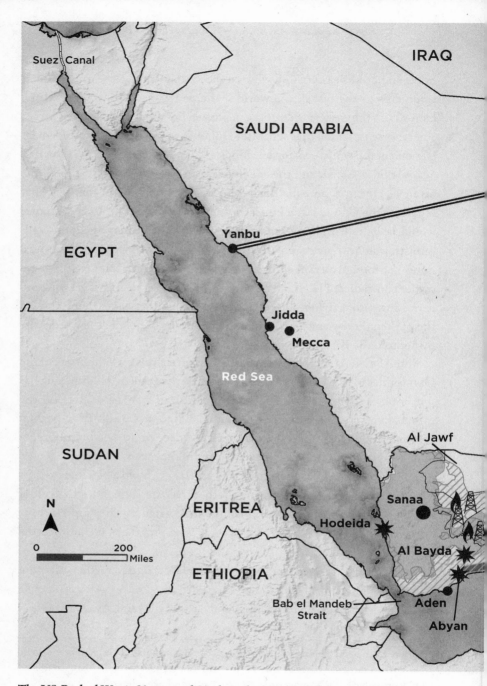

The US-Backed War in Yemen and Saudi Arabia's Proposed Trans-Yemen Pipeline
A trans-Yemen pipeline was conceptualized in 2008 by Saudi Arabia as a way to continue transporting its oil to the Arabian Sea if Iran closed tanker traffic in the strategic Strait of Hormuz. Saudi-funded Al Qaeda forces have been deployed to protect the pipeline route. Problems arose in 2015 when Shiite-backed Houthi rebels

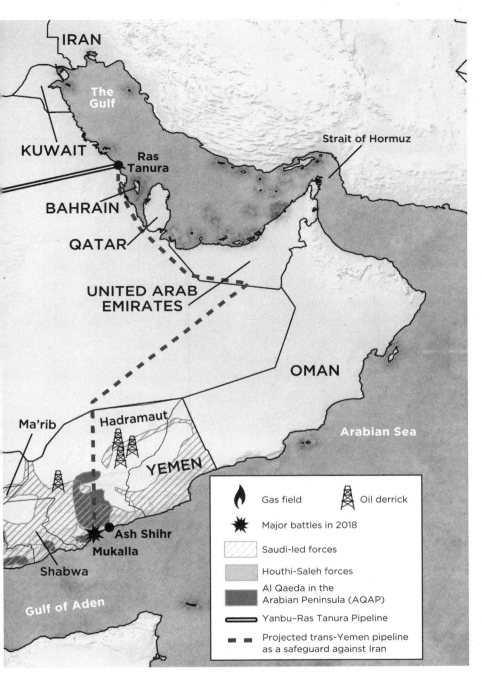

🔥	Gas field	⛏	Oil derrick
✹	Major battles in 2018		

Saudi-led forces

Houthi-Saleh forces

Al Qaeda in the
Arabian Peninsula (AQAP)

Yanbu–Ras Tanura Pipeline

Projected trans-Yemen pipeline
as a safeguard against Iran

gained control over much of northern Yemen and soon began advancing toward the oil-producing province of Ma'rib and toward the Bab el Mandeb Strait, another vital corridor for oil tankers. In 2015 the Saudi crown prince sought US arms to defeat the Houthis. The Saudi-blockaded port of Hodeida is the Houthis' only entry point for arms — and food. Mass starvation and dislocation have created a humanitarian crisis.[36]

Enter Crown Prince Mohammed bin Salman, then the heir apparent to the Saudi throne and grandson of the founder of Saudi Arabia, Abdulaziz Ibn Saud. Just thirty-three years old, dashing, and thoroughly Westernized (to the point of shedding his robes for blue jeans and a motorcycle romp with his Facebook friend Mark Zuckerberg), the prince made several trips to the United States beginning in 2015 to meet with Defense Department officials in the Obama administration. Topic A was countering the threat to regional stability posed by Iranian-backed Houthis who took control of the government of Yemen in 2015. At stake, all present agreed, was the freedom of navigation (particularly tanker navigation) around the Bab el Mandeb Strait at the opening of the Red Sea on the western side of the Arabian Peninsula.[37] Soon, MBS became commander in chief of Saudi air strikes against the Houthis; at the same time, he received billions of dollars' worth of US armaments for the kingdom and promises of US investments.

Simultaneously, Saudi Arabia sent arms and money to proxy fighters in the Hadramaut region of southern Yemen, through which most Yemeni oil exports pass and over which the Saudi pipeline would traverse. Who are the proxy fighters for the Saudis? None other than Al Qaeda in the Arabian Peninsula (AQAP).

Joke Buringa, a senior advisor on Yemen in the Netherlands Ministry of Foreign Affairs, wrote about the proposed Saudi pipeline in 2015, revealing that "Saudi Arabia has been delivering arms to al-Qaeda, who is expanding its sphere of influence."[38] Corroborating that view was Michael Horton, a terrorism analyst with the Jamestown Foundation based in Washington, DC. Saudi Arabia, he observed, used AQAP fighters in a proxy war against the Houthis, which "would mirror the situation in Syria where al-Qaeda affiliate Jabhat al-Nusra has for some time been regarded by Saudi Arabia and other Gulf States as a relatively moderate proxy force to counter the Assad government."[39]

The Saudi pipeline has yet to be built, but protection of its route through Yemen by its Al Qaeda proxies and the massive infusion of armaments from the United States gave Saudi Arabia the confidence that it could weather the disastrous war. But a major turning point may have occurred on August 9, 2018, when Saudi coalition forces bombed a school bus, killing forty children and thirty-two nearby civilians. The outcry was immediate, further inflamed by pictures gone viral of tiny coffins and children standing among them denouncing the bombing. By August 19, CNN was reporting what everyone suspected — that the bomb used in the attack was US-made, a 227-kilogram laser-guided bomb manufactured by Lockheed Martin.[40]

Media attention began to focus on US arms sales to Saudi Arabia, including offers of over $115 billion in weapons by the Obama administration. To his credit, President Obama had ended the sale of guided munition technology to Saudi Arabia after a funeral hall was bombed in October 2016, killing 155 people. The reason, according to the *Guardian*: "Improved precision would not save civilian lives if the Saudi-led coalition were not taking care to avoid hitting non-military targets."[41]

Yet the munition technology sales, the *Guardian* added, "were reinstated by the Trump administration's first secretary of state, Rex Tillerson, in March 2017."

The increase in human suffering that ensued was shocking. By February 2018, a third of the air strikes had hit "nonmilitary" categories including hospitals, medical centers, mosques, bazaars, and water and electricity sites. To add to chronic shortages in food and medical supplies, Yemen was suffering from one of the worst cholera epidemics ever recorded, affecting up to a million people.[42] The Saudis, clearly smarting from the worldwide condemnation incurred from this human catastrophe, renamed their military offensive Operation Renewal of Hope, emphasizing progress in routing out the Houthis in some areas. But hope has vanished for most Yemenis, including those who know that more is at stake for both the Saudis and the Americans in this war than defeating the rebels.

In early November 2018, Geert Cappelaere of the United Nations Children's Fund (UNICEF) announced that the war was contributing to the death of a Yemeni child every ten minutes from disease and starvation due to a Saudi coalition blockade of Yemen's main Red Sea port, where food and supplies would normally enter the country. He noted, "1.8 million children under the age of 5 are suffering from acute malnutrition; 400,000 of these children are suffering the life-threatening form of severe acute malnutrition."[43] In mid-November, another UN body, the United Nations Population Fund, declared its fears that fighting around the Red Sea port of Hodeida could affect a significant portion of the area's estimated 10,000 pregnant women because health facilities were greatly overburdened.[44] Still, the Trump administration continued its support for the Saudis — lucrative weapons sales, refueling assistance, and intelligence sharing.[45]

By early 2019, the human toll of the war was becoming intolerable. According to the United Nations, "24 million people — close to 80 percent of Yemen's population — needed humanitarian assistance or protection." Of those, 3.2 million were teetering on starvation, and far more — 20 million — lacked food security. An estimated 17.8 million didn't have and couldn't obtain safe water. Adequate health care, too, was out of reach for 19.7 million.[46]

Although President Trump had condemned the August 2018 bombing of the school bus as a "horror show" and blamed the Saudis for not knowing how to use their weapons, he made no immediate commitment to lessening US arms sales to Saudi Arabia.[47] After all, the armaments industry was creating a lot of jobs — a fact he repeated numerous times during the October 2018 Khashoggi crisis.

Trump wasted no time in defying Congress. On April 19, he vetoed a Yemen War Powers Act that would have ended US involvement with the Yemen war, claiming there was no US military presence in Yemen "commanding, participating in, or accompanying the military forces of the Saudi-led coalition against the Houthis in hostilities in or affecting Yemen."[48]

Some members of Congress, however, have continued to investigate Trump's relations to Saudi Arabia. Senator Tim Kaine, a member of the Senate Foreign Relations Committee, repeatedly requested information from the Trump administration about the sale of nuclear technology to Saudi Arabia, which is supposed to be approved by Congress and the Department of Energy. Following repeated stonewalling, the Chair of the Senate Foreign Relations Committee, Senator James Risch, issued a directive to the Department of Energy and finally received a response, prompting Kaine to issue a press release on June 4 stating, "It has taken the Trump Administration more than two months to answer a simple question — when did you approve transfers of nuclear expertise from American companies to Saudi Arabia?"

The answer, Kaine's statement revealed, was "shocking." The Trump administration "has approved transfers on seven occasions, the first occurring on December 13, 2017. Notably, the Administration approved two transfers after the Saudi government assassinated Virginia resident and journalist Jamal Khashoggi." Kaine added that he had "serious questions about whether any decisions on nuclear transfers were made based on the Trump family's financial ties rather than the interests of the American people. . . . President Trump's eagerness to give the Saudis anything they want, over bipartisan congressional objection, harms American national security interests and is one of many steps the administration is taking that is fueling a dangerous escalation of tension in the region."[49]

As critical as the trans-Yemen pipeline is to Saudi interests in the country, there is more than a pipeline at stake. Yemen is, in fact, saturated with oil. Yemeni economist Hassan Ali al-Sanaeri revealed in 2016 that the "scientific research and assessments conducted by international drilling companies show that Yemen's oil reserves are more than the combined reserves of all the Persian Gulf states."[50] The area richest in oil is said to be in the western Al Jawf region of Yemen, where much of the bombing raids have taken place.

For this reason alone, the US-Saudi alliance is likely to remain intact during the Trump administration. In Yemen's eastern province of al-Mahrah, also believed to hold lucrative untapped oil resources, residents have begun protesting an increased presence of Saudi troops and military bases as construction on the pipeline proceeds without local approval.[51]

Will MBS Survive?

In the immediate aftermath of the Khashoggi murder, Crown Prince Mohammed bin Salman's reputation was in tatters. In mid-November, the CIA announced that it had reviewed all the evidence and come to the conclusion that the crown prince had ordered Khashoggi's murder.

So it seemed inconceivable that he could regain the power and prestige he had so recently held in Saudi Arabia and the international community. True, he was popular among younger Saudis, but there were already factions in the royal family who had never wanted him to be crown prince.

Opines former British intelligence officer Alastair Crooke, "Both Congress and the Intelligences Services of the US and UK are *already* elbowing into these affairs.* They are not MBS fans. It is no secret that Prince Mohammed bin Nayef was their man."[52]

---

* Not to be confused with the British author and documentarian (*Letter from America*) Alistair Cooke, Crooke describes himself as a British diplomat and "the founder and director of the Conflicts Forum, an organisation that advocates for engagement between political Islam and the West." He is actually a retired officer of Britain's MI6 intelligence service, specializing in the Middle East.

Asia Times reporter Pepe Escobar also gave some credence to this explanation, quoting a businessman close to the royal family who told him that the crown prince's aging father, King Salman, made a "fatal mistake" in choosing MBS as his successor. "The CIA never wanted MBS but [instead] Mohammed bin Nayef. He is still under house arrest and is wise and against terrorism. He should be the next King and that may not be far away." Added the businessman, MBS "has lost the National Guard, the clergy, the royal family and the military through the Yemen misadventure."[53]

According to a 2017 *New York Times* article based on interviews with associates of the Saudi royal family, MBS had plotted to push aside bin Nayef in a transition that "was rockier than has been publicly portrayed." In order to justify this sudden change in the line of succession, some senior princes "were told that Mohammed bin Nayef was unfit to be king because of a drug problem."[54]

After the murder of Khashoggi, concerns about the Saudi succession intensified among the elites in Washington's foreign establishment, for whom security in the Gulf is of premium importance.

In fact, since Trump was elected on promises to rein back globalization and its pet trade agreements — the North American Free Trade Agreement (NAFTA) and the Trans-Pacific Partnership (TPP) — internationalists like those at the Council on Foreign Relations (CFR) have been on high alert. The events that unfolded after Trump came to power and leading up to Khashoggi's murder produced cautious, then worried, then alarmed responses from the CFR. "Mohammad bin Salman isn't just ruining his own reputation," wrote CFR Middle East and Africa fellow Steven Cook, "he's spoiling Washington's policies across the region."

Among Cook's biggest concerns was the war in Yemen, "which was launched to prevent, in the words of Saudi officials, the 'Hezbollah-ization' of that country and the destabilization of the Arabian Peninsula, but has instead pretty much made those outcomes inevitable." He continued, "The United States is confronted with a strategic ally stuck in a war it cannot win, sucking the Saudis of resources and further tipping the regional scale in favor of the Iranians."[55]

Two weeks after Khashoggi's disappearance, longtime CFR president and former US State Department Director of Policy Planning Richard Haass warned, "Washington should resist being drawn in too deeply on the side of Saudi Arabia and the United Arab Emirates in Yemen. The conflict there is fast becoming a military disaster and a humanitarian tragedy, and the fact that the rebels are backed by Iran is insufficient justification for getting trapped in a quagmire." He also outlined steps to contain the building crisis in Saudi Arabia under the crown prince's leadership. Advised Haass, governments should distance themselves from MBS ("no invites to the White House or Downing Street"): "Chief executives, shareholders and workers should reconsider partnering with the government in Riyadh as long as MBS is in charge. The Trump administration or, failing that, the US Congress should place constraints on the use of American-supplied military equipment and intelligence."[56]

Having heard clamors from around the world and from members of Congress to *do something*, Haass opined that "governments should publicly press for an independent and unconstrained investigation of what happened in Istanbul. We should not be distracted by any Saudi attempt to scapegoat the 'rogue element' the government may well claim to be responsible."

And Haass, knowing full well that instability is the scourge of foreign investment and bank loans for development projects, including pipeline construction, advised that it could be "counter-productive and risky to call for the departure of the crown prince," because of MBS's "broad popularity at home." Haass could not come up with an alternative leader at that point, but he cautioned that "broad instability would serve the interests of no one." The most he could suggest was that MBS and others in the royal family should not take Western support for him for granted, while arguing diplomatically, "It is up to the Saudis to sort out their succession." Noted one high-level CIA officer to the author, only the Saudis will determine what happens, regardless of what outsiders may want.

Still, Haass ended his piece with a less-than-subtle warning to the crown prince and his loyal retainers: "It would be ironic if an action apparently carried out to strengthen his control over his country had just the opposite effect."[57]

While the Saudis have not figured out succession, they have put on trial eleven Saudis implicated in Khashoggi's murder. But the trial has been held in secret, causing an international outcry. Agnes Callamard, the UN special rapporteur on extrajudicial executions who is leading an international inquiry into Khashoggi's murder, held a press conference in March 2019 denouncing the kingdom's lack of transparency. "The current proceedings contravene international human rights law according to which the right to a fair trial involves the right to a public hearing," Callamard said.[58]

Louis Charbonneau, UN director at Human Rights Watch, declared, "We can't enable the Saudi government to turn it into a kangaroo court that conveniently finds a bunch of people guilty."[59]

It would seem, at the time of this writing, that most believe that MBS chose to eliminate Khashoggi in a brutal murder to quell the journalist's dissent over Saudi Arabia's policies, especially its war in Yemen. But, as I've learned in my own research, the easiest answers are not always the most reliable, as more facts and analysis emerge over time. And, yes, some analysts are suggesting other scenarios.

Pepe Escobar, for one, seized on a cue that came from Turkish prime minister Erdoğan's chief aide, Yiğit Bulut, who claimed that "Khashoggi's murder was staged to put Saudi Arabia and the king in a very difficult position and to surrender Saudi Arabia completely to the United States." This, Escobar hinted, may have been deemed necessary after MBS began talking to Russian president Vladimir Putin a year ago. What the two agreed upon back then is not fully known, but after the Khashoggi disappearance and his presumed murder, it was Putin whom MBS turned to, not Trump. That, of course, would have triggered a major economic worry long festering in the minds of US officials: "What if Russia — not to mention China — are the wily old king's 'alliance' backup plan," queried Escobar, "as he figured the alliance with the US might finally be dwindling? What if Russia, China and Saudi Arabia should soon start bypassing the petrodollar?"[60]

The Perils of the Petrodollar

Ah, yes, the petrodollar. No discussion of Middle Eastern murders, coups, and intrigues would be complete without bringing up the currency — and trade — wars that have accompanied the major power plays of the twenty-first century. And yes, the wars have been linked to the US command of the oil-based petro*dollar*, much as they have been linked to the control of oil, and most significantly, Saudi oil . . . and oil in Iraq, holder of the second-largest oil reserves, and possibly the oil in Yemen. Yemeni economist Hassan Ali al-Sanaeri says that, with newly discovered reserves in its Al Jawf province, Yemen "could be one of the biggest oil exporters in the region and the world."[61]

On May 13, 2018, the *Wall Street Journal* raised a red flag in an article titled "U.S. Retreat from Trade Deals Poses a New Threat from Dollar." It began (without ever mentioning any oil connection), "Trade friction is emerging as the latest threat to the dollar's position at the heart of the global financial system." Continuing, the article noted:

> For decades, central banks have held the bulk of their foreign ex-change reserves in the dollar, reflecting the dominant role the U.S. and its currency have played in global trade. As the U.S. pulls back from partnerships while countries like Mexico and Japan strike their own trade deals, the dollar's dominance could be undermined, investors and analysts said. That dominance has been referred to as an exorbitant privilege, allowing the U.S. to borrow cheaply and run persistent deficits.

Investors, the *Journal* continued, are now worrying that "the global economy has become too closely tied to the U.S. economy and its curren-cies," while "central banks that traditionally held a large percentage of their reserves [in case of debts not being paid] in dollars are now using other cur-rencies — primarily the euro and the Japanese yen — to make up a growing part of their reserves. At the end of last year, central banks recorded that 63% of their reserves were in dollars — the lowest in four years according to the International Monetary Fund."[62] Readers of the *Wall Street Journal* did not need to be told that the primary source of what is known as "dollar hegemony" is the control of oil.

In fact, leading up to the US invasion of Iraq, some of the world's more astute commentators were pointing out that oil, petrodollars, and the decision of Saddam Hussein in 2000 to convert Iraq's currency reserves from dollars to euros — and his decision to trade in euros instead of dol-lars — were a major reason for that war.

William R. Clark, a professor of political science at the University of Michigan who coined the term *petrodollar warfare*, wrote in January 2003 that the war in Iraq was "in large part an oil currency war." Clark believed that the goal of the Bush administration in the upcoming war was to "pre-vent further Organization of the Petroleum Exporting Countries (OPEC) momentum towards the euro as an oil transaction currency standard. . . . However, in order to pre-empt OPEC, they need to gain geo-strategic control of Iraq along with its 2nd largest proven oil reserves."[63] At the time, Iran had already converted more than half of its foreign reserve fund assets from dollars to euros, China had begun to follow suit, and Russia's central bank had significantly amped its euro holdings.[64]

Noted former diplomat and Berkeley professor Peter Dale Scott, "First Iraq and then Libya decided to challenge the petrodollar system and stop selling all their oil for dollars, shortly before each country was attacked."[65] We all know what happened to Saddam Hussein and Libya's leader, Muammar Gaddafi.

According to Clark, again writing in 2003, a switch by OPEC from a dollar standard to a euro standard would be the Federal Reserve's biggest nightmare. This was unlikely to happen quickly, he said, but over time the transition could be made. Analysts were already fretting that civil unrest in Saudi Arabia, Iran, or other Gulf States could worsen over a prolonged war in Iraq. "Undoubtedly, the Bush administration is acutely aware of these risks. Hence, the neo-conservative framework entails a large and permanent military presence in the Persian Gulf region in a post-Saddam era, just in case we need to surround and control Saudi's large Ghawar oil fields in the event of a Saudi coup by an anti-western group."

Today, civil unrest does exist in Saudi Arabia. And Jamal Khashoggi addressed it.

Turkey's Erdoğan Seizes Another Golden Opportunity

After Khashoggi's murder, certain powers quickly tried to turn his grisly death to their own advantage. Turkey's Erdoğan immediately seized on his friend's death in order to put Saudi Arabia in its place. Commented Alastair Crooke, "Erdogan plainly has loftier ambitions. He is using this Khashoggi leverage now to pitch for leadership of the Islamic world, no less — hoping to snatch it away from Saudi Arabia. After the defeat of the Wahhabis in Syria, Erdogan senses that Sunni Islam is on the cusp: He is brazenly using Ottomanesque language and imagery to assert this prior claim; and op-ed pieces in the Turkish press are adding to this: the demand for Saudi Arabia to give up its 'Wahhabi' hegemony over the holy sites of Mecca and Medina."[66]

While ratcheting up pressure on the Saudis to identify the "puppet masters" responsible for the murder, Erdoğan made overtures to the United States to improve Turkish-US relations, welcoming a US decision to partially exempt Turkey from the harsh sanctions against Iran that went into effect in early November 2018. In return, Erdoğan released an American missionary from prison and sent him back to the United States.

So far, he was playing his hand well. But by mid-November, he may have overplayed it. On November 15, NBC revealed that Erdoğan had also stepped up his demands for the return of exiled Turkish cleric Fethullah Gulen from the United States to face trial in Turkey. President Trump, wishing to placate Erdoğan and possibly lessen Erdoğan's pressures to punish Saudi Arabia, ordered the Justice Department, the FBI, and the Department of Homeland Security to examine the legal status of Gulen, who has a green card and resides in Pennsylvania. When it became clear that Trump was seriously considering Gulen's extradition — a move that would surely end up in his execution, as Erdoğan has blamed him for a 2016 coup attempt — career officials in these departments were livid. The National Security Council issued a statement that it "has not been involved in nor aware of any discussions relating the extradition of Fethullah Gulen to the death of Jamal Khashoggi."[67] The Justice Department issued an identical statement. Since Gulen does not have any charges against him as a resident of the United States, Trump's inquiries were viewed by many officials as totally inappropriate and overreaching. On this Machiavellian maneuver, neither Erdoğan nor Trump were likely to get their way.

Russia, for its part, managed to turn the crisis to its own advantage. On October 27, it emerged as a winner at a mini summit hosted in Istanbul and attended by France and Germany, where it apparently got the two European powers to acknowledge that it controlled Syria's future. In July 2019, Russia began its first shipment of a sophisticated missile system to Turkey, causing outrage in the United States. According to the *New York Times*, Pentagon strategists view this development as "part of President Vladimir V. Putin's plan to divide NATO. American officials are clearly uneasy when asked about the future of the alliance, or even how Turkey could remain an active member of NATO while using Russian-made air defenses."[68]

In that same month Russia also deepened its ties to Saudi Arabia at the "Davos in the Desert" extravaganza in Riyadh, at which its envoys invited Saudi Arabia to join the Russian Direct Investment Fund, to be renamed the Russian-Chinese-Saudi Fund.[69]

As for Mohammed bin Salman's fate, he may very well survive the imbroglio following Khashoggi's murder. Robin Wright, writing in the *New Yorker* just weeks after the scandal, was prescient when she laid out the different possibilities concerning his future. The first scenario, she wrote, "is that the international furor eventually settles down and M.B.S. remains the crown prince and retains his hold on the country's future." She cited Prince Turki al-Faisal, a former chief of Saudi intelligence and a former ambassador to the United States who knew Khashoggi well, in an interview with David Ignatius of the *Washington Post*: "People who think there's going to be any change in the succession are wrong. The more [foreign] criticism there is of the crown prince, the more popular he is in the kingdom."[70]

Like his friend Donald Trump, the crown prince is proving to be remarkably impervious to criticism. In October, 2019 — a year after Khashoggi's murder — MBS staged a second annual Davos in the Desert for the 2019 Future Investment Initiative. This time, Jared Kushner, Treasury Secretary Steven Mnuchin, and top executives from Goldman Sachs, Blackstone, Blackrock, and other financial giants participated in what a *Washington Post* opinion piece derided as "Disgrace in the Desert," especially since no one implicated in Khashoggi's death "has faced any serious punishment or accountability . . . The entire kingdom is now controlled by a ruthless 30-something whose first instinct is to imprison, torture, expropriate and murder."[71]

MBS's resiliency is likely due in large part to his plans to launch an initial public offering (IPO) of Saudi Arabia's gigantic state-owned oil producer, Saudi Aramco, giving foreign investors an opportunity to own a small but highly lucrative part of the world's most profitable oil company. In 2018, the company pulled in $111 billion in net income, five times more than Exxon.[72] But the IPO, too, is not without controversy. Ten environmental groups have warned the world's biggest banks — including JP Morgan Chase, Morgan Stanley, Citigroup, Goldman Sachs, and Bank of America — that "raising tens of billions of dollars for the world's biggest climate polluter" undercuts efforts to address the climate crisis.[73]

Who, I wonder, will emerge victorious and set the world on a new path: world leaders who turn a blind eye to the human suffering the are causing, or an enlightened world citizenry that chooses to put the dignity of human beings and the survival of our planet above all else?

CHAPTER TEN

Reimagining a
New World Order

Reflecting back over the seven decades since my father's death, I find it quite revealing that my government remains obsessed with protecting its special relationship with Saudi Arabia and Israel while containing and defeating the "enemy" — formerly the Soviet Union and now Vladimir Putin's Russia, along with Iran. Russia's and Iran's enormous oil and gas wealth and their ability to make deals with other countries are still viewed as existential threats to the United States. So, too, is any challenge that the United States might face in dominating the region's oil and gas resources and infrastructure, physical or financial. Only now, the United States seems to be losing the game as more countries (Turkey being the latest) are turning to Russia and its ally, Iran.

When President Trump nearly took us to war in Iran in May 2019 over tanker attacks in the Strait of Hormuz, reaction from the American public and even the mainstream media was fiercely negative. The *New York Times* charged Trump and his aides with "trying to gin up a case for war, much as the Bush administration did before the invasion of Iraq in 2003."[1] *Newsweek* went even further, reporting that "Saudi Arabia claimed that the ships were severely damaged by the attack, but satellite imagery of the vessels viewed by the Associated Press showed no major damage," then adding, "Some have said the event is similar to the Gulf of Tonkin incident, when then President Lyndon Johnson used an alleged attack on two U.S. naval destroyers in Vietnam as a pretext for escalating U.S. involvement in the ongoing Vietnam War."[2]

When he tried again in June and then cancelled a military intervention at the last minute, the country that hosts the largest US military base in the

Gulf — Qatar — called for a peaceful settlement of disputes in the Gulf as it drew even closer to an alliance with Iran.[3]

Even some former Bush administration insiders are seeing the folly of a US war on Iran. David Frum, now a staff writer for *The Atlantic*, writes remorsefully, "Inside the Bush administration, we thought we were ready to remake Iraq for the better — but we were not. We were ignorant, arrogant, and unprepared, and we unleashed human suffering that did no good for anyone: not for Americans, not for Iraqis, not for the region."

Frum regrets that "the damage to America's standing in the world from the Iraq War has still not been repaired, let alone that war's economic and human costs to the United States and the Middle East. The idea of repeating such a war, only on a much bigger scale, without allies, without justification, and without any plan at all for what comes next staggers and terrifies the imagination."[4]

In short, the phenomenon of endless wars, fostered by the United States and its NATO allies, is now a subject of debate in the United States and the object of increasing resistance. One of the most significant signs occurred in March 2019, when two US veteran groups representing the left and the right announced that they had merged in a call for the end of "forever wars" in Afghanistan and the Middle East. VoteVets.org and Concerned Veterans for America plan to press Congress to end US presence in Afghanistan, make changes in war-authorization powers, restrain American use of force in foreign policy, and, as the *New York Times* put it, "examine why we are in these endless wars.[5]

Endless Wars in an Overextended Empire

For all the signs of growing opposition to another war in the Middle East, the American public has yet to grasp that endless wars have been deemed necessary to shore up an enormous, overextended empire. And just as the British clung desperately to their empire after World War II, American oil barons will likely do the same, fighting every challenge that comes their way.

If anyone were to doubt that the country that espouses liberty for all is in fact an economic empire backed by military legions, one only needs to look at the number of US troops and military bases that the United States commands around the world: Currently there are 138,000 military troops deployed in more than 800 military bases in more than eighty countries.

By comparison, Russia has approximately 26 to 40 bases in nine countries; the UK, France, and Turkey each have 4 to 10 bases; India, China, Japan, South Korea, Germany, Italy, and the Netherlands each have 1 to 3 bases.[6]

Since our military still relies heavily on oil for its fuel, this presumes a tight relationship between Big Oil, the military, and other branches of the US government. Trump has certainly made big energy companies ever more powerful, to the detriment of American democracy and the survival of our planet, first by appointing ExxonMobil CEO Rex Tillerson to be secretary of state, then by appointing oilmen to head the Interior Department and the Environmental Protection Agency and to fill other critical posts. It's as if the oleaginous diplomacy of the post–World War I and post–World War II era and the George W. Bush administration has returned with a vengeance. At home, Trump rolled back dozens of environmental regulations that protected the environment and public health from the ill effects of oil, gas, and coal extraction and use. In the Middle East, he carried on with the "national" quest for fossil-energy imperialism. As long as there is oil and gas in the ground or under the sea that can be extracted and as long as the United States strives to control oil resources in countries other than Saudi Arabia, the role of America's corporate owners as the world's leading superpower may extend well into the twenty-first century.

As for Saudi Arabia, the murder of Saudi journalist Jamal Khashoggi revealed that the royal dictators in Saudi Arabia are no longer stable or immune from criticism, especially from that country's own people, and the world knows it — a turning point that does not augur well for the long-term survival of an American corporate empire that until recently was able to rely on the vast reserves of Saudi oil to help finance its overseas expansion. The petrodollar is in peril, too. And the long-played "pipeline bypass" game is beginning to turn against the United States, the world's number one superpower, which has bullied its way into one Middle Eastern country after another through military adventures that have become counterproductive. One only needs to look at the massive destruction that has been wrought on Syria, Lebanon, Libya, Gaza, and Yemen. The inhabitants of this region know that the Great Game for Oil is largely responsible for their misery. The assaults on their lives and dignity are fully imprinted on their brains. If someday they may forgive, they will not forget.

Can we really blame all these tragedies solely on oil, you might ask? The answer, of course, is no. Certainly there are other factors,

254 | The Crash of Flight 3804

including long-held grudges among tribes and ethnic groups. But what Middle Easterners often grasp in a way that most Americans still tend to overlook is this: It is those very divisions that imperial powers have always deftly exploited. They have been using divide-and-rule policies to drive a wedge between Muslims, Christians, and Jews for centuries in an effort to control the region's resources. The United States is no different. Only now, divide-and-rule is being inflicted internally, across the United States.

When early US oil barons set their sights on Middle East oil, three forces began to braid together into a rope that could, unless untethered, ultimately hang us all: intelligence, military power, and Big Oil. It is that three-way nexus that my father was beginning to catalyze, wittingly or not, when he reported to Washington on the tensions in the region, explored the most advantageous terminal point for TAPLINE, and wrote in 1944, "We must control the oil at all costs."

That dictum still guides US foreign policy in the Middle East, except the stakes are even larger now. With equally huge oil and gas fields being discovered in Yemen, the Persian Gulf, the Levantine Basin, Egypt, and possibly the Golan Heights, the US militarization of the Eastern Mediterranean and the Gulf has reached unprecedented levels.

The Russians, having helped the Assad regime stay in power, are now building up their military base in Tartus on the northern shores of the Eastern Mediterranean, a fact that must be of some concern to the Israelis. They also appear to be building up their forces in Libya, setting up two military bases in the cities of Torbuk and Benghazi, thereby entrenching their position in the Eastern Mediterranean.[7]

The issue of who controls Syria is central to the battle for control of the Eastern Mediterranean. Although the Russians have emerged as the winners of this war, the Israelis have continued their bombing raids on purported Iranian arms depots in Syria. Israel's Benjamin Netanyahu, having been given the green light by the Trump administration, has broken with decades of restraint imposed on Israel by Western leaders concerned with inflaming the Arab streets.

In April 2019, President Trump, unmindful of the historic tensions in the region, weighed in to help Netanyahu's reelection prospects by asserting US recognition of Israel's sovereignty over the Golan Heights. With this unilateral act, Trump set much of the Middle East on edge.

Black Gold beneath the Golan

There may be another reason for Israel's interest in holding on to the Golan Heights. As early as July 2014, the *Times of Israel* reported that an American oil company, Genie Oil and Gas, was preparing to drill for oil in the Golan Heights. "While the country was focused on the south and the war with Gaza over the summer," the *Times* reported, "the Northern Regional Planning and Building Committee quietly approved a pilot for drilling in the Golan Heights."[8]

Economic forecaster Martin Armstrong described in May 2017 what he called one of the "best kept secrets" in recent years: estimates of "yet more gigantic oil reserves in the highly sensitive Golan Heights, formerly Syrian territory that became part of the Occupied Territories of Israel during the 1967 war."[9] Genie Oil may be a little-known oil company, but it has a star-studded cast on its "strategic advisory board," including former vice president and Haliburton CEO Dick Cheney, News Corp CEO Rupert Murdoch, former CIA director James Woolsey, and financier Jacob Rothschild, chairman of the J. Rothschild Group of Companies and of RIT Capital Partners plc (RITCP), an investment trust company. According to Business Wire, in announcing Murdoch's and Rothschild's respective purchases of 5 percent equity stakes in Genie Energy in 2010, "RITCP is listed on the London Stock Exchange and has a market cap of over £1.7 billion." Lord Rothschild added a note of credibility and confidence in the project by announcing that the "Rothschild family continues to build on its 250-year tradition of leadership in the financing of innovation and growth."[10]

In November 2015, Genie's chief geologist said that three test drillings suggested a "bonanza" of oil lies beneath the rocky Golan soil, potentially yielding "billions of barrels."[11] If this bears out, the likelihood of Israel's ever returning the Golan Heights to Syria is nil, judging by its actions toward Gazan Palestinians over control over the Gaza Marine reserves.

However, according to some Middle East observers, Trump's actions will hurt any prospects for bringing peace to the region. "Giving the Arabs a gut punch with Golan will not help get them to the table," Paul Sullivan, a Middle East expert at Georgetown University's Center for Security Studies, observed. "It shows deep disrespect for the Arabs at large. It is a huge loss of face." Those actions, along with his demeaning statements made in June regarding their alleged inability to rule themselves, pose yet another threat to Jared Kushner's peace plan for the Middle East, part of which proposed running a pipeline from Saudi Arabia to Gaza.[12]

On the subject of the Arab-Israeli conflict, I have come to a conclusion that might make some readers uneasy and others (as has happened in many of my talks) thankful for the clarification: that the creation of a Jewish state in Palestine was part of an overall colonial scheme going back to World War I to divide up the Levant for British and French oil interests invested in the Iraq Petroleum Company and to run pipelines from Iraq to the Eastern Mediterranean. That wasn't the *only* reason for Britain's 1917 Balfour Declaration promising a Jewish homeland in Palestine. Certainly the Jewish people's need to be secure against the scourge of anti-Semitism was a major factor, but here, too, it was exploited by some of the key players in the Great Game, some of whom practiced anti-Semitism against both Arabs and Jews. To ignore this history lets the big powers off the hook and allows conformist scholars to avoid the third rail of the history of Britain and the United States in the struggles for oil and strategic positioning in the Middle East. It also allows current rulers to mislead their peoples into hating "the other" and thinking that the militarization of the Eastern Mediterranean and the Arabian Peninsula is necessary *solely* to protect them against terrorists.

Oil and Gas Wars

Clearly, President Trump's desire to "Make America Great Again" has meant a boost in funding of the US military (and arms industry) and also a green light for the United States' strongest allies in the Middle East — Israel and Saudi Arabia — to "do what it takes" to defeat terrorism. Senator Lindsey Graham, who in early 2018 returned from a trip to Israel, claimed to have been shaken by the Israeli saber-rattling. "Any time you leave a meeting where the major request is 'ammunition, ammunition, ammunition,' that's probably not good," he told reporters. "This was the most unnerving trip I've had in a while." The Israelis, he added, warned that they would have to go into southern Lebanon to wage war on Hezbollah as long as its Iranian-supported militias "keep making rockets that can hit the airport and do a lot of damage to the state of Israel."[13]

Left out of Graham's explanation was the real concern for Israel: Lebanon's claims on "Block 9" offshore gas, one of three blocks located in a maritime area contested by Israel. Israel's then defense minister Avigdor Lieberman challenged Lebanon's claim as "very provocative," warning that Lebanon would "pay the full price" if the two countries went to war.[14] Responded Lebanon's energy minister, Cesar Abi Khalil: "We consider this [Lieberman's statement] as an aggression on Lebanon's sovereignty to practice its natural right to explore our oil resources." Hezbollah also weighed in, declaring Hezbollah's readiness to attack Israel's oil and gas operations in the Levantine Basin.[15]

The prospects for peace in Afghanistan look grim. Trump canceled US peace negotiation with the Taliban in September 2019 following the killing of an American soldier; the United States has subsequently ramped up its attacks on Taliban, ISIS, and Al Qaeda targets, dropping some 948 bombs in September alone.[16] American soldiers are still dying in Afghanistan.[17] During the first half of 2019, US and Afghan troops killed more civilians than the Taliban.[18]

The extent of Afghan victimhood has recently come to light. The chief prosecutor for the International Criminal Court reported that over a million Afghans have submitted statements alleging war crimes and crimes against humanity by Afghan forces, the Taliban, the CIA, and the US military.[19]

Meanwhile, the American people will continue to be kept in the dark about the full horror of this war. According to the *Wall Street Journal*, the US Defense Department has classified all data on civilian air strike casualties, as well as other information on its "progress" in the war, including the size and efficacy of the Afghan forces that have been trained since 2002 at the cost of $75 billion.[20] Explained John F. Sopko, special inspector general for Afghanistan, to the *New York Times*, "The Afghans know what's going on; the Taliban knows what's going on; the U.S. military knows what's going on. The only people who don't know what's going on are the people paying for it."[21]

In an interview with CBS in February 2019, President Trump said that it was important to keep US troops in Iraq in order to keep a close eye on Iran "because Iran is the real problem." The United States, he said, had spent a fortune on upgrading the Ayn al-Asad air base in western Iraq (which he visited in December 2018), and he wanted it to remain "because I want to watch Iran."[22] From that base, American troops could respond to developments in Syria as well.

The Horrors Revisited

Let's look at the costs of these endless wars in terms of human life.

The full human toll of all the wars in the Middle East since World War II is horrific. Figures vary, but the number of dead from wars is clearly in the millions when we count Israel's War of Independence in 1948 (over 8,000 killed);[23] the Israeli, British, and French invasion of Egypt over control of the Suez Canal in 1956 (the British lost 100; the French, 50; the Israelis, 1,100; the Egyptians, 8,000);[24] the Six-Day Arab-Israeli War of 1967 (killing 20,000 Arabs and 800 Israelis);[25] the Yom Kippur War of 1973 (killing 18,000 Arabs and 2,569 Israelis);[26] the Lebanese Civil War of 1975–90 (150,000 dead);[27] the Iran-Iraq War of 1980–88 (one million dead or wounded);[28] and the Gulf War of 1990–91 (382 Americans; 1,500 to 100,000 Iraqis)[29] as well as the wars that still persist at the time of this writing. Each of those ongoing wars — in Afghanistan (ongoing since 2001), in Iraq (since 2003), and in Syria (since 2011) — has claimed approximately 500,000 lives according to the Watson Institute's Cost of War project.[30] The war in Yemen (since 2005) has claimed close to 100,000 lives, as of June 2019.[31]

The Iran-Iraq War's toll may have been significantly higher, with one source estimating the war cost Iran one million lives and Iraq some 250,000 to 500,000 lives. Largely forgotten in the West, this war was described by the *Guardian* as the one in which "Washington wanted both countries to bleed, but it feared Iran more."[32]

The cost of the "War on Terror" is estimated at $5.6 trillion. In June 2019, the Cost of War Project issued a report on the US military's significant contribution to climate change. The report noted that "although the Defense Department has significantly reduced its fossil fuel consumption since the early 2000s, it remains the world's single largest consumer of oil — and as a result, one of the world's top greenhouse gas emitters."[33] The report noted, "this has received little attention."

US involvement in these wars — through intelligence networks, military aid, and troops on the ground — had an overriding aim: to secure oil for the military, to maintain access to the region's oil and prevent Russia and its allies from expanding theirs. In all three of these governmental agencies, personnel acted under orders from what historian Arthur Schlesinger Jr. was the first to call "the Imperial Presidency," guided by foreign policy advisors from corporate and corporate-funded academic backgrounds and think tanks.

Around the time of the 2018 midterm elections, in response to Trump's outrageous comments and actions against immigrants and Muslims, Democrats were calling for the restoration of America's "moral compass."

But I have to ask, where was the moral compass while a million people in the Middle East were slaughtered in the post–9/11 wars? The outcry from both parties (until recently, when the horrifying Khashoggi murder flushed out the repressiveness of Saudi Arabia and the humanitarian crisis in Yemen) has been muted. Indeed, the pervasive censorship regarding the Middle East has been going on since the end of World War II.

Breaking Taboos, Crossing Divides
The American Israel Public Affairs Committee (AIPAC) is one of the most powerful lobbying groups in the United States. Its propaganda apparatus has been far reaching and highly effective, helping to ensure that any criticism of Israeli policies toward Palestinians is tantamount to anti-Semitism.

AIPAC's grip on US public opinion has slipped somewhat over the years due to Israel's more publicized human rights violations and military incursions in Lebanon, Gaza, and the West Bank, but it is ever vigilant. Immediately after the 2018 midterm elections in the United States, for instance, AIPAC proudly announced:

Americans elected a solidly pro-Israel Congress, with many new members. While polarized on many issues, the 116th Congress remains committed to the U.S.-Israel relationship on a bipartisan basis. Virtually all of the new members elected this month have issued position papers and statements reflecting their strong support for Israel's security and her efforts to reach peace with all her neighbors. . . . Members of the pro-Israel community have already begun building relationships with the new members. AIPAC's lay leaders and staff held more than 400 candidate meetings, resulting in more than 300 position papers on the U.S.-Israel relationship in this election cycle.[34]

Now AIPAC's work is being complemented by Saudi lobbyists, who are endeavoring to advance the interests of Saudi Arabia, Israel's new ally. According to the Project on Government Oversight's Lydia Dennett (no known relation to this author), "Saudi Arabia has spent about 19 million dollars on influence campaigns here in the U.S. since the beginning of 2017 and 9 million this year alone." (She made the comment in October 2018.) In 2017, they contacted every US senator, every member of the House Armed Services Committee, and every member of the House Foreign

Affairs Committee to ensure that they would get their arms deals secured. They also engaged in a massive public relations campaign to depict Saudis as reliable allies in the Middle East and stress that the war in Yemen was good for the United States.[35]

Hope in a New Era of Resistance

Despite these well-funded lobbying efforts, there have been significant fissures in the straitjacket on truth in the Middle East.

The election to Congress of two Muslim women (Ilhan Omar of Minnesota and Rashida Tlaib of Michigan) has also generated a much-needed debate over whether criticism of Israel is an expression of anti-Semitism. Influential *New York Times* columnist Thomas Friedman wrote a stunning op-ed, "Ilhan Omar, Aipac and Me," in which he admitted that he shared with Omar a dislike of AIPAC and had "spoken in very blunt language about [AIPAC's] strong-arm political tactics." For many years, he said, AIPAC has "become a rubber stamp on the right-wing policies of Prime Minister Benjamin Netanyahu, which has resulted in tens of thousands of Israeli settlers now ensconced in the heart of the West Bank, imperiling Israel as a democracy."[36]

Shortly after Friedman's piece was published (generating more controversy), AIPAC held its annual meeting in Washington. "This year's confab is playing out in a changed and charged Washington political environment," the *New York Times* reported.

Democrats, the *New York Times* noted, "who for decades have relied on the Jewish vote," would face a tricky task: "They must reiterate their support for the Jewish state without alienating progressives, including millennials and many young Jews who are increasingly willing to accuse Israel of human rights abuses."[37]

A generational divide has also been reported in the Israeli army. On April 2, 2019, the *Jerusalem Post* reported that nine Israeli soldiers had been arrested "for refusing to take part in preparation for a Gaza military campaign." Noted the article, "This is just one of many disciplinary incidents that have been discovered in the unit amid problems between veteran soldiers and the new conscripts."[38]

Meanwhile, back in the United States, many Jews opposed to Israel's brutality toward the Palestinians have aligned themselves with the Washington-based Jewish Voice for Peace. The organization has been circulating a petition that declares, "Israelis and Palestinians deserve freedom, security and the right to sleep in their homes at night without fear of falling bombs. Endless wars on Gaza and endless occupation will not achieve that for anyone."[39]

There are more signs of change, brought on by tragic attacks against both Jews and Muslims in their houses of worship. The brutal attack in November 2018 on the Tree of Life synagogue in Pittsburgh has understandably and appropriately aroused intense concern about growing anti-Semitism in the United States. The massacre of eleven congregants by a lone gunman, considered among the deadliest against the Jewish community in the United States, brought an immediate response from two Muslim organizations. They started an online campaign to support the victims' families, setting their goal at $20,000. Within days, donations had flooded in amounting to $200,000. Commented Chicago activist Tarek El-Messidi, one of the organizers of the online campaign, "Putting our religious differences or even your political differences aside, the core of all of us is that we have a shared humanity. We really wanted to reach out as human beings to help."[40]

Similarly, when a gunman opened fire in a New Zealand mosque, killing forty-four worshippers, Jewish organizations were quick to express their sympathy and support. Stephen Goodman, the president of the New Zealand Jewish Council, sent a message through the Jewish Telegraph Agency that was printed, among other places, in the *Times of Israel*, stating, "We offer our full assistance and support to the Muslim community and stand united with it against the scourge of terrorism and racism, which we must do all we can to banish from New Zealand."[41] Isaac Herzog, the head of the Jewish Agency for Israel, followed up with a tweet: "For the first time in history synagogues in NZ are closed on Shabbat following the shocking massacre of Muslims in Christchurch."

Amid vicious and frightening attacks of racist hatred, victimized communities are finding ways to draw closer together and forge new understandings. I found evidence of this in a blog post by a rabbi from London, Alexander Goldberg, who visited the heavily bombed city of Tripoli, in Lebanon, in January 2019. He made friends, listened to how people in Lebanon still bore emotional scars from so much violence in their lives, and concluded that "while politics has largely failed in the region, I've observed during my encounters that there's a growing grassroots movement calling for peace and reconciliation." As one of his hosts conveyed, "It's up to us, the people, to take effective actions for peacemaking; nobody will do it on our behalf."[42]

History has shown that the oppression of indigenous peoples by occupation forces (and drones) only creates more resentment and more armed resistance. As a result, the pipelines do not get built, because as long as there is instability, banks will not invest in them.

Meanwhile, popular resistance to Western and Israeli pipelines has started in Jordan, Israel, and Gaza. In May 2018, according to *Haaretz*, "a few dozen protesters set fires at several locations on the Gazan side of the Kerem Shalom border crossing with the aim of damaging pipelines that transfer gas and fuel from Israel into the Strip."[43] Those demonstrations have continued every Friday to this day, and as noted earlier in this book, many of those protesters have been killed by Israeli forces.

In July 2018, Jordanian workers carrying signs that read "Our Blood Isn't Worth Gas" and "No to Normalization" protested along a proposed natural gas pipeline route that would carry Israeli gas to Jordan. Organized by one of Jordan's largest and most influential labor unions, the Jordanian Engineers Association argued that Jordan could produce enough alternative energy on its own instead of relying on "stolen gas" from Israel. Ahmad Zoabi, the head of the Jordanian Engineers Association, declared that Jordan could produce enough "solar, wind and shale energy to rid the kingdom of the need to import from the occupied lands."[44]

Meanwhile, Palestinians have begun to make common cause with the "earth warriors" at Standing Rock Indian Reservation in North Dakota protesting the Trump-backed Dakota Access Pipeline, the 1,200-mile construction project that will transfer oil across several states. In November 2016, a *Salon* piece quoted an open letter from a young Palestinian writer and student, Israa Suliman, to indigenous Americans. It read in part:

> *Although we are of different color, religion, culture and place, I have learned, as I read about the protests at Standing Rock, that we have much more in common than differences. When I read your history, I can see myself and my people reflected in yours. I feel in my core that your fight is my fight, and that I am not alone in the battle against injustice.*
>
> *My ancestors were the indigenous people, just like you. And they suffered the same fate as your people. America's policy of occupation and displacement through forced marches like the Trail of Tears, and the gradual transfer of so many of your people to massive, impoverished reservations, hurts me deeply because it is so similar to the ethnic*

*cleansing of my ancestors by the Israeli military occupation in what
we call* al-Nakba *(the catastrophe).*[45]

This amazing letter and all the protests in the Middle East have given
me a renewed sense of hope. The cross-fertilization of ideas from those
who have experienced ethnocide and genocide from opposite ends of the
world is truly happening.

And I am thrilled that nonnative earth warriors in the United States,
such as members of 350.org, have been working tirelessly to recruit
Americans (many of them young college students) to join in their effort to
"keep the oil in the ground." Under the leadership of founder and author
Bill McKibben, they have devised serious educational campaigns showing
how climate interfaces with racism, economic injustice, refugee crises, and
other major issues.

Finding Carat, Putting the Pieces Together

In the process of telling my story, I have gained new insights and discovered their relevance to the endless wars plaguing the Middle East. The
intense rivalries among former World War II allies witnessed by my father
in the late 1940s are still at play, at times resulting in assassinations, regime
change, and all-out war, only on a larger scale with more players. Espionage
continues to play a central role in the Great Game, and, yes, erstwhile allies
still spy on one another.

What surprised me most while writing the sections on my father was
Great Britain's desperate efforts to hold on to — and even expand — its empire after the war, to the point of undermining the United States, at every
turn, whether in Lebanon, Syria, Saudi Arabia, or Ethiopia. I expected
treacherous game-playing by the Soviets, who widely publicized their
alarm over the Truman Doctrine and its Cold War efforts to establish military bases in the Middle East purportedly to contain Soviet expansionism
(while also protecting US oil holdings). But our closest ally, Great Britain?

Although my father considered himself "pro-British by instinct," he
knew that he had to consider the British as opponents of American expansion in their Middle East domain, even though they were allies during the
war. Carat maintained cordial relations with his counterparts in British intelligence, while also keeping tabs on them. Ironically, one of his missions
to British-controlled Jordan — under the cover of a vacation trip with his

wife to the fantastic ruins of Petra — likely resulted in my being conceived in a Bedouin cave inside the ruins. (I was born nine months after my mother dated a letter home, exclaiming "We slept in a cave!") My father made a side trip to Jordan's capital of Amman to more deeply investigate known British influence on King Abdullah of Jordan. The king, he confirmed, espoused a British plan to expand their influence throughout the Levant in what they called Greater Syria — a plan that ran directly counter to US ambitions to win over the loyalties of the Syrians and the Lebanese.[46]

This got me examining more closely his reports — and his attitudes — about the British. Were there any signs of antagonism? Any indication that they would go so far as to sabotage his plane?

In his last letter to my mother about his trip to Saudi Arabia, he expressed his concern about a British model of colonialism (the East India Company) being adopted by the American owners of Aramco. He wrote "Aramco has to a large measure taken over the functions of a legation or government. The King [ibn Saud] doesn't bother with our Minister but deals [directly] with the company, which in a sense is a new American version of the East India Company." Here was a foreboding of the increasing control of corporations — in this case, a powerful oil company — over government officials and functions, including, of course, diplomats. Life at the Aramco compound, he went on, "is a little too paternalistic and I shouldn't enjoy it. Everything is the company's. . . . And since everything belongs to Aramco, one can't do anything without Aramco's permission."

His opinions were apparently shared by Herman Eilts, a contemporary of my father's who began his US diplomatic career in Saudi Arabia from 1947 to 1949. Only Eilts and a member of his diplomatic staff in Jidda, Ernest Latham, took my father's observations one step further, beyond British influence on Aramco (and by extension on TAPLINE, its pipeline company) to TAPLINE's emergence as a power in and of itself. Commented Latham, TAPLINE had assumed the role of "one of the great arteries of Empire, the American Empire in the Middle East I mean. Because that's in fact what it was."[47]

The daughter of a TWA representative working with Saudi Arabia Airlines was also witness to the growing imperiousness of Aramco. She told Robert Kaplan, author of *The Arabists*, about a growing rift between the oil company and the business community in Jidda and the diplomatic corps. The businessmen called the embassy staff the "Dippy Corps," she said, deriding them for having "too many Arab friends," or "ragheads."[48] My father, a member of the diplomatic corps who had many Arab friends, fit the profile. Was his sensitivity to Arab nationalism running counter to the prerogatives of empire espoused by Big Oil? I raise this because of a comment made by the daughter of one of my father's closest Lebanese friends. She told me that whenever my father's name came up in conversations following his death, her father would get very upset and more than once said, "He was killed by one of his own." I have long wondered: Did he mean the Americans, or their "cousins," the British, as they were called in diplomatic cables. Either way, I have been haunted by his words.

Her father, now deceased, was Sheikh Najib Alamuddin, a powerful Druze prince known to the Dennett family as Najib, who used to stay up late talking politics with my father between bridge games in the 1930s when both were instructors at the American University of Beirut. He went on to become a successful businessman and trusted source for my father during his OSS and CIG days in Lebanon, and later became the powerful head of Middle East Airlines after World War II. What Najib remembered about my father in his memoirs, *The Flying Sheikh*, struck me as odd and yet a possible hint that my father did not always get along well with the British. He describes running into my father in the sitting room at a small residential hotel in London in 1937:

> *I was pleasantly surprised to find Dan Dennett, an American friend from my teaching years at the American University of Beirut. Dan had the American love of loudly criticizing everything which differed from the American way of life. Naturally, he saw much to criticize in England, and was quite vociferous about it, especially during mealtimes. Many of the residents at the hotel were retired colonial government officials and their ladies and there was no doubting their failure to appreciate Dan's views, but generally nothing was said. Then, one morning at breakfast, an old lady at the next table said to her companion in a voice to be heard by all: "What do you expect from the Americans, my dear, they are nothing but white natives."*

It was typical of Dan Dennett, Najib continued, "that he greatly enjoyed the old lady's wit." But Najib must have given my father some friendly advice, because "afterwards, he became far more circumspect in his criticism." He ended his brief remembrance by explaining that "Dan returned to Beirut during the Second World War, as a special official of the United States government. Sadly, he was killed in an air crash in the mountains of Ethiopia. His death was a loss to his government and country, and also to the Arab, for he was a true friend."[49]

Why, I had to wonder, with all Najib's memories of Dan Dennett over the years, would he offer this sole anecdote? It was humorous, of course, but I couldn't help but make a mental note about my father's loud anti-British criticism, his colonial listeners' resentment, and in the last sentence, mention of his death.

The Oil Below and the Air Above

As president of the new Middle East Airlines, Najib was intimately familiar with a new arena for postwar commercial rivalry: the development of civil aviation and its ability to penetrate the airspace of lands once held in colonial captivity. He surely had conversations with Dennett about this new phase of competition between the British and the Americans. In many ways, it amounted to the merging of pipeline politics (to control pipeline routes) with "airplane politics" (to control airspace routes), both absolutely vital to American plans for a new postwar world order. Commercial airplanes possessed a unique ability to rapidly reach into new markets while transporting goods, services, and equipment — including aerial cameras, which could photograph oil-bearing terrains and pipeline routes. A new stage in the Great Game was about to begin.

American frustrations with the British had been building ever since the Chicago Convention on International Civil Aviation in December 1944 established the rules of airspace and rights of international travel. Fifty-two states signed on, but final ratification did not occur until March 5, 1947. Among the more contested rights, or "freedoms" established by the Convention was the "Fifth Freedom" — the right of an airline to carry passengers from its country of origin to another country and then a second country and beyond.

By May 1945, Ralph Curren, the US civil air attaché based in Cairo, complained that "British diplomatic personnel in the Middle East countries and British Air Ministry representative have and still do exert every possible influence on local government to refuse American airlines fifth freedom privileges and delay acceptance of bilateral air transport agreements." He reported that in Cairo, British advisors to the Egyptian government were so incensed over US demands for air rights in Egypt that they decided "no dollar exchange would be approved for maintenance by American personnel and that instead BOAC would service and maintain." And in Lebanon, the British Minister to Lebanon "made a definitive statement to Minister Wadsworth that British did not want American airlines to operate in the Middle East."[50]

Carat, reporting from Beirut to Washington and likely relying on some information obtained from one of his most important assets in Lebanon, Najib, who had close ties with the British, stated that "British intelligence has played an important role in opposing during the last six weeks our diplomatic efforts to secure landing privileges [in Lebanon and Syria] for TWA and Pan American. . . . " The British were, he reported, "waging a well-planned campaign to secure every possible economic advantage and all possible political influence." He added that they were becoming adept at intercepting messages about US commercial moves in the region.* "We have discovered that it is a matter of hours only before British have texts of all notes or memoranda or *aide memoirs* which we may leave at either [Lebanese or Syrian] Foreign Office."[51]

My father was well primed for this "war for the air." In his 1944 Analysis of Work, under the heading "Probable American Postwar Interests," Dennett not only wrote about the need to control the oil of Saudi Arabia "at all costs." He followed with this paragraph: "The strategic importance of the region for *air and other transport* is so great that we cannot allow these lands to pass into hostile hands. The threat of such passage should alarm us as much as a challenge to . . ." (emphasis added) The rest of the sentence was redacted as classified by the CIA. Perhaps a reference to our oil holdings?

What followed in his analysis was yet another epiphany: "A hostile threat," he continued, "to our interests cited . . . above may come from two quarters: [a long line is redacted here by the CIA]. The latter may and can become more dangerous than the former."

---

* This comment is important. If the British were intercepting messages, they would have had advance notice of the plans of the US military attaché to fly to Saudi Arabia and Ethiopia in early 1947 to discuss forging closer military ties to both countries and advance American civil aviation.

After decades of investigation, I had to conclude that the two quarters were the British and the Soviets. Certainly by 1947, they were America's — and my father's — most dangerous rivals in the Middle East. The British were trying to hold on to their empire; the Soviets were trying to build theirs. Until the CIA further unredacts that document, I will not know which "quarter" my father considered the most dangerous. But I did know of one country where this dangerous game was playing out at the time of his death: in Ethiopia.

In light of Dennett's second-most vital postwar mission — preventing strategic "air and transport" from falling into hostile hands, it's time to take another look at the events in Ethiopia leading up to his death. John Spencer, the American advisor to the Ethiopian government, had made it clear in an interview with me shortly before his death and in his book, *Ethiopia at Bay*, that the British were deeply concerned about controlling Ethiopia's airspace. The British Overseas Airway Corporation (BOAC) controlled the air tower at the Addis airport. To challenge their monopoly, Spencer sought to establish a government-owned airline in Ethiopia managed by the American-owned TWA. That initiative, he figured, would go a long way toward freeing Ethiopia "from foreign controls over transport and communications, particularly since the country had few roads and was surrounded by nearly impassable deserts."[52] He arranged to have Jack Nichols of TWA meet with the Ethiopian government in August 1945. As noted earlier, Nichols never made it to Addis. After departing Asmara, Eritrea, his plane — traveling the same route as Dennett's Flight 3804 when it took off from Asmara eighteen months later — crashed into the Ethiopian mountains. "It was terrible," Spencer told me. "We had to start [negotiations] all over again."

The British, meanwhile, continued to deny landing rights to the US-backed Ethiopian Air Lines. The British Legation controlled all radio communications in Ethiopia and, according to Spencer, "was seeking to dissuade the U.S. Army Signal corps from setting up a receiving and coding site for radio communications . . . outside Asmara in Eritrea."[53]

Ethiopian Air Lines was finally set up in 1946 with backing from TWA, but by then, British and American relations in Cairo, the Middle East headquarters for both US and British military intelligence, had grown so tense that the office of the US military attaché issued an order that "military personnel would no longer be transported on planes owned and piloted by British Overseas Airways (BOAC). Experience has already demonstrated that use of British Overseas Airways by U.S. military personnel on official missions is highly unsatisfactory and undependable."[54]

The Crash of Flight 3804

When Dennett boarded Flight 3804 in Jidda bound for Asmara on March 19, 1947, it was as if America's players in the new Great Game over oil and airspace converged on this ill-fated C-47 army transport plane. Donald Sullivan, US petroleum attaché, had been traveling throughout the Middle East, most recently in Saudi Arabia, inspecting American oil holdings and prospects; CIG's John Creech was making similar trips, only picking up surplus and top secret wartime radio and communications equipment and delivering them to American legations. Dennett, by virtue of his intelligence training and his recent trip to Saudi Arabia, had to have known the stakes of this trip to Addis were very large. Flight 3804's stated mission, according to the flight records of the US military attaché, was to deliver heavy signals equipment to the US Legation. Beyond that, the Americans' mission was to meet with Sinclair Oil officials in Addis Ababa, to hand over aerial photos taken during the flight, and presumably, to better equip Ethiopian Air Lines with communications and navigational equipment to lessen reliance on BOAC.

After the war, civilian airlines like Ethiopian Air Lines were envisioned to replace the US Army Air Forces as the newest and fastest means of transporting goods and supplies. Aerial surveys once conducted by the Army Air Forces could, after the war, be performed by private carriers. Seen in this light, Ethiopian Air Lines had a vital role to play for US interests, other than breaking Britain's monopoly over Ethiopia's airspace.

According to John Spencer, Sinclair Oil's survey crews met continued resistance from British authorities, especially in the Ogaden region of southeastern Ethiopia, where the largest oil deposits were believed to exist. The region was still under the control of the British military mission. The problem with British obstructionism in the Ogaden "became so severe," wrote Spencer, "that at one point, the company temporarily withdrew its personnel from the Ogaden and proposed canceling the concession. It was only after the withdrawal of the British from the Ogaden (1948) that Sinclair could finally get operations underway."[55]

Aerial surveys, on the other hand, could accomplish from above what survey crews could not accomplish on the ground. A declassified report from

Sinclair Oil to Loy Henderson of the Near East Division dated December 8, 1946, indicates that "through the United States Army, Sinclair has secured air photographs on the Northern Ogaden area."* Furthermore, "efforts to secure additional air photographs which will constitute the basis of all exploration work in Ethiopia have been made and are being continued. . . . These photographs are essential." The report concluded, ". . . if it is found that they [the photos] are not available from any source an investigation will be made to determine the feasibility of flying the area and obtaining photographs through a private undertaking on the part of Sinclair."[56]

The loss of the aerial camera in the crash of 3804 prompted Colonel McNown to send an urgent cable to military intelligence in Washington: "KING TWENTY CAMERA COMPLETELY DAMAGED AIRCRAFT ACCIDENT TWENTY MARCH . . . REPLACEMENT KING TWENTY BE SHIPPED THIS STATION MOST EXPEDITIOUSLY."[57]

More Insights from the Crash Report

Colonel McNown reported that "apparently no person witnessed the crash" but that villagers in the area said the mountain was in a complete cloud and that they heard the plane circle the mountain three times. "Half a dozen natives were insistent in saying the plane circled, trying to explain further by pointing where the plane had gone and where it came from (by sound) just before crashing."

While McNown's official report theorized that the pilot's circling was to find an opening in the clouds, the word *circling* reminded me of my father's last letter to my mother, when he wrote of taking a plane ride "to discover a suitable beachhead between Dharan and Kuwait where pipe for the [Trans-Arabian] line might be landed." Significantly, his airplane "circled round and round, checking maps with topography."[58] I concluded that McNown was not about to offer this interpretation about "circling" in his official report. Like his other omissions (the aerial camera, for instance, or the Americans' planned visit with Sinclair Oil), he chose to leave out any oil connection to Flight 3804.

---

* Interestingly, the Ogaden in 1944 was suggested by Zionists as a location for "mass immigration into various so-called 'empty spaces' of the world," but was "turned down cold." Minister Felix Cole to Clare Timberlake, Chief of the African Division, Department of State, June 17, 1947, RG 59, 884.00/6-1746, NARA.

Still, despite these shortcomings, McNown was adamant in reporting that radio communications between Asmara and Addis on Flight 3804's departure were amiss. In fact, he pointedly laid the blame with the British-controlled BOAC air tower in Addis, which failed to report that the plane did not arrive as scheduled. "All radio contact in the Middle East area . . . is somewhat spontaneous and never reliable," he allowed. "There is no single organized radio control for the Asmara-Addis Ababa route." However, he continued, "The airdome control at Addis Ababa was advised by Asmara radio that 3804 had taken off from Asmara and was proceeding to Addis but did not take any overdue action nor was the message passed on to the American Legation."

In fact, according to McNown's report, the airport manager in Asmara later reported, "[there was] no information received from Addis that this aircraft did not arrive until 24 hours after it was overdue . . . this delay might be very serious."[59]

Serious indeed. A delayed rescue might have meant no survivors as well as looting or tampering with the crash site by whoever got there first. And from what I can determine, the first to arrive at the crash site was an unnamed British Brigadier.

Rescue . . . or Reconnaissance?

According to a message from Minister Cole on March 21, "all six on board reported killed. . . . Local authorities and British military mission Dessie doing utmost." A War Department cable from Cairo dated March 22, stated "UNCONFIRMED REPORT INDICATES BRITISH BRIGADIER WAS FIRST TO REACH SCENE AND REPORTED SIX PERSONS KILLED."[60] This was later relayed to the family of CIG communications expert, John Creech, in the War Department's letter of sympathy. What was not reported was the brigadier's opportunity to survey Creech's heavy load of communications equipment, and any sensitive information in the pockets of the deceased.

McNown's official report does not acknowledge that the British were first on the crash site. Instead, he describes the arrival on March 23 (three days after the crash) of a Swedish-led team sent on the orders of Ethiopian emperor Haile Selassie. It was composed of Captain G. Magnusson of the Imperial Ethiopian Air Force and a Swedish medical doctor by the name of Hallen.[61] The pilot who flew them from Addis to the nearest town of Dessie was Count Carl Gustaf von Rosen, who was ordered by the emperor to head up the investigation. At the time von Rosen was training the Ethiopian air force (and, I recently learned, was believed by the OSS in 1945 to be in the pay of both the Germans and the British).[62]

On March 22, the two Swedes set off by muleback from Dessie for a daylong trek to a village near the crash site. On the way they encountered an Ethiopian group "commanded by Major Lemma Gebre Mariam, who was returning to Dessie with six corpses from the crashed plane." Conceivably, this Ethiopian group was connected to the British Royal Air Force, as a Lebanese newspaper had reported that RAF officers stationed in Dessie were first on the scene.[63] RAF officers, I have learned from Hugh Wilford's *America's Great Game*, worked for British counterintelligence; moreover, Wilford reports, "RAF aerial surveillance had been a crucial technique for enforcing the British mandate, so this was very much an imperial perspective from which to survey the Middle East" — and, no doubt, Ethiopia.[64]

On March 23, the Swedish team arrived at the crash site the same day that First Secretary William Beach and Donald Nicholls of the US Legation in Addis set foot at the site. The Americans were accompanied by an unnamed "British Major of the British Military Mission." This was the second time that a British officer was unnamed.

Magnusson, in his separate report, seemed nonplussed about the cause of the accident. Among Magnusson's findings, upon examining the wreckage: the flaps had not been in downposition as before a normal landing; wheels had not been lowered; propellers had not been feathered; the altimeter was completely destroyed.

He raised the possibility of faulty radio contact. "If the aircraft's radio had been working or not, cannot be cleared up here," he wrote, "but may be explained from a ground station at Asmara. . . . A broken radio connection could form the reason for the bad navigation that caused the C-47 to crash into the side of a mountain."

US military attaché McNown, who arrived the following day from Jidda, added details that suggested that the pilot "did not think he was in trouble." The pilot's, copilot's, and the radio operator's safety belts appeared not to have been fastened. There were about twelve parachutes on board but no evidence of their being used. The flight maps were inaccurate, showing the mountains to be 8,000 feet high, whereas the plane hit a mountain peak at 11,000. However, the pilot knew the maps were inaccurate and had flown the route before.

McNown ended his report vowing that a continuing investigation would be carried out "to determine the possibility of sabotage. The equipment on board was valuable and of a classified nature. No reliable security exists in Cairo, Jidda or Asmara." He also recommended that "a reliable State Department radio network be established in the Middle East so that arrival and departure notices of aircraft can be sent and received without delay."

The Ethiopian Air Lines Connection

McNown itemized the radio communications and navigational equipment in his report, without explaining their usage other than its being "destined for the American legation, Addis Ababa."[65] A cable from McNown's Cairo office dated March 22 verified that the cargo was "signals equipment," which was used during the war to intercept and decipher the most secret communications between adversaries.[66]

Given the reluctance of the British to allow American signals equipment to be used outside of Asmara, the planned delivery of this equipment to the US Legation was likely kept secret from the British. After the plane crashed, however, the top secret cargo was exposed, smashed to pieces on the ground. When McNown completed his on-site investigation, he flew to Addis for a reckoning with "BOAC radio personnel and Mr. Obermiller, American head of the Ethiopian Airlines." McNown knew from the radio logs that BOAC was in control of the Addis tower and had received notice of the plane's departure from Asmara. Yet BOAC failed to take overdue action. When queried by the Asmara control tower how this could have happened, the radio logs also showed BOAC trying to claim that it was Ethiopian Air Lines, not BOAC, that had been informed of the plane's departure from Asmara and expected arrival date. BOAC seemed to be passing the buck. At the post-crash meeting with McNown, BOAC again denied being alerted to Flight 3804's impending arrival on March 20.

Either way, both BOAC and Ethiopian Air Lines were parties of interest in connection to the crash. Two weeks after the crash, new information came in to the American investigators that raised suspicions about Ethiopian Air Lines to a new level.

The Mysterious Mr. X

In a declassified State Department memo dated June 6, 1947, First Secretary William Beach reported from Addis on a conversation he had with a "Mr. X," a radio operator for Ethiopian Air Lines who said that of the twenty-five persons employed there, half of them were Greeks "believed to be communists," and that they were "organized for the purpose of getting control of the communications of the Ethiopian Air Lines."[67]

Mr. X reported that the latest Greek employee to arrive from Cairo was a "meteorologist" who was in the midst of typing a letter to someone called "Duke" when he was called out of the office, "and quite imprudently left the letter in the typewriter." The letter stated, "We are working hard here to get more Greeks down from Cairo. . . . If we send enough," the letter ended ominously with reference to Ethiopian Air Lines, "the Line must go down." Mr. X said he "had felt for some time that 'these Greeks' were Communists, but was unable to give any tangible evidence."

First Secretary Beach inquired if the letter was written in English and Mr. X said it was, and that he assumed "Duke" was possibly a "Russian who did not understand Greek."

"Mr. X," Beach concluded in his report, "spoke of the danger of allowing any one clique to get control over the communications system of the Ethiopian Air Line."

Beach had been involved in the on-site investigation of the crash of Flight 3804, and surely must have read McNown's report. Beach's memo, written less than a month after the crash, seemed to suggest that Greeks manning the EAL command center might have been involved in the downing of Flight 3804 and the scuttling of its mission to deliver top secret communications equipment to the Americans. For me, the question was whether the Greeks were really communists, possibly following orders from the Soviet Union, or if they were working for the British.[68] Why, for instance, was the letter left in the typewriter written in English and directed to someone named "Duke," rather than a "Dimitri"?

Deepening the intrigue in Ethiopia at the time of the crash was an alleged plot by the British to overthrow the pro-American emperor Haile Selassie. US military attaché McNown, who was close to all the men on the plane and was distraught over their loss (according to one of his relatives, whom I interviewed after McNown had died), passed on a top secret message to Washington on April 16, 1947, from an "unquestionable repeat unquestionable source upon which reliance must be placed." McNown proceeded to cable a dire warning:

BETWEEN NOW AND END APRIL A COUP D'ETAT PLANNED ETHIOPIA. BRITISH PLOTTING ASSASSINATION EMPEROR

AND HAVE BOUGHT OUT CROWN PRINCE, WHOSE ACCES-
SION TO THRONE ALSO BACKED BY FOREIGN OIL INTER-
EST BELIEVED TO BE BEHIND THE PLOT THAT WOULD PUT
THE CROWN PRINCE ON THE THRONE. THE SUCCESS OF
THIS PLOT WOULD BE INIMICAL TO AMERICAN INTER-
ESTS IN AFRICA AND MIDEAST . . . ALTHOUGH BRITISH
POSSIBLY NOT REPEAT NOT INVOLVED, SOME FOREIGN
COUNTRY IS INVOLVED.[69]

The crown prince was governor general of the Province of Wollo, which includes the area of Dessie near the plane crash site.

US Minister to Egypt Pinkney Tuck, on receiving McNown's warning, averred that McNown's source (Egypt's King Farouk) "confided to me over two years ago that he believed that the British were responsible for his motor accident at Kassassin and that it was a deliberate attempt on his life."[70]

McNown flew to Addis to directly warn US Minister Cole. Anglophile that he was, Cole adamantly resisted the notion that the British were involved. Perhaps McNown's presence in Addis was just in time, as the coup did not materialize.[71] Interestingly, however, the Ethiopians succeeded in causing Cole's resignation soon afterwards, ostensibly as a result of his colonialist views and perceived insensitivity to Ethiopian customs and culture.[72] Ethiopia's Haile Selassie wanted Cole, an admirer of the interfering British, gone.

Reverberations from the crash of Flight 3804 were felt well into late 1947 and 1948. In October 1947, the Ethiopian president of Ethiopian Air Lines was assured that "a communications system has been designed, constructed and staffed with competent personnel. This system now provides adequate two-way radio communications between Ethiopian Air Lines ground stations and Ethiopian Air Lines airplanes in flight over all the routes of the airline."[73] In March 1948, the Damascus-based US military attaché, Robert Brown, proposed hiring a Lebanese as a handyman-guard for "aircraft assigned to this station." He even proposed having "a reliable Arab" sleep in the aircraft during volatile times. "Attention is called to the extreme vulnerability to sabotage of our aircraft," he wrote, "and to the lack of available US guard personnel."

In August 1948, the Department of State announced that "it is politically wise to recommend a control tower operator [at the Addis Ababa airport] who is an American citizen."[74]

The Russian Factor

McNown's cable about the planned coup against Emperor Selassie suggested that if the British were not behind the plot, "some foreign government is involved." On March 21, 1947 — the day after the crash of Flight 3804 — McNown sent out a message to the War Department reviewing Soviet reaction to the Truman Doctrine announced a week earlier. Moscow radio, his message read, made "two and three broadcasts daily in all Middle East languages. Theme: America betrays UNO (the United Nations); invites war; sells Greco-Turkish democratic cause to reactionary racist clique; dollar diplomacy and American imperialism engulfs Middle East."[75] Some of these concepts, I figured, could have been easily cooked up by Kim Philby, now stationed in Turkey.

Even earlier, in January 1947, Clare Timberlake, the acting chief of the US State Department's Division of African Affairs, had concluded that the USSR was indeed "stepping up its pace to obtain influence in Ethiopia," which was likely "part of a coordinated plan directed at the strategic lower Red Sea area and . . . at the same time, providing an entering wedge into Central Africa." They were setting up a Soviet hospital in Addis that, he surmised, "may be used as a cloak for Soviet intelligence activities."[76] The Soviets, for their part, accused the British of wanting to enlarge their interests by establishing a "Greater Somaliland," much as the British were angling for a Greater Syria to solidify their hold over the entire eastern Mediterranean.[77]

To add to my British-Soviet conundrum, I found another intriguing document in the declassified top secret records of the Department of State, dated August 3, 1947. It indicates that "three terrorists," imprisoned by the British in a prison camp in Eritrea, "escaped Eritrea internment mid-January, entered Ethiopia clandestinely in March, remained hidden in Addis until July 23 and were apprehended for return to the British." Fascinatingly, all "claimed Soviet citizenship shortly after arrest and requested communicat[ion to] Addis Soviet Legation which was not granted." Yet they also had connections to Britain. "Two bore old London Polish Government passports. . . . One bore documents of Captain British RAF."[78] I noted that the terrorists entered Ethiopia in the same month that my father's plane crashed. Whom were they tied to: the Soviets, the British, or both?

The British had indeed imprisoned members of the Irgun Zvai Leumi in a prison camp in Eritrea. American supporters, author Bruce Hoffman notes, "were particularly successful in . . . raising funds for the Irgun, and gaining access . . . to the special British prison for Jewish terrorists in Eritrea."[79] Did the Americans secure the prisoners' releases or aid in their escape? Did the British release some prisoners to perform operations for them, in return for their freedom? Did the Soviets pull off a jailbreak that released the three Irgun members into Ethiopia?[80]

Inevitably, these questions only intensified my interest in learning more about Kim Philby, who worked clandestinely for both the British and the Soviets and had been visiting with the British in Taif and Jidda in January 1947. Might Philby's masters' interests have converged, I wondered, in wanting to blunt the rise of the United States as a superpower thanks to its oil holdings in Saudi Arabia and its efforts to assist Sinclair Oil in Ethiopia?[81] And might they have arranged, through Philby, to have the Irgun Zvai Le'umi or Greek communists to do their dirty work? Philby, working for *both* the Soviets and the British, continued to surface as a suspect in my investigation. He strived, on behalf of the Soviets, to undermine British interests in the Middle East. Yet he had to deliver for the British to remain above suspicion. The one area where both tasks converged to the satisfaction of both his Soviet and British handlers was going after the Americans.

Final Thoughts

Even though I have established the motive for the downing of Flight 3804, I have yet to establish the precise means or identities of the perpetrators. Some skeptics have asked, "Why go to the bother of downing an airplane when there were easier ways, like shooting him on a dark street?" To which I answer, some of the most famous cases of alleged murder by plane crash are still the subject of controversy precisely because proving "whodunit" or how the plane crashed has been so difficult.

Philby has been implicated in the 1943 plane crash that killed Polish premier Wladyslaw Sikorski on his way to the Middle East. The death by plane crash of United Nations Secretary General Dag Hammarskjold in 1961 in what was then the British protectorate of Northern Rhodesia is also still the subject of controversy. According to the *New York Times* in February 2019, conspiracies abound "that colonial-era mining interests, perhaps backed by Western intelligence agencies, had plotted to assassinate him. The inquiries have turned Mr. Hammarskjold's death into the biggest mystery in the history of the United Nations."[82]

Enrico Mattei, who was the founder of the Italian oil company ENI and negotiated oil concessions for Italy in the Middle East, likewise died in a plane crash under mysterious circumstances. The case, which has obsessed Italy for years, was first ruled an accident; three decades later it was determined to be the result of a bomb on the plane. Reported the *Independent*, "with the Cold War over, the Mafia informer Tommaso Buscetta announced three years ago that Mr Mattei had been killed by Cosa Nostra as a favour to its friends in the US business community."* That statement "triggered the latest inquiry, including the exhumation of Mr Mattei's corpse." The autopsy showed "'clear signs of multiple lesions caused by waves from an explosion.'"[83]

My father's body was cremated, so exhumation is not an option.

As revealed in many chapters, due to the secrecy, lying, and deceit that are part and parcel of the Great Game, it is difficult to get at the full truth. A former CIA station chief who has been helpful to me in understanding the basic workings of the agency told me that it would be "extremely difficult" to find out what really happened. And, of course, he said, I would have to take into consideration that the plane itself was the target because of the equipment it was carrying (aerial camera and signals equipment) and not because of my father, or for that matter the other five men on the plane. Whereupon I told him about the importance of understanding context in developing a theory, something that Jan Leestma, a world authority on forensic neuropathology, emphasized: "Facts in isolation," he said, in an interview with CNN, "lead to all sorts of questions," whereas "facts put in a contextual light" enable the investigator to narrow down the causes."[84] "Yes, context is important," the retired CIA chief admitted, "and so is circumstantial evidence, which can be used in a court of law to prove a case." Indeed. If nothing else, I have provided a historical context within which certain patterns are recognizable. One of them is the obsession of the biggest players in the Great Game with "getting the oil at all costs," to the point that any resistance to their agenda can provoke them to manipulate

---

* Mattei, according to the *Independent*, had reportedly "single-handedly built up Italy's state-owned energy sector, to the fury of Italy's Cold War allies who wanted their private companies to be able to exploit the country's oil and natural gas reserves. He also "forged alliances with Middle Eastern clients of the Soviet Union" and "gazumped the multinational oil giants by offering better terms for distribution rights."

proxies into instigating regime changes, assassination attempts, war, and death. I still tend to go with this theory. The Irgun Zvai Leumi may have been only too happy to carry out an act of sabotage against a plane carrying America's only master spy in the Middle East who happened to oppose the partition of Palestine.[85] But it was their masters who released them from prison who may have had a bigger objective: to teach the Americans a lesson that they were getting too big for their new imperial britches. Kim Philby would have been delighted to help out.

As I wrote these closing words, I received an unexpected validation of my father's work as the CIA's "forgotten first star." On April 2, 2019, a phone call came through from Vienna. I hesitated to pick up. Whom did I know from Vienna, Austria? Or maybe it was Vienna, Virginia? I answered the call. The pleasant male voice introduced himself as David Marlowe, assistant director of the CIA's Near East Mission. He told me that the CIA had decided to honor my father at its annual ceremony in May at the Langley headquarters' Memorial Wall. He figured I would want to attend.

I answered, "Yes," and paused, astonished by the call and the identity of the caller. I surprised myself for what I said next, "Thank you. I'm thrilled by the honor." It took over seventy years for this recognition for a man, like so many, who sincerely believed he was risking his life for the American people and their cherished democracy.

AFTERWORD

At All Costs

O n a chilly day in April 2019, three men from the CIA came to our home in Burlington, Vermont. Their ostensible mission was to discuss the Memorial Wall celebration, but the fact that there were three of them suggested that more was on the agenda. One was an agency psychologist who identified himself merely as Lloyd, the second a CIA historian named Mark Schwendler, and the third the assistant director of the CIA's Near East Mission, David Marlowe — the same person who had first reached out to me about honoring my father.

When they showed up at our door, they told us about their very bumpy plane ride to Burlington and how they had joked of the irony if their plane went down. Jerry and I laughed. It was an awkward and unusual ice-breaker, but we instinctively accepted it as genuine. We welcomed them to join us in our living room.

They were dressed in casual suits and were clearly schooled in etiquette: They stood up whenever one of us left the room for a minute and remained standing until we were all together again. Marlowe, a tall, attractive man with closely cropped hair and a slight tan (having recently returned from the Middle East) had an aura of quiet confidence that suggested he was well trained for encounters of this kind. As the meeting proceeded, with the three of them sitting on our L-shaped couch facing us in our chairs and a coffee table between us, a lively discussion ensued.

I joked with the bespectacled Lloyd, the psychologist who identified himself as a part of the agency's medical team and could not reveal his last name. "So you are here to check out my mental stability after seventy years have gone by since my father's death?"

He laughed and said the agency usually sent out a team to talk to recently bereaved families, but acknowledged that this meeting was quite different from the others. I let that one go, sensing that he was still assessing me for . . . whatever.

Then Schwendler, the youthful-looking historian, explained how he had come to research my father. He had worked with Nick Dujmovic, he said, at the Center for the Study of Intelligence, "a CIA think tank." I was, of course, familiar with the name. Back in 2008 Dujmovik had written the tribute to my father as the CIA's "forgotten first star" and he advocated for putting his star on the CIA lobby's Memorial Wall and adding his name to the "Book of Honor" at the annual ceremony honoring the fallen. At some point during the ensuing years, Schwendler explained, "It fell upon me to do follow-up research on your father's career and the circumstances leading up to his death."

Jerry and I couldn't help but wonder — why now? We figured that they surely must have researched us ahead of time and discovered I was writing a book about my father, which I described online. Schwendler handed Jerry and me photocopies of records he obtained from the National Archives about John Creech, the communications expert on Flight 3804 who had also died in the plane crash. Without letting on that I had seen many of these documents before, I listened to what he had to say.

He pointed to specific information he had highlighted in yellow. There was a cable from the assistant military attaché dated March 22, 1947 (two days after the crash), that stated that the mission was to transport signals equipment to the American Legation in Addis, which I knew. The cable went on: "INADEQUATE WEATHER REPORTED FACILITIES FOR ADDIS ABABA. CIVIL PILOTS REPORTED THUNDERSTORMS AND TURBULENCE BETWEEN ASMARA AND ADDIS." This was new to me, and seemed to add weight to the case that Schwendler was making: that weather had caused the crash. Yet I knew that attaché McNown's report, written on March 26, had stated that weather conditions in Asmara had recorded clear skies — CAVU, meaning Ceiling and Visibility Unlimited — and that the crash site was "only one hour and a half away from [the pilot's] CAVU starting point." McNown went on to state that weather reports "cannot be trusted" and that rainy weather "in this area is very rarely a flying hazard."

Flight 3804 took off early to avoid afternoon rains. Besides, and now I was addressing Schwendler, "If there were thunderstorms and turbulence, why weren't the seat belts used?" He had no answer, and I left it at that.

He showed us several cables (one from Teheran, dated March 28, and another from Cairo, dated March 29, from the office of the US military attaché) stating that "CAUSE BELIEVED DUE TO PILOT ERROR WITH PRINCIPAL CONTRIBUTING FACTOR BEING ADVERSE WEATHER." This again was highlighted in yellow. McNown's written caveats — not only about the weather rarely being a flying hazard, but also his comment that "it is extremely difficult to believe a pilot of Lt. Smith's ability and experience could have had an accident of this type" — were missing in the apparent final need for brevity and a cogent explanation for the crash.

In short, what Schwendler was doing with these highlighted documents was making his case — and the agency's official story — that the crash had been an accident. "We aren't hiding anything," he said to his polite but visually skeptical audience. "There is nothing to suggest foul play, and contemporaneous cables from CIG stations show this." At this point, Marlowe broke in, adding, "There is nothing for us to pursue."

Jerry and I rebutted their arguments, reminding them we were investigative journalists, and filled in some context: intense competition from both the British and the Russians over US emergence as a major power in the region; the bombing of Carat's office at the US Legation in Beirut; Greek "communists" being recruited to "bring the Line down"; the possibility of Philby's involvement (the three exchanged silent glances); McNown's discovery of a plot linked to the British to assassinate the United States' new ally, Emperor Haile Selassie (more exchanged glances); the fact that McNown did not rule out sabotage in his accident report (which they apparently had not seen). I had to wonder: With an incident happening over seventy years ago, why was it so important to avoid the possibility of sabotage — and to refuse to turn over other documents seven decades old?

Toward the end, I sensed that our exchange — they gave us something, we gave something back — may have given them pause. Their mission was to convince us that the plane crash was an accident, and it was now clear to them that we knew more than they thought we knew, or perhaps more than even they knew, raising the possibility that sabotage should not be ruled out.

As our meeting was coming to a close, I gave our guests an afternoon snack: apple pie à la mode. It went over well.

"You can't get more American than that!" Lloyd blurted out. Sufficiently put at ease, he even ventured a question that caught me quite by surprise: "Why didn't you join the agency? You are perfect for the job!"

"How is that?" I asked.

"You are curious," he said, then added, "and you are not afraid." Hmm, I thought, if that is his psychological assessment of me, I'll take it. But flattery, as the old adage goes, will get you nowhere.

We chatted briefly about the current state of affairs in the Middle East. Marlowe commented that things really hadn't changed that much, that the agency was still confronting some of the issues my father was dealing with. The meeting ended well, with our guests commenting that it certainly had been unusual and quite enjoyable. As they departed, Marlowe turned to me, promised a tour of the agency's internal spy museum and a visit to his office on the sixth floor (whatever for? I wondered) before the celebration would take place. His parting words, with a strong handshake, were unforgettable: "Welcome to the family. We are *all* family."

After they left, I pondered his words. Was welcoming me into the CIA family an effort to win over my loyalty? Say nice things about the agency?

I wondered what would be said, and left unsaid, at the Memorial Wall Celebration. We were encouraged to send photos and anecdotes about Daniel Dennett. Cindy and Dan sent childhood memories of him. Since I had none, I sent in, with my siblings' approval, a story that my father was fond of recounting, about an experience he had teaching Muslim students at the American University of Beirut in the early 1930s. He was supposed to teach a lesson on "How to Live," and decided to give a lecture on toleration.

First, he gave some shocking examples of Christian intolerance: the Inquisition, the Wars of Religion, the persecution of scientists. From there he went on to Jewish intolerance, citing selections from the Old Testament. But when he got to Muslim intolerance, one of his students stood up and loudly protested his teacher's insulting reflections on Islam.

Toleration, the student said, "is a virtue that is possessed by people who don't believe or are easy going in their faith, a virtue that only those who are rich and prosperous, strong and confident, unafraid of menaces, could afford. But if you believe, and your faith is challenged," the student went on, "if you love your country and see its independence denied, if you have ideals and see them destroyed, then you have two choices: intolerance, or moral extinction."[1]

Dennett accepted the explanation and vowed never to teach toleration again. But the exchange had shaken him profoundly. He would later incorporate the anecdote into a speech, likely given at Clark University, where he taught in 1942. He ended the speech with a warning: "Pray to God that wherever else we may choose to intervene, the United States will be spared the disgrace of intervening in the Near East."

I suspected this anecdote would not be included in the ceremony. A statement giving a sympathetic read on causes of Arab anger over American orientalism could be deemed too political, too controversial.[2] (As it turned out, my hunch was right.)

The Big Day: May 21, 2019

A large black van with the name "Dennett family" on the windshield pulled up at the Marriott Hotel at Tysons Corner, Virginia, and whisked my sister, Cynthia; my brother, Dan; his wife, Susan; Jerry and me off to CIA headquarters in Langley. I was impressed by the size of the building, set back from a long drive with security guards posted along the way. Our guides for the day awaited us at the entrance: two very personable and attractive young women, both of whom had served in Afghanistan.

As we entered, we could see where a whole section had been roped off for the ceremony by the wall. It was scheduled for the afternoon. First on the morning's agenda was a tour of the spy museum, not to be confused with the International Spy Museum in Washington, DC. It was not at all what I expected. I had figured they would keep it limited to displays of spy paraphernalia, but, no, it was a historical tour with photographs, written explanations, and biographies of leaders of US intelligence, from OSS through the CIA. To be sure, some of the spy gear and gadgets were on display, and Schwendler, the historian, made sure to point out to me a very large and heavy-looking piece of communications equipment, circa World War II, and similar to the equipment that had been on Flight 3804.

A retired officer with fifty years of experience in the agency rendered brief accountings of spymanship during major events (World War II, the Korea War, the Bay of Pigs, Vietnam, the Gulf War, the Iraq War). He also showed us a model of the fortified housing complex in Abbottabad, Pakistan, that had sheltered Osama bin Laden until his death, giving us the official story of how Navy SEALs killed the Al Qaeda leader. I could see how this was a popular exhibit in the museum, presented as one of those rare success stories with an outcome praised around the world. I was surprised to see that exhibits described intelligence failures, too.

We stopped at a display case showing a handwritten letter from OSS officer and future CIA director Richard Helms to his young son on Hitler's (stolen) stationery on VE Day. Our guide's voice trembled as he read the letter aloud: "Dear Dennis: The man who might have written on this card once controlled Europe. . . . Today he is dead, his memory despised, his country in ruins. He had a thirst for power, a low opinion of man as an individual, and a fear of intellectual honesty." My mind traveled to thoughts about our current president as our tour leader read. When he finished the letter, he teared up. I couldn't help asking him if there was something in particular that he just recalled, or feelings in general. "In general," he replied. Here was a true believer, I concluded. World War II, with all the enormous sacrifices in blood and treasure, was after all the "good war." It defeated a despot, and destroyed Nazism . . . at least, for the next seven decades.

As the guide took us through the wide halls of CIA headquarters, passing by employees walking to and fro, with their security badges dangling from their necks, a saying on one of its walls seemed designed to keep up their morale: "We are the Nation's first line of defense. We accomplish what others cannot accomplish and we go where others cannot go."

Lunch followed the tour on the sixth floor, compliments of the Near East Mission. Along with the family of fellow crash victim John Creech, also being honored that day, my family was led into a conference room to see a Lebanese mezze of humus, lamb, tabbouleh, and other traditional fare, all laid out on a long table for lunch. Mounted on stands against the back wall stood elegant posters of Creech, the CIG communications specialist, and Dennett, their photos each set against a black background with the headline "Honor Our Fallen Hero" in big white letters. Beneath their photos was a star, their names, and the words, "In honor of those who gave their lives in the service of their country." Below that, "OUR SOLEMN TRIBUTE: We have the honor to represent those who came before us — including all of our fallen heroes. These heroes each have their own story and this is our solemn tribute to them. Each was a warrior, a patriot, a friend, and a professional who answered the call of duty."

Marlowe, as assistant director of the Near East Mission, gave a speech about the two fallen first stars while members of the division crowded around the long table and looked on, including the CIA's station chief from

Lebanon.* Then he surprised us by showing us a plaque that had the names Dennett and Creech engraved on it, to be mounted, he said, on the door of one of the conference rooms that would herein be named in their honor as men whose service should be emulated. Afterward he showed me his office — a large room with huge windows that looked out on the tops of green, swaying trees. "It's great: I love to see the birds flying past," he said. I noticed a large map of the Middle East on a wall and was immediately struck by the location of some of the miniature flags pinned on the map denoting serious trouble spots. They were lined up, like soldiers in a regiment, along the entire coast of the Eastern Mediterranean.

The greatest surprise came when our hosts ushered "the Dennett family" into another room and told us that we would soon be meeting with the director of the CIA, Gina Haspel. This was most definitely not on the agenda. Soon we were entering her spacious office; she greeted us cordially and motioned us to have a seat in a semicircle facing her, with the assistant director of the CIA sitting to my left. Dressed in a modest beige jacket and skirt, her brown hair neatly swept away from her face, Haspel's demeanor was gentle, even friendly.† After welcoming us, she reiterated something Marlowe had said during lunch: that the CIA wanted Daniel Dennett to be a role model for new recruits. She had obviously read of his background, including remembrances that we had sent down for selection at the ceremony. She asked if we had any questions, and brother Dan piped up, politely, "Surely after seventy years you could release more

---

* He later remarked that he was astonished to learn that "the Dennett we were honoring was none other than the father of the philosopher with the same name: One of the smartest men in the world!" he told his colleagues. "I've read many of his books."

† I was so unprepared for this encounter that I only later considered the fact that her confirmation hearings in 2018 had ended with a cloud over her past as a career agency operative. She had reportedly overseen the waterboarding of a key Al Qaeda leader, Abu Zubaydah, at a CIA black site in Thailand. A reporter who was trying to write a profile on her sent me a retraction from ProPublica, which confessed to misreporting the torture charge and also retracted that "she mocked the prisoner's suffering in a private conversation." Wrote ProPublica, "Neither of these assertions is correct and we retract them. It is now clear that Haspel did not take charge of the base until after the interrogation of Zubaydah ended." See Raymond Bonner, "Correction: Trump's Pick to Head CIA Did Not Oversee Waterboarding of Abu Zubaydah," ProPublica, May 15, 2008, https://www.propublica.org/article/cia-cables-detail-its-new-deputy-directors-role-in-torture.

documents." She agreed to do that. I was stunned by the exchange, but seized the opportunity and whipped out of my purse our father's heavily redacted 1944 "Analysis of Work." I had planned to give it to Schwendler, the CIA historian, after the ceremony but couldn't resist handing it to the director of the CIA. "Maybe we can start with this!" I said, smiling.

I didn't mention the largely unredacted paragraph about protecting Saudi oil at all costs, or for that matter, the paragraph that followed which spoke of the need to protect airspace from hostile forces. She surely saw the last two pages, entirely blacked out, and assured me this largely redacted document would be dealt with. And it was! In January 2020, the CIA sent me the entire document with redactions removed along with other declassified documents concerning my father's last months alive.[3]

When it came time to leave, Haspel shook my hand earnestly and said, "Keep at it! Continue on with what you are doing!"

The Ceremony

Before the ceremony began, we were invited to go up to the wall to see where our father's star was newly engraved and where his name had been added to the "Book of Honor" in front of the wall. The families — of Dennett, Creech, and others celebrated that day — were asked in advance not to discuss what was said at the ceremony itself, for obvious security reasons but I feel comfortable giving a general account of what happened. The Dennett and Creech families sat in the front row, directly across from the Memorial Wall. Behind us sat a couple hundred attendees — many of whom had been honored in the past and return every year for this celebration. The ceremony began with a color guard, followed by a bagpipe player, and "Taps." That's when I noticed my sister, sitting next to me, was dabbing her eyes with a handkerchief. Having been a chaplain for the United Church of Christ who had attended many memorials, she later recounted, "The format was familiar. Even including the bagpiper and 'Taps.' But this was so personal — honoring Father's service to our country." The color guard, she added, "the moment of silence, the chaplain's prayer, and the reading of all one hundred thirty-three names of the fallen were poignant reminders of service beyond oneself. The ceremony revealed powerfully that Father and all the others were not forgotten. Music always reaches me. The tunes of 'Amazing Grace' and 'Taps' brought tears!"

Director Haspel read out some remembrances from the families. When she got around to our father, she looked directly at me, again spoke of

Daniel Dennett's being a role model, and then walked over and delivered to me a framed memorial star and a folded quilt with stars on it that had been made by volunteers. We all agreed the quilt would go to Cynthia.

Exactly which aspect of Dennett's service they wanted to emulate, I was unsure. His knowledge of and respect for the Arab world? His intent to secure the oil at all costs? His willingness to take on a very dangerous assignment and even risk his life?

I will long remember that moment and her handshake after the ceremony, reiterating that I should keep on going. A number of other members of "the Family" came up to me, too — as I recall, younger members, mostly women, who warmly thanked me. For what? For persevering to get recognition for my father? I wasn't sure. It later struck me: If something happened to them, wouldn't they want their family to remember them, even find out what happened?

Final Reflections

First the memorial celebration, then an evening dinner put on by the Third Option Foundation with folk songs dedicated to fallen special operations members, gave me a whole different view of the CIA. Call it the "human side" of an agency viewed by many (including me) as unfeeling and often ruthless in carrying out its duties. Here, in contrast, were genuine tributes to unsung heroes who had risked and lost their lives believing in their mission to protect the national security of our country. That was certainly what my father believed during World War II and when he was killed in 1947.

The respect and sensitivity showed us by members of the CIA, including our Burlington visitors and Director Haspel, seemed genuine. These Americans (being part of an oath-taking secretive organization) do not get the same public accolades as our armed forces on Memorial Day, yet they come together every year in a private ceremony to honor the fallen, and to participate in a certain esprit de corps, much needed for families' closure and institutional morale, especially when they come under attack, as is happening now from President Trump.

Let's face it. Intelligence agencies are needed, a fact that has long been recognized: Spying has been called the second-oldest profession. It is dangerous work and often comes with few rewards. I picked up from my day at Langley that members of the CIA may not always feel comfortable in what they are ordered to do, but they strongly believe in the overall mission: that ultimately, they are protecting democracy itself. That became even clearer to me when we ran into Congressman Adam Schiff, head of the House Intelligence Committee, after the ceremony. All of us — Dan, Susan, Cindy, Jerry, and I — thanked him for standing up to the Trump administration and exposing its misdeeds. But above all, we thanked him for trying to save American democracy. "That's what we do, too!" said Marlowe when we told him of the encounter.

Along with Jerry, I have spent years writing about how the prerogatives of empire have distorted American values. My father died before some of the agency's "black ops" that had tarnished its reputation were revealed by journalists (Jerry and me included). I recall what Lloyd, the psychologist, admitted to me at one point: "We appreciate what you've done . . . well, maybe not earlier [he laughed] but . . . " Apparently my wanting to do justice to my father won them over to our patriotism and the sincerity of our work, despite some understandable misgivings about our previous books.

I also recall, with some hope, that it was our intelligence agencies that disagreed with George W. Bush when he said Saddam Hussein was a threat to national security and would have to be removed through war. More recently, I found myself allied with former directors of the CIA as they have sounded the alarm about the rogue presidency of Donald Trump. At this moment of writing (November 2019), I wonder whether saner heads will prevail despite the gung-ho neoconservatives in the Trump administration who seem to be setting us up for war with Iran.

The CIA subscribes to two often conflicting mottoes that are in full display — of all places — on the T-shirts and coffee mugs in the CIA's gift shop. One motto says, "Admit Nothing, Deny Everything." The other, adapted from the biblical testament of John 8:31–32, says, "Ye shall know the truth, and the truth shall set you free." You can guess which memento I took home with me.

There are critical times when the truth is not revealed, sometimes not even to bereaved families, under orders to protect national security. Sometimes the shielding goes too far, and claims of national security are too broad, causing some to ask, "Whose security are we protecting?" Among the questioners is a group of former intelligence officers called VIPS (Veteran Intelligence Professionals for Sanity) who take the CIA to task whenever they think it has overstepped its duties or misjudged a crisis.

Ultimately, it is up to us journalists to try to dig out the truth as part of our First Amendment responsibility to keep the citizens of the republic well-enough informed to enable self-rule. We have our separate missions. But in these times, getting at the truth — and protecting democracy — is vitally important if our democracy is to survive.

In the coming years, I will wonder whether making Daniel Dennett a role model is realistic, or naïve, given the world we live in seven decades after his death.

A reporter who was planning to write a piece on Haspel called me after the ceremony and reminded me of a statement I gave to Congress about the importance of transparency and the Freedom of Information Act. In that testimony, I relayed a statement by one William Thomson, a professor of Arabic at Harvard, in the foreword to my father's book, *Conversion and Poll Tax in Early Islam*.[4] "America lost in Dennett," Thomson wrote, "what we could spare least," and described him as:

> ... *a scholar and teacher, whose wide knowledge of the Near East past and present, and enlightened judgment of its peoples and problems would have served his country well in these days of devious and dubious political activity at the great crossroads of ancient and modern world routes. . . . For lacking a knowledge of these two fields [modern Europe and the Umayyad Caliphate], centuries apart though the eras be, it is scarcely possible to steer an intelligent course in Near Eastern affairs today.*

If the reporter found this on the web, perhaps the CIA had found it, too. Which prompted me to inquire of Marlowe several months after the Memorial Wall celebration: What, in fact, was it about my father that convinced the CIA to choose him as a role model?

Here is how he responded:

> *As I learned about Mr. Dennett and his background, I was struck by the fact that the things that made him successful were the things we most value and cultivate in our officers today. He not only spoke Arabic, he'd committed years of his life to understanding the language in depth along with the culture and history behind it. He was a scholar, but not the kind of person confined to a library.*

He went on to say "his writing reflects the objective honesty we hope for from today's officers. He had a sense of adventure and the confidence to take on challenges that would intimidate most people."

"If he were here today," Marlowe continued, "he'd be one of our most capable operators and most trusted observers of our region's multidimensional mosaic. Even though I never met him, as I read about him, I felt like I missed him."

Well, who could not be moved by such a tribute? But Marlowe added more:

> *Your dad's role was unique, and he is among the very first of our predecessors. As we introduce new officers to our work in the Middle East, he is among the first people they hear about. And what they hear is the nature of the region in which we operate, and the nature of the officers who leave a timeless stamp.*[5]

Words like these, coming from the highest levels of the CIA, made me think that my quest had been worthwhile. They prompted me to ponder: Are we on the cusp of something new? Or the same old story: protecting the oil — and the oil, gas, and air routes — at all costs?

We have witnessed career foreign service officers breaking rank from the Trump administration and testifying about their alarm over his self-serving foreign policy regarding Ukraine, while providing the kind of objective honesty that is so needed. But will the full underlying story of profit-hungry Americans trying to grab Ukraine's natural gas come to light? How much of the military aid will go toward protecting the oil and gas?

The American people seem the wiser, turning up at the polls in large numbers in 2018 while rejecting the unrestrained greed and immorality displayed by the most corrupt president in American history. But have we really turned a page? My father's unease with the imperial drift of Aramco shortly before his death in 1947 has been borne out in ways that he surely could not have envisioned, with Saudi Aramco surpassing the major American oil companies by far as the most profitable company in the world, raking in over $100 billion in profits in a single year. Can a powerhouse that size, now the Biggest of Big Oil surrounded by covetous Big Banks, be restrained by the heartfelt pleas of millions of young climate activists?

As for the CIA, the day after I received Marlowe's statement, a new report came across my email transom that reminded me of some harsh realities in today's Middle East. It was the latest Costs of War report from Brown University — *The CIA's Army: A Threat to Human Rights and an Obstacle to Peace in Afghanistan*. It stated, "the CIA is still running local militias in operations against the Taliban and other Islamist militants. Throughout, the militias reportedly have committed serious human rights abuses, including numerous extrajudicial killings of civilians. CIA sponsorship ensures that their operations are clouded in secrecy. There is virtually no public oversight of their activities or accountability for grave human rights abuses."[6]

This is not what my father would have wanted. And I have to wonder what the CIA's Middle East officers think of these marauding militias killing civilians and frankly undoing all the well-intentioned efforts to win over hearts and minds. In my response to Marlowe's tribute to my father (written before I received the Cost of War report), I expressed my family's hope that there would finally be peace in the Middle East, but in the age of oil, I realized this was a tall order.[7]

At any time there could be another showdown in the Gulf over sabotaged oil tankers. In October and November of 2019, tens of thousands of protesters took to the streets in Iraq and Lebanon against the corruption and mismanagement of their leaders — riots, however legitimate, reminiscent of the beginning stages of the eight-year war in Syria. Iran's supreme leader is blaming Israel and the United States for fomenting the revolts, which in Iraq are also against Iran, and in Lebanon, against Hezbollah.[8]

ISIS warriors, many freed during the withdrawal of US troops in Syria, will regroup and commit more heinous acts in revenge for the killing of their leader, Abu Bakr al-Baghdadi. Trump's description of his demise (he "died like a dog, whimpering and crying and screaming all the way" — yet to be confirmed by the Pentagon) is likely to inflame ISIS even more, for a driving force behind their Islamic jihadism is redemption for the humiliation brought upon them by the West.

When will we ever learn? And yet, I'm an optimist at heart — and my heart wants to tell me that the enormous human and environmental costs may finally figure into the calculations about whether to wage war or peace. But I am also convinced, by history, that this will not happen unless the American people insist on the right to be informed, and on responsibly acting on what they learn.

Ultimately, we stand at the cusp of a history of our own doing.

ACKNOWLEDGMENTS

This book took decades to assemble, and in the end, a year to write. So as I think back over time as to who helped me through the process, there may be some names inadvertently left out, for which I apologize.

My thanks go to Timothy Naftali, now a professor at New York University and former archivist of the Nixon Library, who was doing research at the National Archives in College Park, Maryland, on the X-2 (counterintelligence) division of the OSS and stumbled on my father's papers. He contacted our family and it was his prompting that got me going on my quest through the National Archives.

I am immensely grateful to the archivists at the National Archives (NARA), starting with two posthumous acknowledgments: the late John Taylor, for many years the archivist of the military division, who was very supportive of my research, my FOIA requests at the archives, and who finally suggested I sue the CIA; and the late Larry McDonald, who oversaw the declassified OSS records and brought me to a meeting of retired intelligence officers at Fort Myer, where I learned from a former colleague of my father's that "we always thought [the plane crash] was sabotage but couldn't prove it." John Taylor and Larry McDonald had institutional memories going way back and are sorely missed.

A big thank-you goes to Richard Boylan, NARA's specialist on army records. He found the inches-thick accident report on Flight 3804 — one of my biggest breakthroughs in my investigation into my father's death. The National Archives continues to be very helpful, with special thanks to Huda Dayton. I am also appreciative of the decision by former OSS operative and CIA director under Ronald Reagan, the late William Casey, who in 1985 initiated a declassification program for OSS records, "which would be of greatest historical interest . . . and make possible a more accurate report and fuller understanding of our Nation's history since World War II."[1] Thanks to his order, I was able to follow my father's career from 1944 up to 1946 through hundreds of his written reports. I am awaiting the release of more Central Intelligence Group records (1946–47) anticipated in William Casey's 1985 order and personally pledged to our family by CIA Director Gina Haspel.

Vermont Senator Patrick Leahy, the son of a publisher and a great believer in transparency, continues to be a valued supporter of the Freedom of Information Act and was helpful to me in nudging the CIA along to release documents pursuant to my FOIA request. Washington, DC, attorney Dan Alcorn was indispensable in guiding me once I decided to sue the CIA for my father's documents.

A number of people reviewed and discussed with me the official accident reports of Flight 3804: my brother, Dan Dennett; my sister, Cynthia Yee; Louis Godbout, Harriet Wright (wife of the deceased radio operator on Flight 3804, Donald Tisdall); the von Rosen family of Sweden; Bob Buck; Jack Northrop; Tom Stalcupt; Bob Young; and Hank Hughes (the latter five being pilots or professional accident investigators). I appreciate their observations and insights.

Additional thanks to Dan and his wife, Susan, for hosting a family reunion in Beirut in the spring of 2011, which gave me an invaluable opportunity to witness how Lebanon had fared after fifteen years of civil war and to reflect closely on the regional impact of the growing violence in neighboring Syria.

My friends Judith and (the late) Richard Dewey from Beirut put Jerry and me up in their home while we did research in the Standard Oil of California archives. Richard, a librarian who once worked in Istanbul, was instrumental in getting me access to the archives of the American College for Girls. Terry Dugan and Larry Klein opened hearth and home numerous times during our research trips, as did Kristina Borjesson and Fred Larreur, Michael Lebron and Liz Vega-Lebron, Sue and Phil Wheaton, Barbara Butterworth, and Jeff Weaver.

During our 2005 trip to Beirut, Professor Lamia Shehadeh, the daughter of Carat's most trusted advisor, historian Asad Rustum, with her husband provided exquisite Lebanese hospitality and a tour of Chemlan and environs. Kris Peterson and Mousa Ishaq kindly translated from Arabic portions of Dr. Shehadeh's 2014 biography of her father, *Asad Rustum, Historian of the See of Antioch*, with its mentions of my father.

Dale Harrell, daughter of OSS's Cairo officer Stephen Penrose, kindly shared some of her father's papers with me.

The University of Vermont's Howe Library has proved to be an excellent resource with a fine collection of books on the Middle East.

Two names remain constants throughout the years: my dear friend in Vermont, writer/filmmaker/philanthropist Robin Lloyd, and my husband, Jerry Colby. Robin has been a loyal friend and supporter of our work ever since we arrived in Vermont in 1984, and her support for this book was crucial. As for Jerry, he gets big thanks for forbearance: he accompanied me on numerous research trips to the National Archives, the British Archives, the FDR and Truman Libraries, the Library of Congress, and took time away from his own important research to help me with mine. He accompanied me to Beirut, Istanbul, London, and Stockholm for interviews and more research. He edited different "prospectuses" for publishers, went over submitted chapters, and shared in my disappointment when the rejections came in. As president of the National Writers Union (2004–2009) he warned me that in today's celebrity-driven world of big publishers (which count on known audiences and minimal risk-taking to maximize book sales and profits), snagging a book contract with a big publisher was close to impossible because my father was unknown, the "CIA's Forgotten First Star" who died young and had slipped into obscurity.

So I decided to try a new approach: Take the crash of Flight 3804 and my father's last mission to Saudi Arabia to discuss the route of the Trans-Arabian Pipeline and tie them in with current events and a pressing need to explain the role of pipelines in the Middle East's endless wars. I went to Margo Baldwin of Chelsea Green Publishing, the publisher of my previous book, *The People v. Bush*, because I enjoyed working with the team at Chelsea Green and trusted Margo's integrity as a publisher. Once again, the team was a joy to work with. They were at all times encouraging, patient, and very professional: my wonderful editor, Joni Praded; Chelsea Green's taskmaster extraordinaire, project manager Patricia Stone; copy editor Nancy Ringer; proofreader Eliani Torres; and indexer Shana Milkie. I am counting on savvy Sean Maher to do a bang-up job on promoting the book.

Special thanks to geoscientist and cartographer John Van Hoesen for his painstaking work on the maps and to Vermont graphic artist Anne Linton for getting me started on the maps.

Also thanks to Dr. Nafeez Ahmed, professor and journalist, for reading an early version of the manuscript and making particularly astute suggestions about my chapter on Syria.

296 | *The Crash of Flight 3804*

Writing a book takes a lot of teamwork, and it also takes money to support the author's research and writing. Special thanks go to Chris Lloyd, Lola Moonfrog, Jason Horowitz, the late Bill Preston, Nat Winthrop, Kit Miller, Martin Sheen, the Ben and Jerry's Foundation, Bob Fertik, Amark Foundation and Steve Markoff, Carol Brouillet, Tabard Associates, Louis Godbout, and Dan and Susan Dennett.

I am grateful to filmmaker John Suma for getting me started on a GoFundMe campaign and for producing its video, "Help Me Solve a Mystery." Filmmaker / fellow journalist and my good friend Kristina Borjesson wisely coached me along.

For donors to my GoFundMe campaign, I reached out to childhood friends; classmates from the American Community School in Beirut (class of '65); and Wheaton College (class of '69); fellow progressives and friends in the accountability movement, the labor movement, the women's movement, the peace and justice movement, and the legal community. Here they are, in alphabetical order, with huge thanks: Ida Alamuddin, Bob Alexander, Russ Baker, Andy Barker, Medea Benjamin, Jo Bernard, Barb and Paul Bertocci, Eleanor Becker, Gregory Bloom, Jon Block, Kristina Borjesson, Ann and Scott Brunger, Barbara Butterworth, Candy Bryant, Cheryl Diersch, Dean Corren, Cleo Current, Rickey Gard Diamond, John Douglas, James Eberlein, Joan Ecklein, Marguerite Edelman, Ellen David Friedman, Mary Gable, Mary Beth Gardam, Jackie Harman, Krista Hart, Jeff Hutchins, Kathleen Krevetski, Jason King, Beth Kubly, Michael Lebron and Liz Vegas, Robin Lloyd, Anne McCook, Susan McLucas, Mark Miller, Orm Muilwijk, Susie Moulton, Carol Ormsbee, Mark Palermo, Styliani Pastra-Landis, Cynthia Papermaster, Ed Paquin, Alice and Steve Purington, Jim Rader, Lynn Riley, Lucy Sachs, Lisa Senegal, Mark Seifert, Sue Serpa, Frances Shure, Kate Stevens, Dorothy Tod, Barbara Weeks, Katherine Vose, Eric Weijers, Sue and Phil Wheaton, Bart and Shirley Wilder, Nat Winthrop, Fred Woekener, Anne Wright, and Cynthia D. Yee.

I also had a number of anonymous donors, whom I thank, knowing who you are while respecting your privacy.

Lastly, I wish to thank all who made my one day in May at the CIA (honoring my father) a memorable occasion.

NOTES

The National Archives and Records Administration, College Park, Maryland, is herein abbreviated as NARA.

Chapter 1: Tracking TAPLINE

1. Besides Dennett, the Americans on the plane were US petroleum attaché Donald Sullivan, First Lieutenant Howard G. Smith (pilot), Sergeant Dale M. Holmes (aerial engineer), Sergeant Donald R. Tisdall (radio operator), and First Lieutenant John W. Creech (from the office of the assistant secretary of war). Creech also worked for the Central Intelligence Group and was responsible for transporting top secret communications equipment to Addis Ababa.
2. Max W. Ball, *This Fascinating Oil Business* (New York: Bobbs-Merrill Company, 1940), 17.
3. I would eventually learn that Dennett had been given the code name Carat to distinguish him from other OSS agents with names like "Squirrel," "Pony," and "Stallion." I mention this not to boast, but to convey that someone held in this high regard deserved to be understood and remembered instead of obliterated from history due to his death at the young age of thirty-seven. A CIA historian agrees, as noted in chapter 7.
4. J. Rives Child to Lowell Pinkerton, March 22, 1947. Letter in the author's possession.
5. Daniel C. Dennett, "Memorandum to the Minister at Jidda," March 15, 1947. Memorandum in the author's possession. It has, however, been declassified, as I found a microfilmed copy in the National Archives in Record Group (RG) 59 of State Department records concerning Saudi Arabia. See LM 162, reel 67, US State Department files 1945–49, Saudi Arabia, Internal Affairs.
6. Clifton Daniel, "Pipeline for U.S. Adds to Middle East Issues: Oil Concessions Raise Questions Involving Position of Russia," *New York Times*, March 2, 1947.
7. The Arabs have long bristled over the term *Persian Gulf*, first given by Greek cartographers. With the rise of Arab nationalism and pan-Arabism in the 1960s, the Arabs insisted on calling it the Arabian Gulf. As a compromise, the BBC and the *Times Atlas of the World* refer to it as *the Gulf*. Google Earth uses both names. For the purposes of this book, maps will use the term *the Gulf*.
8. "Our World Role: A Crucial Debate Opens," *New York Times*, March 2, 1947.
9. See Douglas Little's comprehensive paper, "Pipeline Politics: America, TAPLINE, and the Arabs," *Business History Review* 64, no. 2 (1990): 258 (online version).
10. Daniel Dennett to Turner McBaine, "Problems with Cover," May 12, 1944, Declassified Records of the Office of Strategic Services (OSS), RG 226, entry 108A, box 172, NARA. McBaine, while serving as OSS head at Cairo, was general counsel of Standard Oil of California (later Chevron) and later served on the Rockefeller-funded Asia Foundation.

11. During the lead-up to the so-called Levant Crisis in April 1945, US diplomats pondered over France's insistence that it would withdraw its troop from Syria and Lebanon only if it could retain its "special position" in the Levant, which included retention of air bases in Lebanon and Syria. By May 30, 1945, this was further clarified as "retention of control over the pipeline from Mosul [Kirkuk]." See RG 84, Records of Foreign Service Posts of the Department of State, box 13, folder: The Franco-Levant Crisis, NARA.

12. William Eddy to Loy Henderson, October 26, 1945, Department of State, RG 59, Records of the Office of Near Eastern Affairs, lot 54D403, box 12, NARA.

13. It should be noted that I found no reference in Carat's files, either in his reports or in his orders from Washington, to the extreme suffering of Jews placed in European internment camps after the Nazi death camps had been liberated. President Truman announced an Anglo-American Committee of Inquiry in November 1945 to determine whether it was possible to resettle tens of thousands of displaced European Jews in Palestine. In April 1946, the committee recommended the resettlement of 100,000 Jews in Palestine, but according to a 2016 article in *Politico*, Truman's military advisors argued against it, warning that "communists, as many Zionists were believed to be, in a new Jewish state could jeopardize the West's access to Middle Eastern oil." See Andrew Glass, "Truman Weighs Role of Jews in Palestine: Nov. 13, 1945," *Politico*, November 12, 2016, https://www.politico.com/story/2016/11/truman-weighs-role-of-jews-in-palestine-nov-13-1945-231124.

14. The bombings and Dennett's response were described in a letter from Ruth L. Dennett to members of the Dennett family. This letter is in the author's possession. Dennett's investigations were written up in five reports on the bombings. They can be found in the Declassified Records of the Office of Strategic Services (OSS), RG 226, entry 108A, box 173, NARA.

15. "SAINT [Washington] to SAINT HG 1 [Beirut] re: Bombings and Sources," September 25, 1946. The designation SAINT was the OSS's code for "head of section"; HG1 was Carat's official code designation. Records of the Office of Strategic Services (OSS), RG 226, entry108A, box 173, NARA.

16. "SAINT [Beirut] to SAINT [Washington], re: Station Activities Month of July, 1946, 7/24/46 DCD GNX A-59," RG 226, entry 210, box 348, previously withheld documents, NARA.

17. "SAINT HG1 to SAINT Washington, re: Attempts to Penetrate American Legation," April 11, 1946, RG 226, entry 108A, box 173, NARA.

18. Little, "Pipeline Politics," 268.

19. John H. Spencer, *Ethiopia at Bay: A Personal Account of the Haile Selassie Days* (Algonac, Michigan: Reference Publications, 1984), 167. Spencer goes into great detail on the problems he encountered with the British regarding the Sinclair Oil concession and the establishment of Ethiopian Air Lines.

20. "Izvestia Assails Deal," *New York Times*, January 27, 1947.

21. Little, "Pipeline Politics," 279. Little was one of the first to bring to light the CIA's 1949 coup in Syria and to use the term "pipeline politics."

22. Little, 283.

Chapter 2: Seeking Truth, Finding Oil

1. The *Washington Post* initially included this "rumor" about Princess Ashraf in a story it ran in 1979. The *Post* subsequently published its regrets in an article dated January 17,

1979, titled "Pahlavi Fortune: A Staggering Sum." Noted the *Post* in an explanation preceding the article: "In a story from Tehran last week, the *Washington Post* reported persistent rumors that the shah's sister, Princess Ashraf, had been involved in drug smuggling. The *Post* has no substantive evidence that these reports are true, and regrets their inclusion." The students I spoke with insisted that Princess Ashraf's drug smuggling was widely known, but, like the *Post*, I cannot confirm this.

2. Kenneth E. Morris, *Jimmy Carter, American Moralist* (Atlanta: University of Georgia Press, 1996), 276; and "Jimmy Carter for Higher Office," *GQ*, June 26, 2018, http://www.gq.com/story/jimmy-carter-for-higher-office.

3. One month after the war started, the *New York Times* published a story on the disputed oil territory by Thomas C. Hayes, "Confrontation in the Gulf: The Oilfield Lying below the Iraq-Kuwait Dispute," September 3, 1990.

4. Two decades after the war, the controversy reopened as to whether Ambassador Glaspie deliberately misled Saddam Hussein following the release by WikiLeaks of a cable about Hussein's meeting with Glaspie. See Stephen M. Walt, "WikiLeaks, April Glaspie, and Saddam Hussein," *Foreign Policy*, January 9, 2011.

5. For Bush's propaganda war, see John McArthur, *Second Front: Censorship and Propaganda in the 1991 Gulf War* (New York: Hill and Wang, 1992).

Chapter 3: Afghanistan

1. See Daniel Dennett, *Breaking the Spell: Religion as a Natural Phenomenon* (New York: Viking, 2006). As my philosopher brother writes: "The spell that I say must be broken is the taboo against a forthright, scientific, no-holds-barred investigation of religion as one natural phenomenon among many." (p. 17) He approaches this taboo as an atheist, whereas Jerry and I approach it as investigative journalists exploring the power dynamics behind conquest.

2. For an excellent primer on the rise of jihadist violence, See Terence Ward, *The Wahhabi Code: How the Saudis Spread Extremism Globally* (New York: Arcade Publishing, 2017).

3. Ahmed Rashid, *Taliban: Militant Islam, Oil and Fundamentalism in Central Asia* (New Haven: Yale University Press, 2001), 146.

4. Rashid, *Taliban*, 6.

5. Akhilesh Pillalamarri, "Why Is Afghanistan the 'Graveyard of Empires'?" *The Diplomat*, June 30, 2017, https://thediplomat.com/2017/06/why-is-afghanistan-the-graveyard-of-empires/.

6. Rashid, *Taliban*, 21–23

7. Rashid, 1–3.

8. Rashid, 158–60; and interview with Bulgheroni.

9. "Chevron, Shell and ExxonMobil express interest in Ghana's oil," Myjononline.com, May 6, 2014, https://www.myjoyonline.com/business/2014/June-5th/chevron-shell-and-exxon-mobil-express-interest-in-ghanas-oil.php.

10. Steve Coll, *Ghost Wars: The Secret History of the CIA, Afghanistan, and Bin Laden, from the Soviet Invasion to September 10, 2001* (New York: Penguin Press, 2004), 303.

11. Coll, *Ghost Wars*, 304–5.

12. Rashid, *Taliban*, 163.

13. Rashid, 163.

14. Peter Dale Scott, *The Road to 911: Wealth, Empire and the Future of America* (Berkeley: University of California Press, 2007), 72.
15. David Rockefeller, *Memoirs* (New York: Random House, 2002), 417.
16. Brzezinski, quoted in Scott, *The Road*, 72.
17. "Les revelations d'un ancien conseiller de Carter," *Le Nouvel Observateur*, January 15–21, 1998.
18. Scott, *The Road*, 72.
19. Rashid, *Taliban*, 160.
20. Rashid, 161.
21. Stephen Kinzer, "Caspian Competitors in Race for Power on Sea of Oil," *New York Times*, January 24, 1999.
22. Rashid, *Taliban*, 163.
23. Coll, *Ghost Wars*, 310.
24. Coll, 310–11. Coll describes, in footnote 17, an interview he had with Bhutto more than half a decade later. She was still indignant over Simons's heavy- handedness. "They started saying my husband is interested [in Bridas] and that's why I'm not going to [cancel the MOU with Bridas], which made me really, really upset because I felt that because I am a woman they're trying to get back at me through my husband. . . . It had nothing to do with my husband. . . . [Bridas] had come first, I mean, they're wanting us to break a legal contract."
25. Coll, 299.
26. Rashid, *Taliban*, 166.
27. John Burns, "Pakistan's Premier Bhutto Is Put under House Arrest," *New York Times*, November 5, 1996. In 1995, Bhutto had declared that Pakistan was "a front-line state for moderation and pluralism, against the forces of extremism and ignorance; see "Pakistan against Forces of Extremism: PM," Dawn Wire Service, April 13, 1995, https://asianstudies.github.io/area-studies/SouthAsia/SAserials/Dawn/1995/13Ap95.html#extr. Beyond the Unocal-Bridas controversy, I believe her downfall represented an example of a liberal, secular leader (she was educated at Radcliffe and Harvard University) succumbing to constant Islamist efforts to undermine her policies as being too "modernist."
28. Coll, *Ghost Wars*, 308.
29. Coll, 308.
30. Paul Fitzgerald and Elizabeth Gould, "Afghanistan, a New Beginning," a guest op-ed for *Informed Consent* (blog), April 2, 2009, https://www.juancole.com/2009/04/fitzgerald-gould-afghanistan-new.html.
31. Steven Levine, "Unrest in Afghanistan Is Disrupting Plans for Pipeline," *New York Times*, May 30, 1997.
32. Steven Levine, *The Oil and the Glory: The Pursuit of Empire and Fortune on the Caspian Sea* (New York: Random House, 2007), 292.
33. Hugh Pope and Peter Fritsch, "Pipeline Dreams: How Two Firms' Fight for Turkmenistan Gas Landed in Court," *Wall Street Journal*, January 19, 1998, https://www.wsj.com/articles/SB885165209866309000.
34. David Cloud, "Albright Lambastes Taliban over Treatment of Women," *Chicago Tribune*, November 19, 1997, https://www.chicagotribune.com/news/ct-xpm-1997-11-19-9711190061-story.html.
35. Rashid, *Taliban*, 180.

36. Beijing Declaration, Fourth World Conference on Women, United Nations, September 1995, https://www.un.org/womenwatch/daw/beijing/platform/declar.htm.
37. Author's interview with Eleanor Smeal, May 31, 2019.
38. Paul Fitzgerald and Elizabeth Gould, *Afghanistan's Untold Story* (San Francisco: City Lights Press, 2009), 230.
39. Rashid, *Taliban*, 179.
40. "Two U.S. Embassies in East Africa Bombed," *New York Times*, August 8, 1998; CIA, "20th Anniversary of the US Embassy Bombings in East Africa," April 2, 2018, https://www.cia.gov/news-information/featured-story-archive/2018-featured-story-archive/anniversary-of-us-embassy-bombings-in-east-africa.html; and Hovhannes Nikoghosyan, "Book Review: Mercenaries, Extremists, and Islamist Fighters in Karabagh War," *Armenian Weekly*, December 21, 2010, https://armenianweekly.com/2010/12/21/book-review-mercenaries-extremists-and-islamist-fighters-in-karabagh-war/.
41. "The Foundation of the New Terrorism," National Commission on Terrorist Attacks upon the United States, August 24, 2004, https://govinfo.library.unt.edu/911/report/911Report_Ch2.htm.
42. Rashid, *Taliban*, 133.
43. Osama bin Laden, quoted in Robert Fisk, *The Great War for Civilization* (New York: Vintage Press, 2007), 22.
44. Rashid, *Taliban*, 133.
45. David B. Ottaway and Dan Morgan, "Gas Pipeline Bounces between Agendas," *Washington Post*, October 5, 1998.
46. Rashid, *Taliban*, 179.
47. Stephen Kinzer, "Caspian Competitors in Race for Power on Sea of Oil," *New York Times*, January 24, 1999.
48. Steven Levine, "Unocal Quits Afghanistan Pipeline Project," *New York Times*, December 5, 1998.
49. Robert Ebel, "Energy Choices in the Near Abroad. The Haves and Havenots Face the Future," Center for Strategic and International Studies, Washington, DC, April 1997.
50. Kinzer, "Caspian Competitors."
51. Kinzer, "Caspian Competitors."

Chapter 4: Bush's Oil and Pipeline Wars

1. As we note in our 2017 update to *Thy Will Be Done*, the Rockefeller Archives Center newsletter that was released shortly after the 9/11 attacks opined that the attacks were in response to globalization and to the Rockefeller family's involvement in globalization. See Gerard Colby with the author, *Thy Will Be Done: The Conquest of the Amazon: Nelson Rockefeller and Evangelism in the Age of Oil* (New York: Open Road Media, 2017). See "The End of an Era: An Introduction and Brief Update to the 2017 Edition."
2. Frank Viviano, "War Will Be Linked to Control of Oil," *New York Times Service*, carried by *Burlington Free Press*, October 1, 2001.
3. Writes Borjesson, "After interviewing almost two dozen of this country's best journalists, I discovered there is no consensus among them regarding why America preemptively invaded Iraq. This I think is profound. Equally profound is the level of ignorance among the American leadership in Washington and the military in the

Middle East about the region in general and Iraq in particular." See Kristina Borjes-son, *Feet to the Fire: The Media after 9/11. Top Journalists Speak Out* (Amherst, NY: Prometheus, 2005), 17.

4. Marjorie Cohn, "Cheney's Black Gold: Oil Interests May Drive U.S. Foreign Policy," *Chicago Tribune*, August 10, 2000.

5. Jacob Heilbrunn and Michael Lind, "The Third American Empire," *New York Times*, January 2, 1996.

6. Author's interview with Marjorie Cohn, February 12, 2019. See also Cohn's blog post, "The Dark Side of the Bombing of Kosovo," May 21, 1999, https://marjoriecohn.com /the-dark-side-of-the-bombing-of-kosovo/.

7. See George Monbiot, "A Discreet Deal in the Pipeline," *The Guardian*, February 14, 2001, https://www.theguardian.com/business/2001/feb/15/oil.georgemonbiot. See also John Pilger, "Tony Blair Is Deceiving Us," *New Statesman*, April 2, 1999. Pilger writes, "As they bomb Serbia without a shred of legality, they refer to 'an emerging international law.' It is the law of pirates." Pilger goes on to refer to the completion of NATO's "most urgent post-cold war project: the establishment of an oil protectorate all the way from the Persian Gulf to the Caspian Sea."

8. Cohn, "Cheney's 'Black Gold.'"

9. "2000 Election. Transcript of First Presidential Debate between Vice President Al Gore and George W. Bush," *New York Times*, October 4, 2000, https://www.nytimes.com /2000/10/04/us/2000-campaign-transcript-debate-between-vice-president-gore -governor-bush.html. Bush qualified his statement, saying that he wanted to build pipelines "throughout this hemisphere" (i.e., the Americas), but his subsequent wars in Afghanistan and Iraq revealed where his priorities lay.

10. "The Iraq War Was about Oil," *The Guardian*, June 4, 2003. According to this article, Wolfowitz's comments were made during an address to delegates at the Asian security summit in Singapore.

11. "US Oil and Gas Industry Has High Expectations from Bush Administration on Energy Issues," *Oil and Gas Journal*, February 12, 2001.

12. Damien Cave, "The United States of Oil," *Salon*, November 20, 2001, https://www .salon.com/2001/11/19/bush_oil/.

13. The author, "The War on Terror and the Great Game for Oil: How the Media Missed the Context," essay in Kristina Borjesson, ed., *Into the Buzzsaw: Leading Journalists Expose the Myth of a Free Press* (Amherst, NY: Prometheus, 2004), 78.

14. Julio Godoy, "U.S. Policy towards Taliban Influenced by Oil," *Inter Press Service*, November 15, 2001, http://www.ipsnews.net/2001/11/politics-us-policy-towards -taliban-influenced-by-oil-authors/.

15. Ian McWilliam, "Central Asia Pipeline Deal Signed," BBC News, December 27, 2002, http://news.bbc.co.uk/2/hi/south_asia/2608713.stm.

16. John Pilger, "The War on Terror: The Other Victims," *Third World Traveler* (Nov.–Dec. 2001), www.thirdworldtraveler.com/Terrorism/War_On_Terror_Pilger.html.

17. Neela Banerjee with Sabrina Tavernise, "As the War Shifts Alliances, Oil Deals Follow," *New York Times*, December 15, 2001. Banerjee would go on to lead the investigation into Exxon's early climate research, which made her a finalist for the 2016 Pulitzer Prize for Public Service.

18. John Foster, "Afghanistan and the New Great Game," *Toronto Star*, August 12, 2009.

19. John Foster, *A Pipeline through a Troubled Land*, Foreign Policy Series vol. 3, no. 1 (Canadian Centre for Policy Alternatives, June 19, 2008). https://www.policyalternatives.ca/sites/default/files/uploads/publications/National_Office_Pubs/2008/A_Pipeline_Through_a_Troubled_Land.pdf.

20. Foster, *A Pipeline through a Troubled Land.*

21. John Pilger, "Why Are Wars Not Being Reported Honestly?" *The Guardian*, December 10, 2010, https://www.theguardian.com/media/2010/dec/10/war-media-propaganda-iraq-lies.

22. James Sterngold, "Cheney's Grim Vision: Decades of War," *SFGate*, January 15, 2004, https://www.sfgate.com/politics/article/Cheney-s-grim-vision-decades-of-war-Vice-2812372.php.

23. John Omicinski, "General: Capturing bin Laden Is Not Part of Mission," *USA Today*, November 23, 2001. Yet for the next ten years, until bin Laden was pronounced dead in May 2011, "getting bin Laden" was time and again offered as a major reason for keeping US military troops in Afghanistan. Once President Obama announced bin Laden's death, the American public had little stomach for the war and Obama removed troops from Afghanistan that year.

24. Robert Fisk and Martin Bell, "The Lost Art of Reportage," *The Independent*, November 10, 2009.

25. "The Neoconservative Plan for Global Dominance," Project Censored, April 29, 2010, https://www.projectcensored.org/1-the-neoconservative-plan-for-global-dominance/. This Project Censored report draws on the work of five journalists: Neil Mackay, David Armstrong, Robert Dreyfuss, John Pilger, and John Rosenberg. Their articles are sourced at the beginning of the report.

26. "The Neoconservative Plan."

27. A declassified 1994 draft of the *Defense Planning Guidance* report stated that in the Middle East, "our overall objective is to remain the predominant outside power in the region and preserve US and Western access to the region's oil." The report trumpeted the collapse of the Soviet Union and the "new international environment" that had also "been shaped by the victory of the United States and its Coalition allies over Iraqi aggression." It hailed George H. W. Bush's Desert Storm for having wrested a "critical region from the control of a ruthless dictator bent on developing nuclear, biological and chemical weapons and harming Western interests." (This characterization of Saddam Hussein would of course be drawn upon by George W. Bush as he prepared to finish what his father had started: the second war against Iraq.) See *Defense Planning Guidance, FY 1994–1999*, https://www.archives.gov/files/declassification/iscap/pdf/2008-003-docs1-12.pdf.

28. "The Neoconservative Plan."

29. Zbigniew Brzezinski, *The Grand Chessboard: American Primacy and Its Geostrategic Imperatives* (New York: Basic Books, 1997), 133.

30. Noted Brzezinski, "Before the Soviet Union's collapse, the Caspian Sea was in effect a Russian lake, with a small southern sector falling within Iran's perimeter. With the emergence of the independent and strongly nationalist Azerbaijan — reinforced by the influx of eager Western oil investors — and the similarly independent Kazakhstan and Turkmenistan, Russia became only one of five claimants to the riches of the Caspian Sea basin. It could no longer confidently assume that it could dispose of these resources [with its own pipelines] on its own." See Brzezinski, *The Grand Chessboard*, 93.

31. Brzezinski, 211.

32. Nafeez Ahmed, *The War on Freedom: How and Why America Was Attacked* (Joshua Tree, CA: Tree of Life Publications, 2002), 77.

33. "Statement of Principles," Project for a New American Century, web archive, https://web.archive.org/web/20050205041635/http://www.newamericancentury.org/statementofprinciples.htm.

34. Barry Bearaknov, "Scott Ritter's Iraq Complex," *New York Times*, November 24, 2002.

35. To view the map of Iraq oil fields and foreign suitors, see "Maps and Charts of Iraqi Oil Fields" on the Judicial Watch website at https://www.judicialwatch.org/maps-and-charts-of-iraqi-oil-fields/.

36. Simon English, "Cheney Had Iraq in Sights Two Years Ago," *The Telegraph*, July 22, 2003.

37. Rebecca Leung, "Bush Sought 'Way' to Invade Iraq?" *60 Minutes*, January 9, 2004, http://www.cbsnews.com/news/bush-sought-way-to-invade-Iraq.

38. For a lengthy analysis of how Bush's legal team overcame these obstacles, see the author, *The People v. Bush: One Lawyer's Campaign to Bring the President to Justice and the National Grassroots Movement She Encounters along the Way* (White River Junction, VT: Chelsea Green, 2010), 171–80.

39. Sewell Chann, "Ahmed Chalabi, Iraqi Politician Who Pushed for U.S. Invasion, Dies at 71," *New York Times*, November 3, 2015.

40. "Iraqi Oilfields," BBC News, Conflict with Iraq: Key Maps, http://news.bbc.co.uk/2/shared/spl/hi/middle_east/02/iraq_key_maps/html/oil_fields.stm. Zack Beauchamp, Max Fisher, and Dylan Matthews, "27 Maps That Explain the Crisis in Iraq," *Vox*, August 8, 2014, https://www.vox.com/a/maps-explain-crisis-iraq.

41. Ted Vuillamy, "Israel Seeks Pipeline for Iraqi Oil," *The Guardian*, April 20, 2003.

42. Vuillamy, "Israel Seeks Pipeline."

43. Vuillamy, "Israel Seeks Pipeline."

44. Gregory Andrade Diamond, ed., *The Unexpurgated Pike Report: Report of the House Select Committee on Intelligence* (New York: McGraw-Hill, 1976), xiii. "Paramilitary support by the CIA to the Kurdish rebellion against the Iraqi government from 1972 to 1975, which cost some $16 million, was initiated at the request of the Shah of Iran, then engaged in a border dispute with Iraq. Once the Iraqis agreed to a settlement favorable to Iran, the Shah had the support to the Kurds cut off. The rebellion collapsed, over 200,000 Kurds became refugees, and neither Iran nor the US set up adequate refugee assistance. As one high ranking but unidentified witness told the Select Committee, 'covert action should not be confused with missionary work.'" As for Israeli support for Mullah Mustafa, see Trita Parsi, *Treacherous Alliance: The Secret Dealings of Israel, Iran, and the U.S.* (New Haven, CT: Yale University, 2007), 52–53.

45. Robert Fisk, "The Case against War: A Conflict Driven by the Self-interest of America," *The Observer*, Feburary 15, 2003.

46. Richard Perle, *A Clean Break: A New Strategy for Securing the Realm* (Israel: The Institute for Advanced Strategic and Political Studies, 1996).

47. Brown University Costs of War Project, November 2018, https://watson.brown.edu/costsofwar/figures/2018/budgetary-costs-post-911-wars-through-fy2019-59-trillion.

48. Lutz Kleveman, *The New Great Game: Blood and Oil in Central Asia* (New York: Atlantic Monthly Press, 2003), 212.

49. Kleveman, *New Great Game*, 224.

50. Kleveman, 225.

51. Kay Johnson and Hamid Shalizi, "Afghanistan's Karzai Criticizes U.S., Pakistan in Farewell Speech," Reuters, September 29, 2014.

52. Kleveman, *New Great Game*, 257.

53. Bruce Pannier, "Afghan TAPI Construction Kicks Off, but Pipeline Questions Still Unresolved," Radio Free Europe, February 23, 2018, https://www.rferl.org/a/qishloq -ovozi-tapi-pipeine-afghanistan-launch/29059433.html.

54. "Campaign for Afghan Women and Girls," Feminist Campus, Feminist Majority Foundation, updated March 2018, http://feministcampus.org/wp-content/uploads /2018/03/Afghanistan_2018.pdf. Copies can be obtained by contacting the foundation at (703) 522-2214.

55. Sanket Sudhir Kulkarn, "US-Taliban Talks and the Fate of TAPI Pipeline," Observer Research Foundation, May 29, 2019, https://www.orfonline.org/expert-speak/us -taliban-talks-and-the-fate-of-tapi-pipeline-49354/.

56. Editorial Board, "The Unspeakable War," *New York Times*, May 11, 2019, https://www. nytimes.com/2019/05/11/opinion/afghanistan.html.

57. Greg Muttitt, *Fuel on the Fire: Oil and Politics in Occupied Iraq* (New York: New Press, 2012), 122–23.

58. Antonia Juhasz, "Whose Oil Is It, Anyway?" *New York Times*, March 13, 2007, https:// www.nytimes.com/2007/03/13/opinion/13juhasz.html.

59. Tara Copp, "'US Forces Are Needed Here.' After 15 Years, Fight in Iraq Not Over," *Military Times*, March 20, 2018.

60. Philip Issa, "Furious Iraqi Lawmakers Demand US Troop Withdrawal," Associated Press, December 27, 2018; and Mary Clare Jalonick, "Senate Breaks with Trump on Afghanistan, Syria Withdrawal," Associated Press, February 4, 2019.

61. Kleveman, *The New Great Game*, 263.

Chapter 5: Is the Syrian War a Pipeline War?

1. Douglas Laux and Ralph Pezzullo, *Left of Boom: How a Young CIA Case Officer Penetrated the Taliban and Al-Qaeda* (New York: St. Martin's Press, 2016), 264.

2. Letter from Daniel Dennett in the author's possession.

3. Dennett to SI (Cairo), SAINTS (Cairo, Washington, London), "Reaction to local communists and French to Russian Recognition of Lebanon and Syria," August 11, 1944, RG 226, entry 108A, box 172, NARA.

4. A. B. Gauson, *The Anglo-French Clash in Lebanon and Syria, 1940–45* (New York: St. Martin's Press, 1987), 179.

5. Dennett, "Analysis of Work," 1944, declassified and approved for release by the CIA in August 2005 as part of Dennett's FOIA lawsuit against the CIA.

6. Dennett to SAINTS in Cairo, Washington, London, Istanbul, SI in Cairo, "RE: Events in Lattaquia, 5–7 July, 1945, Fighting in Lattaquia/Causes" GNX 117, July 9, 1945, RG 226, entry 108A, box 172, NARA.

7. Alexander Werth, *De Gaulle: A Political Biography* (New York: Simon and Schuster, 1966), 186.

8. "Officers Fire on Crowd as Syrian Protests Grow," *New York Times*, March 20, 2011, https://www.nytimes.com/2011/03/21/world/middleeast/21syria.html.

9. Michael Quentin Morton, "Once Upon a Red Line — the Iraq Petroleum Company Story," *Geo ExPro*, 2013, https://www.geoexpro.com/articles/2013/06/once-upon -a-red-line-the-iraq-petroleum-company-story.

10. The arguments for and against "gas attacks as false flag attacks" are legion, complicated, and — without absolute proof one way or the other — hard to prove. For this reason, I have elected not to weigh in on these arguments until more substantive proof becomes available.

11. "Who Is Really behind the Syrian War?" *The Corbett Report*, August 30, 2013, https://www.youtube.com/watch?v=cCdaExnIpGs.

12. Since writing this 2016 article for *Politico*, Kennedy did a serious investigation of Sirhan's role in the murder of Senator Kennedy and concluded that there was a second gunman and that Sirhan was not the murderer. See Tom Jackman, "Who Killed Bobby Kennedy? His Son RFK Jr. Doesn't Believe It Was Sirhan Sirhan," *Washington Post*, June 5, 2018, https://www.washingtonpost.com/news/retropolis /wp/2018/05/26/who-killed-bobby-kennedy-his-son-rfk-jr-doesnt-believe -it-was-sirhan-sirhan/.

13. Robert Kennedy, "Why the Arabs Don't Want Us in Syria," *Politico Magazine*, February 22, 2016, https://www.politico.com/magazine/story/2016/02/rfk-jr-why-arabs-dont -trust-america-213601.

14. Tyler Durden, "The Oil-Gas War over Syria (in 4 Maps)," *Zero Hedge*, October 25, 2016, https://www.zerohedge.com/news/2016-10-24/oil-gas-war-over-syria-4-maps; and Mnar Muhawesh, "Refugee Crisis and Syria War Fueled by Competing Gas Pipelines," *MintPress News*, September 9, 2015, https://www.mintpressnews.com /migrant-crisis-syria-war-fueled-by-competing-gas-pipelines/209294/.

15. Gareth Porter, "The War against the Assad Regime Is Not a 'Pipeline War,'" Truthout, September 21, 2016, https://truthout.org/articles/the-war-against-the-assad-regime -is-not-a-pipeline-war/. In fact, corroborating evidence that Syria objected to the pipeline because of Russian concerns can be found in Stewart Winer, "Saudi Arabia Tries to Woo Russia Away from Syria with Arms Deal," *Times of Israel*, August 8, 2013.

16. Nafeez Ahmed, *State Propaganda in Syria: From War Crimes to Pipelines* (London: International State Crime Initiative, July 2018), http://statecrime.org/data/2018/07 /Nafeez-Ahmed-State-Propaganda-in-Syria-ISCI-Report-July-2018.pdf.

17. Seymour Hersh, "The Redirection," *New Yorker*, February 25, 2007, https://www .newyorker.com/magazine/2007/03/05/the-redirection.

18. Clark first described this encounter in his 2003 book, *Winning Modern Wars: Iraq, Terrorism, and the American Empire* (New York: PublicAffairs, 2003), 130.

19. Wesley K. Clark, *A Time to Lead: For Duty, Honor and Country* (New York: St. Martin's Press, 2007).

20. Joe Conason, "Seven Countries in Five Years," *Salon*, October 12, 2007, https://www .salon.com/2007/10/12/wesley_clark/.

21. Five of these seven countries (Iraq, Syria, Lebanon, Libya, and Iran) are discussed in detail in this book as being targeted for US intervention since 2001. The United States has become heavily involved in Somalia and Sudan as well. See, for example, "Why Are We in Somalia?" by the editorial board of the *Pittsburgh Post-Gazette* (October 18, 2016), https://www.post-gazette.com/opinion/editorials/2016/10/18/Why-are-we -in-Somalia/stories/201610180013; and "Why Does South Sudan Matter So Much to

the US?" by Karen Allen of the BBC News (August 31, 2015), https://www.bbc
.com/news/world-africa-34083964.

A popular uprising backed by Sudan's military removed President Omar al-Bashir
from office in April 2019, ending his three-decades-old rule. But protesters in May
claimed that the "transitional military council" governing Sudan, backed by Saudi Arabia, the UAE, and Egypt (all US allies) is part of the former regime, causing widespread
strikes demanding civilian rule. "Sudan Protesters Begin Two-Day Strike to Pressure
Military," Al Jazeera, May 28, 2019, https://www.aljazeera.com/news/2019/05
/sudan-braces-strikes-opposition-aim-pressure-army-190528062731737.html.

In July, Al Jazeera reported, the protesters and military councils signed a power-
sharing deal "aimed at forming a joint civilian-military ruling body which, in turn,
would install civilian rule." However, the most powerful Sudanese general met with
Egypt's strongman, Abdel Fattah el-Sisi, to discuss restoring stability to Sudan before
power-sharing discussions were to resume, See "Sudan's Hemeti meets el-Sisi before
resumption of power talks," Al Jazeera, July 29, 2019, https://www.aljazeera.com
/news/2019/07/sudan-hemeti-meets-el-sisi-resumption-power-talks-190729112632551
.html. This was hardly a good omen for the protesters in light of the reemergence of a
military dictatorship in Egypt under el-Sisi after the Arab Spring.

22. See, for example, "Glenn Greenwald on Syria: U.S. & Israel Revving Up War Machine
Won't Help Suffering," *Democracy Now*, April 9, 2018.

23. James Huang, interview with General Wesley Clark, "WHO Exclusive: Gen Wesley
Clark on Oil, War, and Activism," *WhoWhatWhy*, September 24, 2012, https://www
.youtube.com/watch?v=SUw7lbG4QBM.

24. Ed Vuillamy, "Israel Seeks Pipeline for Iraqi Oil," *The Guardian*, April 20, 2003.

25. Steven W. Popper, et al., *Natural Gas and Israel's Energy Future: A Strategic Analysis Under
Conditions of Deep Uncertainty* (Santa Monica, CA: RAND Corporation, 2009) 16,
https://www.rand.org/pubs/technical_reports/TR747
.html. Full report can be downloaded.

26. Craig Whitlock, "U.S. Secretly Backed Syrian Opposition Groups, Cables Released by
WikiLeaks Show," *Washington Post*, April 17, 2011, https://www.washingtonpost.com
/world/us-secretly-backed-syrian-opposition-groups-cables-released-by-wikileaks
-show/2011/04/14/AF1p9hwD_story.html.

27. US State Department, Cable06DAMASCUS5399_a, "Influencing the SARG in the
End of 2006," December 23, 2006, Public Library of US Diplomacy, WikiLeaks,
https://wikileaks.org/plusd/cables/06DAMASCUS5399_a.html.

28. Associated Press, "Syrians Vote for Assad in Uncontested Referendum," *Washington
Post*, May 28, 2007, http://www.washingtonpost.com/wp-dyn/content/article/2007
/05/27/AR2007052701117.html.

29. "How Syria's 'Geeky' President Went from Doctor to Dictator," NBC News, archived
from the original on December 22, 2017. Retrieved April 14, 2018.

30. Reuters, "ConocoPhillips to End Business in Syria, Iran," *Houston Chronicle*, February
10, 2004, https://www.chron.com/business/energy/article/ConocoPhillips-to-end
-business-in-Syria-Iran-1624555.php. ConocoPhilips's explanation for backing out
of Syria (not mentioned in the State Department memo) had to do with its coming
under fire for running a business in a country that promoted terrorism. However,
given the Bush administration's decision to start launching a propaganda campaign

against Syria's Assad in 2005, it can be plausibly argued that ConocoPhillips had insider information that instability in Syria was imminent. For whatever reason, ConocoPhillips turned over its plant to the Syrian Gas Company in 2005 and quit the country. (A decade later, the plant would be occupied by ISIS and eventually liberated by US forces in 2017.) See also Raha Abdulrahman, "U.S.-Backed Syrian Fighters Capture Key Gas Plant from Islamic State," *Washington Post*, September 24, 2017.

31. State Department cable, November 2, 2005, cited in Ahmed, *State Propaganda*, 118; see https://wikileaks.org/plusd/cables/05DAMASCUS5788.html.

32. State Department cable, September 13, 2007, cited in Ahmed, *State Propaganda*, 119; see https://wikileaks.org/plusd/cables/07DAMASCUS931.html.

33. Hersh, "The Redirection."

34. "Text: Obama's Speech in Cairo," *New York Times*, June 4, 2009, https://www.nytimes.com/2009/06/04/us/politics/04obama.text.html.

35. Henry Kissinger, quoted on MSNBC, January 6, 2009. Long before Syria became an issue, Barack Obama had rapidly risen to power with strong support from the liberal wing of the powerful Rockefeller family, particularly Jay Rockefeller, great-grandson of John D. Rockefeller. Senator Jay Rockefeller (D-WV) has been forthright, even proud of his role and that of his influential Chicago-born wife, Sharon Percy Rockefeller, in backing Obama. At a July 2008 fund-raiser at Rockefeller's mansion in Washington, DC, he introduced Obama as a man of "profound intelligence" and confessed to his well-heeled audience that "I've met the man, the only person I've really wanted to see as president." Michael Powell, "Obama Courts Big Donors," blog post, *New York Times* website, July 9, 2008.

36. State Department cable, April 28, 2009, cited in Ahmed, *State Propaganda*, 122; see https://wikileaks.org/plusd/cables/09DAMASCUS306_a.html.

37. The concept of "coercive threats" comes from the following 2009 article on regime change, "Q&A with Melissa Willard-Foster," ed. Beth Maclin, an analysis of forced regime change in Iraq, Harvard Kennedy School Belfer Center for Science and International Affairs, https://www.belfercenter.org/publication/qa-melissa-willard-foster. Willard-Foster goes on to point out, "If states have to resort to force, if they have to remake the targeted state's government to get what they want, then it's a clear sign that coercion has failed."

38. Yoav Stern, "Syria's Four Seas Strategy," *Syria Comment* (blog), October 22, 2009, https://www.joshualandis.com/blog/syrias-four-seas-strategy-by-yoav-stern/.

39. Ahmed, *State Propaganda*, 120.

40. Tamsin Carlisle, "Qatar Seeks Gas Pipeline to Turkey," *The National*, August 26, 2009, https://www.thenational.ae/business/qatar-seeks-gas-pipeline-to-turkey-1.520795.

41. Agence France-Presse, "Moscow Rejects Saudi Offer to Drop Assad for Arms Deal," August 8, 2013, http://www.hurriyetdailynews.com/moscow-rejects-saudi-offer-to-drop-assad-for-arms-deal-52245.

42. Craig Whitlock, "U.S. Secretly Backed Syrian Opposition Groups, Cables Released by WikiLeaks Show," *Washington Post*, April 17, 2011.

43. Sultan Sooud Al Qassemi, "How Saudi Arabia and Qatar Became Friends Again," *Foreign Policy*, July 21, 2011, https://foreignpolicy.com/2011/07/21/how-saudi-arabia-and-qatar-became-friends-again/.

44. "Iran, Iraq, Syria Sign Major Gas Pipeline Deal," Mehr News, July 26, 2011, https://en.mehrnews.com/news/47151/Iran-Iraq-Syria-Sign-major-gas-pipeline-deal.

45. Colum Lynch and Anne Gearan, "At U.N., Qatar Emir Calls on Arab Nations to Intervene in Syria," *Washington Post*, September 25, 2012, https://www.washingtonpost.com/world/national-security/at-un-qatar-emir-calls-on-arab-nations-to-intervene-in-syria/2012/09/25/4bf05a9e-0758-11e2-a10c-fa5a255a9258_story.html.
46. Felix Imonti, "Qatar: Rich and Dangerous," Oilprice.com, September 17, 2012, https://oilprice.com/Energy/Energy-General/Qatar-Rich-and-Dangerous.html. Although Imonti does not address how, exactly, Qatar would avoid the Saudi Barrier, he likely means that Qatar would ship its natural gas beneath the Saudi peninsula through the Gulf of Aden and then up through the Red Sea to reach Israel – but that even so, Syria would still be in the way. Installing the Muslim Brotherhood in Syria would clear the way for the natural gas to reach Turkey.
47. Lynch and Gearan, "At U.N., Qatar Emir Calls on Arab Nations."
48. Ahmed, *State Propaganda*, 125.
49. U.S. Marine Corps forecasting paper, September 12, 2011, cited in Ahmed, *State Propaganda*, 129.
50. "Iran-Syria Gas Pipe to Run through Iraq," *Israel National News*, February 20, 2013.
51. Roula Khalaf and Abigail Fielding Smith, "Qatar Bankrolls Syrian Revolt with Cash and Arms," *Financial Times*, May 16, 2013.
52. Stewart Winer, "Saudi Arabia Tries to Woo Russia Away."
53. Ambrose Evans-Pritchard, "Saudis Offer Russia Secret Oil Deal If It Drops Syria," *The Telegraph*, August 27, 2013.
54. Nafeez Ahmed, "Pentagon Report Says West, Gulf States and Turkey Foresaw Emergency of 'IS,'" *Middle East Eye*, May 29, 2015, https://www.middleeasteye.net/opinion/pentagon-report-says-west-gulf-states-and-turkey-foresaw-emergence.
55. Bethan McKernan, "Hillary Clinton Emails Leak: Wikileaks Documents Claim Democratic Nominee 'Thinks Saudi Arabia and Qatar Fund Isis,'" *The Independent*, October 11, 2016.
56. Ben Norton, "Leaked Hillary Clinton Emails Show U.S. Allies Saudi Arabia and Qatar Supported ISIS," *Salon*, October 11, 2016.
57. Martin Chulov, "Isis Insurgents Seize Control of Iraqi City of Mosul," *The Guardian*, June 10, 2014.
58. Chulov, "Isis Insurgents."
59. Chulov, "Isis Insurgents."
60. Jane Ferguson, "Why the Human Toll for the Battle for Mosul May Never Be Known," *PBS NewsHour*, December 19, 2018. Reported Ferguson, estimates of up to 40,000 civilians died in the battle. In the old city of Mosul, "buildings were pounded into rubble. Rubble was pounded into dust." No one knows, she added, how many bodies still lie beneath.
61. Ben Watson, "What the Largest Military Battle in a Decade Says about the Future of War," *Defense One*, July 8, 2017, https://www.defenseone.com/feature/mosul-largest-battle-decade-future-of-war/.
62. Karen Laub, "Aleppo Confronts Vast Destruction Left by 4 Years of War," *Washington Post*, December 5, 2016.
63. Robert Fisk, "Aleppo's Sheikh Najjar: The Death of a Once-Rich City," *The Independent*, June 6, 2014, https://www.independent.co.uk/news/world/middle-east/aleppos-sheikh-najjar-the-death-of-a-once-rich-city-9503699.html. Residents of Aleppo told Fisk that the rebel forces belonged to Al Qaeda, Jabel el-Nusra, Jihad Islamia, the al-Sham

Brigade, and "remnants of the old 'Free Syria Army.'" Syrian commanders told Fisk how they "had to smash their way into this place of pulverised iron, rubble and ash, [while] hundreds of Islamist suicide fighters blew themselves up en masse rather than surrender."

64. Chulov, "Isis Insurgents."

65. Ahmed, *State Propaganda*, 112.

66. Paul Wood, "What Is Putin's Endgame in Syria?" *The Spectator*, March 3, 2018.

67. Steve Austin, "Oil Prices and the Syrian Civil War," Oil-Price.net, October 14, 2015, http://www.oil-price.net/en/articles/oil-prices-and-syrian-civil-war.php.

68. Ahmed, *State Propaganda*, 115.

69. "Syria Asks Russia to Rebuild Its Energy Sector," RT, May 20, 2016, https://www.rt.com/business/343783-syria-energy-companies-infrastructure/.

70. Viktor Katona, "Russia Is Taking Over Syria's Oil and Gas," Oilprice.com, February 18, 2018, https://oilprice.com/Energy/Energy-General/Russia-Is-Taking-Over-Syrias-Oil-And-Gas.html.

71. Diana Al Rifai and Mohammed Haddad, "What's Left of Syria?" Al Jazeera, March 17, 2015, https://www.aljazeera.com/indepth/interactive/2015/03/left-syria-150317133753354.html.

72. Rifai and Haddad, "What's Left of Syria?"

73. REACH, UNOSAT, "Syrian Cities Damage Atlas – Eight Year Anniversary of the Syrian Civil War: Thematic Assessment of Satellite Identified Damage," March 2019, https://reliefweb.int/report/syrian-arab-republic/syrian-cities-damage-atlas-eight-year-anniversary-syrian-civil-war.

74. Ahmed, *State Propaganda*.

75. "Spy Kid: A Young CIA Officer Breaks Cover and Spills Secrets," NBC News, April 1, 2016, https://www.nbcnews.com/news/us-news/spy-kid-young-cia-officer-breaks-cover-spills-secrets-n548846.

76. Laux and Pezzullo, *Left of Boom*, 281. According to NBC News, "A former senior intelligence official confirms that a version of his plan was recommended in 2012 by then CIA director David Petraeus. It was also backed by Secretary of State Hillary Clinton, as she recounts in her memoir, 'Hard Choices' – but President Obama declined to give it a green light." See "Spy Kid: A Young CIA Officer."

77. Pepe Escobar, interviewed by James Corbett in *The Corbett Report*, August 30, 2013, https://www.youtube.com/watch?v=cCdaExnIpGs.

78. F. William Enghdahl, "The Secret Stupid Saudi-US Deal on Syria. Oil Gas Pipeline War: The Kerry-Abdullah Secret Deal," *Global Research*, October 24, 2014.

79. Thomas Erdbrink, "For Many Iranians, the 'Evidence' Is Clear: ISIS Is an American," *New York Times*, September 10, 2014.

80. Anne Barnard, "Amid a Maze of Alliances, Syrian Kurds Find a Thorny Refuge at the Border," *New York Times*, September 24, 2014.

81. The UN report can be found at http://undocs.org/S/2018/705.

82. Whitney Webb, "UN Report Finds ISIS Given Breathing Space in US-Occupied Areas of Syria," *MintPress News*, August 16, 2018, https://www.mintpressnews.com/un-report-finds-isis-given-breathing-space-in-us-occupied-areas-of-syria/247795/.

83. Webb, "UN Report." See also Joanne Stocker, "Coalition and SDF Thwart 'Pro-Regime' Forces Attack in Deir Ezzor," *Defense Post*, February 8, 2018, https://thedefensepost.com/2018/02/08/coalition-sdf-pro-regime-forces-attack-khusham-deir-ezzor/.

84. "Haley: US Troops to Stay in Syria until Goals Achieved," Al Jazeera, April 15, 2018, https://www.aljazeera.com/news/2018/04/haley-troops-stay-syria-goals-achieved-180415163532771.html.

85. Karen de Young et al., "Trump Decided to Leave Troops in Syria After Conversations About Oil," *Washington Post*, October 25, 2019, https://www.washingtonpost.com/world/us-defense-secretary-mark-esper-says-us-will-leave-forces-in-syria-to-defend-oil-fields-from-islamic-state/2019/10/25/fd131f1a-f723-11e9-829d-87b12c2f85dd_story.html; and Robert Burns and Lolita Baldon, "Trump's Claim to Syrian Oil Raises Many Questions," *Associated Press*, November 1, 2019, https://apnews.com/6b7fad3ff9494b3485c1c56f4d309783.

86. Robert F. Kennedy Jr., "Why the Arabs Don't Want Us in Syria," an interview by Thom Hartmann on the *Thom Hartmann Program*, February 24, 2016, https://www.youtube.com/watch?v=Y1CgNEv4JlE.

Chapter 6: The Turkish Cauldron

1. "We are extremely interested in the use in which the Soviets may be able to make of minority groups such as the Circassians. Would appreciate any further information." In "SAINT (Washington) to SAINT HG 1 (Carat), Subject: The USSR and the Circassians," September 27, 1946, RG 226, 108A, box 173, NARA.

2. "Conditions Among the Kurds," Report by the Central Intelligence Group, dated "End of August, 1946," RG 226, 108A, box 173, NARA.

3. Dennett, "The Kurdish Problem in Syria," October 29, 1946, RG 226, 108A, box 173, NARA.

4. Dennett, "Administration of Public Security in the Jazireh," October 28, 1946, RG 226, 108A, box 173, NARA.

5. Memorandum, HG1 to Arthur Fennel, AH 45, November 6, 1946, in Dennett, "Administration of Public Security in the Jazireh."

6. The author, *The People v. Bush: One Lawyer's Campaign to Bring the President to Justice and the National Grassroots Movement She Encounters along the Way* (White River Junction, VT: Chelsea Green, 2010), 77, citing *Nightline*'s two-part series on pipelines in Central Asia, ABC, April 25, 2002, and May 2, 2002.

7. "Turkey: New Crossroads of Empire," *Z Magazine*, April 2013.

8. BP is the majority owner, with 30.1 percent of the company; the State Oil Company of Azerbaijan controls 25 percent of the share; US companies include Chevron (8.9 percent), ConocoPhillips (2 percent), and Hess (2.36 percent). The pipeline linking Caspian Sea oil to the Eastern Mediterranean was completed and officially inaugurated in July 2006 at the very time Israel began a bombing campaign against another country bordering the Eastern Mediterranean: Lebanon. See chapter 7.

9. Gal Luft, "Baku-Tbilisi-Ceyhan Pipeline: Not Yet Finished and Already Threatened," *Energy Security* (a newsletter of the Institute for the Analysis of Global Energy Security), November 4, 2004, http://www.iags.org/n1104041.htm.

10. Luft, "Baku-Tbilisi-Ceyhan Pipeline."

11. Luft, "Baku-Tbilisi-Ceyhan Pipeline."

12. S. Frederick Starr and Svante E. Cornell, eds., *The Baku-Tbilisi-Ceyhan Pipeline: Oil Window to the West* (Washington, DC: Central Asia-Caucasus Institute & Silk Road Studies Program, 2005), https://www.silkroadstudies.org/resources/pdf/Monographs/2005_01

_MONO_Starr-Cornell_BTC-Pipeline.pdf; and Svante E. Cornell and Fariz Ismailzade, "The Baku-Tbilisi-Ceyhan Pipeline: Implications for Azerbaijan," *Semantics Scholar*, 2005, 78, https://www.semanticscholar.org/paper/The-Baku-Tbilisi-Ceyhan-Pipeline%3A -Implications-for-Cornell-Ismailzade/24aa74828a308c1fc78bbe9954c44b0092340484.

13. Luft, "Baku-Tbilisi-Ceyhan Pipeline."

14. "Baku-Tbilisi-Ceyhan Was Blown Up Not by Kurdish Bomb But by Russian Laptop," *Georgian Journal*, December 18, 2014, citing *Bloomberg Research*, https://www. georgianjournal.ge/military/29027-baku-tbilisi-ceyhan-was-blown-up-not-by -kurdish-bomb-but-by-russian laptop; and "Georgia war," University of Texas map, https://legacy.lib.utexas.edu/maps/georgia_war 2008 html.

15. Luft, "Baku-Tbilisi-Ceyhan Pipeline."

16. Luft, "Baku-Tbilisi-Ceyhan Pipeline."

17. Michael Klare, "Russia and Georgia: All about Oil," Foreign Policy in Focus, August 13, 2008, https://fpif.org/russia_and_georgia_all_about_oil/.

18. "Ceyhan Ceremony Inaugurates BTC Pipeline," Radio Free Europe, July 13, 2006.

19. "Ceyhan Ceremony Inaugurates BTC Pipeline," Radio Free Europe.

20. Marc Champion and Andrew Osborn, "Smoldering Feud, Then War: Tensions at Obscure Border Led to Georgia-Russia Clash," *Wall Street Journal*, August 16, 2008. A subsequent investigation by the European Union faulted both sides. See Marc Champion, "Tbilisi Started '08 War, but Moscow Also at Fault, EU Finds," *Wall Street Journal*, October 1, 2009.

21. Anne Barnard, "Georgia and Russia Nearing All-Out War," *New York Times*, August 10, 2008.

22. Jonah Hull, "Russia-Georgia War: 10 Years Since Conflict," Al Jazeera, August 8, 2018, https://www.aljazeera.com/news/2018/08/russia-georgia-war-10-years-conflict -180808130141965.html.

23. Michael Klare, "Russia and Georgia: All About Oil."

24. George Friedman, "The Medvedev Doctrine and American Strategy," Stratfor Geopolitical Intelligence Report, September 2, 2008.

25. By 1899, all of Europe was abuzz with news of America's unprecedented commercial penetration of Turkey. That year, the US Consul General had managed to negotiate direct steamship service between New York and Constantinople, allowing American products to enter the Ottoman Empire's eastern markets "nearly on equal terms with their European rivals." Products ranging from railway materials and agricultural machinery to oil, beer, and flour were pouring into Turkish ports. European newspapers were quick to alert their readers that "a new and dangerous commercial rival [the US] has entered this field" — a field, noted the *Deutsche Tablatt* of Vienna, that Americans had carefully and methodically prepared by "building educational and philanthropic institutions." I'm including the very college where Elisabeth Redfern would teach within a year: the American College for Girls. See "Charles Dickenson, Consul General, to the Assistant Secretary of State," April 7, 1899, RG 59, Dispatches from U.S. Consuls, 1820–1908, T-194, roll 21, NARA.

26. Daniel Dennett, letter to Horace, September 28, 1931. In the author's possession.

27. By the mid-1870s, Rockefeller's Central Refiners Association controlled all the refining business in Cleveland, New York, and Pittsburgh and determined all rate agreements with the railroads that shipped the oil. By the turn of the century, pipelines began to

replace tank cars. Rockefeller aggressively built and bought pipelines, earning himself a reputation in the United States as the "king of pipelines." By 1877, he controlled all the pipelines in the eastern United States—all the outlets of American oil to the world market. The message to competitors was clear: Join the Standard, or be crushed. Indeed, it was John D. Rockefeller who is said to have coined the phrase "the Great Game." He had become a master player, plowing all his profits into new ventures, building new refineries and pipelines, shipping his oil at reduced rates, outbidding his competitors, capturing more markets, expanding into new territory, buying up the land, and securing the rights-of-way for pipeline routes. See Daniel Yergin, *The Prize: The Epic Quest for Oil, Money and Power* (New York: Touchstone, 1992), 37.

28. Allan Nevins, *Study in Power: John D. Rockefeller*, vol. 2 (New York: Charles Scribner's Sons, 1953), 119

29. Nevins, *Study in Power*, 121.

30. Nevins, 32.

31. Yergin, *Prize*, 42. The Standard Oil men operated in great secrecy and often communicated in code.

32. Smith College's first president, Laurenus Clark Seelye, and his brother Julius, who was president of Amherst College, were part of a family tradition that traveled widely and encouraged good works through religious missions. On one occasion, Seelye singled out the Congregational church for special praise, commemorating the "instrumentalities it has employed to promote Christian living, its charitable and missionary enterprises." Elisabeth and her brother Ralph, who was a graduate of Amherst, were constantly being reminded during their college years of the value of missions abroad. Her brother chose instead to work in the oil fields of Oklahoma, but Elisabeth willingly took up the banner, perhaps because she was better suited to missionary work. As President Seelye pointed out, only educated *women* could break through the cultural barriers facing "women of the heathen world." Educated men, he asserted, had an easier task because "their knowledge of affairs helps them to appreciate the benefits of a superior civilization. But the minds of the women have been starved so long, that their mental capacity has been crippled. Their brains resemble the stunted feet." But once women were educated, he wrote, they could truly "extirpate their ancestral vices" and become leaders in their own right as well as women of "the strongest faith and the highest culture." Education indeed had sparked a cultural revolution of rising expectations among America's upper-class women, many of whom became missionaries. See the papers of Laurenus Clark Seelye, 1837–1924, Smith College Archives, and specifically Box 12, Folder 14.

33. The archives were housed in a private building in New York when I visited them; they have since been transferred to Columbia University.

34. Mary Mills Patrick to the trustees of the American College, December 13, 1909. In the Papers of Carolyn Boyden, archives of the American College for Girls, Columbia University, New York. (Note: The citations provided were from the archives' old location in a private building; they may have changed since the archives moved to Columbia University.)

35. As the president of Ginn and Company working out of its New York headquarters, Plimpton had solid connections among members of the Eastern establishment. Within two years, he would agree to serve on the American College for Girls board of advisors in New York, becoming one of the school's principal liaisons to the richest man in the United States, John D. Rockefeller. There are numerous letters between

Plimpton and the top administrators of the college during this period that can be found in the college archives at Columbia University.

36. The "tainted money scandal" was famous in its time, and much discussed in histories of the Congregational church and early missionary activities. Jerry and I had written about it in *Thy Will Be Done*, not knowing that the money was earmarked for the American College for Girls thanks to the intercessions of my grandmother!

37. By the turn of the century, wood-starved Europe was a growing market for white pine. The wood was flexible but sturdy, floated easily, and made, among other useful items, reliable railroad ties. Germany, I discovered from reading through consular reports in Turkey, was then an "excellent buyer" of American lumber. See "Prices of American Lumber at Rotterdam," Advance sheet, *Consular Reports*, March 17, 1999, Dispatches from U.S. Consuls, 1820–1908, T-194, roll 21, NARA.

38. The Ottoman Turks' empire had been weakened by successful independence movements in the Balkans and North Africa that had been backed by covetous European colonial powers. The Russians had stirred up the Balkan and Transcaucasian people to declare their independence and were constantly provoking the Armenians (who were Christians, like the Russians) to revolt. The French, allies of the Russians, had increased their domination over Tunisia and Syria. The British seized Egypt. The Italians did likewise with Tripoli (Libya). See Edward Earle, *Turkey, the Great Powers, and the Baghdad Railway: A Study in Imperialism* (New York: Macmillan, 1923), 11. Even so, Turkey remained the political and financial hub of a remnant empire comprising today's Turkey, Syria, Lebanon, Jordan, Israel, Palestine, Iraq, and the western territories of Saudi Arabia.

39. Barbara Tuchman, *The Guns of August* (New York: Dell, 1963), 21.

40. One of the trustees, who would go on to become president of the American College for Girls in 1915, was Charles Crane, heir to a Chicago-based plumbing — and pipeline — fortune. He made multiple trips to the Middle East using the college as his base and would lead the legendary 1919 King-Crane commission (officially called the 1919 Inter-Allied Commission on Mandates in Turkey) to the Middle East to determine the wishes of Arabs and Jews prior to the final determinations by the victors of World I of their geographic and political status. From there, he would go on to play a major role in encouraging the United States to invest in Saudi Arabia and its oil. Another trustee was Cleveland Dodge of the Phelps Dodge mining fortune, whose family made major donations to Christian colleges in the Middle East, including the American College for Girls, Robert College, and the Syrian Protestant College, later known as the American University of Beirut. He would become part of Woodrow Wilson's inner circle, advising him on the Middle East, "the Armenian question," and preparations for World War I.

41. Mary Mills Patrick, *Under Five Sultans* (New York: Century, 1929), 180.

42. Roland Greene Usher, "Proposed Berlin to Bagdad Railway" in *The Story of the Great War:1914–1918* (New York: The Macmillan Company, 1919).

43. Liberty Dennett, Letter to the Editor, *Portland Daily Express*, January 19, 1909. Letter in the author's possession.

44. Mary Mills Patrick, *A Bosporus Adventure* (Istanbul: Boğaziçi University Press, 2016), 110–17.

45. Earle, *Baghdad Railway*, 205–23.

46. Yergin, *Prize*, 188.

47. By 1911, all the locomotives traversing Turkey's new railroads had converted to oil — oil purchased from Standard Oil of New Jersey. The administration of the Young Turks was earning revenue from the Anatolian and Baghdad railways, which were now within reach of the great plains of Mesopotamia. Turkey's economic prospects finally seemed to be taking a turn for the better. So, too, did the prospects of the American College for Girls. Construction on the new campus began with the laying of the cornerstone of Gould Hall in November 1911. See Earle, *Baghdad Railway*, 231.

48. R. G. Laffan, *The Serbs: The Guardians of the Gate* (New York: Dorset Press, 1989 [reprint of 1917]), 163–64.

49. Earle, *Baghdad Railway*, 139.

50. Yergin, *Prize*, 187.

51. Letter of Mary Mills Patrick to Grace Dodge, October 22, 1914, in the American College for Girls archives at Columbia University, box 4, folder 7.

52. Mary Mills Patrick to George Plimpton, October 29, 1915, in the American College for Girls archives at Columbia University, box 13, folder 5.

53. "Death March," The Institute for Armenian Studies of Yerevan State University, http://www.armin.am/armeniansgenocide/en/Encyclopedia_Of_armenian_genocide _death_march.

54. The genocide of Armenians in 1914–15 was preceded by Turkish attacks on the southern Turkish town of Adana in 1909, which lay in the path of the Berlin-to-Baghdad railroad. Half the city of 40,000 was made up of Armenians. Well educated and well off, they had become emboldened by the high ideals of multiculturalism and respect for minority rights that the Young Turks had professed. They began to openly question why Christians like themselves couldn't be equal to Muslims under the law. For this, they had been called "pushy" and "aggressive." One year after the Young Turk Revolution of 1908, events beyond their control made them scapegoats for Turkish resentment against Christians, when Christian European nations were again amputating European portions of Muslim Ottoman territory. When the killings in Adana ended, 4,823 homes had been destroyed and some 15,000 to 20,000 inhabitants had died. The vast majority were Armenians. See Peter Balakian, *The Burning Tigris: The Armenian Genocide and America's Response* (New York: HarperCollins, 2003), 148–57.

55. Mary Mills Patrick to George Plimpton, November 21, 1914, in the American College for Girls archives at Columbia University, box 13, folder 7.

56. Joseph L. Grabill, *Protestant Diplomacy and the Near East: Missionary Influence on American Policy, 1810–1927* (Minneapolis: University of Minnesota Press, 1971), 90.

57. "I have tried," Bristol told a Standard Oil executive, "to get our businessmen to reconcile [their] difference with the benevolent institutions" and to make the missionaries realize that "their interests depend very largely upon our American business interests." He considered Armenia a "lemon" in the grand scheme of US foreign policy and confessed privately to a colleague, Admiral William S. Sims, that he believed the Armenian people "are a race like the Jews; they have little or no national spirit and have a poor moral character." See Balakian, *Burning Tigris*, 366.

58. Allen Dulles to Mark Bristol, April 21, 1922, Bristol Papers, Washington, DC, quoted in Balakian, *Burning Tigris*, 369.

59. Balakian, 369.

60. Grabill, *Protestant Diplomacy*, 280.

61. Balakian, *Burning Tigris*, 346.
62. Joseph Grew, *Turbulent Era: A Diplomatic Record of Forty Years 1904–1945* (Boston: Houghton Mifflin, 1952), 707.
63. "Economic Brief: The Blue Stream Gas Pipeline," *Power and Interest Newsletter*, November 22, 2005, https://web.archive.org/web/20070702221045/http://www.pinr.com/report.php?ac=view_report&report_id=403&language_id=1.
64. Torrey Taussig, "The Serpentine Trajectory of Turkish-Russian Relations," Brookings Institution, October 4, 2017, https://www.brookings.edu/blog/order-from-chaos/2017/10/04/the-serpentine-trajectory-of-turkish-russian-relations/.
65. "In the Depths: Drilling for Oil in the Black Sea," Offshore Technology, February 3, 2016, https://www.offshore-technology.com/features/featurein-the-depths-drilling-for-oil-in-the-black-sea-4788063/.
66. "Gas Pipeline: Blue Stream," Gazprom, http://www.gazprom.com/projects/blue-stream/; "How the Annexation of the Crimea Changed Russia's Exclusive Offshore Economic Zones," Lamont-Doherty Earth Observatory, Columbia University; and Kostiantyn Yanchenko, "Black Sea Gas Deposits — an Overlooked Reason for Russia's Occupation of Crimea," *Euromaidan Press*, October 10, 2018, http://euromaidanpress.com/2018/10/10/black-sea-gas-deposits-an-overlooked-reason-for-russias-occupation-of-crimea.

Chapter 7: Mare Nostrum

1. Graham Rayman, "CIA Paranoia and the Lady from Vermont," *Village Voice*, October 19, 2007, http://www.villagevoice.com/news/0743,rayman,78104,2.html.
2. David Painter, *Oil and the American Century* (Baltimore: John Hopkins University Press, 1986), 114.
3. Anthony Cave Brown, *Treason in the Blood: H. St. John Philby, Kim Philby, and the Spy Case of the Century* (New York: Houghton Mifflin, 1994), 379.
4. "Izvestia Assails Deal. Writer Sees in Pipeline a Link in U.S. Military Base Chain," *New York Times*, January 27, 1947.
5. Brown, *Treason in the Blood*, 372.
6. Brown, 371.
7. Brown, 178–79.
8. "Monthly Operations Report" of the military attaché for March 1947. Found in "Army Airforce Report of Major Accident." Documents in the author's possession.
9. US Minister to Egypt Pinkney Tuck had cabled the State Department on March 20, 1947, that Sullivan had just "completed successful regional Arab country survey [on oil] March 16th." Cable found in "Army Airforce Report of Major Accident." Documents in the author's possession.
10. Graham Rayman of the *Village Voice* described the technicality well: "The CIA asked a federal judge to dismiss the lawsuit, saying that it had done everything it could do. The judge agreed. Dennett then mistakenly sent her notice of appeal to the wrong post-office box in the same federal building that houses the District Court and the clerk for the Court of Appeals. The same judge refused to give her more time to file her appeal. That decision created one huge irony: The government was holding her to a procedural miscue, when it had delayed, ignored, and fought her FOIA requests for eight years. In its appellate brief, the government dwells on Dennett's clerical error for four pages. Dennett's error, the government argues, doesn't meet the standard for 'excusable

neglect.' But what about the government's handling of her Freedom of Information Act request? Wasn't that in itself inexcusable neglect?" See Rayman, "CIA Paranoia."

Alan Feuer of the *New York Times* ended his story of my FOIA lawsuit on a poignant note: "Kingdoms can be lost for the lack of a nail. So, too, the truth about a loved one for the lack of a proper address." Alan Feuer, "A Dead Spy, a Daughter's Questions and the C.I.A.," *New York Times*, October 23, 2007.

11. "CIA's Failure of Memory: Daniel Dennett, the Forgotten First Star?" In Nicholas Dujmovic, "Amnesia to Anamnesis: Commemoration of the Dead at CIA," *Studies in Intelligence* 52, no. 3 (2008), https://www.cia.gov/library/center-for-the-study-of-intelligence/csi-publications/csi-studies/studies/vol52no3/amnesia-to-anamnesis.html.

12. Brown, *Treason in the Blood*, 378.

13. Wassim Mroueh, "No Leads in the Case of Kidnapped Estonians — Security Sources," *Daily Star*, March 24, 2011.

14. Rick Rozoff, "Libyan War and Control of the Mediterranean," *Voltaire Network*, March 26, 2011.

15. Bruno Waterfield, "Gaddafi Attacks Sarkozy Plan for Union of the Med," *Telegraph*, July 10, 2008, https://www.telegraph.co.uk/news/worldnews/europe/2277517/Gaddafi-attacks-Sarkozy-plan-for-Union-of-the-Med.html.

16. Adrian Bloomfield, "Libya: Foreign Mercenaries Terrorising Citizens," *Telegraph*, February 23, 2011, https://www.telegraph.co.uk/news/worldnews/africaandindianocean/libya/8343959/Libya-foreign-mercenaries-terrorising-citizens.html; and Josephine Whitaker, "Protestors under Fire from Land, Sea and Air in Libya," Open Democracy, February 21, 2011, https://www.opendemocracy.net/en/opensecurity/210211/.

17. Micah Zenko, "The Big Lie about the Libyan War: The Obama Administration Said It Was Just Trying to Protect Civilians. Its Actions Reveal It Was Looking for Regime Change," *The Atlantic*, March 22, 2016.

18. Ewen MacAskill, "Gaddafi 'Supplies Troops with Viagra to Encourage Mass Rape,' Claims Diplomat," *The Guardian*, April 29, 2011, https://www.theguardian.com/world/2011/apr/29/diplomat-gaddafi-troops-viagra-mass-rape. Rice also took aim at President Assad for "disingenuously blaming outsiders, while seeking Iranian assistance in repressing Syria's citizens, through the same brutal tactics that have been used by the Iranian regime." She declined to provide evidence of Iranian involvement, as did the State Department.

19. Patrick Cockburn, "Amnesty Questions Claim That Gaddafi Ordered Rape as Weapon of War." *The Independent*, June 24, 2011. Writes Cockburn: "Nato leaders, opposition groups and the media have produced a stream of stories since the start of the insurrection on 15 February, claiming the Gaddafi regime has ordered mass rapes, used foreign mercenaries and employed helicopters against civilian protesters. An investigation by Amnesty International has failed to find evidence for these human rights violations and in many cases has discredited or cast doubt on them."

20. Brad Hoff, "Hillary Emails Reveal True Motive for Libya Intervention," *Foreign Policy Journal*, January 6, 2016, https://www.foreignpolicyjournal.com/2016/01/06/new-hillary-emails-reveal-true-motive-for-libya-intervention/.

21. See the website of the United States Africa Command at https://www.africom.mil/what-we-do.

22. *People's Daily*, February 26, 2007, cited in Rozoff, "Libyan War."

23. Florence Gaub, "Lebanon's Civil War: Seven Lessons Forty Years On." *ISSUE Alert*, European Union Institute for Security Studies, April 2015, https://www.iss.europa .eu/sites/default/files/EUISSFiles/Alert_21_Lebanon_civil_war.pdf.

24. David Hirst, *Beware of Small States: Lebanon, Battleground of the Middle East* (New York: Nation Books, 2010), 109.

25. Hirst, *Beware of Small States*, 111.

26. Franklin Lamb, "Lebanon and the Planned US Airbase at Kleiaat," *CounterPunch*, May 30, 2007, https://www.counterpunch.org/2007/05/30/lebanon-and-the-planned-us -airbase-at-kleiaat/.

27. Lamb, "US Airbase at Kleiaat."

28. Nicholas Blanford, "Death Toll Reaches 80 in Lebanon as Troops Shell Palestinian Refugee Camp in Battle with Fatah al-Islam," interview by Amy Goodman, *Democracy Now!*, May 22, 2007, https://www.democracynow.org/2007/5/22/death_toll _reaches_80_in_lebanon.

29. "Here's Hezbollah's Game-Changing Secret Drone Base," *Business Insider*, April 24, 2015, https://www.businessinsider.com/hezbollahs-secret-drone-base-2015-4.

Chapter 8: The Hidden History of Pipeline Politics in Palestine and Israel

1. Ed Vuillamy, "Israel Seeks Pipeline for Iraqi Oil," *The Observer*, April 19, 2003.

2. Daniel Yergin, *The Prize: The Epic Quest for Oil, Money and Power* (New York: Touch-stone, 1992), 188–89.

3. Yergin, *Prize*, 188–89.

4. Marvin Lowenthal, ed., trans., *The Diaries of Theodor Herzl* (New York: Dial Press, 1956), 370.

5. Bernard Avishai, "The Balfour Declaration Century," *New Yorker*, November 2, 2017.

6. The Allied betrayals in the Balfour Declaration and the Sykes-Picot Agreement, released a month later, had proved to be a supreme challenge to British officers as their forces advanced up the Eastern Mediterranean to capture Jerusalem in December 1917. The British managed to keep the release of the Sykes-Picot Agreement secret long enough to secure their military occupation of the Holy City. A month later, the British sent a special envoy to Prince Hussein, the Sharif of Mecca, whom they had titled the King of Hejaz, reassuring him of Britain's undying friendship and its sincere commitment to protecting the Arabs' political and economic rights in Palestine. This was followed up by a formal written declaration to Hussein in February 1918 praising him for his leadership and guidance and reaffirming His Majesty's government's "former pledge regarding the liberation of Arab people." See George Antonius, *The Arab Awakening* (New York: Penguin/Capricorn Books, 1946), 213.

7. William Yale, cited in "Memorandum on the Neareastern Oil Question," April 9, 1920, RG59, 800.6363.166, NARA.

8. Telegram to US Secretary of State from American Mission (Turkey), June 5, 1919, State Department Records of Internal Affairs, 1910–29, microfilm copy 353, roll 67, NARA.

9. Memorandum to the secretary of state from the American consul in charge, Palestine, "International Trade Competition — Oil Concessions in Palestine," October 27, 1921, State Department Records of Internal Affairs, RG 59, 867.6363, 1910–29, microfilm copy 0353, roll 67, NARA.

10. Memo to Mr. Dwight, Mr. Frost, and Mr. Lay from the Office of the Foreign Trade Advisor, US Department of State, February 19, 1920, State Department Records of Internal Affairs, 867.6363, RG 59, 1910–29, microfilm copy 0353, roll 67, NARA.

11. Allen Dulles to Department of State, November 28, 1923, "Memorandum of Conversation with Mr. Thomas of the Standard Oil Company with Regard to Geological Investigations in Palestine." Writes Dulles, "Mr. Thomas told me confidentially that they were somewhat embarrassed at this [British request for a report] as they did not desire to submit their report until the Mesopotamian negotiations were completed. I gathered from Mr. Thomas that they had agreed to turn in their Palestine holdings to the Turkish Petroleum Company and did not desire that company to learn . . . that the Standard Oil investigation had led them to believe that their Palestine claims were of little value as the prospects of oil were not good." State Department Records of Internal Affairs, RG 59, 867.6363/65, 1910–29, microfilm copy 0353, roll 87, NARA.

12. Matthieu Auzanneau, *Oil, Power, and War: A Dark History* (White River Junction, VT: Chelsea Green, 2018), 116.

13. US Holocaust Memorial Museum, "The United States and the Holocaust: Why Auschwitz Was Not Bombed," https://encyclopedia.ushmm.org/content/en/article/the-united-states-and-the-holocaust-why-auschwitz-was-not-bombed.

14. For years McCloy would deny having any involvement in the decision not to bomb Auschwitz, and in a 1983 interview with Morton Mintz of the *Washington Post*, he tried to pass the buck on to General Henry (Hap) Arnold of the Army and Air Force and to President Roosevelt. "I haven't anything on my conscience. . . . I know my conscience is perfectly clear," he told Mintz, who, in the article, pointed out the McCloy "has been an adviser to presidents as well as chairman of Chase Manhattan Bank, the Ford Foundation and the Council on Foreign Relations." See Morton Mintz, "Why Didn't We Bomb Auschwitz," *Washington Post*, April 17, 1983, https://www.washingtonpost.com/archive/opinions/1983/04/17/why-didnt-we-bomb-auschwitz/a9053a8f-eb12-4bd3-9090-0837c4141baf/.

15. Sara J. Bloomfield, "The Bombing of Auschwitz Question," United States Holocaust Memorial Museum, referencing a memory from Elie Wiesel, from his book, *Night*. https://medium.com/@HolocaustMuseum/the-bombing-of-auschwitz-question-cc30e524a9c2.

16. Adolf Berle to Mr. Secretary, April 20, 1943, State Department Subject File, 1938–45, Berle Papers, box 58, Franklin Delano Roosevelt Library, Hyde Park, New York.

17. William Eddy to Loy Henderson, October 26, 1945, Department of State, RG 59, Records of the Office of Near Eastern Affairs, lot 54D403, box 12, NARA.

18. "Notes by J. T. Duce," April 19, 1944, introduced as testimony presented by Socal Aramco before the Senate Oil Policy Committee (executive session), April 19–26, from the archives of Standard Oil of California, box 0373186. At the time, it was expected that the US government would finance the pipeline at a cost of $135 million, saving Aramco considerable expense. Duce replied, "We are, after all, an American company doing our best to develop oil abroad [and] . . . as an American group, we thought we were entitled to Government protection the same as any other citizen." The company would also pay "40% of our profits to the United States Government in income taxes." Not satisfied, Brewster "burst out in a tirade" over concerns that the Russians were getting involved in the region and, with one of his boys already in the army, "he didn't

want to see any American blood spilled." Duce assured Brewster that Aramco did not contemplate "American troops ever being sent to Arabia."

19. George Wadsworth to Loy Henderson, July 11, 1945, 890E.00/7-1145, RG 59, NARA.

20. See a full account in Douglas Little's comprehensive paper, "Pipeline Politics: America, TAPLINE, and the Arabs," *Business History Review* 64, no, 2 (1990): 258 (online version) 264–65.

21. Terry Duce to Sanger, November 4, 1946, 867N.01/11-446, RG 59, NARA.

22. Maya Spitzer, "Haifa Enjoys Benefits of Visiting US Sailors," *Jerusalem Post*, March 3, 2009, https://www.jpost.com/Local-Israel/Around-Israel/Haifa-enjoys-benefits-of-visiting-US-sailors.

23. Joel Beinin, "The U.S. Israel Alliance," in *Wrestling with Zion: Progressive Jewish-American Responses in the Israel-Palestinian Conflict*, eds. Tommy Kusher and Alisa Solomon (New York: Grove Press, 2003), 50.

24. "Nuclear Weapons, Who Has What," Arms Control Association, June 2018, https://www.armscontrol.org/factsheets/Nuclearweaponswhohaswhat.

25. Martha Wenger, "US Aid to Israel: From Handshake to Embrace" *MERIP Reports* 164, 1991.

26. Transcript, "Joint Press Conference with Secretary Gates and Minister Barak from Tel Aviv, Israel," Department of Defense, March 24, 2011, http://archive.defense.gov/transcripts/transcript.aspx?transcriptid=4797.

27. Associated Press, "Incoming U.S. Defense Secretary Tells Senate Panel Israel Has Nuclear Weapons," *Haaretz* (Israel), December 7, 2006, https://www.haaretz.com/1.4937037.

28. For more on arms sales to Israel and the benefits accrued to arms makers and large oil companies (the "weapondollar/petrodollar" coalition), see Jonathan Nitzan and Shimshon Bichler, *The Global Economy of Israel* (London: Pluto Press, 2002), and Steven Fleischman, "Israel Neocolonialism and U.S. Hegemony," *Nature Society and Thought* 17, no. 3 (2004).

29. Reuters and Israel Hayom staff, "Key U.S. Lawmakers Want to Boost Israel's $38 Billion Defense Aid Package," Israel Hayom, February 28, 2018, https://www.israelhayom.com/2018/02/28/key-us-lawmakers-want-to-boost-israels-38b-defense-aid-package/.

30. William Orme Jr., "Arafat Hails Big Gas Find off the Coast of Gaza Strip," *New York Times*, September 28, 2000.

31. Michael Schwartz, "The Great Game in the Holy Land: How Gazan Natural Gas Became the Epicenter of an International Power Struggle," *TomDispatch*, February 25, 2015, https://www.tomdispatch.com/blog/175961/tomgram%3A_michael_schwartz,_israel,_gaza,_and_energy_wars_in_the_middle_east/.

32. Schwartz, "Gazan Natural Gas."

33. Schwartz, "Gazan Natural Gas."

34. "Map of Levant Basin Province, Eastern Mediterranean," US Geological Survey, https://www.usgs.gov/media/images/map-levant-basin-province-eastern-mediterranean; "Western Power Missile Attacks on Syria (April 2018)" and "Syrian Conflict Overview Map (early October 2018), The Energy Consulting Group, http://energy-cg.com/MiddleEast/Syria/Syria%20Oil%20and%20Gas%20Overview.html; and "The Islamic State and the Crisis in Iraq and Syria in Maps," BBC News, March 28, 2018, https://www.bbc.com/news/world-middle-east-27838034.

35. Ari Shavit, "The Enemy Within," *Haaretz*, August 29, 2002.

36. "Israeli Minister Calls Anti-settler Group a 'Virus,'" Reuters, August 19, 2009, https://www.reuters.com/article/idUSLJ180639.

37. Moshe Yaalon, "Does the Prospective Purchase of British Gas from Gaza Threaten Israel's National Security?" *Jerusalem Issue Briefs* 7, no. 17 (October 19, 2007), http://jcpa.org/article/does-the-prospective-purchase-of-british-gas-from-gaza-threaten-israel%E2%80%99s-national-security/.

38. Uri Blau, "GO Southern Command: IDF Will Send Gaza Back Decades," *Haaretz*, December 12, 2008, https://www.haaretz.com/1.5078956.

39. "Gaza Crisis: Toll of Operations in Gaza," BBC News, September 1, 2014, https://www.bbc.com/news/world-middle-east-28439404.

40. Schwartz, "Gazan Natural Gas"; and Nafeez Ahmed, "IDF's Gaza Assault Is to Control Palestinian Gas, Avert Israeli Energy Crisis," *The Guardian*, July 9, 2014. During this period, Israel sought to drive a wedge between Hamas and Fatah, the more moderate Palestinian faction that controlled the West Bank. According to Mark Turner, founder of the Research Journalism Initiative, "by leveraging political tensions between the two parties, arming forces loyal to Abbas and the selective resumption of financial aid, Israel and the United States effectively re-installed Fatah in the West Bank, projected the party back onto the international stage and revived the possibility of concluding the energy deal." See Turner, "Gaza Siege Intensified after Collapse of Natural Gas Deal, *Electronic Intifada*, January 22, 2008, https://electronicintifada.net/content/gaza-siege-intensified-after-collapse-natural-gas-deal/7312. In other words, Israel used divide-and-rule tactics, driving a wedge between Hamas and Fatah, and made the more moderate Fatah the "official group" to negotiate energy deals. NB: This tactic was often used on American Indians sitting atop oil: The more "moderate" tribes or tribal leaders were manipulated and bought off, as they were more likely to cut a deal to the energy companies' liking.

41. Barak Ravid, "U.S. Backs Lebanon on Maritime Border Dispute with Israel," *Haaretz*, July 10, 2011.

42. Chris Lo, "Timeline: Game-Changing Gas Discoveries in the Eastern Mediterranean," *Offshore Technology*, December 13, 2017, https://www.offshore-technology.com/features/timeline-game-changing-gas-discoveries-eastern-mediterranean/.

43. Gal Luft, "Energy Security Challenges for Israel following the Gaza War," *Journal of Energy Security*, February 19, 2009.

44. Luft, "Energy Security Challenges."

45. "New Energy and Peace Triangle in the Eastern Mediterranean: Israel-Cyprus-Turkey," Hazar Strategy Institute, February 2014.

46. "Gaza Crisis," BBC News.

47. Isabel Kershner and Rick Gladstone, "Gaza Militants Targeted Jerusalem with Rockets for First Time in Conflict," *New York Times*, November 17, 2012.

48. Ethan Bronner, "Israel, on New Battlefield, Sticks to New Approach," *New York Times*, November 12, 2012.

49. Bronner, "Israel, on New Battlefield."

50. Helene Cooper, "US Fears a Ground War in Gaza Could Hurt Israel and Help Hamas," *New York Times*, November 16, 2012.

51. Isabel Kershner, "Israel, Facing Criticism, to Investigate Possible Military Misconduct in Gaza," *New York Times*, September 11, 2014.

52. Nafeez Ahmed, "IDF's Gaza Assault."

53. Jonathan Cook, "Everyone Washes Their Hands as Gaza's Economy Goes into Freefall," *CounterPunch*, October 2, 2018.

54. *Report of the Independent International Commission of Inquiry on the Protests in the Occupied Palestinian Territory* (United Nations Human Rights Council, February 28, 2019), https://www.ohchr.org/EN/HRBodies/HRC/CoIOPT/Pages/Report2018OPT.aspx.

55. Nick Cumming-Bruce, "Israelis May Have Committed Crimes against Humanity in Gaza Protests, U.N. Says," *New York Times*, February 28, 2019.

56. Bethan McKernan, "Palestinians Ask ICC to Consider Israeli War Crimes and Crimes against Humanity," *Independent*, May 22, 2018, https://www.independent.co.uk/news/world/middle-east/gaza-protests-icc-israel-palestine-petition-war-crimes-against-humanity-deaths-a8363706.html.

57. Steve Holland, "Trump Administration Takes Aim at International Criminal Court, PLO," Reuters, September 9, 2018, https://www.reuters.com/article/us-usa-trump-icc/trump-administration-takes-aim-at-international-criminal-court-plo-idUSKCN1LQ076; and Adam Taylor, "John Bolton Hates the International Criminal Court. That Might Make Other Countries Love It," *Washington Post*, September 10, 2018, https://www.washingtonpost.com/world/2018/09/10/john-bolton-hates-international-criminal-court-that-might-make-other-countries-love-it/.

58. Rachel Elbaum, "Israel's Netanyahu, Hamas, Both Boosted by Gaza Violence," NBC News, May 6, 2019, https://www.nbcnews.com/news/world/israel-s-netanyahu-hamas-both-boosted-gaza-violence-n1002271.

59. Grace Wermenbol, "Why is Bahrain Hosting the Middle East Peace Conference?," *MENASource* (blog), *Atlantic Council*, May 30, 2019, https://www.atlanticcouncil.org/blogs/menasource/why-is-bahrain-hosting-the-mideast-peace-conference.

60. Jonathan Swan, "Exclusive: Jared Kushner on MBS, Refugees, Racism and Trump's Legacy," *Axios*, June 2, 2019, https://www.axios.com/kushner-mbs-refugees-racism-trump-legacy-a92d1982-4b6f-4164-a0e0-57d0a746c68e.html.

61. See, for instance, the opinion piece by Muhammad Shehada, "Jared Kushner Just Killed the Palestinian Peace Camp," in *Haaretz*, June 4, 2019, https://www.haaretz.com/us-news/.premium-jared-kushner-just-killed-the-palestinian-peace-camp-1.7317109.

62. Wharton School, "Why Developing Israel's Leviathan Gas Field Is a Mammoth Task," Knowledge@Wharton, August 25, 2017, https://knowledge.wharton.upenn.edu/article/developing-israels-leviathan-gas-field-proven-mammoth-task/.

63. Wharton School, "Developing Israel's Leviathan."

64. Wharton School, "Developing Israel's Leviathan."

65. Agence France-Presse, "Erdogan Accuses US, Israel of 'Meddling' in Iran, Pakistan," *Times of Israel*, January 5, 2018, https://www.timesofisrael.com/erdogan-accuses-us-israel-of-meddling-in-iran-pakistan/.

66. Schwartz, "Gazan Natural Gas."

67. Wharton School, "Developing Israel's Leviathan."

68. Wharton School, "Developing Israel's Leviathan."

69. The gas is supposed to be supplied from the gas fields Tamar and Leviathan, which are owned by an Israeli company, Delek, together with the American energy company Noble. See Noa Landau, "Israeli Natural Gas Giant Signs $15 Billion Export Deal with Egypt," *Haaretz*, February 19, 2018.

70. David Rosenberg, "Why Isn't Egypt Joining Israel's Natural Gas Deal Party?" *Haaretz*, February 20, 2018.

71. Shahira Amin, "Egypt Faces Public Backlash after Signing $15 Billion Gas Deal with Israel," *Al-Monitor*, February 23, 2018.

72. Rosenberg, "Why Isn't Egypt Joining?"

73. Rosenberg, "Why Isn't Egypt Joining?"

74. Simon Henderson, "Israeli Gas is Almost Ashore, but Challenges Remain," Washington Institute, September 7, 2018, www.washingtoninstitute.org/policy-analysis/view/israeli -gas-is-almost-ashore-but-challenges-remain. The Washington Institute is a nonprofit organization whose mission "is to advance a balanced and realistic understanding of American interests in the Middle East and to promote the policies that secure them."

75. Mathew Hoare, "Assessing the Future Potential of Gaza Marine Field," *Egypt Oil and Gas*, April 5, 2018.

76. Hoare, "Assessing the Future."

77. Reuters, "Shell Gives Up on Gaza's Offshore Gas Field," *Yahoo! Finance*, March 5, 2018, https://finance.yahoo.com/news/shell-gives-gazas-offshore-gas-153520384.html.

78. Shadia Nasralla, "Energean Ready to Take Gaza Marine Gas Field Stake if Israel, Palestinians Agree," Reuters, July 6, 2018, https://www.reuters.com/article/us-gaza -gas-energean-israel/energean-ready-to-take-gaza-marine-gas-field-stake-if-israel -palestinians-agree-idUSKBN1JW1D8.

79. Mark Landler and David M. Halbfinger, "Trump, with Netanyahu, Formally Recognizes Israel's Authority over Golan Heights," *New York Times*, March 25, 2019.

80. Whitney Webb of *MintPress News* was one of the few reporters to draw attention to a bill introduced to Congress by Senator Ted Cruz in February 2019 that would not only have the United States recognizing Israel's sovereigny over the Golan Heights but also support "joint projects" with Israel in the Golan, including "industrial research and development." Comments *MintPress*, "This is sure to result in joint U.S.-Israeli efforts to extract the large oil reserves recently discovered in the Golan Heights, as the rights to extract that oil were granted to the joint U.S.-Israeli venture Genie Energy soon after its discovery was made public." See Whitney Webb, "With Oil, Water and Iran as Targets, US on Brink of Recognizing Israeli Sovereignty over Golan Heights," *MintPress News*, February 27, 2019.

81. David Hearst, "Bin Salman 'Tried to Persuade Netanyahu to Go to War in Gaza' Say Sources," *Middle East Eye*, November 13, 2018, https://www.middleeasteye.net/news /bin-salman-tried-persuade-netanyahu-go-war-gaza-say-sources.

Chapter 9: Pipeline Politics, Assassinations, and the West's War on Yemen

1. Aaron C. David and Aaron Williams, "12 Saudis Appear to Have Ties to Security Forces," *Washington Post,* October 18, 2018.

2. "Jamal Khashoggi: All You Need to Know about Saudi Journalist's Death," BBC News, December 11, 2018, https://www.bbc.com/news/world-europe-45812399. This is a useful reference answering many questions about events up through December 2018.

3. "Jamal Khashoggi's Killing Took Seven Minutes," *Middle East Monitor*, October 16, 2018.

4. Ben Hubbard and David D. Kirkpatrick, "For Khashoggi, a Tangled Mix of Royal Service and Islamist Sympathies," *New York Times*, October 14, 2018, https://www .nytimes.com/2018/10/14/world/middleeast/jamal-khashoggi-saudi-arabia.html.

5. Peter Nicholas and Rebecca Ballhaus, "White House Defends Saudi Ties," *Wall Street Journal*, October 23, 2018.

6. Nicholas and Ballhaus, "White House Defends."

7. Anthony Cave Brown, *Treason in the Blood: H. St. John Philby, Kim Philby, and the Spy Case of the Century* (New York: Houghton Mifflin, 1994), 159–60.

8. Brown, *Treason in the Blood*, 159–60.

9. See *The Magnes-Philby Negotiations, 1929. The Historical Record* (Jerusalem: The Magnes Press, The Hebrew University, 1998)

10. In addition to Hoffman, see Calder Walton, *Empire of Secrets: British Intelligence, the Cold War, and the Twilight of the Empire* (New York: Overlook Press, 2013), and his article, "How Zionist Extremism Became British Spies' Biggest Enemy," *Foreign Policy*, January 1, 2014, https://foreignpolicy.com/2014/01/01/how-zionist-extremism -became-british-spies-biggest-enemy/, adapted from his book.

11. Bruce Hoffman, *Anonymous Soldiers: The Struggle for Israel, 1917–1947* (New York: Knopf, 2015), 315.

12. Ruth Dennett, "Dear Families," letter in possession of the author.

13. Dennett to the Secretary of State, "Progress, and Investigation into the Bombing Outrage at American Legation," GNX 463, August 19, 1946, RG 226, entry 108A, box 173, NARA. See also Memo from Wadsworth to Dennett, August 16, 1946, in box 173, NARA.

14. Brown, *Treason in the Blood*, 293 and 298.

15. Bruce Kuniholm is among those American historians who, citing State Department documents, understandably believed that US-British competition over the Middle East receded beginning in 1944, "because of the empire's increasing weakness relative to Russia." Great Britain, he wrote in 1980, "chose to bury differences with the United States over vital oil interests in the Near East in order to protect them." See Bruce Kuniholm, *The Origins of the Cold War in the Near East* (Princeton, New Jersey: 1980), 204. Likewise, Phillip J. Baram asserted that in 1944, "The Department's oil policy crystallized" and that among its objectives were "1) the demotion of Britain's role from senior partnership in developing and controlling Middle Eastern oil to junior partnership with the United States and 2) together with Britain, the prevention of a postwar scramble for Middle East oil, a scramble that would predictably include the USSR." See Phillip J. Baram, *The Department of State in the Middle East, 1919–1945* (University of Pennsylvania Press, 1978), 112. Yet as revealed in this book, through declassified OSS documents, the very year when Dennett was posted to Lebanon as Carat (1944), the rivalry remained intense, with Dennett discovering that the British would be a major "danger point" and that a "real free for all" among allies was about to begin.

16. Paul Fitzgerald and Elizabeth Gould, "The Khashoggi Gambit," *CounterPunch*, November 2, 2018.

17. Hoffman, *Anonymous Soldiers*, 369.

18. Hoffman, 209.

19. "America and the Saudis," *Wall Street Journal*, October 22, 2018.

20. "Saudi Arabia's 'Davos in the Desert' Is Still Going On. Here's Who Went," *Bloomberg*, October 24, 2018; and David Ignatius, "Why Was MBS So Afraid of Jamal Khashoggi?" *Washington Post*, October 25, 2018.

21. Mark Landler and Kate Kelly, "Saudi Prince's Showcase Tarnished by Grisly Report. Global Conference in Tatters," *New York Times*, October 14, 2018.

22. "In Search of Investors, Saudi Arabia's Crown Prince Is Coming to America," *Forbes*, February 27, 2018.

23. John Hudson, "Saudis Transfer Millions in Pledged Funds to U.S. Said Khashoggi Critics," *Washington Post*, October 18, 2018.

24. Vicky Ward, *Kushner, Inc.: Greed. Ambition. Corruption. The Extraordinary Story of Jared Kushner and Ivanka Trump.* (New York: St. Martin's Press, 2019), 149.

25. "U.S. Seeks Answers in Khashoggi Case," *Washington Post*, October 17, 2008.

26. Summer Said, Margherita Stancati, and Justi Scheck, "Heir to Saudi Throne Jolted by Backlash," *Wall Street Journal*, October 22, 2018.

27. Richard Hall, "Britain Continued Seeking Arms Deals with Saudi Arabia in Weeks after Khashoggi Was Murdered," *The Independent*, January 1, 2019, https://www.independent.co.uk/news/world/middle-east/saudi-arabia-britain-arms-sales-jamal-khashoggi-murder-yemen-a8706651.html.

28. Anna Stavrianakis, "History Won't Look Kindly on Britain over Arms Sales Feeding War in Yemen," *The Guardian*, November 30, 2018, https://www.theguardian.com/global-development/2018/nov/30/history-will-not-look-kindly-on-britain-over-arms-sales-feeding-war-in-yemen.

29. Jamal Khashoggi, "Saudi Arabia's Crown Prince Must Restore Dignity to His Country — by Ending Yemen's Cruel War," *Washington Post*, September 11, 2018.

30. David Ignatius, "Khashoggi Was Part of a Long Tradition of Brave Arab Journalists," *RealClearPolitics*, October 26, 2018, https://www.realclearpolitics.com/articles/2018/10/26/khashoggi_was_part_of_a_long_tradition_of_brave_arab_journalists_138467.html.

31. Ben Hubbard and David D. Kirkpatrick, "For Khashoggi, a Tangled Mix of Royal Service and Islamist Sympathies," *New York Times*, October 14, 2018.

32. Alexander Downer, "Jamal Khashoggi Was a Player, Not a Bleeding Heart Liberal," *Financial Review*, November 4, 2018, https://www.afr.com/news/economy/jamal-khashoggi-was-a-player-not-a-bleeding-heart-liberal-alexander-downer-20181104-h17h9k.

33. "Conflict in Yemen," *C-SPAN*, panel discussion hosted by the Brookings Institution, filmed October 25, 2018, in Washington, DC, https://www.c-span.org/video/?453579-1/brookings-forum-examines-us-policy-war-yemen.

34. J. M. Sharp and C. M. Blanchard, *Congress and the War in Yemen: Oversight and Legislation, 2015–2019* (Washington, DC: Congressional Research Service, updated February 1, 2019), https://fas.org/sgp/crs/mideast/R45046.pdf.

35. Simon Denyer and Carol Morello, "Japanese Ship Owner Contradicts U.S. Account of How Tanker Was Attacked," *Washington Post*, June 14, 2019, https://www.washingtonpost.com/world/japanese-ship-owner-contradicts-us-account-of-how-tanker-was-attacked/2019/06/14/7ea347d0-8eba-11e9-b6f4-033356502dce_story.html.

36. "Houtie's Revenge: Saudi Arabia Says Oil Stations Attacked by Armed Drones," *News of Asia*, May 14, 2019, http://newsofasia.net/houties-revenge-saudi-arabia-says-oil-stations-attacked-by-armed-drones/; and "Military Situation in Yemen on December 11, 2018," South Front, https://southfront.org/military-situation-in-yemen-on-december-11-2018-map-update/.

37. For a thoughtful analysis of the Obama administration's challenges regarding Yemen, see Andrew Exum, "What's Really at Stake for America in Yemen's Conflict," *The Atlantic*, April 14, 2017, https://www.theatlantic.com/international/archive/2017/04/yemen-trump-aqap/522957/.

38. Joke Buringa, quoted in Christina Lin, *Saudi Arabia and Turkey's Pipeline Wars in Yemen and Syria*, ISPSW Strategy Series: Focus on Defense and International Security, no. 429 (Berlin: ISPSW, June 12, 2016). Buringa's blog on the pipeline is no longer online, but can be viewed here: http://web.archive.org/web/20150701113930/www.jokeburinga.com/divide-and-rule-saudi-arabia-oil-and-yemen-3/.

39. Lin, *Saudi Arabia and Turkey's Pipeline Wars*.

40. Julian Borger, "US Supplied Bomb That Killed 40 Children on Yemen School Bus," *The Guardian*, August 19, 2018.

41. Borger, "US Supplied Bomb."

42. Ben Watson, "The War in Yemen and the Making of a Chaos State," *The Economist*, February 3, 2018.

43. "Malnutrition amongst Children in Yemen at an All-Time High, Warns UNICEF," press release, UNICEF, December 12, 2016, https://www.unicef.org/press-releases/malnutrition-amongst-children-yemen-all-time-high-warns-unicef.

44. Luay Shabaneh, "1,500 Pregnant Women at Risk of Death as Main Hospital in Hodeidah Becomes Inaccessible," United Nations Population Fund report, November 14, 2018, https://reliefweb.int/report/yemen/1500-pregnant-women-risk-death-main-hospital-hodeidah-becomes-inaccessible-enar.

45. Amy Goodman, "U.N.: A Yemeni Child Dies Every 10 Min. from War-Caused Disease, Hunger," *Democracy Now!*, November 5, 2018.

46. UN News, "Humanitarian Crisis in Yemen Remains the Worst in the World, Warns UN," United Nations, February 14, 2019, https://news.un.org/en/story/2019/02/1032811.

47. Alex Wayne, "Trump Says Saudis Misused U.S. Weapons in 'Terrible' Yemen War," Bloomberg News, November 4, 2018.

48. Alice Malloy, "Trump Vetoes Yemen War Powers Resolution," CNN, April 17, 2019, https://www.cnn.com/2019/04/16/politics/trump-vetoes-yemen-war-powers-resolution/index.html.

49. "Kaine Statement on Transfers of Nuclear Technical Expertise to Saudi Arabia," statement posted on Senator Tim Kaine's website, June 4, 2019, https://www.kaine.senate.gov/press-releases-kaine-statement-on-transfers-of-nuclear-technical-expertise-to-saudi-arabia.

50. "Economic Expert Discloses US-Saudi Arabia Agreement on Yemen's Oil Reserves," *Teheran Times*, December 11, 2016, https://www.tehrantimes.com/news/409031/Economic-Expert-Discloses-US-Saudi-Arabia-Agreement-on-Yemen-s-Oil-Reserves.

51. Ahmed Abdulkareem, "Seeking New Routes for Oil Delivery Saudi Arabia Tightens Its Grip on Eastern Yemen," *MintPress News*, July 16, 2019, https://www.mintpressnews.com/new-routes-oil-pipeline-saudi-arabia-tightens-grip-al-mahrah-yemen/260572/.

52. Alastair Crooke, "The Unraveling of the Netanyahu Project for the Middle East," Strategic Culture Foundation online journal, November 5, 2018, https://www.strategic-culture.org/news/2018/11/05/unraveling-netanyahu-project-for-middle-east.html.

53. Pepe Escobar, "Summit in Istanbul as Ramifications of the Khashoggi Debacle Roll On," *Asia Times*, October 27, 2018, https://en.reseauinternational.net/summit-in-istanbul-as-ramifications-of-the-khashoggi-debacle-roll-on/.

54. Ben Hubbard, Mark Mazzetti, and Eric Schmitt, "Saudi King's Son Plotted Effort to Oust His Rival," *New York Times*, July 18, 2017, https://www.nytimes.com/2017/07/18/world/middleeast/saudi-arabia-mohammed-bin-nayef-mohammed-bin-salman.html.

55. Steven A. Cook, "The Saudis Are Killing America's Middle East Policy," Council on Foreign Relations, October 31, 2018, https://www.cfr.org/article/saudis-are-killing-americas-middle-east-policy.

56. Richard Haass, "U.S. Must Shed Its Illusions about Saudi Arabia's Crown Prince," Council on Foreign Relations, October 1, 2018, https://www.cfr.org/article/us-must-shed-its-illusions-about-saudi-arabias-crown-prince.

57. Haass, "U.S. Must Shed."

58. Stephanie Nebehay "U.N. Investigator Urges Saudi Arabia to Open Up Khashoggi Murder Trial," Reuters, March 28, 2019, https://www.reuters.com/article/us-saudi-khashoggi-un/u-n-investigator-calls-on-saudi-arabia-to-open-khashoggi-murder-trial-idUSKCN1R9251.

59. Nebehay, "UN Investigator."

60. Escobar, "Summit in Istanbul."

61. "Saudi Arabia Stealing 65% of Yemen's Oil in Collaboration with Total: Report," *American Herald Tribune*, March 5, 2017, https://ahtribune.com/world/north-africa-south-west-asia/war-on-yemen/1537-saudi-arabia-yemen-oil-total.html. According to Yemeni economist Mohammad Abdolrahman Sharafeddin, also quoted in this article, "63% of Yemen's crude production is being stolen by Saudi Arabia in cooperation with Mansour Hadi, the fugitive Yemeni president, and his mercenaries. Saudi Arabia has set up an oil base in collaboration with the French Total company in the Southern parts of Kharkhir region near the Saudi border province of Najran and is exploiting oil from the wells in the region."

62. Chelsey Dulaney and Joshua Zumbrun, "U.S. Retreat from Trade Deals Poses a New Threat to Dollar," *Wall Street Journal*, May 13, 2018.

63. William Clark, "The Real Reasons for the Upcoming War with Iraq: A Macroeconomic and Geostrategic Analysis of the Unspoken Truth," Researchgate.org, January 2003, https://www.researchgate.net/publication/242216258_The_real_reasons_for_the_upcoming_war_with_Iraq_A_macroeconomic_and_geostrategic_analysis_of_the_unspoken_truth/citation/download.

64. Clark, "The Real Reasons."

65. Peter Dale Scott, "The Libyan War, American Power and the Decline of the Petrodollar System," *Asia Pacific Journal* 9, issue 18, no. 2 (updated May 15, 2011), https://apjjf.org/-Peter-Dale-Scott/3522/article.pdf.

66. Alastair Crooke, "Khashoggi's Murder — At the Complex Intersection of Three Points of Inflection," Strategic Culture Foundation online journal, October 23, 2018, https://www.strategic-culture.org/news/2018/10/23/khashoggi-murder-complex-intersection-three-points-inflection/.

67. Carol E. Lee, Julia Ainsley, and Courtney Kube, "To Ease Turkish Pressures on Saudi Arabia, White House Weighs Expelling Erdogan Foe," NBC News, November 15, 2018.

68. Carlotta Gall, "Turkey Gets Shipment of Russian Missile System, Defying U.S.," *New York Times*, July 12, 2019.

69. Nicolas Parasie and Asa Fitch, "Saudi 'Davos in the Desert' Lowers Its Profile," *Wall Street Journal*, October 22, 2018, https://www.wsj.com/articles/saudi-davos-in-the -desert-lowers-its-profile-1540153042.

70. Robin Wright, "Can Saudi Arabia's Crown Prince, Mohammed bin Salman, Survive the Jamal Khashoggi Murder?" *New Yorker*, October 25, 2018, https://www.new yorker.com/news/news-desk/can-saudi-arabias-crown-prince-mohammed-bin -salman-survive-the-jamal-khashoggi-murder.

71. Ali Ahmad, "Disgrace in the Desert: The Shameless Return of Business and Govern-ment Leaders to Saudi Arabia," *Washington Post*, October 31, 2019, https://www .washingtonpost.com/opinions/2019/10/31/disgrace-desert-shameless-return -business-government-leaders-saudi-arabia/.

72. Holly Ellyatt, "4 Reasons Why Analysts Are Cautious of Saudi Aramco's IPO," CNBC, November 4, 2019, https://www.cnbc.com/2019/11/04/4-reasons-why-analysts-are -cautious-of-saudi-aramcos-ipo.html.

73. Jillian Ambrose, "Banks Warned over Saudi Aramco by Environmental Groups," *The Guardian*, October 17, 2019, https://www.theguardian.com/business/2019/oct/17 /banks-warned-over-saudi-aramco-by-environmental-groups.

Chapter 10: Reimagining a New World Order

1. Declan Walsh, "Iran Crisis or 'Circus'? A Weary Middle East Wonders," *New York Times*, May 19, 2019, https://www.nytimes.com/2019/05/16/world/middleeast/iran-war -fears.html.

2. Cristina Maza, "Iran Crisis Is Similar to Controversial Incident That Escalated U.S. Role in Vietnam War, Analysts Argue," *Newsweek*, May 14, 2019, https://www.newsweek .com/iran-crisis-similar-vietnam-war-analysts-argue-1425484.

3. In 2017, Saudi Arabia and its allies (the UAE, Bahrain, and Egypt) tried to isolate Qatar for not being sufficiently anti-Iranian by imposing a blockade on the tiny gas-rich emirate. But their actions backfired, drawing Qatar closer to Iran and, with help from Turkey, China and Pakistan and "help(ing) Qatar endure its neighbors' economic stranglehold." See Joseph Hinck, *Time*, "How U.S. Allies in the Middle East are Responding to Rising Tensions with Iran," June 18, 2009.

4. David Frum, "Take It from an Iraq War Supporter — War with Iran Would Be a Disas-ter," *The Atlantic*, May 15, 2019. https://www.theatlantic.com/ideas/archive /2019/05/the-iraq-war-was-a-failurewar-with-iran-would-be-worse/589534/.

5. Jennifer Steinhauer, "Two Veterans Groups, Left and Right, Join Forces against the Forever Wars," *New York Times*, March 16, 2019.

6. Alice Slater, "The US Has Military Bases in 80 Countries," *The Nation*, January 24, 2018.

7. Micha'el Tanchum, "Russia's Intervention in Libya Would Realign the Eastern Mediter-ranean," *Jerusalem Post*, March 16, 2017. See also, Tom Newton Dunn, "Russia Sends Troops and Missiles into Libya in Bid to Enforce Stranglehold on the West," *The Sun*, October 8, 2018 (updated October 9, 2018), https://www.thesun.co.uk/news /7448072/russia-missiles-libya-warlord/.

8. Melanie Lidman, "Israel Oil War Shifts to the Golan Heights," *Times of Israel*, September 18, 2014, https://www.timesofisrael.com/israels-oil-wars-shift-to-the-golan-heights/.

9. Martin Armstrong, "Is There Really More Oil in the Golan Heights than in Saudi Arabia? Who's Genie Energy?" *Armstrong Economics*, May 3, 2017, http://www.armstrong

economics.com/international-news/middle_east/is-there-really-more-oil-in-the
-golan-heights-than-is-saudi-arabia.

10. "Business and Financial Leaders Lord Rothschild and Rupert Murdoch Invest in Genie Oil
& Gas," Business Wire, November 15, 2010, https://www.businesswire.com/news/home
/20101115007704/en/Business-Financial-Leaders-Lord-Rothschild-Rupert-Murdoch.

11. "Black Gold under the Golan," *The Economist*, November 7, 2015, https://www
.economist.com/middle-east-and-africa/2015/11/07/black-gold-under-the-golan.

12. Glen Carey, "Trump's Golan Move Means His 'Deal of the Century' May Be
Dead," Bloomberg News, April 1, 2019, https://www.bloomberg.com/news/
articles/2019-04-01/trump-s-golan-move-means-his-deal-of-the-century-may
-be-dead; and Vicky Ward, *Kushner, Inc.: Greed. Ambition. Corruption. The Extraordinary
Story of Jared Kushner and Ivanka Trump* (New York: St. Martin's Press, 2019), 149.

13. "Lindsey Graham Says Israel Warned Him of Imminent War with Hezbollah in
Lebanon," *Middle East Monitor*, March 1, 2018.

14. "Israel, Lebanon Step Up War Talk over Mediterranean Oil, Gas Fields," *The Iran Project*, February 5, 2018, https://theiranproject.com/blog/2018/02/05/israel-lebanon
-step-war-talk-mediterranean-oil-gas-fields/.

15. "Israel, Lebanon Step Up," *The Iran Project*.

16. Ryan Browne, "US Ramped up Strikes in Afghanistan Following Collapse of Taliban
Peace Talks," CNN, October 30, 2019, https://www.cnn.com/2019/10/30/politics
/us-afghanistan-strikes/index.html.

17. David Zucchino "U.S. Service Member Is Reported Killed in Afghanistan," *New York
Times*, July 13, 2019, https://www.nytimes.com/2019/07/13/world/asia/afghanistan
-us-service-member-killed.html.

18. Mujib Mashal, "Afghan and U.S. Forces Blamed for Killing More Civilians This Year
Than Taliban Have," *New York Times*, July 30, 2019, https://www.nytimes.com
/2019/07/30/world/asia/afghanistan-civilian-casualties.html.

19. "Court Received 1.17 Million War Crimes Claims from Afghans," *US News and World
Report*, February 15, 2018.

20. "U.S. Classified Afghan War Data," *Wall Street Journal*, January 30, 2018. See also
Thomas Gibbons-Neff, "Afghan War Data, Once Public, Is Censored in U.S. Military
Report," *New York Times*, October 30, 2017.

21. Tom O'Connor, "US Report on War in Afghanistan Shows Historic Losses, but Hides
Death Toll, Previously Made Public," *Newsweek*, October 13, 2017, https://www
.newsweek.com/us-report-war-afghanistan-historic-losses-hides-death-toll-made
-public-697776.

22. Domina Chiacu, "Trump Wants US Military in Iraq to 'Watch Iran': CBS interview,"
Reuters, February 3, 2019.

23. For casualties in Israel's War of Indepence, see "Casualties of Mideast War," *Los Angeles
Times*, March 8, 1991, https://www.latimes.com/archives/la-xpm-1991-03-08-mn
-2592-story.html.

24. Michael Peck, "In 1956, Russia Almost Launched a Nuclear War against Britain,
France and Israel," *National Interest*, January 18, 2017, https://nationalinterest
.org/blog/the-buzz/1956-russia-almost-launched-nuclear-war-against-britain-18978.

25. "The Six Day War," History.com, August 21, 2008, https://www.history.com/topics
/middle-east/six-day-war.

26. "Casualties," *Los Angeles Times.*

27. "Casualties," *Los Angeles Times.*

28. "Casualties," *Los Angeles Times.*

29. "Gulf War Fast Facts," CNN, July 30, 2019, https://www.cnn.com/2013/09/15/world /meast/gulf-war-fast-facts/index.html.

30. Neta Crawford, "Human Cost of the Post 911 Wars," Watson Institute Cost of War Project, November 8, 2018, https://watson.brown.edu/costsofwar/files/cow/imce /papers/2018/Human%20Costs%2C%20Nov%208%202018%20CoW.pdf.

31. Rod Austin, "Human Cost of Yemen War Laid Bare as the Death Toll Nears 100,000," *The Guardian*, June 20, 2019, https://www.theguardian.com/global-development/2019 /jun/20/human-cost-of-yemen-war-laid-bare-as-civilian-death-toll-put-at-100000.

32. Ian Black, "Iran and Iraq Remember War That Cost More Than a Million Lives," *The Guardian*, September 23, 2010.

33. "Pentagon Fuel Use, Climate Change, and the Costs of War," Watson Institute for International and Public Affairs, Brown University, June 2019, https://watson.brown .edu/costsofwar/papers/ClimateChangeandCostofWar.

34. AIPAC, "The New Congress Remains Solidly Pro-Israel, but More Work Lies Ahead," *Near East Report*, November 2018, https://www.aipac.org/-/media/publications /policy-and-politics/aipac-periodicals/near-east-report/2018/near-east-report -nov-2018.pdf.

35. Mary Louise Kelley interview with Lydia Dennett, "How Much Saudi Arabia Spends to Influence Public Opinion in the U.S.," NPR, November 17, 2018, https://www.npr .org/2018/10/17/658253810/how-much-saudi-arabia-spends-to-influence-public -opinion-in-the-u-s.

36. Thomas Friedman, "Ilhan Omar, Aipac and Me," *New York Times*, March 6, 2019, https://www.nytimes.com/2019/03/06/opinion/israel-ilhan-omar.html.

37. Sheryl Gay Stolberg, "Israel Lobby Convenes in Washington amid Fraying Bipartisan-ship and Rising Tension," *New York Times*, March 23, 2019, https://www.nytimes .com/2019/03/23/us/politics/aipac-israel-trump-democrats.html.

38. Anna Ahronheim, "Nine Golani Soldiers Incarcerated for Refusing Orders while on Gaza Front," *Jerusalem Post*, April 2, 2019.

39. See the Jewish Voice for Peace website at https://jewishvoiceforpeace.org.

40. Matthew Haag, "Muslim Groups Raise Thousands for Pittsburgh Synagogue Shooting Victims," *New York Times*, October 29, 2018, https://www.nytimes.com/2018/10/29 /us/muslims-raise-money-pittsburgh-synagogue.html.

41. "In Solidarity with Muslims, NZ Jews Shut Synagogues on Shabbat for First Time," *Times of Israel*, March 15, 2019, https://www.timesofisrael.com/in-solidarity -with-muslims-nz-jews-shut-synagogues-on-shabbat-for-first-time/.

42. Alexander Goldberg, "A Rabbi in Lebanon: Finding Common Cause during My Trip to Tripoli," *Jewish News*, January 25, 2019, https://blogs.timesofisrael.com/a-rabbi -in-lebanon-finding-common-cause-during-my-trip-to-Tripoli.

43. Jack Khoury and Yaniv Kubovich, "Palestinians Set Fires at Israel-Gaza Crossing: 70 Wounded by Israeli Fire in Border Protests," *Haaretz*, May 4, 2018.

44. "Jordanians Rally against 'Normalization' with Israel over Gas Pipeline," *Times of Israel*, July 27, 2018.

45. Ben Norton, "Palestinians Support Indigenous Dakota Pipeline Protests: 'We Stand with Standing Rock,'" *Salon*, November 18, 2016, https://www.salon.com/2016/11/18 /palestinians-support-indigenous-nodapl-protests-we-stand-with-standing-rock/.

46. Dennett, "Amir Abdullah of TranJordan," GNX 319, May 1, 1946, RG 226, entry 108A, box 173, NARA.

47. Ernest Latham quoted in Richard D. Kaplan, *The Arabists: The Romance of an American Elite* (New York: The Free Press, 1993), 135.

48. Kaplan, *The Arabists*, 136.

49. Najib Alamuddin, *The Flying Sheikh* (London: Quartet Books, 1987), 17.

50. Ralph Curren to Aviation Division, Department of State, May 8, 1945, in Foreign Relations of the United States, US State Department, Volume VIII, The Near East and Africa, 69.

51. HG 1 to SAINT, Washington, "Subject: Monthly Progress Report for August," September 5, 1945, RG 226, entry 108A, box 173, NARA.

52. John H. Spencer, *Ethiopia at Bay: A Personal Account of the Haile Selassie Days* (Algonac, Michigan: Reference Publications, 1984), 165–7.

53. Spencer, *Ethiopia at Bay*, 104.

54. Memo from Col. F. M. Hinshow to the Director of Intelligence re: Assignment of ATC Pilot on Temporary Duty to MAA, Egypt, November 21, 1946, RG 319, Army-Intelligence Project decimal file, 1946–48, Egypt, box 11, NARA.

55. Spencer, *Ethiopia at Bay*, 192.

56. P. C. Spender, Sinclair Oil Company to Loy W. Henderson, December 18, 1946, Declassified, "Report Summarizing the Geological Work of Sinclair," RG 59 884.6363/12-1746, box 7169, NARA.

57. Cable from McNown to Washington, June 7, 1947, RG 319, box 1, "Egypt," NARA.

58. Letter from Dennett to Ruth Dennett in the author's possession.

59. Cable from J. S. Grant, BOAC Asmara to Senior Control Officer, Sudan, March 22, 1947, RG 319 (Army decimal file), entry 47, "MID 360.33 Ethiopia," box 143, NARA. Letter contained in the accident report.

60. Cable from Cairo to Washington, March 22, 1947, RG 226, Names file, Creech, NARA.

61. The two Swedes had been ordered by His Imperial Majesty's Chancellor to "constitute an Investigation Commission" along with Count von Rosen. (The Swedes had been helpful to the emperor in modernizing his army before the Italian invasion in the mid-1930s; after the war he turned to them again because, according to a State Department memo dated January 28, 1947, he wanted "experts from countries that had something to impart but did not aspire to foreign territory." Count Carl Gustaf von Rosen's mission was to reorganize the country's air force and train a cadre of pilots and officers who would one day train the Ethiopian air force. Magnusson's report is included in the official US accident report filed by McNown, which can be found at RG 319 (Army decimal file), entry 47, "MID 360.33 Ethiopia," Box 143, NARA.

62. Profile on Carl Gustaf von Rosen, Records of Sweden OSS/X-2, RG 226, entry 120A, box 13, February 12, 1945, document X-2861, NARA. (His father, the aristocratic Eric von Rosen, became the brother-in-law to Hermann Göring, a leader in the Nazi Party, when his wife's sister, Carin von Kantzow, married Göring.)

63. A Lebanese newspaper reported, "Some people of the country reported to the RAF [British Royal Air Force] station, half way between Asmara and Addis Ababa, that there had been a wreck. When the RAF officers went to the scene of the accident,

they discovered that Daniel Dennett and the military men with him had been killed. It took nine hours to bring the bodies back to the nearest town, where they were properly identified." "Death of Daniel Clement Dennet, Jr.," *Al-Kulliyaa*, April 1947, Archives of the American University of Beirut.

64. Hugh Wilford, *America's Great Game: The CIA's Secret Arabists and the Shaping of the Modern Middle East* (New York: Basic Books, 2013), 44–45.

65. McNown lists the equipment as being "1000 lbs of teletype, 1200 lbs Transmitter; 329 lbs Transformer for AN/Equipment; 100 lbs Receiver Antenna for AN/Equipment; 450 lbs Reciever AN/FRE-3 and 450 lbs terminal equipment AN/FGC-3."

66. John Creech, "OSS Personnel," RG 226, box 153, NARA.

67. Memo from Minister Felix Cole enclosing report by William Beach on "Communist Activities in Addis Ababa, Ethiopian Airlines," June 6, 1947, RG 59, 861.20284/6-647, NARA.

68. I found a January 1948 cable from Minister Cole to the Secretary of State that stated "there are indications that Greek community in Ethiopia is most susceptible of foreign groups to Communist penetration and efforts have already been made to plant agents from other countries among them." Cable, Felix Cole to Secretary of State, January 12, 1948, RG 59, 861.20284/1-1248, NARA. That would suggest that Greek communists truly were penetrating Ethiopian Air Lines. On the other hand, Jerry and I were told by some fellow journalists in Athens that the British used Greek communists imprisoned by them during the civil war in Greece (1946–49) to do special ops for the British in return for their release from prison. In April 2019, I made some further inquiries to some Greek scholars I had met through the National Archives, and the most they could tell me was that there was a large Greek community in Cairo during the war, including royalists and Greek soldiers. A number of Greeks living there had joined the British armed forced in Cairo.

69. Top Secret Message from American Legation, Addis Ababa to Department of State, April 16, 1947, Declassified State Department Documents RG 59, 884.00/4-1647, box 1766, NARA.

70. Cable, Pinckney Tuck to Secretary of State regarding views on McNown warning, April 19, 1947, Declassified State Department Documents, RG 59, 884.00/4-1847, Box 1766, NARA.

71. Spencer, *Ethiopia at Bay*, 188.

72. Spencer, 168–9. See also "Memorandum for the President," from Acting Secretary of State, April 16, 1947, Official Files 308, box 997, Truman Library.

73. Memo to the President of Ethiopian Airlines, October 21, 1947, RG 59, box 7170, Commercial accidents, box 7170, NARA.

74. Memorandum from the Department of State to the Officer in Charge of the American Mission, Cairo, August 4, 1948, RG 59, 884.7962/7-2648, box 7170, NARA.

75. Cable from McNown to Washington, March 21, 1947, RG 319, box 11, "Egypt," NARA.

76. Clare Timberlake to Felix Cole, January 30, 1947, RG 59, 861.20284/1-3047, NARA.

77. Timberlake, January 30, 1947.

78. Cable from Addis Ababa to Secretary of State, August 3, 1947, Declassified State Department Documents, RG 59, 884.00/8-147, box 1766, NARA.

79. Bruce Hoffman, *Anonymous Soldiers: The Struggle for Israel, 1917–1947* (New York: Knopf, 2015), 483.

80. Even if the Irgun prisoners were released to sabotage an American airplane in the mountains of Ethiopia, how much advance information would they have needed of the plane's flight plan? McNown made several trips to Ethiopia in the preceding month, and since his departure from Cairo bound for Jidda was known to Dennett by March 10 (who was then staying in Taif, location of a major British military base), McNown's trip to Jidda on March 19 (delayed a week) was to meet with his British counterparts in Jidda (one of whom, Captain Cubitt, rode with him on the plane from Cairo to Jidda that day). In short, the British were informed in advance of McNown's plans. And one of the biggest mysteries still remains: Why did McNown get off the plane rather than continue on to Ethiopia as originally planned?

81. This was not that far-fetched an assumption. Regarding British rivalry with the United States, James Barr, author of *Lords of the Desert*, shows just how threatened the British were by TAPLINE, a competing US pipeline. Barr's recent book is the first, to my knowledge, that notes that "Tapline's one drawback was that it put the United States on a collision course with the British." As Barr explained further, "ARAMCO's pipeline would compete with that already operated by the British controlled Iraq Petroleum Company, which pumped Iraqi oil from Kirkuk to Haifa, and it would extend Saudi influence into a region that the Iraqis and their British allies regarded as their backyard." James Barr, "Once upon a Time, America Needed Syria," *Foreign Policy*, September 18, 2018. Article adapted from Barr's book, *Lords of the Desert: The Battle Between the United States and Great Britain for Supremacy in the Modern Middle East* (New York: Basic Books, 2018). As for the Soviets, it will be remembered that they viewed TAPLINE as a dangerous "auxiliary enterprise of the American System of world-wide military bases." "Izvestia Assails Deal," *New York Times*, January 27, 1947.

82. Rick Gladstone and Alan Cowell, "More Clues, and Questions in 1961 Crash That Killed Dag Hammarskjold," *New York Times*, February 17, 2019, https://www.nytimes.com/2019/02/17/world/africa/hammarskjold-crash-mystery.html.

83. Andrew Gumbel, "Autopsy May Solve Deadly Mystery of the Mattei Affair," *The Independent*, August 29, 1997, https://www.independent.co.uk/news/world/autopsy-may-solve-deadly-mystery-of-the-mattei-affair-1247785.html.

84. Jan Leestma cited in the author's essay "The War on Terror and the Great Game for Oil: How the Media Missed the Context," in Kristina Borjesson, ed., *Into the Buzzsaw: Leading Journalists Expose the Myth of a Free Press* (Amherst, N.Y.: Prometheus, 2004), 68.

85. During World War II, Zionist forces, acutely aware of upper-class anti-Semitism among Americans as well as the British, would be just as likely to target American diplomats as British diplomats whom they deemed unsympathetic to their cause. Hugh Wilford writes of "a group of Middle East–born OSS officers who, during the 1940s, had worked secretly to bring the United States and the Arab states closer together and to head off the partition of Palestine. Descended from nineteenth-century American missionaries in the Arab world, these men were anti-Zionist less because of any inherent prejudice against Jews and more because of a fierce — in some cases almost mystical — belief in the overriding importance American-Arab, and Christian-Muslim, relations." Hugh Wilford, *America's Great Game: The CIA's Secret Arabists and the Shaping of the Modern Middle East* (New York: Basic Books, 2013), xx. My father was not born in the Middle East, nor did he harbor mystical beliefs, but he shared a deep connection to the region through his mother, a missionary-educator in Turkey.

I know, from conversations overheard among old family friends, that he thought the partition of Palestine into a Jewish and Arab state was a bad idea and would cause all sorts of complications in the future.

Afterword: At All Costs

1. The copy of the speech was found among Dennett's writings in a family scrapbook. My mother wrote on the back, "Dan's speech at [AUB] Staffite meeting, Beirut, 1933 or 34?" But she added "probably 1942," most likely due to its reference to events in the Levant that occurred that year. Dennett was an instructor at Clark University in 1942 and the speech was likely made to an audience at Clark.
2. Edward W. Said, *Orientalism* (New York: Vintage Press, 1979).
3. The documents arrived just days before this book was to go to print and I am still digesting their contents, but can divulge the following: In his now declassified 1944 analysis, my father identified oil as the "vital factor" regarding America's postwar interests. He anticipated a "hostile threat" to American oil and air rights might "come from two quarters: a foreign power and from a native government." He identified possible "post-war sources of friction" as being France, Zionism, the British, and the Russians, with detailed descriptions of their anticipated efforts to undermine American interests. As it turned out, all became his deadly rivals in the Great Game for Oil. Last, another declassified 1944 document written by OSS agent Carlton Coon to OSS Director Donovan on "Intelligence Work in Arab Countries" identified my father as a "Moslem expert" and Britain's Lt. Col. St. John Philby — Kim Philby's father — as a "menace" capable of wrecking American expeditions to Arabia, if not politically than "by less agreeable means." Always remember, Coon wrote, that Philby could get any number of Saudi Arabs "to do any dirty work he desires for him." Coon concluded, "only exceedingly well-trained men can hope to handle the Philby problem."
4. Walter Thomson, Introduction to Daniel C. Dennett, *Conversion and Poll Tax in Early Islam* (Cambridge: Harvard University Press, 1950).
5. David Marlowe to the author, August 20, 2019.
6. Astri Suhrke and Antonio De Lauri, "The CIA's 'Army': A Threat to Human Rights and an Obstacle to Peace in Afghanistan," Brown University, Watson Institute's Cost of War Project, August 21, 2019, https://watson.brown.edu/costsofwar/files/cow/imce/papers/2019/Costs%20of%20War%2C%20CIA%20Afghanistan_Aug%2021%2C%202019.pdf.
7. The author to Marlowe, August 20, 2019.
8. Sune Engel Rasmussen, Ghassan Adnan, and Nazih Osseiran, "Iran Finds Itself in Crosshairs of Arab Protesters," *Wall Street Journal*, November 4, 2019, https://www.wsj.com/articles/iran-finds-itself-in-cross-hairs-of-arab-protesters-11572890538.

Acknowledgments

1. William Casey, Memorandum for All [CIA] Employees re Historical Review Program, June 18, 1985.

INDEX

Note: Page numbers in *italics* refer to maps. The initials "CD" refer to the author. The initials "DCD" refer to the author's father, Daniel C. Dennett, Jr.

350 | *The Crash of Flight 3804*

Truman, Harry (*continued*)
  endorsement of Jewish state, 203
  recognition of Israel, 202
  Truman Doctrine announcement, 12, 31, 171, 178, 191
  understanding of the Eastern Mediterranean's importance, 191
Truman Doctrine
  announcement of, 12, 31, 133, 171, 178, 191
  Soviet reaction to, 276
Trump, Donald
  accusations against Iran, 237
  al-Baghdadi, Abu Bakr death, 292
  attacks on the CIA, 288
  attempts to withdraw troops from Iraq and Afghanistan, 93
  cancellation of Taliban peace talks, 257
  cuts to Palestinian relief aid, 214, 215
  declaration of Golan Heights as part of Israel, 220, 232, 254, 255
  election of, 244
  Erdoğan, Recep Tayyip relationship, 249
  increased military funding, 256
  Khashoggi, Jamal killing, 222, 223–24, 231–33, 242
  misdeeds of, 289
  misinformation about extent of Taliban presence, 91–92
  potential military intervention in Iran, 251–52, 257
  quest for fossil-energy imperialism, 253
  recognition of Jerusalem as Israel's capital, 215
  remarks against immigrants and Muslims, 258
  support for Israel, 221
  support for Saudi Arabia, 241–43, 245
  ties with neoconservatives, 289
  Ukraine foreign policy, 291
  use of AUMF, 64n
  withdrawal of troops from Syria, xiii, 132
Tuck, Pinkney, 275, 316n9
Tunisia
  Arab Spring involvement, 97, 179, 180, 181
  French domination of, 314n38
  as Muslim-majority nation, 217
Turkey
  Armenian genocide, 156–162
  attacks on Adana, 315n54
  Black Sea exploration, 165
  border with Syria, 135
  completion of the BTC pipeline, 136–141, *138–39*
  complexities of developing the Leviathan natural gas field, 216, 219
  Cyprus dispute, 216
  Erdoğan, Recep Tayyip leadership, 164–65, 168
  geographical significance of, 133
  historical world commerce in, 146
  military training by the US, 136
  pipeline project proposals, 62, 120
  post-WWI geography of, 143n
  post-WWI reforms, 162–64
  railroad development, 315n47
  repression of Kurds, 134
  role as regional policeman, 121
  settling of borders, 162
  Soviet plans for autonomous Kurdish state, 134–35
  strengthening of ties with Russia, 164–65, 168, 249
  support for opposition in Syria, 123, 129, 130, 131
  US commerce in, 144, 312n25
  See also Qatar–Turkey pipeline proposal
Turkish Petroleum Company (TPC), 157, 163, 197, 199
  See also Iraq Petroleum Company (IPC)
Turkish Republic, formation of, 154
Turkmenistan
  Bridas Oil Company investments in, 44
  Caspian Sea competing oil claims, 303n30
  conflicts over pipeline routes, 45
  dance between dictators and oil barons, 41
  support for the Taliban, 46
  TAPI pipeline project, 70, 71, *72–73*, 89–90
  Unocal pipeline projects, 45–46, 50
  US efforts to help develop oil and mineral resources, 50, 78–79
TurkStream pipeline, 165, 166–67, *166–67*, 168
TWA (Transcontinental & Western Air), 17, 267, 268

Ukraine
  annexation of Crimea by Russia, 166–67
  Black Sea exploration, 165, 166
  Trump, Donald foreign policy, 291
United Islamic Front for the Salvation of Afghanistan. *See* Northern Alliance (Afghanistan)
United Kingdom (UK). *See* Britain
United Nations
  monitoring of Iraq's weapons of mass destruction, 80
  secret peace negotiations with the Taliban, 90–91
United States (US)
  air travel competition with Britain, 266–69
  arms sales to Saudi Arabia, 241, 242
  battle for influence in the Middle East, 13, 30–31, 94, 256, 282, 324n15, 333n81
  China's rivalry with, 61, 78, 183, 246
  conflicts with Britain, 8, 13, 15, 36, 263–64, 266, 324n15
  East vs. West oil rivalry, 7, 8, 12, 13, 31, 146–47
  efforts to destabilize the Soviet Union, 48–49
  efforts to improve relations with Russia, 49–50
  embassy bombings of 1998, 58–59, 60
  endless wars phenomenon, 252–54
  extensive military troops and bases overseas, 252–53
  Franco-Russian whisper campaign against, 15–16
  growing anti-Semitism in, 261
  historical influence in Syria, 95
  legation bombing of 1946, 15, 16, 36, 227–29, 282
  misinformation about the Middle East, 47
  neoconservative plan for global dominance, 76–80, 110
  oil concession in Saudi Arabia, 1, 13, 45n, 203, 225, 319–320n18
  special relationship with Britain, 231
  special relationship with Israel, 200–202, 204–6, 230–31, 259
  special relationship with Saudi Arabia, *10–11*, 11, 231–33

ABOUT THE AUTHOR

KATHERINE VOSE

C harlotte Dennett, a former reporter in the Middle East, is an investigative journalist and an attorney. She described her campaign to prosecute George W. Bush in *The People v. Bush: One Lawyer's Campaign to Bring the President to Justice and the National Grassroots Movement She Encounters along the Way*. She coauthored with her husband and fellow investigative journalist, Gerard Colby, *Thy Will Be Done: The Conquest of the Amazon: Nelson Rockefeller and Evangelism in the Age of Oil*. She lives in Vermont with her husband.